Wall Street People

Wall Street People

True Stories of Today's Masters and Moguls

Charles D. Ellis
with
James R. Vertin

JOHN WILEY & SONS, INC.

New York • Chichester • Weinheim • Brisbane • Singapore • Toronto

ISBN 0-471-23809-0

Printed in the United States of America.

10 9 8 7 6 5 4 3 2 1

J. Richardson Dilworth

Thank you, Dick, for giving me in my early career years your inspiring example of high standards of performance in service to America's institutions in business, education, and the arts—with your gifts of professional skill, personal grace, and infectious good humor.

Preface

Enjoyment—and a little learning—are the goals with which this anthology has been put together. We hope each reader will share the pleasure we've had in learning more about the fascinating people who have made a significant difference—for good or ill—as they performed their parts—sometimes comedy, sometimes tragedy—in the theater of investment and finance in which we too play our parts.

This anthology is *not* history. The pieces presented here are colorful tiles, but they are not a coherent mosaic. And certainly not a complete one: Many more colorful tiles or stories are yet to be told. Still—after five years of searching and reading—this book contains less than 1 percent of all that was examined and considered. There are a few patterns we've found worth noting:

- Fame is fast fleeting and most players are soon forgotten. Surely most of those included from this century would not be included 100 years hence.

- Celebrity is not nearly equal to significance: Many of the most important contributors to the development of our profession and industry have not been celebrated; while, due to curious circumstances, several minor characters were.

- Notoriety comes most readily to those who misbehave—while thousands upon thousands of able people go about their work conscientiously, effectively, and anonymously.

- Finally, the study of significant people refreshes our modesty: Many exceptional people have played important roles very well. While sharing in their adventures, we learn the power of great commitments sustained over long periods of time, particularly in favorable environments. We may also learn how to calibrate our own ventures and achievements.

While this collection is certainly not presented as "scholarship," a reasonable effort has been made to get the stories right and to get the right stories. Myths grow quickly and familiarity can give false confidence in their validity—as can our delight in hearing a story told in the familiar way we've learned to like best. Such a problem was presented by a popular Dutch Admiral named Piet Hein—the legendary hero of a favorite Dutch drinking song, which toasts: "Piet Hein: His name is short; his deeds are tall. He won the silver fleet!"

Enthusiasm for including Admiral Piet Hein in this collection originated with hearing this story: After capturing a huge treasure-laden Spanish fleet in 1628 as it returned from the New World—instead of engaging in a boisterous celebration of triumph—Piet Hein retired to his cabin, solemnly wrote a letter to his wife at The Hague, and then instructed a skilled young lieutenant to set sail in a small, fast boat and take the Admiral's letter directly to Madame Hein.

When he sailed into harbor at The Hague, so the story went, the lieutenant dashed up the dock and ran to the Admiral's home where he pounded on the door. When Madame Hein opened the top of the half-door, he eagerly thrust the crucial letter at her. Surprised to see her read it so calmly, the lieutenant was even more surprised to see her calmly tuck it into her bodice, smile, thank him—and gently, but firmly, bid him good day as she closed the door.

What the young lieutenant wouldn't see as he walked away was the great burst of energy within the home as Madame Hein—following the careful instructions she'd just read in the Admiral's letter—dashed about, collecting all their cash and every piece of silver, pewter, or brass that could be pawned. She went directly to the pawnbroker where she raised all the cash she could in a hurry and then on to the coffee house where the crowd bought and sold shares in the common stock of the Dutch West India Company—her husband's employer. Soberly, Mrs. Hein purchased what we would recognize today as call options on a large block of that common stock.

A few days later, when news of Admiral Hein's triumphant victory finally arrived, the common stock of the company rose and rose—and rose to record highs. And the Hein's call options soared—creating what is still today one of the great family fortunes in the Netherlands.

But is it true? Or did the Admiral's fortune come simply from the sale of his share of the loot? I don't know and have been unable to find out. (We do know the shares of his company rose 225 percent during the period immediately following the victory; the options would surely have soared!)

Some other stories have eluded me: When Kleinwort Benson ran short of cash during a business recession, Rex Benson is said to have gone to Monte Carlo and gambled boldly with what was left in the till, enjoyed a splendid run of luck, and returned to London with plenty to meet the firm's payroll for several weeks.

Some stories that might have been included are left out because they involve taking—rather than making—a fortune. One of the most amazing, if true, is of General Tomoyuki Yamashita,* "The Tiger of Malaya," who captured Singapore and looted temples, bank vaults, and private fortunes throughout Southeast Asia. He allegedly hid the loot in 172 different sites on some of the 7,100 islands of the Philippines. None has been found in the half century since, but the Yamashita treasure is estimated by believers to be worth at least $100 billion and perhaps as much as $2 trillion. (*Esquire*, June 1995, p. 34.)

Some of the pieces in this collection were discovered in quite serendipitous ways. One example began on Pall Mall, where Karl Van Horn and I were standing on the sidewalk, engaged in the semiserious conversation of friends. I noticed a burly policeman stopping traffic, apparently for a lady standing just off the Mall, and was pleased as four lanes of traffic came to a halt, thinking how considerate of one another Londoners are. Assuming the constable had stopped the traffic to enable the lady to cross, I was puzzled when she did not move; she simply stood with her bicycle. Just short of commenting to Karl, I realized the reason the woman, the policeman, and four lanes of traffic stopped: A mother duck with six ducklings in a row behind her were waddling their way across Pall Mall so they could reach their pond. Delighted, I waved to the lady as she rode her bike along the path to where Karl and I were standing. She stopped, smiled, and asked what was on my mind.

"Have you ever read Robert McClusky's *Make Way for Ducklings?*" I asked. She'd not. I explained it was a children's book that told a similar tale set in Boston. She was pleased; I said I'd like to send her a copy and asked her name and address. A month later, I received a letter from Helen Mann of *The Economist* acknowledging receipt of McClusky's book and explaining it was en route to her grandchildren living in Australia.

Helen Mann received a letter from me a few years later on asking for help on obtaining a profile of Walter Bagehot,† the great editor of *The Economist*. She very generously sent me the full history of that superb newspaper, which had the best profile I've found on Bagehot.‡

My career over the past 40 years—nearly three decades as a partner of Greenwich Associates in consulting on strategy and its successful implementation with senior executives at the world's leading financial service

---

* Executed on February 23, 1946, as a War Criminal.

† Two years later, driving through Chelsea in a Deux Chevaux with a wonderful sculptor named Almuth Trebenoff, whose work had caught my eye while on display in the area in front of the *The Economist's* offices, I mentioned a comment about her work made to me by a woman at *The Economist*, and we were soon exchanging happy thoughts about what a fine person is Helen Mann, who had sponsored the show.

‡ *Lombard Street*, in which Bagehot explains why central bank reserves must be used boldly and decisively, is a long-time favorite.

organizations—has given me an unusual series of opportunities to become acquainted with and to work closely with a wide range of interesting
people who have made significant contributions to the investment profession and the business of finance. I've enjoyed personal acquaintance with
more than half the major figures profiled here. They've enriched my life
quite wonderfully.

One of my real low points was the day I was obliged to tell Gus Levy—
then Chairman of the NYSE and Managing Partner of Goldman Sachs
(among many other positions of power)—that it was too late to become a
client in our firm's program for the year because the offering period was
past and the report was no longer available—even to Goldman Sachs,
whom we all admired and hoped to serve in the very near future. "You
know and I know it can't cost you $50 to make another copy," said the most
powerful man on Wall Street. "And you know I can get what I need on
Wall Street." I explained meekly that we had a specific offering period—
like an underwriting—and, like an underwriter, we'd committed explicitly
to a closing date and that all our importuning to Goldman Sachs had been
for naught and that we'd have to wait until next year.*

The conversation was over. He turned to other matters, and I left
Gus Levy's glass office on the trading floor, afraid I'd put the kibosh on
our fledgling firm's possible relationship with Goldman Sachs. Much to
my relief, Bob Menschel, Levy's partner, bumped into me a week later and
had the kindness to tell me, "I hear you met with Gus. He thought you
were OK." Sure enough, Goldman Sachs became our client the next year
and was one of our largest and most consequential clients over the next
quarter century.

I never met Siegmund Warburg, but I certainly bumped into him. I'd
delivered to S.G. Warburg & Co. an analysis of their merchant banking
business across Europe, which contained the documented assertion
that S.G. Warburg had no major business relationships in Germany. Siegmund Warburg read it and concluded our firm was *non grata*.

His reasoning was clear and decisive. We *must* be wrong. Why, Herman Abs and several others were very good friends of his and of his firm's.
Of course, they had important relationships. It apparently did not occur to
Siegmund Warburg that *he* could have a great and important *personal* relationship with a very senior, retired executive and yet his *firm* might not
have an important *working* relationship with that same executive's corporation. No matter: We were precluded from doing business with S.G. Warburg for three years—until Siegmund Warburg retired. Today, our firm
works with Siegmund Warburg's firm on three continents in five different
lines of business, and Peter Darling, who built Warburg's Mercury Asset

---

* We were in our first year of business and would not get above break-even until our seventh. We were certainly not "dealing from strength."

Management into the United Kingdom's leading investment management organization, is a Director of our firm.

Ben Graham* and I met twice at Donaldson, Lufkin & Jenrette's series of three-day conference-seminars of two dozen leading investment managers, which it has been my privilege to lead for more than a quarter century. (He came with his beautiful and charming Malou; he was in his 80s; she in her early 60s.) We both enjoyed innovations and rigorous discussion and developed a delightful friendship. Still, we would not agree on everything. Ben could not convince me to invest at least one-third in bonds. Equally, I could not convince Ben that the real reason Jacob Bronowski *appeared* to get every word correctly in his TV program was that the Bronowski book Ben was reading from as he followed Bronowski's TV performance had been made *after* the TV program. Ben was familiar with movies made from books. It did not—and even with my verbal assurances would not—ring true to him that the TV program was taperecorded *first* and the transcript was made—and published as a book—*after* the video. As Alan Greenspan's official escort at the Yale graduation at which he received his honorary degree, it was my responsibility to make engaging small talk with the man the whole world knows is expert at saying nothing. We had a 20 minute procession through crowds of observant onlookers. Even well prepared, the challenge of sustaining apparent discourse was daunting.

Dick Jenrette, a gracious team-building play-maker in business and in private life one of the world's finest antiquarians and restorers of lovely homes, has achieved a great success in rebuilding The Equitable. It pleases me to know this good man, at the appropriate time, *de*-mutualized The Equitable—the peak achievement of Dwight Morrow, another good man, having been to *mutualize* The Equitable. Dwight Morrow will appear in Volume II of *Wall Street People*.

Among my light-hearted memories is the evening *Institutional Investor* celebrated its tenth anniversary at The Four Seasons restaurant in New York. I was at a table of four with Heidi Fiske and Fidelity's remarkable Mr. Johnson. Bored by the speeches, Mr. Johnson and I entertained ourselves by floating more than a dozen wine glasses in the lighted pool in the center of the dining room, delighting in the light that came from below the water's surface, caught the dark red wine remnants and projected flickering wine-red color splashes across the ceiling of the room. Mr. Johnson loved it.

Some of the great stories are not yet ready for telling. Many of the truly wonderful people have hidden from view. Among those I wish were included here—and anticipate will be included in a future compilation—are Bob Barker, Gary Brinson, Bob Rubin, John Mack, Tom Luddy,

---

* David Dodd, his co-author, entrusted to my care his own copy of the First Edition of *Security Analysis*—now on loan to Roger Murray.

Jim Rothenberg, David Swensen, Marty Liebowitz, Larry Lasser, David Fisher, John Chalsty, and Bill Elfers.

Also missing are the several brilliant researchers who have so greatly changed Wall Street investing and finance: Fischer Black, Dick Brealey, Colyer Crum, Gene Fama, Bob Merton, Merton Miller, Franco Modigliani, Paul Samuelson, Myron Scholes, Bill Sharpe, and Jack Treynor. We'll all miss Fischer, correctly identified by *The Economist* as the intellectual godfather of modern derivatives markets.

Friends have been wonderfully helpful in making this book possible. Two superb authors have been particularly generous in allowing the use of their work: John Train and Ron Chernow. Dan Chabris gave up his entire collection of trade magazines (neatly tied in bundles, they filled a station wagon). Barbara Lathrop helpfully dug through the files in the Kress collection of rare books at Harvard Business School. Juanita Bosee pursued many obscure pieces whose value had been hinted at elsewhere. Carol Loomis, one of Wall Street's most admired and appreciated journalists, was both the first and last person to help put this collection together. Carol gave generously of her time and her knowledge of *Fortune's* writers and writing. Her professionalism and engaging good humor influenced the outcome considerably.

Arthur Zeikel, who built Merrill Lynch Asset Management, and Peter Stormonth Darling, who built Mercury Asset Management in London, joined in the search—as did several others. It pleases to know their two firms are now joined together.

Nancy Dickerson Whitehead, responding to a plea for help, encouraged her husband John to cooperate wonderfully in developing the profile written specifically for this book, and his co-head of Goldman Sachs, John Weinberg, gave generously of his time so a comparable profile could be written. Justly proud but quite modest men, neither had allowed a biographical sketch to be written before.

Roy Neuberger and Benno Schmidt were remarkably forthright during our interviews. And visiting with Schmidt's former partner Don Ackerman renewed a warm friendship that began when we were classmates at Harvard Business School. Over and over again, the glue that brought this collection together was the bonding of friendship.

Heidi Fiske, Wally Stern, Patricia Woolf, Ed Ryan, Patrick Gifford, Maureen Caswell, Dick Dilworth, and Don Ackerman each gave time and caring comments and encouragement for which I am deeply grateful.

With ever-encouraging good will and patience, Kimberly Breed, Geertrund Mensinga, Lucy Carino, Jaynee Dudley, Lori Dameron, Mary Whalen, and Lori Bowman did the considerable typing required.

Jim Vertin, my co-editor for this (and our two previous books, *Classics I* and *II*) had witnessed as an executive at Wells Fargo Bank a protracted angry confrontation between computer "know-it-alls" and the "traditional" investors who were his friends and colleagues. The computer types forced and lost the confrontation in 1970. Instead of joining the victory celebration of the "traditional" investment professionals, Vertin urged the traditionalists to recognize the good parts of their bullying opponents' ideas and find a way to make them truly useful. Volunteering to stake his career on the uncertain possibilities, he organized Wells Fargo Investment Advisors. The firm pioneered the application of quantitative methods in investing and led the major movement by pension and endowment funds into indexed investing. When Wells Fargo sold it to Barclays 25 years later, it had a market value of $500 million.

My warm and caring friend for more than a quarter century, Jim Vertin has again provided that extraordinary combination of inspiring perception of what *might* be done in the abstract with tenacious insistence that it *must* be done in all details to make this collection ready for reading.

The strong personal friendship that has now engaged Jim Vertin and me in producing this anthology has extended over 25 years of conversations, meetings, and correspondence about and on behalf of the Chartered Financial Analysts, the CFA Research Foundation, and the Association for Investment Management and Research. While individually sometimes somewhat tenacious on specifics, we have enjoyed together a very happy agreement on the major themes and objectives.

An expert marksman, Jim is known to take only as many shells as equals the legal limit when hunting ducks—because he virtually never misses—and is rumored to select his fast-flying targets by their age, to assure the best flavor when eating. Jim is also a very experienced outdoorsman, has precise habits and practices, and expects appropriate conformance to the exact program he has carefully worked out over the several prior months. The pleasures of our friendship were beautifully illuminated by Jim's taking me on a ten-day tour above the tree-line in the High Sierra California wilderness.

We went fishing in different pocket lakes each day—mostly for rainbows and brooks in lakes that would see only a few people each week. Exacting as usual, Jim would give strict instruction each morning as to the exact size of fish he intended to cook that day. As a tyro, I tested not only Jim's knowledge and his ability to teach, but also his gentle patience.

When fishing was over, he began guiding me through the intricacies of dominoes, the favorite game of all true San Franciscans. Again, the patient good humor of an experienced expert was sorely tested, but I loved being with Jim—in his country and learning.

After one of our games of dominoes, the concept developed in our amiable give-and-take for this anthology about *people*—to follow the anthology we'd just completed together on investment *ideas*. Investing is, after all, a "people business." The concept took shape and we agreed we would go for it. The searching and assembling has been fun—and we have been joined by other friends.

Some potentially splendid pieces have been unavoidably left out because they are not yet known. We can only hope knowledgeable readers will take up the invitation to make their nominations known so they can be included in a future edition. The two guidelines on selection are simple: First, the *person* must be interesting in what she or he has done, and second, the *piece* must be well written and, hopefully, answer well John F. Kennedy's thoughtful challenge to any biographer: "What was he *really* like?"

CHARLES D. ELLIS

Greenwich, Connecticut
February 2001

Contents

(By Order of Appearance)

Contents

(In Alphabetical Order)

MASTERS OF INVESTING

Bernard M. Baruch

BERNARD M. BARUCH

Here, we are introduced to Bernard Baruch, who made a substantial fortune—and a national reputation—from a small start on Wall Street. For many years, he served as an informal counselor to the mighty, including Winston Churchill. Even filtered through the 40 years since it was written down, how fresh and "now" his philosophy remains!

In evaluating individual companies three main factors should be examined.

First, there are the real assets of a company, the cash it has on hand over its indebtedness and what its physical properties are worth.

Second, there is the franchise to do business that a company holds, which is another way of saying whether or not it makes something or performs a service that people want or must have.

I have often thought that perhaps the strongest force that starts an economy upward after it has hit bottom is the simple fact that all of us must somehow find a way to live. Even when we are sunk in the blackest despair, we have to work and eat and clothe ourselves; and this activity starts the economic wheels turning anew. It is not too difficult to determine the things people must have if they are to continue to live. Such fields usually open up investments which are likely to hold their value over the long run.

Third, and most important is the character and brains of management. I'd rather have good management and less money than poor managers with a lot of money. Poor managers can ruin even a good proposition.

• • •

I have defined a speculator as a man who observes the future and acts before it occurs. To be able to do this successfully—and it is an ability of priceless value in all human affairs, including the making of peace and war—three things are necessary:

First, one must get the facts of a situation or problem.

Second, one must form a judgment as to what those facts portend.

Third, one must act in time—before it is too late.

• • •

What registers in the stock market's fluctuations are not the events themselves but the human reactions to these events, how millions of individual men and women feel these happenings may affect the future.

• • •

[This is a] practice I was to develop ever more systematically as my operations grew in size. After each major undertaking—and particularly when things had turned sour—I would shake loose from Wall Street and go off to some quiet place where I could review what I had done and where I had gone wrong. At such times I never sought to excuse myself but was concerned solely with guarding against a repetition of the same error.

• • •

The longer I operated in Wall Street the more distrustful I became of tips and "inside" information of every kind. Given time, I believed that "inside" information can break the Bank of England or the United States Treasury.

It is not simply that inside information is often manufactured to mislead the gullible. Even when insiders know what their companies are doing, they are likely to make serious blunders just because they are in the know.

• • •

If anything, too much information may be available today. The problem has become less one of digging out information than to separate the irrelevant detail from the essential facts and to determine what those facts mean. More than ever before what is needed is sound judgment.

• • •

Outside my old office in Wall Street there used to be an old beggar to whom I often gave gratuities. One day during the 1929 madness he stopped me and said, "I have a good tip for you."

When beggars and shoeshine boys, barbers and beauticians can tell you how to get rich it is time to remind yourself that there is no more dangerous illusion than the belief that one can get something for nothing.

• • •

In speculation, our emotions are constantly setting traps for our reasoning powers. It is far more difficult, for example, to know when to sell a stock than when to buy.

• • •

Other people's mistakes, I have noticed, often make us only more eager to try to do the same thing. Perhaps it is because in the breast of every man there burns not only that divine spark of discontent but the urge to "beat the game" and show himself smarter than the other fellow. In any case, only after we have repeated these errors for ourselves does their instructive effect sink home.

Being so skeptical about the usefulness of advice, I have been reluctant to lay down any "rules" or guidelines on how to invest or speculate wisely. Still, there are a number of things I have learned from my own experience which might be worth listing for those who are able to muster the necessary self-discipline:

1. Don't speculate unless you can make it a full-time job.

2. Beware of barbers, beauticians, waiters—or anyone—bringing gifts of "inside" information or "tips."

3. Before you buy a security, find out everything you can about the company, its management and competitors, its earnings and possibilities for growth.

4. Don't try to buy at the bottom and sell at the top. This can't be done—except by liars.

5. Learn how to take your losses quickly and cleanly. Don't expect to be right all the time. If you have made a mistake, cut your losses as quickly as possible.

6. Don't buy too many different securities. Better have only a few investments which can be watched.

7. Make a periodic reappraisal of all your investments to see whether changing developments have altered their prospects.

8. Study your tax position to know when you can sell to greatest advantage.

9. Always keep a good part of your capital in a cash reserve. Never invest all your funds.

10. Don't try to be a jack of all investments. Stick to the field you know best.

These "rules" mainly reflect two lessons that experience has taught me—that getting the facts of a situation before acting is of crucial importance, and that getting these facts is a continuous job which requires eternal vigilance.

Albert J. Hettinger Jr.

CARY REICH

Al Hettinger, after a full academic career, made a fortune as an analyst-
investor at Lazard Frères. He began the process at an age when most investors are thinking of slowing down, not speeding up, and continued it
well into his 80s.

When it came to his investments, [André] Meyer did trust one person
implicitly: Albert J. Hettinger Jr., the lanky, pipe-puffing ex-Harvard
professor whom Meyer hired shortly after taking over Lazard. In fact,
Meyer's support of Hettinger was probably the shrewdest investment decision Meyer ever made.

What Cézanne was to painting, what Rodin was to sculpture, Al Hettinger was to undervalued stocks. No one, not even Meyer, could match
Hettinger's artistry at ferreting them out. Partly, his skill was rooted in
native shrewdness, but mostly, it was the product of sheer doggedness—
Hettinger probably read more annual reports than any other investor in
America—and a devotion to business fundamentals. Hettinger had never
forgotten what he had learned from his first investment in 1921: two shares
of the National Biscuit Company. Hettinger sold the stock when he thought
it had reached its peak, but he had neglected one very important point—that
Nabisco, with the help of the rather informal accounting standards of those
pre-SEC days, was deducting its plants as expenses rather than charging
them as a capital investment. The stock, thanks to those write-offs, zoomed
upwards. Hettinger resolved never again to overlook the fundamentals.

Having steered Meyer and Lazard into their first real postwar bonanza,
the undervalued utility stock investments, Hettinger began to study the insurance industry. The more annual reports he read, the more he became
convinced that insurance companies were the stock market's equivalent to
King Solomon's Mines. Peering through the underbrush of the insurers'
mundane underwriting business, Hettinger was one of the first to get a
glimpse of the glittering unrealized values in the companies' investment
portfolios. His first big plunge was in Connecticut General, around 1948,
and in the succeeding years he began loading up on the stock of other insurers. By the late 1950s, thanks largely to his insurance holdings, Hettinger

Reprinted from *Financier: The Biography of André Meyer* by Cary Reich (William Morrow,
1983; John Wiley & Sons, 1998), Chapter 12, pp. 152–154, by permission of the Estate of
Cary Reich © 1983 by Cary Reich.

was a multimillionaire—and André Meyer, who tagged along on most of those investments, was a lot wealthier, too.

That was only the beginning. Hettinger's attention was drawn to the Japanese insurance industry. Once again, he saw investment portfolios ripe with unrealized values; and once again, he and Meyer moved into the market in a big way. Patiently, Hettinger and Meyer waited for the buds to blossom—and with the inevitability of tulips in the spring, they all did. An investment in Tokyo Marine, which cost Hettinger in the neighborhood of $3 million when he first bought it in the early 1960s, was worth at least $35 million a decade later. And, with gritty persistence, Hettinger kept accumulating more and more stock as the price went up. According to a former aide, Hettinger maintained accounts at the Chase Manhattan Bank that automatically invested $10,000, $20,000, and more *a week* in a selected list of Japanese issues. "The way he worked it," says this aide, "if the market went down, he simply bought more shares."

By the 1970s, this former professor, once scorned by his Wall Street peers as a hopelessly weird, head-in-the-clouds old drone, was said to have been worth in excess of $100 million. And, perhaps most astounding of all, he had done it all after the age of 57. . . .

As demonic a workhorse as Meyer was, Hettinger was even more so. In his seventies and eighties, he could still be found in his little office poring over his annual reports, long after men 30 and 40 years his junior had gone for the day. Once, tiring from his labors, he stretched out on the floor of his office to take a nap. The cleaning woman came by, spotted the old man sprawled on the floor, and promptly called for an ambulance. Even the 1977 New York blackout couldn't stop Het, as he was affectionately known around Lazard; with the elevators out of commission, he climbed 32 floors to his office. He was 86 years old at the time. . . .

While there was never any doubt as to why Meyer stuck with Hettinger, it was never quite so evident why Hettinger, once he had made his initial fortune, continued to hang his hat at Lazard. One reason, no doubt, was sheer gratitude to Meyer for the base of operations he had been given and for the faith Meyer had shown in him. Then there were the contacts that Meyer and other well-connected Lazard partners like George Murnane generated; Hettinger was shrewd enough to realize that there was more to ferreting out investment opportunities than just reading thousands of annual reports.

Finally, there was the aura of André Meyer: like so many others, Hettinger was at once spellbound and unnerved by the Frenchman. In Meyer's presence, this supremely self-confident investor would become completely unwound, his fingers nervously working the fabric of his pockets. Sometimes Hettinger would say something, and Meyer would immediately dismiss it out of hand, snapping, "That is too cavalier." (This was one of Meyer's favorite expressions.) Hettinger would promptly apologize. "He never seemed able to separate himself from a fierce unbending abnegation to André Meyer," says a man who worked for them both.

Indeed, as late as 1979, in a conversation with the author, the then-87-year-old Hettinger still seemed almost embarrassingly awestruck by Meyer. "There is no living man I revere as much as André," Hettinger said then. "No one is infallible, but André came as close to being infallible as anyone I can conceive of. I can't emphasize too strongly that he was Lazard and the rest of us were miles behind him. Anything he wanted me to do, I was his to command."

Roy Neuberger

CHARLES D. ELLIS

> Every so often—but only at very long intervals—an extraordinary investor appears. Such people are successful, in the sense that they make lots of money, but they are also much more than this. They add to the tradition and the lore of the business at the same time that they add unique, intriguing, and very genuine personas to the investment milieu they occupy. This profile introduces one such person, an extraordinary investor named Roy Neuberger.

"Are you interested in the market?" Roy Neuberger asks his visitors as the DJIA is advancing vigorously beyond 3400 in the mid-1990s. "I guess you *have* to be interested in this market—at least a little. I don't trust the market any more than two rattlesnakes—not because it's dishonest or anything like that, but because institutions all act like sheep. And so often just because one analyst changes a recommendation from 'Buy' to 'Hold' or even from 'Strong Buy' to 'Buy.' It's very interesting, the market."

Roy Neuberger has been a leading investor and, more importantly to him, a leading collector of contemporary art for over half a century. In 1944, the Museum of Modern Art named his the most interesting contemporary art collection in New York City. "That turned my head a little bit."

Now 90, his green-brown eyes radiate warmth and good humor as he looks steadily into his companion's eyes; his conversation is peppered with specific names and exact dates across 70 years of remembered experiences; and in his selections of paintings and investments, he is very contemporary—always looking ahead, looking for what's new. (Having discovered a new shoe design which he likes particularly, he has just bought six pairs.)

Balancing his skillful, knowledgeable engagement with the new are such enduring commitments as 50 years with one company, Neuberger Berman, and over 60 years of marriage with Marie Neuberger.

Sharing his views on investing, Roy counsels that "One should fall in love with ideas, with people, or with idealism based on the possibilities that exist in this adventuresome world. In my book, the last thing to fall in love with is a particular security. It is after all just a sheet of paper indicating a part ownership in a corporation and its use is purely mercenary. The fact that a number of people have been extremely fortunate in the past by falling in love with something that went their way is not necessarily proof that it will always be that way. Stay in love with a security until the security gets overvalued, then let somebody else fall in love."

Asked how he got into investing, Roy begins with the beginning and explains that after graduating from Dewitt Clinton High School, where he captained the tennis team, he went to NYU—"primarily to play on their tennis team," allowing his companions to wonder whether this was an early example of his admired originality of mind and capacity to comment to his own decisions—or the retrospective humor of a wise elder.

"After a while at NYU, I got a job at B. Altman's, where I advanced to being the buyer of upholstery fabrics at 19. I'd been reading Galsworthy's *The Forsyte Saga*, where I learned that young people from good families were sent abroad for the grand tour of Europe. Since I was orphaned and on my own, I decided I would treat myself to a tour of the Continent for what became three months.

"I liked France very much; so I went back and stayed there from 1925 to 1929." That's when he, "Played and beat the great tennis champion, Fred Perry."

After a pause to let this triumph sink in, he leans forward to acknowledge: "Of course, I was 22 and Perry was only 16 at the time. Later it would have been different."

During that time, I went to the Louvre two or three times a week. And I read many, many books, including *Ulysses*—it first came out in 1922—and a book that had just been written in French about Van Gogh." Moving to a bookshelf, Roy takes the frayed book from its shelf to share it. "Reading this book, I learned Van Gogh never sold a painting during his lifetime. That made quite an impression on me. Oh, his brother *said* he'd sold one and sent the $150 to Van Gogh, but that was just his brother trying to make him feel better.

"That was when I decided on a major life purpose: to buy the work of living artists.

"After all, even Michelangelo was a living artist at one time. That decision meant I'd need to make some real money. So, I returned from Europe, planning to go to Wall Street. My father knew Bear of Bear Stearns who introduced me to Jerome Danzig. Alison Danzig wrote about tennis. Maybe that helped a bit. They had no place for me but helped me get a start at Halle & Stieglitz on March 8th of 1929 at $15 a week. I was there 11 years.

"My father, who had run a miniature Brooks Brothers out in Michigan, had left my sister, brothers, and me some 'guaranteed first mortgage bonds.' How's that for a name for a security? Who guaranteed those? They all disappeared in the 1930s—guarantee or no guarantee.

"There were very few government bonds in those days. So I had a modest portfolio of good blue-chip stocks. And in 1929 the market for these good stocks kept going down, not a lot, but a little every day in September. Meanwhile, Radio Corporation of America was where all the excitement was, and it seemed to keep going up. And up. And up. It got to $574. Far and away, it was the most active stock."

Roy pauses in the storytelling to give some historical perspective: "My own portfolio has been for many years 'market neutral,' but I would not recommend the procedure of being 'short' some stocks and 'long' others at the same time for more than a very small percentage of investors. One has to have a stubborn, perverse, and patient attitude in selling short securities that are too high in one's eyes. Also, it's nearly impossible to be perfectly 'market neutral.' Your long and short positions are very different entities. But, if it is done methodically and continuously, it is an excellent method to help in the accumulation of capital—and education. Here are the advantages: (1) It gives one more patience to hold on to undervalued long positions. (2) It makes one less concerned with the psychology of fear that dominates the market from time to time, and it permits you to have an 'anchor to windward.' Even if things go down—you benefit.

"I would prefer not to make too much of this philosophy. In remembrance of things past, however, it stood me in good stead in late September of 1929. My portfolio was down about 12 percent and I had an uneasy feeling about the market and conditions in general. Those were the days of 10 percent margin, and I studied the lists carefully for a stock that was overvalued in my opinion and which I could sell short as a hedge. I focused on Radio [Corporation of America] at about $100 per share. It had recently split 5 for 1 and appeared overvalued. There were no dividends, little income, a low net worth, and a weak financial position. Its only bullish aspect was hope for the future age of radio! I sold short a dollar value of this stock equal to the dollar value of my long portfolio. The last short was at $98.* (You could short then on a down tick.) It proved to be a timely and profitable move.

"Some people try to guess what the crowd will do, believing they can be swept along in a favorable current. But this is dangerous. The crowd may be very late in acting. Suppose it's an institutional crowd. Sometimes they

---

* In 1932, Radio sold for just $2.50 a share.

over-influence each other and are the victims of their own habits. Personally, I like to be contrary. When things look awful, I become optimistic. When the crowd and the world look most rosy, I like to be a seller, perhaps prematurely, but usually profitable.

"Rarely can securities be valued correctly at over 20 times earnings, because rarely is there any clear prospect that a company's earnings will grow sufficiently in the future to make it worth that price. We know that there are exceptions, but they account for perhaps 1 percent of the cases. So the odds are against you when you pay a very high multiple.

"The 1929 market was quite an education, but I didn't have to pay for it, being market neutral. (Usually, you should pay for your education. You learn more.) The bear market that occurred in 1930–1932 made it imperative to sell short if you wanted to make a profit. The habit has become somewhat ingrained in me by now, although it is quite possible to do well without it."

Switching topics with an easy abruptness that reminds his partners of Casey Stagel, Roy is talking without pause about Neuberger & Berman's flagship mutual fund which Roy managed very successfully for more than a quarter century. "Guardian was, I think, one of the first publicly offered, no-load mutual funds when we introduced it on June 1, 1950. . . . The ethics of charging an 8½ percent sales load bothered me. T. Rowe Price was working on the same idea and may have been first. We began with $150,000. Now it's almost $2 billion. Others are much bigger, of course, but the fund has done well."

Roy managed Guardian until 1978—one of the longest runs with a single mutual fund by any investment manager—and then turned it over to a younger man who wanted "to have a turn." Roy was at loose ends without his own fund to run. Trying to be helpful to the firm's other portfolio managers, he was something of a nuisance. When managing Guardian, he could lead by example, but couldn't "help" others more directly in managing money. As one partner, Dick Cantor, observed: "Roy knows and understands a lot I don't know or understand, but I don't know how much I could actually *learn* from Roy. He's *very* intuitive. I'm not sure even he knows all that goes into his thinking. Roy gets his information on different channels than the rest of us. And I've seen him sometimes say the reason he did something was X because maybe he was a little reluctant to say what really was his reason and thought some BS from *Business Week* would somehow sound better."

Another partner, Joe Lasser, explains it this way: "Like many of the most successful investors, Roy is multifaceted. He is not only an art connoisseur and patron—and a benevolent human being—he has read widely and perceptively in history, politics, economics, et cetera, and he can and does bring the distillation of a broad range of knowledge to his investment style and decisions. At times it is surprising how many factors he has considered when he has made a commitment—and he can give an impressive array of facts and logic as to how he arrived at his conclusions—*if* you press him to do so, or if he feels conversational. But for most people who live in and are satisfied with a world of one-liners, Roy can and does offer simple explanations for his actions that make him look as if he is acting intuitively rather than analytically. He's much more complex than he appears because he is charming, friendly, and multifaceted—but don't be fooled, his mind is in gear and moving at supersonic speed."

After Roy turned over the management of Guardian, Dick Cantor realized Roy was looking for something to *do* and called Rusty Olsen at Kodak to ask if he would be interested in having part of their pension fund managed by one of the firm's very senior seniors. "You mean Roy? You bet!"

But Roy wasn't going for it, telling Cantor, "No, No, I'm through with that business. I'm going to do other things." But that night he couldn't sleep at all well. Early the next morning he was in Cantor's office. "Dick, I've been thinking all night about your suggestion. Can I reconsider? I think I better do it if I want to keep active in a positive way. I don't want to end up like some other guys have, making fools of themselves."

The Kodak relationship began in the spring of 1979. This was a very active account: turnover was over 200 percent. For eight years, it went very well. But in 1987, Roy was in deep trouble, trailing all other managers at the firm *and* at Kodak. Others were up 35 percent in the year. Roy was almost flat. The market kept rising, and Roy was *very* short of S&P futures. Hundreds of millions of futures. Then came October. Into the sharpest market break in history, Roy sold his futures and went from the bottom of the league tables to the top, finishing the year up 18½ percent.

The next July he turned over the account to others saying with a smile how nice it was to quit while still winning. Over the decade that he managed the account it was up fourfold—3 percent annually (net of fees) *ahead* of the S&P—and all in large-cap stocks.

"Roy is truly revered around here," observes Cantor, "but not for making money or for business acumen. And Roy has not been a traditional 'driving force' to build the business of the firm. It's something else. Something more important. When we were considering the link-up we've since made with Banque Nationale de Paris, Roy listened to a lot of talk about concerns and complexities. Then he spoke to the partners and said he was ashamed of them. 'This can be a great *adventure*. Don't worry over the details. This will be *fun*. It's *important*. Let's do *it!*'"

Roy is quick to pay respect to others. "Buffett has to be regarded as a genius. Gary Brinson is impressive. So are Peter Lynch and John Templeton. Al Hettinger was really brilliant. At one time in the early 1960s, he had 33 percent of his own portfolio—which was about $100 million—invested in Japanese stocks. But I felt uncomfortable with selecting individual stocks in Japan so we owned 5 percent of the Japan Fund." . . .

"One of the best ways to be a good investor is to be in good physical condition. And by good physical condition, I also mean good mental condition. Early to bed and early to rise is perhaps too ideal. To drink in moderation is perhaps better than not to drink at all and to eat in moderation is certainly better than not to eat at all. In any case, to walk at least one hour a day, either by yourself or with someone else, is a good way to improve your investing ideas. Walking is better than running; you can't work out an idea running." Roy walked more than 40 blocks daily from his apartment across Fifth Avenue from the Metropolitan Museum of Art to his offices at 43rd Street. Typically, when arriving at work he was the first one in. Even when the firm moved to 39th Street and Third Avenue, Roy still walked, always pondering the market —or art.

"A sizable part of the Wall Street community has in recent years developed an obsession. It appears to be over-zealous in finding out what is happening minute by minute to corporate earnings. The fever has spread as well to corporation executives, who appear to worry excessively over reported quarter-to-quarter earnings. The greatest game among a number of stock research firms seems to be to determine the next quarter's earnings before someone else does. This focus on short-term earnings appears to ignore the significance of longer-term trends in earnings.

"A speculator or investor is often successful because he is willing to commit large sums on the buy side when the market is very weak and he gets a lot of securities for his money. On the opposite side he creates his eventual buying power by having the guts to sell in the very strong markets where you sell comparatively few securities for high prices and get large sums. That's a very simple principle. I use the word 'guts,' but it's really more a matter of sticking to a common sense viewpoint."

Turning back to the art market, Roy shares his concern that "It's not the right climate for collecting now. Too much of the interest is in prices. Art shouldn't be bought to make a profit, although of course you can. Art should be bought for its creative quality."

Benjamin Graham

JOHN TRAIN

> Benjamin Graham set an example of professional diligence and skill, and contributed more than any other person to the development of security analysis and investment management. Two of his great books, *The Intelligent Investor* and *Security Analysis,* continue to be "must reads" a full half-century after their initial publication dates. Most of his fortune was made through an investment in GEICO. It was an investment made at a P/E multiple well beyond anything sanctioned by his investment philosophy but one to which he felt he had obligated himself—even as others in his investor group shied away.

Benjamin Graham ranks as this century's (and perhaps history's) most important thinker on applied portfolio investment, taking it from an art, based on impressions, inside information, and flair, to a proto-science, an orderly discipline. He applied great astuteness, hard experience, and infinitely detailed labor to a field full of superstition, tips, and guesswork, one in which most people who have something to say also have an incentive to deceive the listener. Employing analysis of published records, Graham explained and demolished fallacy after fallacy—often as neatly as if opening a letter.

Graham's *summa,* after more than 50 years still the basic text of the profession, is his *Security Analysis.* More useful for most readers, however, and indeed the best book ever written for the stockholder, is *The Intelligent Investor.* One is ill advised to the point of folly to buy a bond or a share of stock without having read its three hundred pages. Many people, including experienced businessmen and professionals, have been financially shipwrecked because they trustingly set forth in a leaky craft captained by an incompetent. *The Intelligent Investor* would be unlikely to suffer this fate. . . .

Benjamin Graham . . . came to New York from England with his parents in 1895 when he was a year old. His father represented the family chinaware firm, Grossbaum & Sons. (The family name was changed to Graham during World War I.) He grew up in Manhattan and Brooklyn, the youngest of three boys. After the death of his father, when Ben was nine, the family was greatly reduced in circumstances. His mother never adjusted to the change, and her anxieties undoubtedly contributed to Ben's subsequent preoccupation with achieving financial security.

He was an industrious student, and almost too good a boy. In his high-school years, when he took jobs to help support his family, he studied Greek and Latin, which became a lasting joy to him. After graduating from Columbia in the class of 1914, Ben was offered teaching fellowships in English and mathematics; instead he went to work as a messenger in Wall Street for Newburger, Henderson & Loeb. He soon progressed to doing write-ups and analyses, and during this period he married the first of three wives. By 1917 he was earning respect as an analyst, and started publishing in financial magazines. He became a partner of the firm in 1920.

Graham was a small, stocky man who became thinner as he aged. He had an odd round face, with heavy lips and light blue eyes. A complex person of boundless energy, he loved literature—Proust, Virgil, Chateaubriand, Victor Hugo, the German poets—and was a fountain of apposite quotations.

By Wall Street standards he had unusually wide interests: the Greek and Latin classics, philosophy, languages. He translated a book from the Portuguese, wrote several books himself, admired Marcus Aurelius, and identified himself with Tennyson's free spirit, Ulysses, a wily and thoughtful adventurer who traveled far, leaving his wife lonely.

Once at a family gathering for his birthday he delivered this remarkable and revealing piece of self-analysis:

One of the great heroes of my childhood reading was Ulysses, or Odysseus. In spite of the great praise heaped on the *Iliad* as the world's foremost poem, I must confess that I have never been able to read it through—although some passages, such as Hector's farewell to Andromache, have long been my favorites. But the *Odyssey* has fascinated me from the beginning, nor has that fascination diminished through the years. The wiliness and the courage, the sufferings and the triumphs, of its protagonist carried an appeal which I never could quite understand. At first I thought it was the attraction of opposites—Ulysses enthralled me because both his character and his fate were so different from my own. Only after I had long passed my maturity did I begin to realize that there were quite a bit of the typically Odyssean faults and virtues in my own makeup. . . .

While Graham sought women, he was not suited to marriage. His second wife was a secretary, and his third, Estelle, worked for him. The French . . . [woman, Malov,] with whom he spent his final years he took over from one of his own sons. He developed a passion for dancing and signed up for several thousand dollars' worth of lessons, eventually giving it up and offering the unused time to his brother, Victor.

His interest in his own children only really started when they became concerned with ideas; then he became their walking encyclopedia. A born teacher, he liked to invent stories for them and answer their questions on any subject.

Generous and kind . . . he was liked by the people he came in contact with, but had few intimate friends. In a self-description he quoted Estelle's judgment that he was "humane, but not human." Although an agnostic who held for no organized faith, he was interested in religious philosophy. He became a skier when that was an unusual skill, and a keen tennis player. As a friend says, he had no *minor* faults: he didn't smoke or drink, and ate sparingly. He was absentminded and did not like to drive a car. He lived modestly but comfortably, and after he achieved financial security he was little concerned with money. Late in life he moved from New York to La Jolla, California, but in his very last years preferred the south of France.

Graham loved mathematics, and his approach to investment is mathematical, quantitative. In fact, he may well have been concerned with security analysis primarily as a branch of mathematics. Certainly no earlier investment thinker approached the subject solely through figures, without concern for the quality of the business or the character of management.

In 1926 he formed a pool, the Benjamin Graham Joint Account, which grew to $2.5 million within three years and which he managed in return for a share of the profits. During the first year he was joined by Jerome Newman, with whom he remained associated throughout his business career.

During this period Graham encountered Bernard Baruch, and was instrumental in his making a number of investments. A person close to the situation adds, "Baruch was lavish with praise privately but that was all; the relationship was all take and no give on the part of Baruch." Baruch is believed to have offered Graham a profit-sharing association, but not on a basis that Graham found attractive.

When the market collapsed in 1929 and 1930, the Joint Account sustained severe losses; from 1929 to 1932 it declined 70 percent as compared to 74 percent for the Dow Jones Industrials and 64 percent for the Standard & Poor's 500. But since the Joint Account had been using substantial margin at the beginning of the period Graham's stock-picking record was better than it seemed. Nevertheless, he personally was wiped out in the Crash. Having ducked the 1929 cataclysm, he was enticed back into the market before the final bottom.

From 1928 to 1956 Graham taught a popular evening course at Columbia Business School. In 1934, with Professor David L. Dodd, he published the monumental *Security Analysis*, the basic text for all serious students of investing, which has sold over 100,000 copies so far and seems likely to sell forever. (As a curiosity, and an indication of Graham's skill, the value of the list of undervalued special situations in the 1940 edition advanced over 250 percent in the next eight years, compared to a one-third increase in the Standard & Poor's Industrials.)

In 1944, Graham published *Storage and Stability*, offering a plan to stabilize food surpluses, world commodities, and world currencies. *The*

Interpretation of Financial Statements appeared in 1947, and in 1949 *The Intelligent Investor.*

Graham's greatness as an investor may well have consisted in knowing how to say no. One of his assistants in Graham-Newman has described to me ruefully what it was like proposing a list of carefully selected and re-searched opportunities for Graham's consideration, only to have him find something substantive to object to in every one. He felt no compulsion to invest at all unless everything was in his favor.

When he finally did buy he was sure of what he was doing. His idea of a good, safe investment was simply buying a dollar for 50 cents over and over again. In any specific case something may go wrong, but if you do it dozens of times the procedure is virtually infallible. Diversification—a multiplic-ity of transactions—is thus a key to the method, just as in insurance.

And even as he bought, Graham always kept one foot out the door, ready to run if his calculations went awry. But this intrinsic caution robbed him of the flair necessary to catch major market moves. Besides reentering the market too soon in the thirties and getting cleaned out, he missed the great bull move beginning in 1950, even advising one of his protégés not to go to work in Wall Street in 1951 because the market was so high.

However, in the 1973 edition of *The Intelligent Investor* he was right: "We think the investor must be prepared for difficult times ahead—per-haps in the form of a fairly quick replay of the 1969–1970 decline, or per-haps in the form of another bull market fling, to be followed by a more catastrophic collapse." And indeed, the 1973–1974 collapse was the most severe since the great crash of 1929–1932—creating the best buying op-portunity since that time.

• • •

All his professional life Graham sought explainable, specific techniques that he could teach to others to enable them to select safe and profitable investments. He wanted a method that was entirely *quantitative*, that did not depend on things one couldn't be sure about, such as social trends, a company's future success in bringing out new products, or qual-ity of management.

He also wanted a method that could be used by anybody, and which therefore depended entirely on readily available published material, partic-ularly the company's own reports.

He and his associates, after working for years, finally, in that prodigious compendium, *Security Analysis*, did give the investor the tools he needed.

• • •

Graham constantly underlines the distinction between "investment" and "speculation." Investment must be based upon *thorough analysis*, and must promise *safety of principal* and a *satisfactory return*. A holding may fail to be an investment, and thus be a mere speculation, because the analysis, the safety or the return is lacking.

• • •

In 1948 Graham-Newman Corporation and Newman & Graham, a companion partnership, put $720,000, one-quarter of their assets, into buying a half-interest in Government Employees Insurance Company. GEICO . . . sells automobile insurance to government employees, but always directly, by mail. It has no agency force. It can offer unusually attractive rates, since its costs are low, and experience shows that this class of driver has relatively few accidents.

Although, for SEC reasons, most of this investment had to be spun off to the Graham-Newman Corporation shareholders, the value in GEICO stock received by Graham's group eventually reached half a billion dollars! GEICO then fell on very hard times, and at the dead low in 1977 lost 95 percent of its value; but it has made a considerable recovery since.

Excluding the GEICO stock received by his investors, Graham was never managing more than $20 million at any one time—an inconsiderable sum by today's institutional investment standards, since there are now hundreds of portfolios worth over $1 billion. By distributing to his shareholders the cash received from holdings that were liquidated, he kept his company from growing. That was because he was not confident of being able to discover more than $20 million of grossly undervalued situations at a time. If he had allowed the money to build up in the company, it would have grown to a very considerable sum—on the order of $100 million—and the results would probably have been affected.

Graham's explicit followers have always managed a limited amount of money. I would guess that even today it amounts to less than $100 million, and quite possibly much less. With the availability of computer readouts on demand, the game will become much easier to play, and thus more competitive and less profitable.

David L. Babson

EVERETT MATTLIN

David Babson is a folk hero to investment people of a certain age. He developed a concept of investing with which he built a respected firm. He also understood profoundly the concept of professionalism, for which he provided leadership to a generation. Along the way, he wrote some of the best-ever commentary about investing, and also had some fun. This piece dates from 1970, immediately following collapse of the "go-go years" bubble.

As the gunslingers were shot down en masse at the corner of Broad and Wall over the past year, the few left to swagger into Oscar's to celebrate were some of the old boys who had almost been forgotten in all the excitement of the past few years. Leading them was David L. Babson, whose fund ranked fifth in 1969 for U.S. funds with assets of over $10 million, with a slight gain in a year when minuses prevailed. Babson, 58, a dogged, somewhat stooped, pipe-smoking New Englander, has for years been wagging his finger at the performance boys and what he calls their "speculative orgy." It was as if old-fashioned virtue had finally triumphed in the marketplace.

Babson is a gentle man, but he has never been shy about speaking up against what he considers evil. In articles and speeches he has railed against what he has called at times "the performance fad" and at other, more emotional times, the "performance psychosis." He has blasted mutual funds that indulge in "outright gambling with other people's money" and who have turned the market into a "national crap game." Repeatedly he has condemned professional investors who behave like tape-watching speculators, the churning of fund portfolios, the analysts who substitute stories and chart reading for solid research, the liquidity problems that the continuous shifting of huge blocks of stocks is bringing about, the unlikelihood of "hundreds and thousands of smart guys trying to outsmart other smart guys as coming out anything but a draw," the questionable tactics of funds pushing up the price of thin stocks, the disreputability of "managing earnings" by accounting gimmicks, the possible decline of public confidence in the free enterprise system and

Excerpted from *The Institutional Investor 4* (February 1970), pp. 61–66. This copyrighted material is reprinted with permission from: **Institutional Investor, Inc.**, 488 Madison Avenue, New York, NY 10022.

the probability of eventual government intervention if the whole "gigantic pari-mutuel operation" doesn't stop.

• • •

It is ironic that Babson should now be labeled a conservative; when he opened his counseling office 25 years ago, the Boston investment community thought him rather far-out, and possibly unsound. Babson graduated from Harvard in 1932 on the day that the Dow-Jones hit its low mark of the century. "Steel mills were running at 8 percent of capacity that week," he recalls. But somehow the Depression and the War years didn't sour him on the stock market the way it did so many of his contemporaries. "After the War," he says, "I was the first, along with T. Rowe Price, to push growth stocks, when I might add, most of today's 'performance investors' were happily frolicking in their play pens."

That Babson could have a hard time convincing anyone to invest in stocks in the late 1940s now seems hard to believe, but he can remember those days clearly. "Everyone expected a big drop, like 1920–1921. Most people who had been through the 1920s were still thinking of a cyclical approach to the market. People were scared. There was no interest in stocks; they were selling four, five and six times earnings. I remember one day when only 130,000 shares were traded on the New York Stock Exchange. I stood on the floor of the Chicago Exchange and watched the boys playing ball on the floor. The ticker didn't move at all. Finally 200 shares of Armour crossed—at two dollars a share."

Investment counselors at other firms thought Babson irresponsible to recommend stocks in such a climate, but he kept writing in his weekly staff letters that "we are on the threshold of the greatest prosperity in our history." He argued that the stabilizers built into the economy since the Depression would really have an impact. He predicted that a sustained birth rate, inflationary pressures, government spending, higher standards of living, and great advances from new technology would assure an expanding economy. "Sure it's commonplace now, but they called me a radical then."

He was also an aggressive investor. "I never put money into bonds unless the account had to have them." He bought growth instead of dividends—3M, Honeywell, Merck, Pfizer, and Corning Glass—for his clients. "I bought Polaroid when it was running out of a garage in Cambridge. I bought IBM from 1948 on and I don't know as I ever told anyone to sell it. I've always believed in buying only stocks that you want to keep. There may be nothing very exciting about buying for the long pull," he says, "but it works."

Babson's approach to the market was probably inevitable, given his thoroughly New England heritage. He believes, as do a good many of the old-time Boston counselors and money managers, that those who handle money should function in the Boston prudent trustee tradition, and a trustee doesn't fool around with someone else's money. Babson's ancestors settled in Massachusetts in 1630. He was born on a farm near Gloucester; his father was a veterinarian as well as a farmer. Babson went to grade and high school in Gloucester and worked summers on the farm. After skipping a couple of lower grades, he graduated from Harvard at the age of 20—with a major in history and a cum laude honors thesis pronounced the best in its division for that year. . . .

Babson is a facile expository writer, able to clarify and simplify complicated economic issues, and an inveterate communicator. Out of Harvard, he started writing at Babson's Reports for his cousin, the late Roger Babson. . . . He still writes a widely quoted weekly newsletter on economic and investment policy trends that is mailed to some 7,000 clients and interested parties. "I've been writing something once a week for 37 years now." . . .

In 1940, when he was 29, he left Roger to found his own firm. "Roger was tough to work for—and I was with him eight years. I really don't like to have anyone control me. Anyway, I was writing an investment newsletter when I thought what people really needed was personal attention. It's like reading a medical report in the paper instead of seeing a doctor. Counseling was still in its infancy then. There were only about a half dozen firms in the field. It was rough going at first. It's tough to come to a man and say, 'Mr. Smith, if you decided to become my client, you'll be the first.'"

• • •

Investment decisions are based on the same principles that have applied since the firm began: to buy quality stocks for the long haul and not worry about short-term forecasting. But a Yankee is shrewd as well as cautious, and Babson has never played it super-safe by sticking to blue chips. He has always preached growth. His method of sniffing out growth situations is standard: his analysts look for a major industry, one growing faster than the economy, then seek the leaders in that industry, companies with progressive management, a low ratio of labor costs to sales, high profit margins, little government regulation and strong R&D which should result in new products and processes. . . .

Life is more relaxed for the man who buys for the long haul, who doesn't have to worry about daily portfolio switches, and there is no hurry about Babson—he even speaks slowly.

Philip Fisher

JOHN TRAIN

Philip Fisher was one of the first, if not *the* first, to declare that growth stocks had identifiable characteristics that made them different from ordinary stocks. He wrote one of the best-ever books on investing, sharing with his readers the benefits of his extraordinary thinking-through of the why and the how of long-term growth stock investing. Such is his stature that when he turned 80 in 1987, a commemorative interview in *Forbes* was published with an introduction written by Warren Buffett, himself a legend in his own time.

Philip Fisher is the most famous of the older generation of investment counselors in San Francisco, although he has always kept the number of his clients to a minimum. "Oh yes, *Common Stocks and Uncommon Profits*," people will say, referring to his first book. His experience and thoroughness give him the confidence to be original and, above all, patient. If you tell an experienced investor that Fisher took a major position for his accounts in the original private placement of Texas Instruments, and has kept the stock ever since, he will be awestruck.

Fisher is a friendly man with an easy, courteous manner. Of medium height, he is sparely built and slightly stooped. His thin, scholarly face, with dark brown eyes behind rimless glasses, is topped with a high forehead and receding hairline. He has a humorous mouth and large, pointed ears. He was always tallish and slim. Since his hair has never turned gray, he looks much younger than his 70-plus years.

His father, who was a surgeon, provided his early schooling, and apparently did a good job: Fisher entered college at 15. Because his father believed that one should have something hot for breakfast, Fisher, who doesn't like tea or coffee, starts the day with a bowl of soup, accompanied by an orange and a piece of toast. Once a week, year in, year out, he brews up his soup supply for the next seven days, always using the same formula: two cans of Campbell's pea soup, two cans of tomato, and one can of . . . he couldn't remember what. "My wife buys it for me," he explained.

For lunch he sends his secretary out for some French bread; he used to spread peanut butter on it from a jar kept in a drawer but found that procedure messy. Now, instead, he takes it with a bite of chocolate, like a French schoolchild. He has a weakness for cookies, but drinks little. He has no hobbies, favorite games, or strong outside interests, except science and some weekend gardening. When he comes home he changes into an old blue sport shirt and trousers and settles down to read murder mysteries.

He set up shop as an investment counselor almost 50 years ago, and has spent 35 years in his present office building. During that time neither he nor his office has changed much. His reputation as an original, profound, and remorselessly thorough investment thinker has continued to grow, as has the value of the handful of portfolios he manages.

His small, unmarked office on the eighteenth floor of the Mills building in San Francisco contains the simplest steel and plastic furniture. On his plain, worn desk is a white leatherette pen and pencil holder—nothing else. A beige wall-to-wall carpet is underfoot. The walls are embellished by a watercolor of Chinatown painted by a friend, another of a bright red pagoda, and a pseudomosiac depicting a bonsai tree and a Japanese lantern assembled by his wife. No equipment is visible except for a telephone and a digital clock (set seven minutes fast)—no files, no calculator, no In and Out boxes, no photographs, memorabilia, or knicknacks. It is believed in some investment circles that Fisher's office has no windows, but that's not so: he looks out on San Francisco's business district.

Fisher doesn't like expensive things. For years he wore an overcoat from decades earlier and drove a 1966 Oldsmobile-6 without a radio or frills. It's not that he particularly liked the car, he just didn't see the need for a newer one. Utterly logical in this, as in all else, he is often highly original. . . .

Philip Fisher first hung up his shingle as an investment counselor on March 1, 1931. After a year at Stanford Business School he had gone to work in the security analysis department (then called the statistical department) of a San Francisco bank. Shortly after Hoover's announcement that prosperity was just around the corner Fisher switched to a stock exchange firm. Unfortunately, the firm could not wait for Hoover's prediction to come true, and Fisher found himself once again on the street. For some time he had thought that he would like to be independent and so seized this occasion to start his own firm.

He found two unexpected advantages in beginning his career when he did. First, he talked to businessmen, and since they often had so little to do, they were delighted to chat. One executive he called on said he had finished the sports page and didn't want to go home yet, and so had asked himself, "Why don't I just let this monkey in to see me?" He became a long-time client, and later confided that a year later he couldn't have seen Fisher: he'd become too busy.

The other advantage of starting in 1931 was that almost every potential client was dissatisfied with his existing advisor—if he had any capital left at all. . . .

Fisher's first office, which he rented for $25 with the telephone thrown in, had no outside windows, only a glass partition separating it from the people he leased it from. In 1932 he earned an average of $2.99 a month. In 1933 he averaged about $30 a month—still not quite as well as he could have done if he had been selling newspapers. In 1934 he was already doing better, and by 1935 he was on his way.

Fisher likes to say he spent World War II in every red tape job in the Army Air Corps. . . . During his slack periods he had a chance to think about what he would do after the war ended, and he resolved that when he went back to his professional practice his first order of business would be to identify the best chemical company in the United States.

After he was discharged he spent nine months looking them all over, finally winnowing the list down to three. In the end he decided that Dow Chemical was the pick of the lot, and he bought some stock in 1946.

In the spring of 1947 he was introduced to Dow itself through one of its important customers. After meeting with the management he decided that these people were among the most remarkable he'd ever encountered, and, he says, he has never had occasion to change his view. For approximately seven years in the late 1950s the company did not perform outstandingly, but Fisher did not lose confidence or patience, or sell any stock. Since then the company's success has been legendary, and it long remained one of Fisher's important holdings.

Stephen Horton, a field analyst for Standard & Poor's, first mentioned Texas Instruments to Fisher in 1954, after which Fisher talked to many people about the company, becoming increasingly interested in it. One day he was talking to Emmett Solomon, later president of San Francisco's Crocker National Bank and at that time manager of the Provident Securities Company, a Crocker family holding company. He told Solomon that while he didn't know enough about this small Dallas company to invest in it, still, what he had learned so far was very exciting. Solomon was struck by this, since he and his wife had just met Erik Jonsson, the head of the company, on a cruise to Hawaii, where they'd had adjacent cabins. Solomon had been intrigued enough to resolve to visit Jonsson's company, and invited Fisher to go with him.

Morgan Stanley had just advised the four founders of Texas Instruments to sell a small amount of their stock for estate planning purposes. After Solomon and Fisher's visit, the Provident Securities Company and Fisher's clients became two of the three purchasers of that placement. With additions bought near the bottom of three market breaks, it has since become one of Fisher's largest holdings.

Fisher discovered Motorola in a similar way. An investment man passing through San Francisco mentioned to him that Motorola seemed most remarkable. Fisher visited the company, representing both himself and friends in Fireman's Fund Insurance. Very much impressed, Fisher and Fireman's Fund both bought Motorola stock. A year or so later Fireman's

Fund told Fisher that they had hired a New York bank to go over their portfolio. The bank ranked all their holdings as "very attractive," "attractive," or "unattractive"—all except Motorola, which was not ranked since, said the bank, it was not the kind of company worth spending time on. Later still, however, Fireman's Fund told Fisher that Motorola had been their best-acting stock.

These stocks have been big holdings in Fisher's portfolios, which decline about as fast as the averages in a bear market, but have done much better in static or rising markets.

Fisher the investor is quite a different figure from Fisher the investment writer, who sets forth criteria by which one can judge almost any company and determine if it is worth investing in. Expressing one of his key principles, Fisher the investor says, "I don't want a lot of good investments; I want a few outstanding ones." He focuses his attention on a narrow range of enterprises and is unwilling even to consider most companies. He wants above all not to try to be a jack-of-all-trades and master of none. . . .

Fisher's general feeling about investments that are of interest to him is that the company in question should combine outstanding business management with a strong technological lead in most of what it does. He won't invest in companies that depend on the taste of the mass consumer, influenced by advertising; though he agrees that there is a technology of influencing the consumer, he does not feel he understands it. . . .

Fisher's key idea is that *you can make a lot of money by investing in an outstanding enterprise and holding it for years and years as it becomes bigger and better.* At the end your share in the enterprise is worth a great deal more than at the beginning. *Almost certainly the market price of your share will rise to reflect its higher intrinsic worth.* And, certainly, you should concentrate on growth in intrinsic worth: without that there's no reason for the stock to go up rather than down.

He ridicules short-term thinking. Throughout his life, he says, he's only known one in-and-out trader who made money consistently. (Many professional investors don't know any.) Pursuing short-term goals Fisher regards as the worst possible mistake, both for the investor and for the company he has a stake in. He therefore insists that *management must first and foremost be working to build the company over the long term.* Growth only happens because management is profoundly dedicated to bringing it about and directs all its activities to that objective.

Fisher redefines the word *conservative* around this concept. To him, a conservative investor is one who makes his capital grow in a practical, realizable way, not in a way that can't succeed. People often describe large, well-known companies as conservative investments. But for Fisher, old and famous companies that have passed their prime and are losing ground in the jungle of international business are by no means conservative holdings. Rather, the conservative investor is one who owns winners—dynamic, well-managed enterprises, that because they are well situated and do almost everything right continue to prosper, grow, and build value year after year.

The owners of such companies don't have to worry about market values, since the assets are building: things are going the right way. Market recognition will follow.

Charles Allen Jr.

ROBERT SHEEHAN

Charlie Allen began Allen & Co. with no capital, no connections, and no backers. Not so many years later, it was one of the richest firms on Wall Street, still innovating, still private, and still effective.

People who pride themselves on a knack for appraising character at a glance might try their talents on Charles Allen Jr., founder and senior partner of the New York investment banking house of Allen & Co. Here is a firm—a watchword in Wall Street for its aggressiveness and agility. And here is the head of the firm—a blondish, blue-eyed, gentle-mannered man of fifty-one, a very youthful fifty-one, who seems to have little relish for the drama and conflict of business. To those who deal with Allen, the casual, almost abstract air with which he will accept or reject an important proposition is sometimes quite disconcerting. And he is a man who, if he can be induced to talk at all about his financial adventures, will do so pleasantly enough, but in tones so subdued and terms so self-depreciatory as to suggest a certain diffidence toward the topic.

This is how diffident he is: Charlie Allen quit school to be a Wall Street runner at fifteen, started his own investment firm at nineteen, and made—and lost—nearly a million dollars by the time he was twenty-six. During the depression he picked his way through the rubble of the market, buying and selling securities with such boldness and skill as to accumulate a fresh $1-million stake. Today the capital of Allen & Co. is over $20 million. In recent years he has emerged as one of the few investment bankers with the old-time creative flair for buying and merging companies and exerting a hand in their rehabilitation and development. From the Rockefellers he

Excerpted from *Fortune* (May 1954), pp. 124–126, 170, 172, 175. © Time Inc. All rights reserved.

bought control of the slumbering Colorado Fuel & Iron Corp., quadrupled its sales, and raised it to ninth position in the steel industry. He bought control of the family-owned Arma Corp. of Brooklyn, maker of precision instruments for the military, then fitted it into American Bosch, acquired from the Office of Alien Property, to start an interesting electronics complex. He is the principal factor in large real-estate developments in Kansas City, Chicago, and Riverside, California, controls two small but thriving railroads, a steamship company, several bus lines and an automotive-manufacturing company (ACF-Brill). Along the way, of course, Allen & Co. has occasionally stirred up controversy. But the achievement, in sum, is an impressive one, and the aggregate assets of corporations now under Allen & Co.'s wing exceed $500 million.

• • •

As a firm, Allen & Co. is built to Charlie's measure, and there is no other house on Wall Street quite like it (actually Allen & Co.'s offices are not on Wall but Broad Street). Charles Allen says the firm is "a combination of investment banking with a risk thrust," a definition that will do as well as any other. The activities, in order of importance, are (1) buying and controlling companies, (2) investing in securities for the account of Allen & Co., (3) underwriting, and (4) a small amount of trading performed principally as an accommodation for certain customers and contacts.

Wall Streeters say that the firm is "99 percent Charlie Allen," a statement that perhaps conveys the basic situation but certainly discounts unduly the value of his partners and staff. The only general partners in addition to Charles are his younger brothers, Herbert, forty-seven, and Harold, forty-four. Herbert and Harold Allen have considerable initiative of their own and have made important contributions to the firm's profits. . . .

Charles likes to see his people make a buck, and for the past nine years Allen & Co. has paid a bonus amounting to 100 percent of salary to all employees with five years' service. . . .

Most of Allen & Co.'s large capital is always vigorously at work. Allen & Co. is not, however, a member of any stock exchange. The firm is thus free from numerous regulations that could hamper its maneuverability in certain situations. Allen & Co. is not interested in doing a commission business, and by employing other firms for its transactions in listed securities it creates friends and a climate for reciprocal favors. The firm doesn't do very much business with the public directly, nor does it, except for the largest of deals, often act with partners or syndicates. Charlie Allen is happiest when he is using his own money and running the show in his own way.

If there seems to be an incompatibility here between the apparent mildness of Charles Allen's personality and the vigor of his performance, it should not be construed as a pose of some sort. With him it is rather a question of style. Charles Allen is not a man who got ahead by whirlwind salesmanship, by exerting dominance over others, by terrific organizing ability, or anything like that. His success is based on a marked talent for evaluating securities and special situations, and for acting on these judgments at the right time. An extraordinary number of highly placed Wall Street veterans solemnly affirm that Charlie Allen has an "instinct" for the market and will gladly follow him up any alley on blind faith. Allen himself shyly confesses that he has to have a "feeling" for a thing or he will not put his money into it regardless of how the figures fall. . . .

When it comes to suiting the action to the thought, however, Charlie Allen is one of the swiftest men on the Street to announce his decision and put his money on the line. He believes it is better to move quickly, even in error, than to dawdle over a proposition, consuming time and energy while other opportunities pass by. This willingness to say "Yes" or "No" is one of the reasons why so many deals are brought to him, and why his office is often the first port of call for brokers and finders and even big wheeler-dealers. . . . That is not to say that Allen's decisions are made in ignorance of the facts. "We like to know *all* the faults of a company," says Charlie, "and *one* good reason for going into it." Faults, indeed, are his hobby. Their presence knocks the price down, their eventual correction shoots the value up. But he does not buy any dogs. His special situations, though speculative, are genuinely "special," and he has the fortitude to let them sit and hatch.

• • •

Charles Allen's start was strictly from scratch—not a dime of other people's money, not an iota of influence. The late Charles Allen Sr. was more of an artisan than a businessman—he developed a few minor patents in camera lenses—and the family lived in very moderate circumstances in various rented apartments on New York's upper West Side. Charles was the third of seven children. He had had two years of high school when he hit the bricks of Wall Street, first as a runner, later as a boy bond trader barking bid and asked prices into the telephone for Sartorius & Co. He did well on the job but detested the routine and the necessity of deferring to his superiors on every little point of judgment. So at nineteen, with less than $1,000 in savings as capital, he set up his own one-room trading office.

Charlie hired a few other boys, not much older than himself, to work on commission as over-the-counter traders. Their "contacts" consisted of a score or more lower-rung traders in the various houses along the Street, some of whom were known to them only as familiar voices at the other end of the wire. Margin requirements were so low then—10 to 15 percent—that for a few hundred dollars Charlie could buy several thousand dollars worth of bonds being offered by one house, and peddle them to another house at a profit of an eighth or a quarter of a point. But it was a cumulative thing, and as Charlie's capital grew, he utilized it boldly. His brother,

Herbert, who had by then learned the ropes in one of the larger houses, joined him in 1928, and at the peak of the 1929 bull market Allen & Co. was worth nearly $1 million. The boys lost it all in the crash, and at one point were $250,000 in the red.

Charlie Allen insists that much of the credit for the firm's subsequent recovery belongs to Herbert Allen, and the still younger Harold, who became a partner in 1932. Herbert and Harold developed a rewarding interest in insurance stocks, a class of investment that, because of the actuarial abracadabra involved in the evaluation of the shares, few Wall Street brokers knew anything about. Allen & Co., quickly became the Street's No. 1 specialist in insurance securities, which are traded almost exclusively in the over-the-counter market, and made many a good killing in large blocks of these shares that had been kicking around at bargain prices.

• • •

But it was unquestionably Charles's large-scale speculations, particularly in the late thirties and the early forties, that made Allen & Co. powerful and rich. Charlie has, today, a curious lack of interest in these sensational coups, and has to jog his memory for the details—"It's only the failures that remain in your mind." But a few of his plays will suggest the trend. In this year's market, for example, many investors are congratulating themselves on making a few points on Missouri Pacific preferred. Charlie Allen took his big position—150,000 shares—in Mopac back in 1938, when the road was hopelessly in the toils of bankruptcy. He bought at 22 cents and sold at about $10. Similarly with I.T.&T. stock. Allen went into "I.T." when it was well under $3 a share and also bought a lot of the bonds at $20 and less; his eventual profits on disposal were in excess of $1 million. Back in the Thirties, Allen & Co. bought from Phoenix Securities a million shares of the old Whelan stock—before the merger with United Cigar—at 60 cents a share. Charlie stuck with this for seven or eight years, sold off his first chunk at $2.40 a share and other blocks at prices ranging up to $3.50 for a total profit on this single investment of more than $2 million. His reasons for buying these particular securities, as he recalls them now, do not sound overly profound—"Mopac was bound to be revived . . . I.T.&T. should never have been priced so low," etc. And, of course, he had a feeling for them.

These were big hits. There were losses too, but never on a scale remotely comparable to his winnings. That is because Charles Allen is as quick to pull out of a wrong deal as a cat is to run from rain. He hangs on to nothing because of sentiment or stubborn pride in his initial judgment. By the same realistic reasoning he dislikes a fight, and will rarely engage in one from choice. This is certainly not because he lacks courage—his career offers the lie to any such assumption—but as he says quite simply, "A fight takes up too much time. There are so many other ways of making money you don't have to do it."

• • •

For a long time the Rockefellers had wanted out of Colorado Fuel & Iron provided they would find the right party and get the right price. For years they had been self-conscious about the company's identification with the scandalous "Ludlow Massacre" back in 1914, when 33 lives were lost in a pitched battle between strikers and the state militia. The Rockefellers weren't really much interested in steel, but felt a family responsibility for seeing that the property did not pass on to parties that would break the company up. Henry Kaiser had once been interested in the company, and Republic Steel had also been interested, but nothing jelled. Finally, in 1944, a finder brought the deal to Allen & Co.

After a few months of conversations, Allen was told by Rockefeller intermediaries on December 10, 1944, that he could have the company if the deal could be closed by the end of the year. For the Rockefellers' 50.8 percent of the common stock, Allen agreed to pay approximately $8 million; he also agreed to take some $5 million of income bonds at par. Previous prospective buyers had balked at taking the bonds, but Allen was confident he could refund them (the operation was eventually worked out through the Bank of America, and Marine Midland Trust Co. of New York). Allen formed a syndicate, in which Floyd Odlum's Atlas Corp., among others, participated, and whipped through the C.F. & I deal by December 22. (One for the book: The closing, in the offices of the Chase National Bank, started about 1:00 P.M. and Allen's check was not handed over until shortly after 3:00 P.M. Whereupon the Rockefeller representative, pointing out that his client had lost a day's use of the money, requested—and received— the appropriate interest, about $1,000.)

What happened to C.F. & I. at the hands of the smooth young speculator from Wall Street should happen to a lot of the tired U.S. corporations. When acquired, C.F. & I.'s plant was badly rundown, its labor situation was not good, and because 70 percent of its production was in rails the company was almost totally dependent on the railroads for sales. Under Chairman Allen's hand (though he rarely put in a personal appearance) the properties were refurbished and rebuilt at a cost of more than $55 million. Colorado Fuel was merged with Wickwire Spencer and several of Wickwire's ambitious young steelman were transferred to top posts. . . .

Sales rose in the ten-year period from $56 million to $249 million; net income from $1,700,000 to $8 million.

In this considerable achievement, Charles Allen's role has been that of strategist and banker. From operations he remains, for the most part, discreetly aloof. The managers of Colorado Fuel, and other Allen companies, appear to receive from him a minimum of interference, a maximum of support, and excellent remuneration. . . .

A few years ago Allen had a serious illness, and it was thought that he would sharply curb his pace. But he rebounded remarkably, and as the record shows, he has since done more rather than less. As an aid to convalescence, he took up golf, his first and only hobby outside business.

Charlie Allen has no interest in politics (he contributes amiably to friends in both parties) and though he is a charitable man, he shuns any and all offices in public organizations. He has never wanted to live anywhere but in New York City, and his cooperative apartment on Fifth Avenue is the only home he now owns. He is devoted to his mother, a lively, 77-year-old lady who likes to bet on the horses, and to his three children by his former wife, Rita Allen, the theatrical producer. They were divorced in 1950; Charles was remarried in 1952. . . .

Charlie Allen is, at fifty-one, a man with a large fortune and the simplest of wants. But it is probably a good bet that he will continue to make interesting business news, to invest and divest, and to buy and build up many more special situations in the corporate field. For as a Wall Street friend puts it, "Charlie has no interest in money except making it."

John Hay Whitney

E.J. KAHN JR.

Here, in sketches from 1951 and 1964, we meet and follow the career of Jock Whitney, an exemplary and extraordinary patrician. After serving in Army intelligence in World War II he established J. H. Whitney & Co., the first-ever true venture capital firm, through which—with his partners—he made a lasting contribution to invesing in America. Whitney also found a novel way to use his fortune for philanthropy, published the *Herald Tribune*, was our exceptional ambassador to the Court of St. James, collected art and was a trustee of Yale.

I

John Hay Whitney, a protean man of means, has spent most of his 46 years grappling with the problems that confront any recipient or prospective recipient of a very large inheritance. For more than ten years now, Whitney, a dark, ruddy-faced, heavysct man who has been known since boyhood as Jock, has had an annual taxable income of well over a million dollars. During each of the last six years, he has parted with at least 90 percent of this in the form of federal income taxes and charitable contributions.

Part I excerpted from *The New Yorker* 27 (August 11, 1951), pp. 32, 33, 46–49. Reprinted by permission; © 1951 E.J. Kahn Jr. Originally in *The New Yorker*. All rights reserved.

Whitney has been aware nearly all his life that he was, or would someday be, awfully rich. His earliest memory of having more money than most people goes back to a day when, as a small boy, he was taken by his parents, the late Mr. and Mrs. Payne Whitney, to a department store to buy a toy he wanted. He doesn't recall what the toy was, but he does recall that after getting it his covetous eye lit on a handsome and probably expensive tricycle, and that he expressed a greedy hankering for that, too. "I remember that my parents gave it to me without wincing or protesting," he said recently. "I was absolutely staggered."

As a man who has never had to concern himself with where the rent money was coming from, Whitney has been free to do more or less whatever he has wanted to.

Whitney is a thoughtful man, and he has much pondered the question of finding a pattern of existence for himself compatible with both his resources and his inclinations. Soon after the end of the Second World War, during which he reached the age of 40 and, in accordance with the terms of his father's will, came into complete control of his inheritance, he took two big steps in a self-satisfying direction. For one, he established a $10 million foundation, now known as the John Hay Whitney Foundation, which is one of the few institutions of its kind to have been set up so far in advance of the probable death of its patron. "I'm trying to learn about giving during my lifetime," Whitney explained to a retired banker who asked him what the hurry was." . . . Whitney's other step, also a $10 million stride, consisted of organizing, in 1946, the firm of J. H. Whitney & Co., a partnership dedicated to the propagation of the free-enterprise system by the furnishing of financial backing for new, underdeveloped, and risky businesses that might have trouble attracting investment capital through more conservative channels.

II

Whitney comes by his wealth (an estimated $250 million) partly through inheritance but also through the exercise of a kind of logic that is often unique and quite often correct. He has had an important part in a series of financial successes, ranging from *Gone With the Wind* to Freeport Sulphur, Minute Maid (orange juice), Morton Packing (meat pies). Most of his industrial ventures have been developed through J. H. Whitney & Co., the investment firm he started in 1946 and that he still heads.

• • •

Part II excerpted from *Fortune* (October 1964). New York: The Time Magazine Company. All rights reserved.

Whitney is something of an enigma to the business community. He does not consider himself an ordinary businessman, but rather, as he says, "avowedly an entrepreneur, but not an easily classifiable one." He prefers to remain in the background of any undertaking he finances. . . .

A blend of boldness and reserve characterizes him. As a youth, hampered by a stammer, Jock Whitney plunged into dramatics at Groton and Yale, forcing himself to conquer the impediment and in the course of doing so becoming the first freshman at Yale to make the drama society. He took up polo and played it well enough to earn a six-goal rating and ride in games with the late, famed Tommy Hitchcock. During the war, he unhesitatingly risked his neck to escape from his German captors, jumping at night from a moving train and dodging German troops in the open French countryside until he could gain the protection of the Maquis.

• • •

Whitney has never been heard to complain about the burdens imposed on him by his great fortune. He stands on the Hay family motto, *Quod Habco Desidero* (freely translated, "I like what I have.") Yet he resists the idea that his riches should deny him, as a man in his own right and for his own abilities, the respect and companionship of his fellow men. His friendships are scattered fairly widely among men of wealth and of modest income. He rides in elevators and stands in lines with crowds even in buildings he owns, and talks easily with lower-level employees. He made his greatest influence felt as ambassador to Great Britain by the freedom and frequency with which he moved about the country and the hospitality he showed to all classes in a class-conscious nation.

• • •

World War II brought to a halt the pleasant life of socialite and businessman. Whitney turned his investments over to the guidance of a specialist, Samuel C. Park Jr., enlisted in the service, and rose to the rank of colonel in Air Force intelligence.

While stationed in London, he ruminated on the role he should pursue in the postwar world, a problem he hashed over at length with William H. Jackson, then a fellow officer. Jackson had been a young lawyer in the law firm handling the estate of Jock's father and had become deeply engaged in Whitney's affairs, including his ventures into film production. They held lengthy bull sessions about the responsibilities of a man of great wealth in a world of violence and conflicting ideologies.

Whitney came to the conclusion that what he had been doing on a haphazard basis should be done in a more organized way. He should supply venture capital to create new economic entities, even financing projects that were obviously not going to be great moneymakers but might fill a social or economic need. Whitney and Jackson believed that after the war most of the big corporations would be devoting their capital to conversion to peacetime production. Whitney felt that capitalists like himself had an obligation to supply the capital to encourage inventions and new concepts. He also felt that a man of great wealth should not only invest money in such causes but should give it away, although again in an organized, carefully thought-out way.

In 1946, J. H. Whitney & Co. was formed with a capital of $10 million. In addition to Whitney there were four partners—Richard G. Croft, Samuel Park, Malcolm Smith, Webster B. Todd, and, shortly, Benno Schmidt, most of them lawyers or investment bankers. Its purpose was to provide a reservoir of capital for whatever type of business enterprise the partnership found interesting, attractive, and constructive. Since there were few guidelines for the firm to use at the beginning, there was some initial floundering and uncertainty. . . .

Since its founding, J. H. Whitney & Co. has received 8,000 proposals ranging from plans to manufacture adjustable steps for mobile homes to development of 73,000 acres of Dutch Guiana, TV pilot films, ski lifts, a meat-processing plant in Alaska, a roll-up ladder, a new type of ruler with a sliding marker, and a system for improving the quality of egg production. Although large sums are sometimes spent investigating such projects, the partnership has actually invested in only about 75 ventures. It is difficult to calculate precisely the performance of the company's original $10 million because substantial assets, such as Corinthian Broadcasting, have been spun off, and partners have withdrawn participation profits of millions of dollars. But it can be roughly estimated that the original capital has multiplied itself 10 to 12 times in the course of 18 years. Eighty-five percent of that growth came from seven investments.

• • •

There's some indication—though Whitney himself is elusive on the question—that Whitney's enthusiasm over the accomplishments of J. H. Whitney & Co. began to slacken almost as soon as its initial ventures began to prosper. It was Dwight Eisenhower, in the middle Fifties, who propelled Whitney into a new life.

President Eisenhower had developed a personal fondness for Whitney. The two men shared an interest in golf, bridge, and game-bird shooting. On many occasions Ike had attempted to lure Whitney into government service. Whitney, with more than enough activities to consume his time, resisted the Ike charm. In 1956, however, both Ike and ailing Secretary of State Dulles were distraught over relations with the British and felt that they needed a representative there who could establish a better rapport with both the officials and the people than had Winthrop Aldrich, an older man with ways and attitudes fixed by a long career in the banking industry. Whitney, a prominent social figure who had attended Oxford and was well known in racing circles (a sport the British love), looked like just the person.

Eisenhower made a special plea to Whitney and Whitney accepted the post of ambassador.

No American or British observer can pinpoint an act or incident during Whitney's four-year sojourn in London in which he played a decisive part. Yet all agree that he put the best American foot forward, and that he was particularly effective in healing the wound caused by U.S. opposition to Britain's invasion of the Suez Canal Zone. A [British Prime Minister] Macmillan aide says: "The prime function of an ambassador is to get on such intimate terms with the top management of a country that on the one or two occasions when it is necessary to say something that needs to be said but is somewhat delicate he can say it in a way that is perfectly frank and clearly understood. Jock Whitney established himself on these terms with the British Government."

Benno Schmidt

CHARLES D. ELLIS

Benno Schmidt led, for many years, the first investment firm devoted to venture capital and also was a leader in America's war on cancer. He was a formidable man. While his son was serving as President of Yale University, his young grandson—named Benno Schmidt III—cautiously cautioned: "Grandfather is the first Benno Schmidt and I know my father is Benno Schmidt II, but I'm not the third Benno Schmidt."

"My name is John Hay . . . Whitney," explained the friendly but unfamiliar voice calling Benno Schmidt on the telephone that day late in 1945, and then went on, "You may have heard of me as 'Jock.'" Friends who knew Whitney would not have been surprised to learn he was calling Schmidt on an important matter of great personal interest—and promise: the formation of America's first venture capital firm and a transformation of the way that potentially exciting new companies are financed, nurtured and developed.

After graduating from the University of Texas Law School, where he immediately joined the faculty and taught for four years, Benno Schmidt had gone to Harvard Law School as a Thayer Teaching Fellow. He volunteered for Army duty in 1942 and rose from Lieutenant to Colonel by 1945, receiving along the way the Legion of Merit, a Bronze Star, the Croix de Guerre, the Legion d'Honneur, and the French Medal of Merit. (Honors continued to come in later years, including a knighthood for services to Australia.) Schmidt was in Washington when Whitney's call came; the war was over and it was time to decide on a career.

And so Benno Schmidt and Jock Whitney met for dinner, and before the evening was over, they had agreed he would join a few others in organizing what was to become the first and one of the most successful venture capital firms, inspiring a significant change in the way America finances prospectively exciting new companies.

Over dinner, Whitney explained that during the war in lengthy discussions in London with his fellow officer and family lawyer William H. Jackson, he had thought through what he would do with his life—if and when he got out. One decision was to commit $10 million of his considerable inherited fortune to a fund that would help people in serious trouble. A second decision was that another $10 million would be used to finance new companies capitalizing on the remarkable changes wrought during the war—changes that might fill a social or economic need.

Whitney had checked on the merit of his idea and had been strongly warned off by Sidney Weinberg of Goldman Sachs and Henry Alexander of Morgan. As he engagingly put it to Schmidt, "Before you decide, you might want to know that two very wise observers in finance say it just won't work. They feel you need a steady business like brokerage or banking to cover the overhead and that investments in new and unproven companies should be treated as just a sideline."

Schmidt recounts Whitney saying, "If I am wrong and my plan doesn't work, I will be $10 million worse off, but that will not change my life materially. However, you should give some thought to where you would be if the proposed organization is unsuccessful." To this Schmidt replied: "In the first place, I believe that the business as you have outlined it will succeed. Secondly, if it doesn't succeed, you will be $10 million worse off, I will be right where I am. So I believe I can handle the risk part okay. However, there is one thing you should know." "What is that?" Whitney asked. "That I've never had a day of business experience in my life, unless you call roughnecking or rig building in the old field business experience." Whitney's immediate reply was: "Why don't you just decide whether or not you'd like to come with us and leave it to me to pass on your credentials." "Fair enough," Schmidt replied. "I just didn't want anyone to be surprised if they got out a balance sheet and I said, 'What's that?'" Whitney replied: "We'll learn together," with that wonderful modesty, quiet wry smile and sense of humor that Schmidt later came to know so well. Before dinner was over, Schmidt had decided to join with Whitney.

In the early days of J.H. Whitney & Co., Schmidt explains, "We went around to all the banks, explaining what we wanted to do and how we'd like their help with financing good companies—and their help in identifying them. "One day, we heard from The First National Bank about a Kansan named Kenneth Spencer who had been operating a nitrate explosives plant near Pittsburgh, Kansas. Under the surplus property program, he would have the right of first refusal to buy that facility at the government's set price. Spencer wanted to convert the plant to manufacture ammonium-nitrate for fertilizer. The bank was ready to lend Spencer a big part of the purchase price, but they were quite properly insisting on his getting $1,500,000 of working capital. "That one transaction would take over 15% of our total capital, but we could see it was the right sort of investment for us. "We worked it out at $1,250,000 of preferred and $250,000 of common—and we were in business with one-third ownership.

"Spencer Chemical was a fine deal right from the start. Fertilizer was in very short supply and the business was booming. The preferred was fully paid out in the first year, and we were to make more on the equity than the $10 million of capital with which Jock had started the firm. So we were off to a very strong start right away."

Asked how the term "venture capital" originated, Schmidt explains that in the partners' dining room, he and Whitney were sitting together talking with some of the other partners about the best way to explain the firm's purpose to others. The *New York Times*, when referring to the firm, called it an investment banking firm, but "Since we were not investment bankers, the reference was incorrect. Jock particularly disliked being referred to as an investment banking firm, and said, 'We've got to find a better description for ourselves.'" "Very early in our life, Jock described our business in the simplest terms: 'We are here to invest in companies that we believe can succeed, companies with both managements and purposes which we can wholeheartedly embrace, companies that will be fun to work with as we build, and companies which we will be justly proud of when we succeed.'" "Alex Standish felt the designation should make clear the *risks* we were incurring. Bill Jackson said he thought our business was an *adventure*. He wanted the excitement to be captured." "So I suggested 'How about private venture capital investment firm?'—and it caught on, particularly after the *New York Times* began using the term in their stories, not only to describe J.H. Whitney & Co. but also to describe the group that followed our pattern, such as Payson Trask and American Research & Development."

Asked how Whitney had chosen him, Schmidt's soft blue eyes twinkle below thick, long gray eyebrows as he shifts his large frame gently in recollected amusement. "It was more than a year after we'd gotten started that I asked Jock the same question. He'd been asking around, he said, and had the same recommendation from three different sources at three different times." "His family lawyer and friend, Bill Alexander has recommended me. So had Russell Forgan of Glore, Forgan. So, as he said, I was 'endorsed by an intellectual snob and by a social snob.'" "Then he was talking with Roxy, who had begun as a theater usher and had made a fortune developing the movie and theater company, and he recommended me too. So with three such different recommendations, he decided he'd like to meet me, and we did." "Actually, the decision to work together was made *again* a few years later. I got a call from Pug Ismay, [a NATO officer], saying he wanted me to join up with him as his deputy. This was pretty heady stuff—and a call to duty. So I called Jock to tell him what it was all about and ask his advice. He told me that he recognized I would do what I must do; that he wasn't sure he'd have made the commitments in such and such companies without my direct involvement; but that of course I should do what I felt I must. "With a man like that, of course I turned down the NATO job. After all, I wasn't going to save the world. Why not concentrate right here on what I knew I could do?

"One day, Professor Georges Doriot at Harvard wrote to say he'd like to come visit and get to know how we operated. At our invitation, he came for a week and studied everything as he was organizing American Research & Development. An important difference was he raised his capital by going to the public. "We observed AR&D and their investments pretty closely in those early years and concluded they really weren't very good investments. But AR&D's [investment in] Digital Equipment covered over all the other problems. "Interestingly, Doriot was quite opposed to putting more money into Digital Equipment when it needed enough additional capital to convert from being a testing company to being a computer company. In the end, the decision to invest was based primarily on their sense of responsibility to an individual, Professor Olsen."

Among investments J.H. Whitney made in companies at early stages in their development were: Storage Technology, Compaq Computer, Memorex, Global Marine, several ventures in oil (particularly New Zealand Offshore), a group of broadcasters that were later spun off and combined with the Herald Tribune as part of Whitney Communications, and in Minute Maid whose novel frozen concentrate was being taste tested by Whitney and others during a luncheon at Bankers Trust. Unable to find a can opener, Whitney opened the cans with pliers and a screw driver. Having only wine glasses available, they were used. Urbane Jock Whitney feigned a connoisseur's pensive expression, sipped carefully from his glass after swirling the orange liquid as though it were a fine wine and gave this mock-serious judgment: "Good, but intense flavor. Seems a little 'tinny,' but that may be from the can."

By 1964, the firm had received 8,000 proposals—and made investments in 75, or less than 1%—and had multiplied its original capital 10–12 times over 18 years (85% of the gains were made in just seven investments).

Over the span of nearly 50 years, J.H. Whitney Co.'s initial investments were made in this pattern:

1946–49—17	1970–79—23
1950–59—53	1980–89—89
1960–69—53	1990–93—20

The typical size of an initial investment was increased greatly—from $300,000 in the '40s to $3 million in the '80s. The 1970s represent a low level of activity—at least partly due to a lack of liquidity while earlier investments were being "worked out" of difficulties and cash which might have been available for new investments was "tied up." Investments were made on the basis of finding and backing the right people rather than on calculated rates of return. "Jock Whitney always believed business should be fun. There are a million ways to make money where we simply don't want to get personally involved," says Schmidt. "We always look for the value added." The original policy was to invest only in new products or new processes—and to avoid service companies.

Schmidt became Managing Partner in 1959 when Walter Thayer left to become president of Whitney Communications. Most of the marketable securities were distributed, the firm's capital was again about $10 million and Schmidt had a young team to work with.

Schmidt had no set approach to venture investing, believing the best way, perhaps the only way, was to have a tremendous flow of possible deals to select from—and then be highly selective. "Out of five investments," says Schmidt, "you may get one home run and two of a moderate return, maybe eventually doubling your money. And two will fail—and take up most of your time. So cut back early and don't wait around in the land of the living dead." Planning was anathema and Schmidt was clearly *the* principal on *all* decisions. "It's important to Benno to be in complete control," says one observer. "He did not want partners to meet together—even socially—when he was not there." Clearly also *the* spokesman for the firm, he was the only contact with the Whitneys and, until recently, did not allow partners to develop personal closeness with him. One probable consequence has been considerable turnover among the partners. Over nearly 50 years, J.H. Whitney & Co. has had some 50 partners. Schmidt seldom, if ever, said "No" to a partner who wanted to make an investment. A current partner describes the process: "You'd ask any of the other partners or other people in venture capital if they could be helpful. Then you'd spend as much as two or three hours with Benno discussing every aspect—while *he* was determining the level of *your* conviction. There's no beating it to death. Benno can tell by the look in your eyes and the sound of your voice just how confident you really are. If you had *any* brains, you'd realize when to back away."

Venture capital investors learn to be tough on task and to avoid "sentimentality" but as objective as he is, Schmidt shows another dimension—a highly responsible 'nobless oblige' aspect—in his thinking. A colleague recounts their experience with Parsons Forest Industries which had been financed with industrial revenue bonds to provide employment in a depressed region of West Virginia. "The business went very sour and looked sure to stay sour. All the other investors wanted to run for cover. Benno asks, 'Who owns the revenue bonds?' Well, they'd been sold by a Pittsburgh bank to widows and other trust beneficiaries. So Benno says, 'It would be one thing if those bonds were owned by some big bank that could take the loss, but we won't let that happen to people who can't take the loss.' The firm arranged a lease and sub-lease with a small Ohio company involved in making pallets—using the workers' hardwood working skills and machinery. And 13 years later, those bondholders were fully serviced and paid out—and the firm recovered its capital. I like being in a firm with that kind of character."

During the 1970s, Memorex—a major investment—had grave troubles and the stock price plunged from $130 to $1, so J.H. Whitney couldn't liquidate its position. As a result, the firm had little liquid capital available for investment. It was during this decade—when the firm had only limited activity in making new investments and he himself made no venture investments—that Schmidt devoted substantial time to cancer research as a national commitment. One result of his focus on cancer was that Schmidt was wonderfully well prepared—in his own understanding as well as in his network of contacts—for a surge of activity during the 1980s in bio-tech investing. Schmidt explains, "We are in the early stages of a new biomedical revolution today, and progress in biomedical research has reached a point where there can be little, if any, doubt that this revolution will be viewed in history as one of America's greatest contributions to civilization in this century. "Unlike the last biomedical revolution—the discovery and use of antibiotics—the present revolution is far more broadly based and destined to be far more extensive in its reach. As a result of 20 years of the highest quality fundamental research, we are now beginning for the first time to deal with diseases on the basis of a fundamental understanding of life at the cellular, molecular and even atomic levels. As we better understand the origin and cause of the diseases that compose today's medical agenda, we can develop far more satisfactory approaches to prevention, amelioration, or cure. "This biomedical revolution is quintessentially American and, while it was originally based largely upon funding by the Federal government of fundamental basic research, the level of understanding has now reached the point that hundreds of millions of dollars of private sector money are going into the conversion of this knowledge into pharmaceutical products. Biomedical science is one remaining area of high technology where America is still the undisputed leader."

Don Ackerman, Schmidt's partner at J.H. Whitney for 25 years sums up Schmidt as follows: "Benno Schmidt is the most remarkable man I ever met." "He has a memory that is the oral equivalent of a photographic memory. Without notes, he could and would recall—and repeat with extraordinary precision—conversations from five, even ten years before. "He has splendid intuition, particularly in sizing up people. He has great sensitivity and is able to see through to the real person, looking right through whatever protective barriers a person might put up—even sensing emotional problems—or high blood pressure.

"Benno has a commanding, sometimes even overpowering intellect. With very little information he can reason quickly through to a logical conclusion that others would later—sometimes *much* later—come to see and agree with. Of course, he is well aware of this capability. At law school, he apparently read very little, but listened so very well that he performed quite well on examinations. "Benno has almost always been the acknowledged leader of whatever group he was in, even with groups of quite prominent people. "Stringently non-political, in his public activities, he is always *very* aware of and sensitive to political matters. When the Mets and Jets got into a messy squabble over sharing Shea Stadium, Governor Carey asked him to mediate the dispute. He agreed, explaining he knew many of the people on both sides and stipulated only that there would never be any mention of his name in public and that if any progress were made, it would be announced by New York's Mayor Beame.

"He has an aura of profound probity as well as warmth and charm. After a dinner talk by Franklin Thomas (now head of the Ford Foundation), Thomas' mother spoke with Benno and later said to her son, 'I like that man. I trust that man.' That's how all sorts of people relate to him.

"He has a wonderful sense of humor, particularly with words and their meaning. But he can sometimes seem almost overbearing, speaking right through you—and whatever you might have to say. It's not that he won't listen to others; he's just so extraordinarily focused on what he's thinking and saying that he doesn't even realize you're talking."

Fayez Sarofim

HUGH AYNESWORTH

Born in Egypt but long a Texan, Fayez Sarofim has been a successful investor and a successful money manager for more than 40 years, enjoying the esteem of his professional colleagues the entire time. He built Houston's leading investment firm based on optimism and an appreciation of strong-willed entrepreneurs. This piece introduces an established, confident Fayez.

The man generally regarded as the leading money manager in Texas bears little resemblance to the state's archetype: he doesn't have a ranch, he is not flamboyant and earthy and he doesn't even wear a Stetson. He is, in fact, an

Excerpted from *Institutional Investor 4* (April 1970), pp. 57–58, 60, 94. This copyrighted material is reprinted with permission from: **Institutional Investor, Inc.**, 488 Madison Avenue, New York, NY 10022.

urbane, vested Egyptian who speaks with the slight hint of a southern accent, surrounds much of what he does in mystery, and answers to the name of Fayez Sarofim. Some of his friends call him "The Sphinx."

Sarofim's 11-year-old firm of Fayez Sarofim & Co. runs in excess of $1.2 [b]illion, not that anyone would know it. His fourteenth-floor office, tucked away in the corner of a Houston office building, doesn't even have a name on the door. ("We don't get a lot of drop-in business," he says.) And Sarofim himself is singularly wary of discussing his high-powered list of clients. . . .

Sitting behind a marble football-shaped desk in his brightly decorated office, which features 100 different works of art and sculpture, Sarofim, 41, explains, "When you seek publicity, it takes away from your productive efforts. It might accelerate your growth curve to where it might disrupt your business." Then, straightening a crease in his conservative blue pin-striped suit, he grinned. "We have a nice business," he says, matter-of-factly, as if to lay the whole subject to rest.

• • •

Sarofim attributes his success . . . to timing and emphasis. "We don't try to hit a home run every time," he says. "We try for consistent performance because we're managing huge sums of money for people and we treat that money very seriously."

But whether he goes for the roundtripper every time or not, Sarofim thinks there are a lot of singles, doubles and triples around and the opportunities are limited only by careful study and planning. (He himself will visit as many as 200 companies in a given year.) He frankly admits that he is an optimist and offers several reasons why. "It's interesting," he says, looking through a thick looseleaf book which reminds one of a pro football quarterback's playbook, "that the first 10 years I was in business the gross national product went up from $447 billion to $860 billion. Corporate profits after taxes were up from $22 billion to $51 billion. Dividends went up from $11.6 billion to $24.5 billion. "Now if you were ready to invest in 1958 and I told you that the president of the United States would be assassinated, you'd have a missile crisis in Cuba, and you'd have a war in Vietnam that would divide the nation, you'd probably say, 'I won't invest it.'"

Sarofim believes that in making such assessments, as a foreigner, he has a real edge. "A person born abroad has a greater feel for the strengths of this country and not its weaknesses," he says. "Every country in the world has pluses and minuses and you have to be able to decide where the plus outweighs the minus."

The son of a prosperous pharmaceutical and agricultural products distributor in Egypt, Sarofim attended an English boarding school in Cairo until 1945. In 1946 his father dispatched him, at 17, to the University of California at Berkeley to study food technology. He was somewhat of a reluctant student, and notes that "coming here was quite a transition.

When you live in an underdeveloped country the only things you are exposed to involve food, shelter and clothing." He graduated in three years, and despite a rather complete disinterest in matters of finance, succumbed to parental pressure to enter the Harvard Business School. "My father said I could leave after a week," he recalls, "but I soon called him and said, 'This is my love and what I've been looking for.'"

Upon graduation in 1951 he was offered—and he accepted—a training job with Anderson, Clayton . . . a Houston-based firm of cotton merchants with interests in Egypt. The idea was that Sarofim would eventually represent the firm in Egypt. But a lot changed during the seven years Sarofim was with Anderson, Clayton. For one thing, the firm was an early leader in seeking market performance for its pension money and Sarofim took on the responsibility in this area, becoming "the only nonexecutive on the executive committee." His father began turning to him for portfolio advice, too, and of course, Nasser took power in Egypt.

Thus, armed with an optimistic philosophy about growth and little else, Sarofim opened his own firm in August 1958. His first client came in the back door when he called to offer Sarofim a job. "He asked what I was doing and I told him I was managing money. Now in 1958, managing money for performance for individuals was not too well known." But when Sarofim explained it, he won his first account, which eventually amounted to $3 million.

• • •

Sarofim's biggest early successes stemmed directly from his days at the Harvard Business School. One of his closest friends in the class of 1951 was Arthur J. Rock of San Francisco. When Rock put together his venture capital firm of Davis & Rock in 1962, Sarofim advised several of his larger clients to back Rock. They did, and when Rock got in on the ground floor in Teledyne and Scientific Data Systems, so did Sarofim and a host of his clients.

Not only did Sarofim get in on SDS when it came out at 25, he picked up a large interest long before the firm went public. "That cost only a few cents a share," he recalls happily. SDS then split a couple of times shortly after it went public in 1963, and when the merger with Xerox came about they got 1½ shares of Xerox for each one of SDS. "Our investment in Xerox today is in excess of $100 million," he says.

The old B school network produced another of Sarofim's major winners. "We've done well with a company called Electronic Memories & Magnetics run by another friend and classmate of mine," he says. As with SDS, he bought this early, and then it went public. Present holdings are worth more than $10 million.

"Basically we bet on people," Sarofim says in explaining his approach. But, needless to say, the "old boy" network, while probably very reliable about people, does not produce enough investment ideas to satisfy a billion dollar portfolio. Hence, his money is primarily in large and well-known companies; hence, too, he and his top aides travel continually throughout the country. (He has a staff of 26, most of them secretaries.) "We all try to do research and counseling," he says, "and I think that's a very strong point. This keeps us fresh. It gives us a better understanding of an industry. In making recommendations, you have a much stronger feel after visiting with the managers."

• • •

Sarofim seldom moves for short-term plays. "We have just found it is very difficult to make money on the short-term. I think that if you will look at the history of the wealth created in this country you'll find very few fortunes have been built on trading. Most of them have been built by investing in the right company and staying with it." To identify those companies, Sarofim has some extremely bright young men in his firm. The aides read and compile memos which often go into his playbook. "I can read this on a plane or on nights at home. It really keeps me up to date," he says. Money is committed by the firm along fairly typical procedures. "The key people in the organization," he explains, "sit down to review as often as need be, which is several times a week." They discuss the potentials, the state of the economy, and projections of the type of stock under consideration. "We try to find the specific investment which will give us the proper, portfolio investment mix."

Still, Sarofim makes almost all of the final decisions himself. Even when he is out of town, he's on the telephone to the home office early in the morning, planning out the work schedule for his assistants. Some observers who have carefully watched Sarofim's operation suggest this is something of a problem, that even though he is terribly overworked he doesn't delegate enough authority. They point out that last year he lost two promising aides for this very reason. Further, these critics suggest that no matter how talented Sarofim is—and there is universal respect for that talent—his performance is bound to suffer because his firm has become too big for one man to handle.

• • •

Sarofim lives about a ten-minute drive from his office. . . . He lives with his wife Louisa, the adopted daughter of Herman Brown of the large construction firm Brown & Root. They have two children, Christopher, six and a half, and Allison, almost two. Sarofim plays a bit of tennis at the local country club and he and his wife are active in local art circles; he is on the board of the Museum of Fine Arts and she . . . is on the boards of the Society for the Performing Arts and the Houston Ballet Foundation.

But if Sarofim has become a well-known figure in the Houston art community, he remains quite a bit less so in other quarters. Not long ago, a well-dressed businessman wandered rather perplexedly around the fourteenth floor of the First City National Bank building in Houston and began asking if anyone knew where Sarofim's office was. No one he asked could tell him.

Michael Steinhardt

JULIE ROHRER

Michael Steinhardt was an extraordinarily active—and ferociously effective—money manager who did, thank you, rather well for many years—and then did not and stopped.

There are, really, two Michael Steinhardts. One is Michael Steinhardt after the close of the market: relaxed, charming, discussing his investments with a low-key objectivity, almost a bored weariness, as though he had seen and survived too many market battles to care very much about the current vagaries of the Dow. This is Michael Steinhardt the devoted family man, father of three, the gracious host, the ready and substantial contributor to many philanthropies.

But then there is the other Michael Steinhardt, the Steinhardt of the trading day. Standing at a desk that was designed by an architect friend in the shape of a ship's bow, storming in and out of the trading room, he presides over his firm with the monomania of Captain Ahab aboard the *Pequod*. He scowls. He fumes. He grunts. He bellows. He has little ability, if any, to put the market or his performance in perspective. "He has an overriding need to win every day," says one of his former analysts. And when he isn't winning, adds another, "he suffers as though a major tragedy has occurred." As Steinhardt himself admits when he has slipped back into his laid-back persona: "Too much of my self-image fluctuates with my performance. I don't think I am terribly good at being proportioned or reasoned."

• • •

And no one wields more clout with Wall Street. Time after time, it is on Steinhardt that the Street bestows its most sought-after of gifts: the "first call." Small wonder: While Steinhardt's assets under management are

Excerpted from *Institutional Investor 18* (September 1984), pp. 105–106. This copyrighted material is reprinted with permission from: **Institutional Investor, Inc.**, 488 Madison Avenue, New York, NY 10022.

relatively small compared with other institutions', his shorting and leveraging activity combined with enormously high turnover—he won't even
put a number on it and says simply that it's "off the page"—make him one
of the biggest commission payers on Wall Street. Steinhardt himself has
put commissions generated by his funds at a probably conservative $15
million a year. As a result, the attention and service—and, at times, reverence—accorded him by the Street borders on idolatry. Says one trader:
"Michael is king. Everybody wants to make money for Michael." . . .

Like other monarchs of the Street, Steinhardt came from humble beginnings, growing up in a lower-middle-class neighborhood in Brooklyn
and attending New York City's public schools. His IQ was high enough to
enable him to qualify for a program that allowed him to graduate from
high school at the age of sixteen. Then, at his father's behest, he attended
the Wharton School of the University of Pennsylvania, graduating in
three years.

At nineteen, then, he was ready to launch a career—and there was no
doubt in his mind as to what it would be. For his bar mitzvah, his father,
who Steinhardt says was a confirmed gambler, had given him 100 shares
each of Penn Dixie Cement and Columbia Gas System stock instead of
cash. (His mother and father were divorced when Steinhardt was one year
old.) Steinhardt recalls that at the age of thirteen, "I knew nothing about
the stock market, and nobody I knew knew anything about the stock market." But undaunted, he sent for various advisory reports, began reading the
World Telegram, scanning the noon prices, the 2:00 prices and the closing
prices. While other kids were playing stickball after school, Steinhardt was
hanging out at the local Merrill Lynch retail office in downtown Brooklyn
with the "old men smoking their cigars and watching the tape. It became a
fascination for me," he remembers. By the time he was fourteen, he was
hooked on trading stocks.

With his college diploma in hand in 1960, Steinhardt headed for Wall
Street. He first worked for about two years as a research assistant at the
Calvin Bullock mutual fund organization and then did a stint in the U.S.
Army reserves. Subsequently, for a brief period, he was a writer for the publication *Financial World*. A large part of his job there was to respond to in-
quiries from subscribers asking for investment advice, ranging from "What
is your view of General Motors?" to more esoteric and difficult questions
there were time-consuming and hard to research and answer. As time went
by, Steinhardt's diligence waned, and letters began to pile up on his desk.
One day they were discovered by his boss, and Steinhardt was fired. "It was
awful," he recalls. "I thought my career on Wall Street was over."

Although he was subsequently rehired, Steinhardt soon took a job as a
research analyst at Loeb Rhoades & Co., and it was there—in the mid-
1960s—that his name began to be reckoned with on the Street. In the
heyday of the conglomerate stocks, one of Steinhardt's first recommendations was Gulf+Western Industries, which subsequently tripled. Other

impressive recommendations followed, and before long Steinhardt was known as one of Wall Street's top special situations analysts.

• • •

Soon, Steinhardt began swapping information with another hot special situations researcher, Howard Berkowitz, who was at A.G. Becker. Berkowitz had been a fraternity brother of Jerrold Fine at the University of Pennsylvania. (Ironically, all three attended Pennsylvania at the same time, although neither Berkowitz nor Fine knew Steinhardt there.) Fine, too, was already a star in his own right, managing the partners' capital at Dominick & Dominick. Berkowitz introduced Fine to Steinhardt, and on July 10, 1967, the three opened up Steinhardt, Fine & Berkowitz, with initial capital of about $7.7 million.

"It was a euphoric period. There was a sense of optimism that existed at the time that things were growing and moving. It was within that context that the firm was begun," Steinhardt recalls. Indeed, within about two-and-a-half months . . . the capital had appreciated by more than 30 percent, compared with a gain in the market of 6.5 percent. In the next fiscal year, when the market rose 9 percent, the partnership was up a riveting 100 percent (83.7 percent, when adjusted for general partners' fees). By the end of fiscal 1969, when the partnership dipped by about 1.4 percent versus a decline in the market of 6.2 percent, Steinhardt, Fine & Berkowitz had close to $30 million in capital, and its founders, all under 30 years of age, were millionaires.

Laurence A. Tisch

WILLIAM R. SHELTON

Larry Tisch, described by *Time* in 1986 as "cautious where others are carefree, daring while others are timid," is tenaciously cost-conscious and a tough negotiator. He "finds business very relaxing" and with his brother Preston R. (Bob) Tisch has built a family fortune of more than $2 billion by buying businesses—like CBS—that they'd "be proud to own." They are *active* owners, often bringing a new management team to a new property. This profile dates from their early years.

Of all the builders of great fortunes in the years since World War II, perhaps the unlikeliest are two amiable young brothers named Tisch. They began operating in 1946 with a stake of about $125,000. Today they boast a net worth of $65 million or $7 million a year, i.e., they earn about 10 percent on their money. Aside from the magnitude of their success, there are several grounds for regarding the Tisches with wonder. They are only in their mid-thirties—though a dozen-odd years of big-time deals, and heavy losses of hair on top, have left them looking somewhat more mature. None of the conventional images of the get-rich-quick artist seem to fit them. They are obviously not flamboyant promoters who have fast-talked their way into the big money, nor are they wild gamblers who simply hit the jackpot. They are, in fact, remarkably unpretentious, low-pressure types. Until last year—when they invested something over $6 million in Loew's Theatres, Inc., apparently gaining control of that enterprise—their names were scarcely known in the business community.

At present their largest single asset is the splendid Americana Hotel just outside Miami, Florida. The Americana has been practically debt-free since the Tisches built it three years ago; recently they turned down an offer of $28 million for it. In addition, they have large interests in three sizable housing developments in Florida. They operate the Traymore and Ambassador hotels in Atlantic City, New Jersey, and own the elegant Colony Motel there. In New York City they own two office buildings and manage the Belmont Plaza Hotel. All these assets as well as a few other hotels, the Loew's Theatres stock, and about $10 million in U.S. government bonds, are owned by the Tisch Hotel-Motel Corp., and by several other holding companies, of which the brothers are sole owners.

When they are prevailed upon to recount their own business history, the Tisches tend to be disarmingly bland and matter of fact; indeed, they almost seem at times to be suggesting that any young man with a little luck and some intelligence can make $65 million. This is an engaging notion, but not exactly borne out by the Tisches' whole story.

A certain measure of their success must, of course, be laid to the fact that they happened along just when the greatest boom in U.S. history was getting under way. But the resort-hotel business was, and is, a treacherous way to make a living, and even in the postwar years a fair number of entrepreneurs have gone broke trying it. . . . Whereas both resort hotels and motels tended to be rather unbusinesslike propositions before the war, run by gregarious Ma's and Pa's with only the foggiest notions about scientific management, the postwar years have produced a breed of businesslike operators who know exactly how to apply cost-accounting procedures, know how to take advantage of the tax laws, and not the least, have a flair for promotion.

• • •

The Tisches are typical of this new breed, except that they have displayed a most untypical daring in some of their ventures. There are very few young men who would have had the audacity to sink most of the family's savings in a venerable hotel in Lakewood, New Jersey, as Laurence Tisch did in 1946. There are also few families that would have let their sons make such an investment. Neither Larry Tisch nor his parents had had any experience in the hotel business; indeed, it was not until he heard about the Lakewood hotel that Larry decided hotels were to be his career. He had attended public schools in New York City, studied economics at New York University's School of Banking and Finance (graduating *cum laude* at 18), taken a master's degree in industry and management at the University of Pennsylvania's Wharton School, and spent three years in the Army, attached to the Office of Strategic Services' decoding section in Washington. Six months at Harvard Law School after that were enough to convince him that it was time to acquire a business. He was then 23.

The Tisches were able to start him off with about $125,000 in cash: $80,000 from the sale of a summer camp the family had operated for a number of years in the Poconos, and $45,000 accumulated from a clothing manufacturing company that Al Tisch, Larry's father, had operated on New York's Union Square. He entrusted the money to his son, who applied himself to a search for business opportunities and in April, 1946, spotted an advertisement in the New York *Times* which indicated that a hotel called Laurel-in-the-Pines, in Lakewood, was on the market.

Father and son took an exploratory drive down to the Jersey resort. The deal looked like a sure thing. The $375,000 price worked out to $1,250 a room, which was very low for an established old hotel; and the annual gross was well above the price. Only $175,000 of cash was required; a friend of Al Tisch's put up $50,000 of this amount and received a one-fourth interest. In the final analysis, the deal hinged on the sellers' and the buyers' differing estimates of the hotel business in Lakewood. The sellers, a family named Seiden feared that the wartime boom was over, and that Lakewood no longer had much to offer; even the gambling houses that had long flourished in the area were now being closed down by the state. The Tisches thought the boom was just beginning, and that the Laurel-in-the-Pines occupancy rate could be stabilized by developing a broader clientele base.

The Tisches went to work. They installed an indoor swimming pool and an artificial outdoor ice rink, on which, as a promotional stunt, they staged a basketball game on skates. They also imported three reindeer from Finland to pull the hotel sleighs. The hotel was an immediate success. The Tisches made enough the first year to buy out their partner. In 1948, Larry's younger brother, Preston Robert Tisch, graduated from the University of Michigan and joined the enterprise, and that year they made enough from the Laurel-in-the-Pines to buy the Grand Hotel, a summer-resort establishment in Highmount, New York. . . . In 1950, leaving a relative of the Seidens in charge of their two hotels, they went out in pursuit of bigger game.

• • •

The game they found was the stately old 575-room Traymore Hotel, an Atlantic City landmark since 1915. The Traymore was then owned by a man named Frank Gravatt, who was in his sixties and owned a sizable number of properties in Atlantic City—and who was increasingly concerned about the unliquid state of his holdings. In an effort to sell the Traymore, he had 160 copies of a specially written brochure mailed out to anyone he thought might be interested. Larry Tisch, on seeing the statement, was immediately intrigued. He observed that the Traymore was grossing more than $3 million but that its expenses were extraordinarily high, so that it was showing a steady loss. He concluded, after extensive analysis, that he could clear $750,000 if he had a chance to manage the hotel himself. When he and Gravatt were unable to come to terms on a purchase price, they compromised by agreeing that Tisch could lease the hotel, with an option to meet any other purchaser's price. Meanwhile, the rent paid by the Tisches was $520,000, which meant that Larry felt reasonably sure of clearing $230,000 that first year. The lessees also had to put up a security deposit of $500,000, and the Tisches had only $100,000. They persuaded a bank in Asbury Park, New Jersey, to lend them another $100,000 and signed a note for the remaining $300,000.

They took over the Traymore at 9:00 A.M. on May 1, 1950. Two hours later, the hotel's general manager announced that he was resigning, and in the next few hours the maître d'hôtel and other key personnel followed him. These resignations seem to have been principally a vote of no confidence in the callow new management (the Tisch boys were then in their mid-twenties), although anti-Semitism may have played a part; there had not previously been any big hotels in Atlantic City under Jewish management. In any case, the resignations left the Tisch boys out on a long limb . . . .

They overhauled the Traymore and its operations in fairly drastic fashion. They cut the staff and brought in less expensive entertainment, but they vastly improved the quality of the food—principally by turning the operation of the dining room over to a young man from the hotel-management consulting firm of Harris-Kerr-Foster. The firm had been retained by Gravatt to study the hotel's dining room, and when the Tisches read the report they hired its author and gave him a long-term contract.

Meanwhile, Gravatt was still eager to sell the hotel, and after their first year of operations the Tisches talked him into accepting their terms. The purchase price that was agreed on was $4,350,000 but only $700,000 in cash; and $500,000 of that would be represented by the Tisches' original security. The beauty of the deal was the new tax shelter it would give the Tisches. Of the $4,350,000, about $3,500,000 would be depreciable—over twelve and a half years, on the average. Under the 150 percent accelerated-depreciation formula allowed by the tax laws, they would be able to depreciate this amount at a rate of 12 percent a year—that is, for $200,000 of additional investment, they would get $420,000 in annual depreciation allowance. . . . The Traymore proved to be every bit as profitable as the Tisch boys thought it would be. They added an ice-skating rink and indoor and outdoor swimming pools, modernized the marquee, the entranceway, the lobby, and most of the rooms, and then raised their room rates an average of 25 percent. Even at the higher rates they were able to increase the levels of occupancy, so that in the following five years the hotel's annual net averaged around a million dollars.

Their spectacular success nerved them to try again. In 1951 they signed a 30-year lease on the 700-room Ambassador Hotel in Atlantic City, which, like the Traymore, had a record of steady losses. Here again the Tisches showed an astute sense of timing. They signed the Ambassador lease and took charge in October 1951, but got an agreement that rental payments would not begin until after April 30, 1952—when the Tisch Hotels, Inc., fiscal year ended. This meant that the corporation's heavy earnings, now consisting principally of Traymore profits, would get an additional tax sheltering from the predictable operating losses of the Ambassador in the off-season months; eventually these losses came to $200,000, which brought the corporation's shelter over income that year to $620,000. But the Tisches' major objective, of course, was to make the Ambassador a money-maker like the Traymore, and this, after another extensive overhauling of property and management, they succeeded in doing. Beginning in fiscal 1953, the Ambassador had an average net of $750,000 a year for three years.

By the mid-1950s the boys found themselves in a position to begin realizing some substantial gains. In 1956 they sold the Traymore for $15 million, and at the same time negotiated a contract that left them in charge of its management; in addition, they retained a parcel of the Traymore's land, worth about $250,000, some of which they have leased out for $25,000 a year. In the same year they sold their Ambassador lease for $5 million, though they retained control of the Ambassador management too.

• • •

Meanwhile the boys had also made their first forays into the hotel business in New York City, and found it possible to pick up a few fast millions there too. Their first big deal involved the massive, 1,500-room McAlpin Hotel, at Broadway and Thirty-fourth Street. One day at a cocktail party Larry and Bob met Joe Levy, who owned both the McAlpin and the Crawford Clothes chain. Levy took a liking to them, and on the spot proposed, soberly, that they lease the McAlpin from him; he would not even ask them for any security deposit. The deal made sense for Levy because his hotel, which did a $4-million business, was not making enough to satisfy him, and he was anxious to bring in a new management that might help him build it up. The Tisches, who were also sober (Larry is a teetotaler), accepted his offer.

Levy also persuaded them, without much difficulty, to take over leases on two office buildings adjacent to the McAlpin, originally acquired to protect the view from the hotel's upper stories. In the next year or so, the Tisches invested about $1 million in redecorating and rehabilitating the hotel. The changes enabled them to raise the room rates an average of 30 percent and to raise the occupancy rate some 20 percent. Over a thirty-month period, the Tisches netted $1,500,000 for themselves; meanwhile, the hotel had become a much more valuable property, and in 1954, Levy sold it to the Sheraton chain for $9 million. The Tisches obligingly took the two office buildings off his hands for $500,000. Today the buildings are worth at least twice that.

• • •

At about the time they were sold out of the McAlpin, Larry and Bob heard about an interesting situation at the 800-room Belmont Plaza Hotel, also in New York . . .

Two things made the Belmont seem attractive to the Tisches. First, it was only a block from Third Avenue; the old Third Avenue elevated railway was soon to be torn down, and they surmised that real estate in that part of New York's East Side would become much more attractive. Second, the Belmont was across the street from the Waldorf-Astoria on Lexington Avenue, and might, if it were cleaned up, get a lot of the Waldorf's convention business overflow.

The Tisches spent about $1 million in renovating the Belmont; they built a new bar and dining room, stripped off the green paint that covered the oak in the lobby, refurnished the rooms, and outfitted them with television sets. They converted the two top floors to office space, and raised the room rates on the other floors an average of 20 percent, which enabled them to recover virtually all of their investment in two years. . . . In December 1956, the Tisches sold their lease for $1,700,000—most of which was clear profit.

• • •

Nineteen fifty-six was a milestone of sorts for the Tisches. The long succession of profitable deals had made millionaires of them—together they were worth perhaps $30 million—and they were receiving an increasing number of propositions from hotel owners. Any proposition that looked good for a return of at least 12 percent (before taxes) still received their close attention, but by this time the boys were looking for something more than those fast in-and-out deals. . . . And so they began to search around for some ventures they might find more challenging.

In 1955 they had laid out $1,350,000 in cash to buy ten acres of oceanfront property at Bal Harbour, Florida—about four miles from the main cluster of luxury hotels in Miami Beach. Early in 1956 they began building the Americana Hotel on the property. While Bob supervised their properties in the North, Larry took charge in Florida. He moved his wife and four boys down to Miami Beach, bought himself a bicycle to ride to work on, and set out to get the hotel finished that year.

Larry wanted, and was prepared to pay for, a resort hotel that would be extraordinarily luxurious even by the fleshpot standards of Miami Beach. The Tisches built the Americana for $17 million, without a mortgage, and without acquiring any other long-term debt. (Later they spent another $7,500,000 expanding the Americana, and this time they did take a $4-million first mortgage.) There were several other remarkable aspects to the building of the Americana. The hotel was built without any overtime costs; and despite a jurisdictional dispute between the plumbers, carpenters, and tile workers over the right to install toothbrush holders in the bathrooms, the hotel was finished on schedule. It opened for business on December 1, 1956. . . .

At the opening night festivities were such famous personages as Gina Lollobrigida, Groucho Marx, and Florida Governor LeRoy Collins.

The opulence of the hotel was unabashed. Just inside the entrance, guests found a sizable glass-enclosed garden with orchids and several varieties of lush foliage; when it rained, these were doused through an open roof. There was a rock pool on the ground floor in which alligators slithered; as fast as they died from eating plastic toothpicks that the guests thoughtlessly tossed in the water, they were replaced. (Guests also toss in an average of $100 a week in coins.) Scattered about the lobby was $100,000 worth of paintings. The lobby was done in Italian travertine marble, the balconies in Panamanian tile, the fixtures mostly in Venetian blown glass and brass. Outside the hotel, a recreational area ran some 600 feet along the ocean. Spotted on the grounds were "lanai suites" (i.e., Hawaiian cottages that included a bedroom, living room, two baths, and a galley) renting for $68 a day. Rooms in the hotel rented for $32 a day, with meals extra. Morris Lapidus, the distinguished architect who designed the Americana, spoke at the opening-day ceremonies and said that the hotel was "more dedicated to the spirit of play than any hotel I have ever created." . . .

• • •

When the Americana was properly launched, the Tisches took a long stride into the motel business—something they had been thinking of doing for years . . . .

Indeed, the future of downtown motels may have been very much on their minds a year ago, when they suddenly began to buy heavily into Loew's, Inc. Their real objective was to gain control of Loew's Theatres, a subsidiary corporation that, in the wake of a federal anti-trust suit, was being spun off from the parent film-producing company.

Loew's Theatres owned a vast amount of property, mostly motion-picture houses, on rather expensive real estate in downtown city areas. The corporation reported its book value at about $60 million, but this was a fairly conservative reckoning, since the fixed assets were carried either at original cost (less depreciation) or at their 1925 appraisal value; the real market value of the corporation's net assets might be $80 million. On this, the corporation earned only $2 million in the year ending August 31, 1959. It was obvious that many of those theatres could be put to better use.

Larry Tisch began buying Loew's just before the spinoff; thus far, he has acquired more than 450,000 shares (17 percent) of the theatre company's stock at an average price of $14. The stated book value works out to $22 a share, and the Tisches are convinced that, with proper management, the corporation should certainly earn 10 percent of that, i.e., about $2.20 a share—which presumably would bring the market price well over $14. Larry went onto the board of Loew's Theatres, with no real opposition, early last fall, and at the same time moved his family from Florida to Scarsdale, New York, in order to devote himself more or less full time to boosting Loew's earnings.

This will take time, obviously, since it will involve the renovation of some theatres, the razing of others, and the erection of new buildings— possibly Tisch-managed hotels and motels—on the theatres' old sites. It is certainly hard to believe that the Tisches will be able to multiply their money quite so rapidly in Loew's as they did in some of their earlier hotel deals. But then, it is only natural that they should be slowing up a little. After all, they will be 40 in a few more years.

Warren Buffett

ROBERT LENZNER

Warren Buffett continues to dazzle those who don't know him with the results he achieves as an investor. Those who do know him are even more dazzled by the extraordinary talent and discipline with which he does his work. This profile commemorates the 1993 occasion of his becoming America's wealthiest individual.

On the night of August 17, a steady stream of young baseball fans approached a middle-aged businessman wearing a red polo shirt who was sitting near the field at Omaha's Rosenblatt Stadium. Often shyly, always deferentially, they asked him to sign their scorecards. Warren Buffett accommodated them—in such numbers as to almost guarantee the famous financier's signature won't bring premium prices on the autograph market.

Except for the polite autograph seekers, there were no indications that this pale, slightly bulging Omaha native was the richest person in America and an investment genius on a scale that the world rarely sees. There were

Excerpted from *Forbes* (October 18, 1993), pp. 40–45. Reprinted by permission of *Forbes Magazine*. © Forbes Inc., 1993.

no fawning retainers or hangers-on, no bodyguards to drive off paparazzi and supplicants. Buffett is 25 percent owner of the Omaha Royals, and by all appearances that day you would have thought that is all he is. His close friend, Charles Munger, puts it this way: "One of the reasons Warren is so cheerful is that he doesn't have to remember his lines"—meaning that the public Buffett and the private Buffett are the same man.

Except for his company's private plane—more a business tool than a luxury—there is nothing of self-importance about him. He drives his own car, lives in a nondescript house, hardly ever vacations and just last month passed up an invitation from his close friend, former Washington Post chairman Katharine Graham, to dine with President Clinton on Martha's Vineyard. Buffett will travel a long way for a good bridge game, but he'll scarcely bother to cross the street for the sake of rubbing shoulders with celebrities.

"I have in life all I want right here," he says. "I love every day. I mean, I tap dance in here and work with nothing but people I like. I don't have to work with people I don't like." Buffett caps the statement with a typically Midwestern cackle.

That's Warren Buffett, living proof that nice guys sometimes do finish first. And we do mean first. . . .

This folksy, only-in-America character was worth—as [we] went to press—$8.3 billion in the form of 42 percent of his investment company, Berkshire Hathaway, whose shares at $16,600 each are the highest priced on the New York Stock Exchange.

Berkshire Hathaway owns 48 percent of GEICO Corp., a big insurance company; 18 percent of Capital Cities/ABC, Inc.; 11 percent of Gillette Co.; 8.2 percent of Federal Home Loan Mortgage Corp.; 12 percent of Wells Fargo & Co.; about 7 percent of the Coca-Cola Co.; 15 percent of the Washington Post Co.; 14 percent of General Dynamics; 14 percent of the voting power in Wall Street's Salomon Inc. We could go on, but we won't, except to add the *Buffalo News*, a newspaper he bought for $32.5 million in 1977 and that now throws off more cash before taxes each year than he paid for it. . . .

Berkshire Hathaway has spread its investments across a broad range: media, soft drinks, manufacturing, insurance, banking, finance, consumer goods. As long as the economy grows, you can count on his fortune continuing to grow.

It's almost equally certain that when this 63-year-old is called to his reward, he will have set the stage for the biggest charitable foundation ever, one that easily will dwarf the legacies of Rockefeller, Ford, and Carnegie. Over the past 23 years, Buffett's investments have compounded his wealth at an average annual rate of 29 percent. He probably can't keep that up. But give him 15 percent. If he lives another 20 years and does 15 percent, the Buffett Foundation will have well over $100 billion. If, as is quite possible, he lives a good deal longer . . . well, you get the picture. . . .

We asked him [what he thought of the market], but knowing he hates the question, we did it in a slightly roundabout fashion. What would his hero and mentor, Benjamin Graham, say about the stock market today?

Not missing a beat, Buffett shot back with the response Graham gave when he appeared before the 1955 Fulbright hearings in Washington: "'Common stocks look high and are high, but they are not as high as they look.' And my guess is that he [Graham] would say the same thing today."

That's about the limit of the specific investment advice Buffett is willing to give: high but not too high.

In dodging the question, Buffett is not just being evasive. Like Graham and the famous British economist and brilliant stock market investor John Maynard Keynes, whose thinking he greatly admires, Buffett believes that all there is to investing is picking good stocks at good prices and staying with them as long as they remain good companies. He doesn't try to time the market or to catch swings. . . . Buffett: "Keynes essentially said don't try and figure out what the market is doing. Figure out business you understand, and concentrate. Diversification is protection against ignorance, but if you don't feel ignorant, the need for it goes down drastically." . . .

His most basic rule is: Don't put too many eggs in your basket and pick them carefully.

Buffett: "I believe every business school graduate should sign an unbreakable contract promising not to make more than 20 major decisions in a lifetime. In a 40-year career you would make a decision every two years."

Buffett points out that he's not prescribing for all investors. Others can make money out of frenetic trading. "It's doing what you understand and what you are psychologically comfortable with. . . ."

Technology stocks are definitely not what Buffett feels comfortable with. "Bill Gates is a good friend, and I think he may be the smartest guy I've ever met. But, I don't know what those little things do."

Except for a position in Guinness Plc., the international spirits concern, Berkshire owns no foreign stocks—ignoring as usual the latest Wall Street fad. "If I can't make money in a $4 trillion market [the U.S.], then I shouldn't be in this business. I get $150 million earnings pass-through from international operations of Gillette and Coca-Cola. That's my international portfolio."

Again, it's staying with what he feels comfortable with. If some guys own the only newspaper in Hong Kong or Sydney, Australia and it's at the right price, I'm perfectly willing to buy it."

Those papers may be in foreign climes, but they are in a business he well understands. That gets close to the heart of the way Buffett, your quintessential Midwesterner, thinks: not in concepts or theories but in intensely practical terms. Buffett doesn't buy stocks; stocks are an abstraction. He buys businesses—or parts of businesses, if the whole thing is not for sale. "I've no desire to try and play some huge trend of a national nature," is the way he puts it.

Buffett's disdain for trends, concepts and the slogans so beloved on Wall Street grows in part from a simple realization that neither he nor any other man can see the future. It also grows from his extreme inner self-confidence: He has not the psychological need for the constant wheeling and dealing, buying and selling that afflicts so many successful business and financial people. When he believes in something, he does not require immediate market upticks to confirm his judgment.

"What I like is economic strength in an area where I understand it and where I think it will last. It's very difficult to think of two companies in the world in important areas that have the presence and acceptance of Coke and Gillette," two of Berkshire Hathaway's core holdings.

Some smart investors like to say they invest in people, not in businesses. Buffett is skeptical. He says, in his wry way: "When a manager with a reputation for brilliance tackles a business with a reputation for bad economics, the reputation of the business remains intact."

It's not that Buffett doesn't think managers matter. He does. But he doesn't invest on people alone. "If you put those same guys to work in a buggy whip company, it wouldn't have made much difference."

His credo, though he doesn't call it that, can be expressed [as] . . . "I am a better investor because I am a businessman, and a better businessman because I am an investor." He's saying a great deal in this seemingly cryptic statement: that business and finance are not two separate activities but intimately connected. A good businessman thinks like an investor. A good investor thinks like a businessman.

There's a fine line here, however. Buffett doesn't try to run the businesses he invests in. As he puts it, "The executives regard me as an investing partner. I'm somewhat involved, talking over leadership succession, potential acquisitions and   other important matters. Managers know I think about these things and they talk to me."

To keep himself posted he relies very little on the gossip some people think is inside information. He does spend five or six hours a day reading, with lesser periods on the phone. He hates meetings. Berkshire Hathaway's board meets once a year. But Buffett does quite faithfully attend directors meetings at Gillette, Capital Cities/ABC, Salomon Inc., USAir Group and Coca-Cola each month.

While Buffett's character and investing style are all his own, they owe a lot to three influences. "If I were to give credit in terms of how I've done it in investments, my Dad would be number one, and Ben Graham would be number two. Charlie Munger would be number three."

He credits his father, Howard Buffett, a stockbroker and onetime congressman, with setting an example of how to behave. "He taught me to do nothing that could be put on the front page of a newspaper. I have never known a better human being than my Dad."

He credits Graham with giving him "an intellectual framework for investing and a temperamental model, the ability to stand back and not be influenced by a crowd, not be fearful if stocks go down." He sums up Graham's teaching: "When proper temperament joins with proper intellectual framework, then you get rational behavior."

Charles Munger is Buffett's sidekick, vice chairman of Berkshire Hathaway and, after Buffett and his wife, its largest stockholder, with 1.8 percent of the stock. He lives in Los Angeles, but he and Buffett are on the phone almost daily. "Charlie made me focus on the merits of a great business with tremendously growing earning power, but only when you can be sure of it—not like Texas Instruments or Polaroid, where the earning power was hypothetical. Charlie is rational, very rational. Essentially we have never had an argument, though occasional disagreements."

Disagreements? Munger says that there are times when he has to prod Buffett away from his old Ben Graham attitudes about what constitutes a bargain. Munger: "Warren was a little slower to realize that a very great business can sell for less than it's worth. After all, Warren worshiped Ben Graham, who wanted to buy companies at a fraction of the liquidation value, and it's hard to go beyond your mentor. Sure, I convinced him we should pay up for good businesses."

Today, Buffett realizes that "when you find a really good business run by first-class people, chances are a price that looks high isn't high. The combination is rare enough, it's worth a pretty good price." In almost every instance that pretty good price gets even better after he buys the stock.

One thing Munger doesn't have to twist Buffett's arm on: They both believe you should never sell those great businesses as long as they stay great, almost regardless of how high the stock price gets. What would be the point? You would have to reinvest the money in something less great.

Buffett has received FTC permission to raise his stake in Salomon Inc. from 14 percent to 25 percent, even though Salomon shares have already more than doubled since its Treasury bond scandal. Why did he wait so long to increase his stake? He felt it wasn't fair to buy more shares when he was involved in turning the company around.

Are great investor/businessmen like Buffett made or born? In this case, the verdict would have to be the genetic one. As a kid he traded on a small scale, buying Coca-Cola from his grandfather's store and reselling it to neighbors. When he was 20 and a student at Columbia University, he started studying the insurance industry. His hero and professor, Benjamin Graham, was chairman of GEICO, Government Employees Insurance Co., based in Washington, DC. Wanting to know more about a company Graham had invested in, one Saturday Buffett paid a cold call on GEICO, and was treated to a five-hour sermon by Lorimer Davidson, then vice president of finance, on how the insurance business worked.

Buffett then had about $9,800 in capital. He proceeded to invest three quarters of it in Geico stock. "It was a company with a huge competitive advantage, managed by the guy that was my God."

In those days Buffett was devouring financial tomes the way most people his age consumed the sports pages or mystery novels. While working for his father's brokerage firm in Omaha, he would go to Lincoln, Nebraska, the state capital, and read through the convention reports, or statistical histories of insurance companies. "I read from page to page. I didn't read brokers' reports or anything. I just looked at raw data. And I would get all excited about these things. I'd find Kansas City Life at 3 times earnings, Western Insurance Securities at 1 times earnings. I never had enough money and I didn't like to borrow money. So I sold something too soon to buy something else."

Even though his lack of capital sometimes led him to sell too soon, Buffett prospered. Geico and Western Insurance Securities were huge winners.

In the early days of his career, he followed Graham's quantitative guidelines obsessively. Graham figured you couldn't lose and would probably gain if you bought a stock for less than the value of its working capital alone. "I bought into an anthracite company. I bought into a windmill company. I bought into a street railway company, or more than one." But, these cheap stocks were cheap for a reason; the businesses were dying.

Buffett soon realized that instead of seeking sure-thing statistical bargains, he would have to find companies that were undervalued for reasons that might not appear on the balance sheet—things like valuable brand names or strong market positions. As a professional money manager he began to make spectacular returns for his clients, with killings in such stocks as American Express and Disney.

But in 1969 he took down his shingle, returned his partners' money and concentrated on his own investments. In retrospect the timing was brilliant. The first post-World War II bull market had essentially ended, though few people realized it. Although a handful of stocks continued to rise until 1973 and 1974, the bull was exhausted.

Aha! So Buffett really is a market timer? No, he says. He simply couldn't find any stocks he wanted to buy at those prices. If it comes to the same thing either way, you can see that Buffett thinks in terms of companies, not in terms of markets. "I felt like an oversexed guy on a desert island," he quips, "I couldn't find anything to buy."

But after the crash of 1974, which took the DJI down nearly 50 percent from its previous high, he had plenty of stimulation in his search for bargains. Reversing the quip, in November 1974 he . . . [said] he felt "like an oversexed guy in a harem."

In the mid-1960s, he had bought control of a down-at-the-heels textile operation in New Bedford, Massachusetts It looked cheap in that he paid less than the book value of the assets. Only it turned out those assets weren't worth what the books said they were. Says Buffett: "I thought it was a so-so textile business, but it was a terrible business."

Yet, ever the opportunist, Buffett used the base as a vehicle for slaking his passion for stocks in a market where the Dow Jones industrial average was well below 1000. Of Berkshire Hathaway, he says: "We worked our way out of it by growing the other capital, but in the late [19]60s half our capital was in a lousy business and that is not smart."

Gradually, Buffett moved away from pure Ben Graham to modified Ben Graham. It was then that he made his fat payoff investments in companies like the Washington Post that were then undervalued, not because they had lots of cash and physical assets but because they had valuable franchises that were not recognized by the market. He describes the change in parameters: "Ben Graham wanted everything to be a quantitative bargain. I want it to be a quantitative bargain in terms of future streams of cash. My guess is the last big time to do it Ben's way was in 1973 or 1974, when you could have done it quite easily."

Is Warren Buffett infallible? No way. He readily concedes he left $2 billion on the table by getting out of Fannie Mae too early. He didn't buy as much as he set out to and sold too early. Why? He shakes his head. "It was too easy to analyze. It was within my circle of competence. And for one reason or another, I quit. I wish I could give you a good answer."

He also sold part of Berkshire's position in Affiliated Publications, the owner of the *Boston Globe* newspaper, because he did not fully grasp the value of Affiliated's big position in McCaw Cellular. He is less miffed about this mistake than about the FNMA one. "I missed the play in cellular because cellular is outside of my circle of competence."

What does Buffett think of politics? Buffett was a registered Republican, like his father, but he switched parties in the early 1960s. "I became a Democrat basically because I felt the Democrats were closer by a considerable margin to what I felt in the early 1960s about civil rights. I don't vote the party line. But, I probably vote for more Democrats than Republicans."

There's a general impression that Buffett plans to cut off his three children, forcing them to fend for themselves. Nonsense, he says. "They've gotten gifts right along, but they're not going to live the life of the superrich. I think they probably feel pretty good about how they've been brought up. They all function well, and they all are independent, in that they don't feel obligated to kowtow to me in anyway." He puts modest amounts each year in the Sherwood Foundation, which is used by his children to give money away in Omaha. Another family foundation gives $4 million a year to support programs promoting population control.

Beyond that, Buffett has sometimes been criticized for not giving away bigger chunks of his great fortune—even when pressed by friends and associates. He explains: "I wouldn't want to transfer Berkshire Hathaway shares to anyone while I'm alive. If I owned a wide portfolio of securities I could give them away. But, I don't want to give up control of Berkshire Hathaway."

But when death does force his hand, his legacy is going to be a whopper. He plans to leave 100 percent of his Berkshire Hathaway holding to his separated but not estranged wife Susan. He has no written contract with

Susan that the shares will go into a foundation, but that is the understanding between them. Says he: "She has the same values I do." The deal is whoever dies last will leave the Berkshire Hathaway shares to a foundation with no strings attached.

"When I am dead, I assume there'll still be serious problems of a social nature as there are now. Society will get a greater benefit from my money later than if I do it now." Any hints as to where he'd like to see the money go? Control of nuclear proliferation is very much on his mind. "Who knows how many psychotics in the world will have the ability to do something with nuclear knowledge that could wreak havoc on the rest of the world?"

It's a little hard to see how money can deal with that problem, but Buffett points out that money could do a lot for what he regards as another major problem: excessive population growth.

"I have got a very few superhigh-grade, very intelligent people in charge of deciding how to spend the money. They [will] have total authority. There are no restrictions. And all they are supposed to do is use it as a smart high-grade person would do under the circumstances that exist when it comes into play, which I hope is not soon."

The trustees of his will include his wife, Susan, his daughter, Susan, his son Peter, Tom Murphy, chairman of Capital Cities/ABC, and *Fortune*'s Carol Loomis.

It's very much in harmony with his pragmatic nature that Buffett plans on putting few strings on the money. Just so long as they don't turn it into a conventional bureaucratic foundation. "If they build an edifice and become traditional I'll come back to haunt them," he declares.

Charles T. Munger

CAROL J. LOOMIS

Charlie Munger and Warren Buffett were both boys in Omaha, but didn't know each other. When they met as young adults, it was Buffett who influenced Munger. Since 1975, however, Munger has been Buffett's influential partner, serving nominally as vice chairman of Berkshire Hathaway, mostly by telephone from Los Angeles. This piece profiles the not-so-well-known member of the team.

[Warren] Buffett considers himself to have been nudged, prodded, and shoved toward a steady, rather than intermittent, appreciation of good

Excerpted from *Fortune* (April 11, 1988), p. 32. © Time Inc. All rights reserved.

business by Charles T. Munger, 64, vice chairman of Berkshire and the "Charlie" of Buffett's annual reports. In the U.S. corporate system, vice chairmen have a way of often not being important. That is decidedly not the case at Berkshire Hathaway.

Munger's mental ability is probably up to Buffett's, and the two can talk as equals. They differ, however, in political views—Munger is a traditional Republican, Buffett a fiscally conservative Democrat—and in demeanor. Though sometimes cutting in his annual report, Buffett employs great tact when doling out criticism in person. Munger can be incisively frank. Last year, chairing the annual meeting of Wesco, a California savings and loan 80 percent owned by Berkshire, Munger delivered a self-appraisal: "In my whole life nobody has ever accused me of being humble. Although humility is a trait I much admire, I don't think I quite got my full share."

Like Buffett, Munger is a native of Omaha, but as boys the two did not know each other. After getting the equivalent of a college degree in the Army Air Force and graduating from Harvard law school, Munger went to Los Angeles, where he started the law firm now known as Munger Tolles & Olson. On a visit back to Omaha in 1959, Munger attended a dinner party that also included Buffett. Munger had heard tales of this 29-year-old who was remaking the Omaha investment scene and was prepared to be unimpressed. Instead, he was bowled over by Buffett's intellect. "I would have to say," says Munger, "that I recognized almost instantly what a remarkable person Warren is."

Buffett's reaction was that of a proselytizer. Convinced that the law was a slow boat to wealth, he began arguing that Munger should give up his practice and start his own investment partnership. Finally, in 1962, Munger made the move, though he hedged his bets by also keeping a hand in the law. His partnership was much smaller than Buffett's, more highly concentrated, and much more volatile. Nonetheless, in the partnership's 13-year history, extending through 1975, Munger achieved an annual average gain, compounded, of 19.8 percent. His wealth expanded as Buffett expected: Among other holdings, he owns nearly 2 percent of Berkshire, recently worth about $70 million.*

When he met Buffett, Munger had already formed strong opinions about the chasms between good businesses and bad. He served as a director of an International Harvester dealership in Bakersfield and saw how difficult it was to fix up an intrinsically mediocre business; as an Angeleno, he observed the splendid prosperity of the Los Angeles *Times;* in his head he did not carry a creed about "bargains" that had to be unlearned. So in conversations with Buffett over the years he preached the virtues of good businesses, and in time Buffett totally accepted the logic of the case. By 1972, Blue Chip Stamps, a Berkshire affiliate that has since been

---

Ed. note: Shares were then selling at $3,100. In 2001, they were over twenty times higher.

merged into the parent, was paying three times book value to buy See's Candies, and the good-business era was launched. "I have been shaped tremendously by Charlie," says Buffett. "Boy, if I had listened only to Ben [Graham], would I ever be a lot poorer."

Last year at a Los Angeles party, Munger's dinner partner turned to him and coolly asked, "Tell me, what one quality most accounts for your enormous success?" Recalling this delicious moment later, Munger said, "Can you imagine such a wonderful question? And so I looked at this marvelous creature—whom I certainly hope to sit by at every dinner party—and said, 'I'm rational. That's my answer. I'm rational.'"

Jack Dreyfus

MARSHALL SMITH

Jack Dreyfus was a gifted and effective Wall Street original. In creating Dreyfus & Co., he contributed importantly to the development of mutual funds, created a great brand and logo, and was one of the first to play the money game. Having given up golf, cards, and the Dreyfus Fund because he was too intense about them, he took up tennis—and, of course, played it also with grim intensity.

Jack Dreyfus is founder of the billion-dollar Dreyfus Fund, whose lion stalks so imperturbably across the TV tube, and president of the brokerage firm plugged by a pair of old TV coots who play languid ping pong while discussing the fantastic view of the harbor offered by Dreyfus & Co. He is a quite implausible creature to be found maneuvering among Wall Street's bulls and bears. A slender, soft-spoken perfectionist of 52, he has thrived on the extreme competitive pressures of his environment. Indeed, many of his contemporaries regard him as an overcompetitor—not only in the realm of high finance but in almost anything else he lays a hand to—including golf, tennis, horse racing, bridge and gin rummy, at all of which he has been enormously successful. Yet he has the eye and ear of an artist and the impulses of a beatnik.

For almost two decades Dreyfus has taken impish delight in stepping on Wall Street's respectable corns. He has been called an upstart, an interloper and a genius. Yet he is, without question, the most singular and effective personality to appear in Wall Street since the days of Joseph Kennedy and Bernard Baruch.

Excerpted from *Life* (1966), pp. 10 and 13. © 1966 Time Inc. Reprinted by permission.

Dreyfus first shook up the Old Guard 15 years ago with a bold new approach to investment-house advertising. His ads, and later his market letters, were written in bright, brisk English instead of the traditional Wall Street Choctaw.

At a time when mass participation in the stock market was really beginning to burgeon—until, today, one of every six Americans is involved in some way—Dreyfus decided to woo the public with whimsy, TV cartoons and wry admissions of fallibility. "Management can see things clearly and still be wrong, you understand," he once advised his shareholders, going on to characterize a certain action the fund had taken as "an admission-of-ignorance position. . . . Had we been smarter, we would not have taken the . . . position at all."

Under different circumstances Dreyfus' tradition-shattering methods might have been considered frivolous and beneath note. But the fact is that Dreyfus has excelled at the one thing Wall Street really respects—making big money—ever since, at the age of 32, he first focused his enormous intelligence on the market.

His ability to [predict] stock market dips and rises has made Dreyfus preposterously rich. It has also made millionaires of a number of his friends and added substantially to the worth of several hundred thousand ordinary citizens who own shares in the Dreyfus Fund, the institution which made Dreyfus' name in the Street. . . .

"I'm an accident down here," he admits. "I don't really belong." He avoids the haunts of other brokers. He hates pomp and protocol. He hasn't worn a tuxedo—or, for that matter, an overcoat—in more than 20 years. His wardrobe consists of 40 expensive suits, all of them dark blue, a hue which serves to give his trim figure a particularly natty look when he chooses to mingle formally with the rest of the human race.

Dreyfus resents being cooped up in offices, even his own plus establishment at No. 2 Broadway with its soothing modern decor. Whenever he feels the urge to escape, he simply takes the elevator down 29 floors and walks across the street to Battery Park. On nice days he divests himself of jacket, tie and shoes. "My brain expands when I take my shoes off," he says. In winter, when the weather discourages this practice, he huddles against the biting winds in a niche in what is left of the park's old aquarium.

Dreyfus possesses at least two qualities rarely seen in busy and successful men. His associates maintain that he is overconscientious about almost everything and that he goes to great lengths to avoid hurting people's feelings. He also has an obsession about finding homes for lost dogs. He chases them on sight the way little boys once used to chase fire engines.

One day not long ago, as he was peering through the brass telescope he keeps in his office for viewing the Statue of Liberty and other harbor sights, he spotted a stray loping along lower Broadway and dodging traffic. Dreyfus promptly dashed for a down elevator and took off in pursuit. After a determined chase through the streets, Dreyfus caught up with the snarling mongrel and, using his belt and his tie as a makeshift leash, returned to the office in triumph with the mutt.

Dreyfus has found homes for at least 50 stray dogs, but his compassion applies to other animals as well. Once, on a business trip to Miami, he came across 14 cats cooped up in an old monkey cage on the grounds of a swank hotel. Dreyfus instantly made arrangements to have them cared for on his 1,200-acre thoroughbred horse farm near Ocala, Florida.

He is the owner of a large stable of race horses and sometimes gives the impression that he prefers their company to that of people. The stable is called Hobeau Farm. Dreyfus picked the name himself because the idea of being a knight of the road has always appealed to him—"Just a bum with no responsibilities." In all his life, however, he has never quite been able to achieve this goal.

As a toddler in Montgomery, Alabama, Dreyfus showed distressing signs of being a natural-born overcompetitor. When he was 5, he was beating his grandfather in dominos. The old man, an immigrant from Alsace-Lorraine, was a first cousin to Captain Alfred Dreyfus, the famous French prisoner of Devils Island. Dreyfus recalls his grandfather as a fiery old codger with fierce mustachios who drank a quart of corn liquor a day and hated to lose at anything.

Dreyfus' father was in the candy business in Montgomery and fancied himself as a bridge player. But every week, when the elder Dreyfus tried to solve the bridge problem printed in *Collier's* magazine, he would give up in disgust and offer 25¢ to anyone who could come up with the answer. By the time young Jack was 8 he was earning a steady income from his father solving these problems. But his first real obsession was golf.

The boy began attacking the game in earnest at age 13. At the Standard Club, where his father was a member, Dreyfus spent up to five hours a day on the practice tee struggling with his temper and an unsound swing. For him golf became more of an exercise in mental discipline than a game—and his mastery of his emotions later helped him not only at cards but in the stock market as well. At 16 he was both club champion and city champion of Montgomery.

At Lehigh University, he barely got passing grades. College contained no challenge for him except as a member of the golf team; his only other real interest in life was bridge. By the middle 1930s he had drifted to New York and into and out of a succession of unexciting jobs. In 1937, when he was 25, Dreyfus joined Manhattan's cardplaying Cavendish Club and decided to devote himself to cards and golf.

"I never became a 100 percent bridge bum," he says. But the distinction is a fine one. Although he had finally accepted a routine job in Wall Street, Dreyfus couldn't wait for the market to close each day at 3:30 P.M. so he could dash uptown to the Cavendish. He had been a first-rate player back home, but what he encountered in this habitat of bridge champions distressed him.

"Part of their game was to make you feel like an idiot," he says. "I was terrified every time I drew one of the big names of the game as a partner. I found myself bidding what I thought he wanted me to instead of using my own judgment."

In a game where ego is crucial Dreyfus suffered acutely. Lack of confidence made him a "caddie" rather than a "personality"—as he puts it—until one day, quite unexpectedly, he solved the riddle of another card game. He was kibitzing a gin rummy session at the Cavendish, mentally computing the odds on various methods of discard, when the revelation came. What he discovered was an advantageous system for discarding what an opponent was not likely to need. . . .

With his bit of knowledge—which he kept to himself—plus his highly developed card sense and intuition, Dreyfus became practically unbeatable at gin rummy. One by one the experts gave up challenging him. Later, when he let his opponents in on the secret, two of the better-known pros, Oswald Jacoby and John Crawford, wrote books on gin rummy using Dreyfus' system as a basic theme. His superiority at gin also gave him back his confidence at bridge. . . .

Between cards and weekend golf Dreyfus had little time for Wall Street. "I had a good instinct for trading and I was pretty good at charts," he says.

But as a customers' broker he was timid and retiring. "He wasn't very good," says his old boss. Then, in 1946, Dreyfus' life changed suddenly. One of his wealthy golfing pals, a department store executive named Jerry Ohrbach, helped him buy a seat on the New York Stock Exchange. Within two years he was head of his own brokerage house.

But 2½ years after that the young firm of Dreyfus & Co. was on the verge of collapse.

"I was trying to run a business with very little knowledge and very little experience," Dreyfus says. In addition to limited knowledge Dreyfus had no research department and no equity. All he did have was a black eye in the trade. A trading infraction by an employee caused Dreyfus to be suspended by the Curb Exchange (now the American Stock Exchange) for three months. Customers drifted away. . . .

Dreyfus reacted by deciding that the time had come for him to either put up or shut up. He cut his own salary to zero and lived for the next year on some small savings and on his considerable winnings at gin rummy. With $20,000 of borrowed money—roughly what he had been making as senior partner of his firm—he embarked on the advertising campaign that was to make his name in Wall Street. . . .

The unorthodox approach paid off. "We weren't doing any business," says Dreyfus. "Then all of a sudden we were." In 1951 the now prosperous firm won the Standard & Poor's award for advertising. But by that time its ingenious and thoroughly aroused proprietor was already moving in a wholly new direction. Dreyfus had become fascinated with the idea of mutual funds. Why, he wondered, weren't brokerage houses sponsoring more mutual funds? Quite apart from the slice of the premiums paid by buyers of fund shares to the operators of the fund, there would be the healthy annual management fee paid by the fund to its operators and also the considerable commissions that would, of course, accrue to the brokerage house as it handled the fund's day-to-day transactions in the market. In 1951, prompted by this twofold attraction, he had taken over the small and faltering Nesbett Fund, set up a corporation to manage it with himself as president and changed the name to Dreyfus Fund.

The fund's policy, he decided, would be flexible, not to say aggressive. "We're interested in outcome [capital gains] and not income [dividends]," he said. His policy would be to operate on what is known as the "technical side" of the market, playing its ups and downs. But for almost two years, while he was working out a system for doing this, Dreyfus marked time with his fledgling fund.

He applied himself, as though he were coping with a problem in cards, to the problem of discovering what made the stock market go up and down. "The same laws of percentages and probabilities are involved," he explains. "And, people's emotions come into it, too."

As a first step Dreyfus divided all buyers and sellers of stocks into two categories—speculators and investors. Upon further study he concluded that while the investors (those hoping that the prices of their stocks would increase over the long pull) far outnumbered the speculators (those who traded for the quick profit), the latter exerted far greater influence on market fluctuations. The speculators, to Dreyfus' mind, were the Jeb Stuarts of Wall Street. They acted in concert, getting in and out of the market very fast. By using the pyramiding effect of margin and credit, they caused the upward surges and triggered the downward spins.

Dreyfus decided to operate against the speculators. But to play this risky game he needed a special intelligence system—some beacons and barometers that would give him a special advantage. The ordinary clues wouldn't do—indicators like housing starts, machine-tool orders, railroad carloadings or unemployment. "The obvious just doesn't work in the market," he says. "If it's obvious, everybody sees it and there's not much advantage."

The first clue Dreyfus seized upon was what he called the short interest. . . .

Until Dreyfus started studying the matter, a large short interest was generally regarded as a pessimistic sign. But Dreyfus interpreted it simply as backed up buying power and therefore a manifestation of strength. In October of 1953, when the size of the short interest suddenly increased by 700,000 shares in one month, he made his first significant move with his fund.

Within a few days he shifted the fund's position from a 50 percent investment in common stock to 93 percent—and caught the market taking off on an upward spiral. But in Dreyfus' system what stocks he bought was less important than *when* he bought them—the exact timing of the purchase.

Knowing when to sell was just as vital. Dreyfus discovered that the most effective clue for the selling phase of his operation was an overabundance of optimism.

In 1957, after four years of rising prices, Dreyfus suspected that Wall Street had reached just such a critical condition. He checked his intuition against timing devices he had adopted for this purpose—including statistics on customers' debits and credits—and found the speculators to be dangerously overextended and devoid of buying power. Dreyfus took this as a signal to start selling.

Once again his timing was perfect. When the plunge developed in October that year, driving down the Dow Jones industrial averages to the lowest level in two years, Dreyfus had cut back the fund to being only 43 percent invested in common stock. The rest of its assets were in cash and government bonds. Early the following year, when he felt that the atmosphere had cleared, he had the common-stock figure back up to 90 percent.

By that time the fund was six years old and it had grown from less than $1 million to $37 million (still small compared to its present size of $1.3 billion) and was causing a stir in The Street. Some rivals were accusing Dreyfus of "churning". . . .

The competition also cried that he was running a "one-man fund," but this was so obvious that even Dreyfus never bothered to deny it. Although the fund had an investment committee, and at least two members of it were supposed to approve every transaction, Dreyfus ran the show. He was also the fund's administrative head, its top salesman, its idea man, copywriter, artistic genius and general handyman. It was his idea to animate the lion and, in March 1958, to present the fund's prospectus as a special 14-page supplement in the New York *Sunday Times*—a previously unheard-of way for attracting investors. . . .

Just about everything Dreyfus set about doing during this period had its special touch. At the office he kept two unusual specialists on the payroll— a gardener to tend the flowers that he insisted be grown on the premises and a psychiatrist to smooth over personality differences among partners and employees. "It's important in business that the atmosphere be peaceful and harmonious."

He hired his executives with the same disregard for convention. The man he picked as chief assistant and understudy had been a serious student of the violin at Juilliard School of Music. A former hotel man who had an easy way of handling people was made the fund's sales manager. Dreyfus' way of indoctrinating his key personnel into the appropriate orbit of thought was equally original.

"We would have meetings in the park," one of them recalled recently. "Everybody would sit around in a circle on the ground and Jack would have sandwiches sent over."

All this time, Dreyfus recalls, his secret dream at these meetings was to escape—to have no worries, no responsibilities. "If you're lucky enough to be reasonably successful, your problems seem to multiply," he says. About seven years ago Dreyfus' problems seemed to him to be multiplying so rapidly that he could not keep up with them. Fearing that he was on the verge of a nervous breakdown, he started a conscious campaign to abandon all those pursuits which fed his passion for perfection.

The first to go was golf. . . . Dreyfus also quit the bridge table and gave up gin rummy. But walking away from the fund was not so easy. It was one thing to swear off games; it was something else to abandon a fund with obligations to churches, hospitals, orphanages, colleges and fraternal groups—to say nothing of the hundreds of thousands of individual investors.

But from his bench in the park Dreyfus began teaching with a new, more intense purpose—to mold his successors so that someday he *could* get away.

Bit by bit the teacher became less involved in the running of the fund. But he found he needed "counterirritants" to help him live with the one great irritant—the stock market. At the age of 46 Dreyfus took up tennis as a means of working off his tensions and, despite himself, became quite good at the game.

He began frequenting the race tracks and, there too, everything he did turned up roses. This soothed him. "It makes you feel like a little boy at Christmas," he says.

After work he would go to the night trotting races wearing sneakers and a sports shirt and bet an average of $4,000 a night on the daily double. He won too regularly to avoid notice. When word got back to him that he was getting a name as the biggest bettor in the New York area, Dreyfus regretfully stopped attending the trotting races. As the head of the fund he couldn't afford such publicity. . . .

In the middle of last year Dreyfus decided that the time had come for him to get out. Howard Stein, the former violinist, had been elevated to the rank of president and was running the fund exactly as Dreyfus thought it should be run. Convinced that he could withdraw without jeopardizing his shareholders' interests, Dreyfus began proceedings which would give Wall Street one last surprise. He told the Securities and Exchange Commission that he intended to sell the management corporation which operated the Dreyfus Fund.

Shares in the Dreyfus Corporation were put on the market at public offering. Dreyfus' personal share came to $26 million. The money, however, was not the most important consideration. What really excited him—even though he agreed to make himself available as a consultant for five years—was that the biggest obstacle between him and his professed ambition of doing nothing, of "being a bum," had been eliminated.

For openers he thought he might travel, slowly, around the world. But that was five months ago and he hasn't started off yet. Most of his friends doubt that he ever will.

Howard Stein

'ADAM SMITH'

Moving on from where Jack Dreyfus left off, Howard Stein built Dreyfus into one of America's largest money managers while maintaining a low profile and earning the respect of competitors and professional colleagues alike. Here is a brief look at Stein the investor and at Stein the person, who once commuted daily to a week's appointments in London from a Paris hotel because he preferred French cooking.

Off Wall Street, surprisingly few people know who Howard Stein is. He is not listed in *Who's Who* ("Nobody ever asked me," he explains). He is rarely interviewed, and he is seldom quoted in periodic financial press roundups of what prominent money managers are thinking.

The reason is that Stein is the Successor to a Founder, a position that never seems to fail to produce instant obscurity. Stein is manager of perhaps the country's second-largest and probably best known mutual fund, the Dreyfus Fund. . . .

[Jack] Dreyfus withdrew totally from the fund eight years ago, and turned it over to Stein, who was immediately branded—and still continues to be thought of as—a caretaker. Stein justifiably feels this assessment is unfair. Under his direction, he points out, "Our assets have grown from $310 million to $2.5 billion. For a caretaker, that's like turning a cottage into a mansion."

Obviously, Stein has been doing something right. . . . [He] has tried steadfastly to avoid the encumbering bureaucracy that an organization the size of Dreyfus almost inevitably develops . . . [and] has tried to create the kind of free-form atmosphere in which highly talented people can comfortably operate. "The style of management is chaotic," Stein admits. "I am not an organized person. I just kind of like people to be enthused, and excited, and to be able to think freely. I think when you put in too much organization, you hinder the willingness of people to take risks."

Two measures of his success are that the Dreyfus Fund, despite its huge size, has continued to compile an excellent record and that . . . alumni from Stein's anti-organizational system now hold high positions all over Wall Street. Stein's accomplishments in the area of what might

Excerpted from *The Money Managers* (New York: Random House, 1969), pp. 123–127, by permission of Random House, Inc. ©1969 by Institutional Investor Systems, Inc.

be called administrative pioneering flow directly from his own personality, which is unusually instinctive and, for the financial world, quite unconventional.

The words most often used to describe Howard Stein as an investment manager are "intuitive" and "flexible." . . .

Stein is an omnivorous listener who believes that he can learn more from a dialogue than from the printed word. He does not read the painstakingly produced outpourings of the institutional research brokers, for as one colleague states finally, "He doesn't read a bloody thing." Nor is he often swayed by the traditional convincers: numbers. Stein is so unconventional in his approach that his research staff has learned to follow suit. A former vice-president of research said recently, "We never had a traditional research staff. We never had a bunch of guys cranking out a lot of numbers. Howard wants to know what you think in words." Dreyfus has only nine analysts of research. None of them are "technicians" and the group uses no computer, although they do of course subscribe to various services that provide charts and statistical analysis.

Outside the Dreyfus Corp., there are a handful of men on Wall Street with whom Stein has regular telephone sessions and on whom he sounds out his ideas. Stein also likes to talk to people off Wall Street, especially people in government and politics, because he thinks that government exerts vast influence on the market.

In March of 1968, when Stein sensed that Senator Eugene McCarthy's candidacy would effectively galvanize antiwar sentiment, and could lead the Johnson administration toward more direct action to end the war, he took a six-month leave of absence to serve as McCarthy's national finance chairman. Stein personally opposed the war, and important to his decision in helping McCarthy was his belief that the war was taking its toll on the economy and the stock market.

By ear or osmosis, when Stein uncovers an attractive investment idea he uses it as his own (occasionally to the chagrin of its originator) and, more importantly, he acts upon it. . . . Stein operates by no rule book. Two former Dreyfus vice-presidents find it hard to define Stein's investment philosophy, but imply that part of his secret is that he has no investment hang-ups. One says, "Howard is hard to characterize. He is quite a flexible person, and if you provide him with an original peg to hang it on, he'll buy almost anything. Afterwards, if it looks like a bad idea, I've seen him spin on a dime and get out within twenty-four hours." Says another, "The best way to describe Howard's investment thinking is that he is not inhibited."

Stein looks much younger than his age, which is forty-three. Handsome, trim and angular, with pale blue eyes and his dark hair fully intact, he could easily pass for a man in his early thirties. His pictures show a dour and ascetic-looking man, but they are deceiving. Stein's manner with his colleagues is relaxed and easy, his style often humorously self-deprecatory. . . .

He uses the telephone often, and so effectively that he goes to his office only three or four days a week.

Outsiders unfamiliar with Stein's habits may still call the Dreyfus switchboard and speak to Stein, without ever realizing that the person on the other end is stretched comfortably in a hammock under the trees behind his 180-year-old French farmhouse in Cross River, New York. In the winter, when Stein moves inside, the Dreyfus phone rings in his greenhouse.

. . . Janet Stein, asked to describe how her husband spends his spare time when he is not on the telephone, responds cheerily, "If you are looking for anything that's off the phone, you can rule it out. He's always on the phone; he likes being close to the action. The only thing I've ever known him to drop the phone for is a good meal."

Though work is Stein's only real hobby, he does enjoy good food. As a colleague says, "He is not the yacht type."

John Templeton

JOHN TRAIN

Deeply religious and a self-made man, John Templeton earned a knighthood and a billion-dollar fortune. In the first of these two short glimpses we get a quick overview of a master of the game, an international investor who established a distinguished record in investment management. The profile ends in 1978, just as he was hitting his full stride. Then, we skip to a 1990 follow-up: at that time, nearing 80, Templeton had recently sold his firm and had established The Templeton Prize for progress in religion, offering the largest cash award of any prize, "because progress in religion is more important than in any other area."

I

One day in 1939, just after war had broken out in Europe, a young man named John Templeton called his broker at Fenner & Beane and gave one of the oddest and most annoying orders a broker could ever hope to receive.

"I want you to buy me a hundred dollars' worth of every single stock on both major exchanges that is selling for no more than one dollar a share."

Selected excerpts from pages 158–160 from *The Money Masters* by John Train. Copyright © 1980, 1989 by John Train. Reprinted by permission of HarperCollins Publishers, Inc.

The broker might have refused the order, which was a nightmare to execute and a most unsatisfactory way to earn a negligible commission, except that Templeton had worked for him as a trainee two years earlier.

After a while he reported that he had bought Templeton a hundred dollars' worth of every stock on either exchange that was not entirely bankrupt.

"No, no," said Templeton, "I want them *all*. Every last one, bankrupt or not." Grudgingly the broker went back to work and finally completed the order. When it was all over, Templeton had bought a junkpile of 104 companies in roughly $100 lots, of which 34 were bankrupt. He held each stock for an average of four years before selling. The result was no joke at all: he got over $40,000 for the kit—four times his cost.

Some of the transactions were startling. He bought Standard Gas $7 Preferred at $1 and sold it at $40. He bought 800 shares of Missouri Pacific Preferred—in bankruptcy—at twelve cents and eventually sold out at $5. (It eventually went over $100: had he sold at the top, that particular $100 would have turned not into $4,000 but $80,000!)

A singular aspect of this transaction was that Templeton didn't have $10,000 in cash. He was convinced that stocks were dirt cheap, and that of them all the neglected cats and dogs selling for less than $1 were the best values. When the war started in Europe he reasoned that that, if anything, was going to pull America out of its economic slump, and virtually all stocks would rise. So he had gone to his boss and borrowed the entire amount.

John Templeton was poor. He came from Winchester, Tennessee. During the Depression, while he was in his second year at Yale, his father told him that he could not give him any more money for his education. So Templeton worked his way through college, with the aid of scholarships. After that he won a Rhodes scholarship and went to Oxford for two years, seeing Europe during his vacations. Then he came back to Tennessee and eventually went to New York, first as a trainee at Fenner & Beane, one of the predecessors of Merrill Lynch, and after that in a seismic exploration company.

There he was when World War II began and he became convinced that the 10-year slump in stock prices was over and everything would boom—especially the Cinderellas that nobody considered as suitable investments.

That one extraordinary transaction set the pattern for Templeton's later ones.

First, *he insisted on buying only what was being thrown away.*

Second, *he held the stocks he had bought for an average of four years.*

That usually gives a bargain enough time to be recognized, so you can make the big revaluation when a stock moves to a higher multiple of higher earnings, the "double-play" profit. (Of course, you completely miss the 20-year run of the great growth stock in its prime, which for most investors is their best hope of stock market profits. There are very

few Templetons who succeed in buying undiscovered values and selling
them again in a four-year cycle.)

After his coup Templeton had some money, so two years later, when he
learned that an elderly investment counselor wanted to retire and sell his
business, which had only eight clients, he wrote him a check for $5,000 and
took over the firm. The clients stayed, but eight isn't many, so Templeton
had a bad time of it at first, and had to live off his savings. Then, however,
word of his abilities began to spread, and he has never lacked for clients—or
income—since.

His firm—Templeton, Dobbrow & Vance—eventually grew to manage
$300 million, including eight mutual funds. The trouble was that having
so many different clients left Templeton working so hard that he didn't
have time enough to think. Finally he and his associates sold their firm to
Piedmont Management, keeping only Templeton Growth Fund, which
Piedmont didn't want because it was based in Canada and couldn't be distributed in the United States.

At 56, John Templeton started all over again. He resolved first that he
would never let himself get so busy that he ran out of time. Not only time to
think about investments but also to reflect on the larger world, particularly
the various approaches to religion. So he moved to Nassau, and on the
grounds of the Lyford Cay Club built a white house in the southern style,
with columns on all four sides. There he assembled his securities files and
started giving his attention to managing his one tiny remaining fund, of
which he and some of his old clients owned most of the shares. The record
of this fund in the next years proved that John Templeton is one of the great
investors.

Over the 20 years ending December 31, 1978, a $1,000 investment in
his fund became worth about $20,000, if all distributions had been rein-
vested in more shares—which made it the top performer of all funds.

• • •

II

His favourite parable is that of the talents. "When I was 19 studying economics at Yale I kept asking myself, what talents do I have which would be
useful."

His voice is calm and soft. He considered politics and the church but
decided his talents lay in judgment and valuation. "I thought if I could use
my talent to judge values I could help investors to get in when the price
was low."

Although he relinquished day-to-day control of Templeton, Galbraith
[Templeton's last firm] five years ago, he still works every day—"and
evenings and weekends." He sees his position as co-ordinator of research.
"I have to be careful every security analyst we bring in is the best possible, and they use the best methods." But no-one makes a strategic move

without him. "And he does not always let them do what they want to do," says one banker.

Templeton was born in 1912 in a small town in Tennessee. His father was a lawyer and cotton grower. He has one older brother who has devoted the past 23 years to building racing cars. "At 81 he is still racing them and winning," says Templeton with child-like pleasure.

At six, he developed a passion for butterflies, collecting the eggs and hatching them out. "I think butterflies are a reminder of resurrection. Caterpillars have no idea they are going to be reborn into the most beautiful creatures." These days he buys other people's collections.

Going to church was a way of life and Templeton took to it from the start, becoming superintendent of the Sunday school at 15. He set his heart on Yale University, trained himself for the exams, and won a place in 1930 to read economics.

The following year his father lost most of his money and told the young Templeton he could not give him a dollar more. "I thought it was a tragedy, but it turned out to be a marvelous benefit." A variety of jobs helped pay the expenses, and he also won scholarships.

"To get scholarships you had to have top grades, so I began to learn I could do much more than I thought." At the end of his course he was the top scholar at Yale.

A Rhodes scholarship took him to Balliol, Oxford, as he prepared to be "a student of large corporations."

Before starting work he set off with a friend to travel the world. "We spent seven months travelling through 25 nations on £90 each." Their average expense for hotels was a shilling a night. "It was a great preparation for investing worldwide," he says. He started on Wall Street in 1937 and three years later set up his own fund management company.

It was not an instant success and he did not pay himself a salary for two years. But that did not stop him marrying and he and his wife set about furnishing a five-room flat in New York for $25 a room. At auctions if someone bid for a chair they would keep quiet. "If nobody bid, we'd say '10-cents'."

Does he regard himself as patient? He laughs: "I would say that is right. If you find shares that are low in price, they don't suddenly go up. Our average holding period is five years."

Templeton is famous for his contrarian approach. "Actually, all he does is try to buy shares at the bottom and sell at the top like the rest of us," says one rival.

When I first met him he was keen on the "bottom up" technique, studying companies first, followed by sectors and global areas. He still maintains its value: it involves so much work that few use it as a technique.

"We have to say to ourselves each day, 'where is there a share selling at the lowest possible price to net worth.' We have to study thousands of corporations and make a value of each one." He believes you cannot stay ahead of the game unless you change and adopt new methods because once they become popular they cease to work.

Don't they ever get it wrong?

"Oh yes. Our analysts make new valuations two or three times a year. But even then, we do sometimes hold companies which go bust."

Templeton and his first wife had three children before she was killed in a cycling accident. "Of course I was grief striken [sic] and I wouldn't advise anyone to make an important decision after a tragedy like that," he says, suddenly sombre. He was a widower for eight years, employing two women to look after the children. But it was still a strain. "I had to go to parent/teachers meetings, the ball games, the school plays as well as building up a business."

Then one day his seven-year-old invited himself to tea with a playmate. On sitting down at the table he addressed his friend's widowed mother, Irene. "If you are ever thinking about getting married again, would you please consider my father." Two years later they married.

To unite the family they set off on a seven-week tour of Europe in a hired bus. Each child was put in charge of something to prevent squabbling—one looked after hotels, the other money and so on. "For ourselves we reserved the most difficult task—keeping our mouths shut. I would advise the experiment for every family, but only once."

Such tales show a wise, logical man with great understanding about the human condition. He believes in discipline and thrift—although he lives in Lyford Cay in the Bahamas and drives an ancient blue Rolls-Royce, he travels economy class on aircraft and genuinely abhors waste.

When I tackle him about living in a tax haven he patiently explains he is taxed where he earns his money and withholding tax in America and Britain is higher than if he were a resident.

He likes Britain and became naturalised some years ago. He was knighted in 1986 for services to charity. He funded Templeton College at Oxford and chose the Duke of Edinburgh to present the first Templeton prize in 1973. "He can be quite a snob," says one associate, "he loves mixing with royalty and people with titles."

Well, even saints have their failings and what I really like about him is his optimism. He believes progress is being made on all fronts, including financial ethical standards. When he started, fund managers sat on the boards of the companies they bought shares in and nobody thought it wrong. "Now its not only immoral but illegal."

What would he most like to be remembered for? "I would like to think I did my best to leave the world a better place than I found it."

Paul Miller

PETER LANDAU

Paul Miller stunned informed Wall Street opinion when he quit as CEO
of Drexel Harriman Ripley to found a new, unregistered investment
management boutique. In only a few years time, however, Miller, Anderson & Sherrerd had grown to be one of the field's leading firms. Recently, it was sold to Morgan Stanley & Co. for $350 million. Here,
Miller tells about the firm and its culture.

We started up on a shoestring in the fall of 1969. I remember visiting the
offices of some other money management firms at the time and feeling very
inferior. One firm in particular that opened around the same time we did
had spent about a million-and-a-half bucks on their offices, as I recall. They
had a winding stairway going from one floor to the next and some nice paneling. I'd come back to the orange crates in our offices and think to myself,
"Are we dumb, or are they dumb?" Because we were spending nothing like
that. We didn't have it to spend.

We didn't need great surroundings because we didn't have any clients
when we opened. Not a single account. And here we were, asking for a
minimum account size of $20 million, which was pretty audacious in those
days. But the business came in, especially once we established a record. A
lot of the clients we got in the early 1970s never even came to our offices
to kick the tires before they signed up. Actually, a couple of them never
even interviewed us. We knew they were looking at us and we sent them
some written material and, lo and behold, we got the business. One account for $200 million came to us that way.

We were approaching a billion dollars in assets by 1980. . . . Suddenly, the
dam broke. We had one of the best five-year records in the business at that
point. And like it or not, five-year records still sell pretty well. I think it's
ridiculous, but they do. Basically, what you're doing is buying people—people with whom you're comfortable, people in whom you have confidence that
they're going to do a workmanlike job. You have no remote idea how well
they're going to do in the future. You know how many five-year records
have been blown apart?

Excerpted from *Institutional Investor* (June 1987), pp. 228–230. This copyrighted material
is reprinted with permission from **Institutional Investor, Inc.**, 488 Madison Avenue,
New York, NY 10022.

Anyway, we just sort of exploded. And one other thing happened: We began an intensive fixed-income effort, which was one of our better business decisions and has been very successful. . . . I can't remember precisely, but I think we went from $1 billion to . . . $12 billion in assets. . . .

If you look at our record, and I think this holds true of other firms that are also more durable in the business, we never shoot the lights out in up markets. We tend to be very good at preserving capital in down markets. And we tend to beat the modest up markets and the modest down markets by bigger amounts. I think that's a comfortable style.

When you go back and analyze our successes, so often they were the result of strategic decisions. . . .

There's something else that has contributed to our success. We've bred an atmosphere where people don't feel as though they're in competition with each other. I've seen a lot of organizations that are just blown apart by incentive systems that pit one investment manager versus another. We've never had any of that. I don't think it pays off because inevitably people begin to hate each other. We have a culture in which people make investment decisions as part of a group but also give some independence to make decisions of their own that aren't measured against everyone else's. The main thing [our structure] has done is to let people be creative on their own. They have a portion of every portfolio to manage. They aren't sat on by a committee, and yet they're a part of a group decision.

I think it's important that we don't have a hierarchical structure. I don't like hierarchies. We've always had equals here. When we started this business, Jay Sherrerd and Clay Anderson and I had equal percentage interests. Everybody probably thought Miller owns the damn thing. . . . I made the decision that the firm wouldn't prosper as well if I did. We started off with that philosophy and we've always kept it.

Claude Rosenberg

NANCY BELLIVEAU MCCONNELL

Claude Rosenberg, one of the investment profession's most enjoyable and respected practitioners, has established two organizations that compete effectively in four different asset classes. He has also written five books including *Wealthy and Wise*, captained the group that launched the AIMR standards for presenting investment performance records, and is a modest, persistent "student" of the profession.

Claude Rosenberg . . . a man whose style, both personal and professional, is decidedly low-key in the pension asset management business. Yet he has emerged after 18 years as one of its most durable, well-respected and truly successful practitioners: His firm, RCM Capital Management, now runs some $11.6 billion in stocks and bonds for 94 of the nation's blue-chip corporations, public funds and university endowments.

Rosenberg's persona explains and, in a sense, defines his firm's success. Claude Rosenberg strikes everyone who knows him as a nice guy, the kind of honest, unassuming, earnest, reliable individual who can absolutely be counted on not to scare his clients with any nasty surprises. His career is a nearly perfect case study in how to prosper through consistency: a consistent investment strategy, consistent performance numbers—never spectacular, but never really bad—consistent growth and almost unbelievably low turnover among both clients and employees. Put another way, Claude Rosenberg has built a highly successful business by averting many of the excesses that have felled—or at least slowed—some of his competitors. . . .

Nearly a dozen of his current accounts, major companies such as Xerox, Boeing Co. and J.C. Penney Co., have been with him almost since the beginning, sticking with him through many years when growth stocks—the firm's equity specialty—were decidedly out of favor and arrogant young consultants crawled all over his clients, offering them value managers or quantitative disciplines or index funds. Over the past 18 years, Rosenberg has lost only seven important clients because of unhappiness with his firm's performance.

• • •

Those who stuck around have had their loyalty rewarded. One longtime client calculates that over a dozen years, Rosenberg has earned his company

Excerpted from *Institutional Investor* (October 1988), pp. 195–208. This copyrighted material is reprinted with permission from: **Institutional Investor, Inc.**, 488 Madison Avenue, New York, NY 10022.

$270 million on its $66 million investment; of the six managers the client has kept during that time, Rosenberg was the top performer only once, but never ranked at the bottom. For the full 12 years, however, Rosenberg was No. 1. Indeed, Claude Rosenberg seems nothing less than living proof that steady but unspectacular short-term numbers can add up to a very good long-term performance record. . . .

From the start, Rosenberg has been blessed with a good—some might say superb—sense of timing. In 1962, after earning both a BA and an MBA from Stanford University and serving two years with the navy, he joined the small, old-line San Francisco brokerage of J. Barth & Co.—when the professional money management business was still in its infancy—and built the firm's research department into one of the largest and most respected institutional efforts in the West. . . . Then, in 1970, just as U.S. pension funds were about to enter the period of their most explosive change and growth, Rosenberg left J. Barth to set up his own firm; he was joined by . . . a team that, with the exception of [the late Robert] Sutton, is still involved in running RCM today.

The Rosenberg partners quickly began to attract an impressive list of pension clients, based on their reputation as good, solid growth-stock investors who would probably lag the averages a bit in frothy markets but could be depended upon to shield clients from disaster in downdrafts; in the debacle years 1973 and 1974, for example, Rosenberg's portfolios were down one and ten percentage points less than the Standard & Poor's 500 index, respectively.

It soon became apparent that the firm's most powerful marketing tool was Rosenberg himself, whose strong research background and ability to speak the language of corporate executives new to the money management game gave him real credibility.

• • •

Early on, Rosenberg announced that his firm would pursue a "slow growth" business strategy, closing its doors to new business if cash flow from current clients was in the neighborhood of 10 percent each year—a move he now says was prompted by his experience with Wall Street's well-known 80-20 rule: "You do 80 percent of your business with 20 percent of your clients and the other 20 percent with the 80 percent who drive you crazy.". . .

Like many "closed door" policies, however, Rosenberg left some wondering if the door wasn't just slightly ajar; one longtime client, who now has more than $300 million with the firm, remembers being told that when his account reached $50 million, the firm would like him to cut off cash flow. Nevertheless, Rosenberg did average a slow, steady yearly growth rate of about three new clients—all of whom felt exceedingly lucky to be on board, given the firm's reputation for choosiness. One executive who hired Rosenberg more than a decade ago remembers being somewhat puzzled "at the partners' comments to the effect that they would decide whether *they* would accept *us* as a client."

Restraining growth allowed the firm to maintain its reputation for superb client servicing—though the partners openly admit they have little time for hand-holding and, in fact, have looked for clients who require a minimum of it. But Rosenberg explains that the primary reason for a careful screening procedure was to weed out trigger-happy clients: "If an account has been jumping from manager to manager, we say simply, 'Look, we're just going to be one of a string,' and that's where humility in taking on business is important." Indeed, the policy probably does help explain the firm's stable client base—but in another important respect as well. As . . . another old Rosenberg friend tells it, "One of the best ways to develop a really strong relationship with clients is to show them you are working for *them* as a priority rather than building up business as a priority." And not incidentally, of course, the policy proved to be a superb marketing tool; one early Rosenberg client swears he got frequent phone calls from fellow pension officers "who wanted to get into Rosenberg and wondered if I had any influence." . . .

Another decision Rosenberg made early on was to diversify away from stock picking. He is perhaps most admired by competitors for his astuteness in building what one calls "one of the most solid businesses in this industry." In 1973 Rosenberg acted on a brochure he received from a social acquaintance, San Francisco real estate syndicator Paul Sack. The result was Rosenberg Real Estate Equity Fund, a pioneering series of closed-end real estate funds designed specifically for pension assets. Observes [Robert] Evans of Xerox: "Like everything else he does, Claude put a lot of thought into how he structured the funds. They were the first ones set up from the viewpoint of what's good for the client, not the real estate manager." Sack recalls, for example, that the initial fee structure he suggested to Rosenberg was "4 percent the first year, when you do most of the work, then half a percent for the middle years when we hardly do anything, and then 2 percent for the year we sell the properties." Sack laughs at the recollection: "Claude said, 'That would be great for you guys, but who's gonna give you a 4 percent fee to buy property?' So we scaled it back to a constant 1 percent per year." Today RREEF manages some $3.5 billion in pension real estate assets (apart from RCM's assets) and is a major money earner for RCM—which started out owning half the firm but is now a minority partner with a less than 30 percent stake.

Key to RREEF's success, say clients, was Rosenberg's decision to hire good, experienced real estate people and, except for giving occasional business advice, leave them alone. And that also is a major reason, clients add, that Rosenberg has been one of only a handful of equity managers in the country to really succeed at bond management.

• • •

This careful, pragmatic approach to investing seems to reflect the personality of Rosenberg himself. . . . Over the years, for example, Claude Rosenberg the quality growth-stock investor has evolved into Claude Rosenberg the *rotational* growth-stock investor, as he has added stocks of a more cyclical and contrarian, sometimes small-cap and even value, nature to RCM's portfolios—a recognition of the fact, in his words, that market realities dictate that "there's a limit to how much [of] the growth game you can play."

One sign of Rosenberg's increasingly contrarian approach is Grassroots Research, a unique national opinion-gathering effort to uncover the truth about companies and their products. . . . Another contrarian tool is Straw Hat, a complex computerized system for gathering massive amounts of Street research, both verbal and written, as well as information on institutional ownership of stocks that interest the firm. . . .

• • •

The tons of data gathered by the RCM network eventually find their way into the firm's computers and from there into RCM's "War Room," where the information can be called up on a giant screen by one of the partners pushing the buttons of a Star Wars-like console during the daily investment committee meetings. The group of six general partners uses a highly disciplined voting system that it claims eliminates much of the political backbiting, personality clashes, long-winded discussions and fuzzy thinking that too often impair decision making at firms organized like theirs.

• • •

Some get the distinct feeling that Rosenberg, in fact, is the primary reason the system works so well. "Claude runs his group of people like a board of directors and is able to lead it to a conclusion without being as strong an autocrat as others in the business," says one client. The emphasis on teamwork at times seems almost obsessive at RCM and, say clients, probably helps explain the reassuring lack of employee turnover. From the beginning, they report, Rosenberg has always made sure that his partners are highly visible to clients and has emphasized that there are no "stars" at RCM—including himself. In fact, Rosenberg insists, this is one reason the firm has never pushed into the lucrative field of international investing: It would probably have meant hiring a "star" to mastermind the effort. "There is a certain type of individual who won't fit in this firm," he observes, "a highly egocentric person who is not a team player." . . .

Still, despite the emphasis on teamwork at RCM, as one client puts it, "Claude is the franchise." What [one] consultant . . . calls Rosenberg's "essential characteristic of believability, a relaxed kind of confidence," is the envy, and sometimes the bane, of his competitors. One of them recalls, for example, sitting in on a meeting of the Stanford University investment committee in the mid-1970s, when Rosenberg was having performance problems. (In 1975 and 1976 growth stocks were out of favor and RCM mistimed the market recovery; it posted the worst equity performance in its history—18 and 8 points below the S&P, respectively.) "The statement was made," recalls this competitor, "that several managers had been let go due to poor performance, and that Claude's performance was way down as well. But 'That's Claude,' they said. 'He'll come back.'. . . They were more willing to forgive him simply because they tended to have more confidence in his ability."

This confidence is bolstered by Rosenberg's image as an authority on investing. He has written four books on the subject—one of them, *Psycho-Cybernetics and the Stock Market*, tying a low self-image to underperformance. He has also earned a reputation as one of the "statesmen" of the money management business; his latest book, *How to Invest with the Best*, takes his own industry to task for many of its abuses, and he recently assumed the somewhat thankless job of heading a committee to publish performance reporting standards under the auspices of the [Association for Investment Management & Research]. . . .

Rosenberg never projects know-it-all arrogance, though. On the contrary, his plainspokenness scores big points with pension executives turned off by the more flamboyant or self-centered characters in money management. . . . Indeed, what seems to solidify Rosenberg's image with clients is that he comes across as a genuinely *nice* individual, a genial, caring fellow who pursues his hobbies—tennis, fly-fishing and composing original lyrics to popular songs for family and firm celebrations—with the same enthusiasm as his work. He is unabashedly patriotic and sentimental, spending vacations on World War II and Civil War battlefields and writing, and recording, corny love songs for his second wife, "Weezy," on the occasion of his 60th birthday.

• • •

Two years ago, one year before turning 60, Rosenberg sold his firm to Primerica Corp., which is a limited partner until 1990, when it assumes full ownership. And at the same time, somewhat symbolically, the firm's name was changed to the rather strange redundancy, RCM Capital Management—a sign, many felt, that Rosenberg was anxious to back away from the "one-man firm" image that has persisted over the years despite the fact that he has always made it clear that all partners are equal.

Then, in August, Primerica was in turn acquired by . . . Commercial Credit Group. What does all this mean for the future of RCM, a firm that's long been linked to the image of one man and driven by partners with a real stake in its outcome? Not much, answers Rosenberg. . . .

Besides, muses Rosenberg, tilting back his desk chair and gazing out at the magnificent panorama of San Francisco Bay and the Golden Gate Bridge below him, he and his partners ceased working purely for money a long time ago. It's the challenge of doing things better, and feeling creative, that keep them in the business. On top of that, he says, he's been "spoiled" by RCM's enormous information-gathering system and can't imagine taking his winnings and starting up a new, small shop. As for the alternative, "I know exactly what would happen to me if I retired," sighs Rosenberg. "The first three months, I would play myself into a tennis elbow. For the next three or four I would probably write and my wife and I would travel. And by the eighth or ninth month, I'd be getting real *itchy*. . . ."

And it would be time to start tinkering again.

Robert Kirby

HEIDI S. FISKE

Bob Kirby entertained and encouraged genuine thinking among clients, friends, and his cohorts at Capital Group by asking thoughtful and thought-provoking questions. He did so in a most engaging and self-effacing way, never failing to evoke an appreciative response. He retired recently as chairman of Capital Guardian Trust but continues to manage portfolios for the firm. Much that is classic Kirby—especially the final paragraphs where, no doubt with a broad smile, he succinctly characterizes the investment management profession—appears here in his own words.

The $64 billion question that haunts me most is whether money management is really a business at all. Or is it like other strange things that have come and gone—the lost cities of the Toltec and the Aztec, for instance, where they find these empty buildings and they can't figure out why anybody left?

After all, there isn't much history yet. "Money management" didn't really exist until the late 1960s; it was all custodianship, really. The big banks had all the money, and their charge was to be careful and produce an income. They didn't have to beat the S&P 500 or anything else. I blame the creation of this whole business on Jack Dreyfus, because he was the first guy who publicized investment returns—known today as "performance."

Reprinted from *Institutional Investor* (June 1987): pp. 35–37. This copyrighted material is reprinted with permission from: **Institutional Investor, Inc.**, 488 Madison Avenue, New York, NY 10022.

In the late 1960s the lion began to tell everybody what return Dreyfus had gotten. And so some director would stand up in a company's board meeting and say, "How big is our pension fund?" And the response came back, "$300 million." And everybody gasped and said: "My God, that's equal to the net worth of the whole company. Does anybody pay any attention to it?" And the answer was no. And somebody said, "Well, then, why don't we call up the bank and ask how they've done with it?"

And, of course, the CEO of the bank was one of the directors, which is why the bank was the trustee of the fund. So somebody called him and said, "Joe, how is your bank doing with our pension fund?" And he said, "I haven't the foggiest idea." So there was a great scramble, and they found out that the money was 75 percent in bonds, and the bond market had been going straight south for 15 years. So the performance was terrible, to put it politely. Then somebody said: "Look what this Dreyfus Fund has done. My God, if we had been there, we'd have four times this much money."

General Mills started the avalanche that followed when they hired a bunch of bright-eyed, bushy-tailed Harvard Business School guys in the mid-1960s and told them, "Let's have our money managed in a more innovative, imaginative, and so on, way." All euphemisms for, you know, "Let 'em roll the dice." And so these guys looked at the records of people who had been managing money for a while to find the best records, and the mutual funds of the Capital Group showed up. They called us up and asked, "Would you be interested in managing a pension fund?" And we said: "Gosh, I don't know. We never thought about that."

I had been hired from Scudder in 1966 specifically to set up an investment counseling arm—kind of a Scudder-type business, but concentrating on large portfolios—but we thought that would be mostly high-net-worth individuals or hospitals and colleges in southern California. We really didn't think IBM was ever going to hire us to run their pension fund. So General Mills said, "Well, would you talk to us about it?" And we said sure, and they hired us in late 1967 or early 1968.

And all of a sudden—whammo! In no time at all every big company just said, "If that's good enough for General Mills, that's sure good enough for us." You know, big corporations are the ultimate run-sheep-run guys. We went from *no-thin'*, like a rocket ship, to a billion-and-a-half dollars under management. We got approached by people we never made a presentation to.

One day I was in [the late Capital Guardian Trust president] Ned Bailey's office when a call came in from Phillips Academy in Andover, Massachusetts. And the caller said, "Our finance committee met today, and we'd like to talk to you about possibly managing a third of our endowment." And Ned said: "Gee, that's wonderful. What are the circumstances?" They described everything and concluded, "And it's $12 million." And Ned said: "Well, gosh, I'm sorry. Our minimum account is $20 million, and we can't do this."

There was a long pause. Then this very indignant guy on the other end of the line said, "Do you realize this is Phillips . . . Academy . . . at . . . Andover, and I'm telling you as chairman of the finance committee at Phillips . . . Academy . . . at Andover that we're thinking of hiring you?" And Ned said, "Well, this is Ned M. Bailey of the Cleveland Union High School, and I'm telling you that you don't meet our minimum."

Our second big early pension client was L.A. County. Right after the California legislature allowed public retirement systems to buy common stocks, I got a call from the L.A. County treasurer, whom I knew. "You're perfect for us," he said. "Please bid on our fund." I told him, thanks anyway, but to forget it. "There'll be guys in there with fees that are literally one tenth as high as ours," I said. "You simply won't be able to hire us." Well, months went by, and one day the treasurer called again and asked me to come and see him in his office. When I sat down, he gestured behind him and pointed to three flags—one for L.A. County, one for California and a U.S. flag. "Look at the U.S. flag," he said. It was red, white—and purple. "That's what competitive bidding got us," sighed the treasurer. "Now, please, bid on our account." And we bid at our usual rates, and, by gosh, we got it.

You know, we really thought we were magic. We all felt like World War I fighter pilots. You know—daring young men off pushing out the frontiers. We spun in from nowhere and were eating the big banks' lunch. It was the thrill of victory more than anything else. At the time, we felt that we were doing things that mortal men would never dare to do, and succeeding: running all-equity portfolios and buying stocks that didn't have "General" in the name and unbelievable stuff like that. We went from managing $100 million to $1.5 billion still in crazy stuff like Mohawk Data Sciences and bizarre Brand X junky companies.

We were crazy to allow ourselves to grow as rapidly as we did. But how can you say no when somebody says this is Whirlpool or Armco Steel or Merck calling? We were hiring people left, right and sideways. A guy would get hired, and before he found out where the men's room was, he was managing $300 million. And Smith managed money this way and Jones managed it some other way, and there was no coordination. Anyway, we did everything wrong that was conceivable to do.

So during the adjustment phase in 1970–1974, our numbers were just awful. In mid-1974 ITT invited a lot of institutional investors on a tour where we were running around so frantically that I hadn't looked at anything for two weeks. When we got back, I couldn't believe how much prices had changed. When I punched out my portfolio on the Quotron, I turned to Ned and said, "Gee, look at that: All my stocks split 2-for-1 while I was in Europe." We went from $1.5 billion down to something like $600 million, helped partly by the crash of 1973–1974 but helped a lot more by clients departing at the speed of light. We were in a terminal power dive where you expected Spencer Tracy to cry out "Buffetting! Buffetting!"

I discovered during that period that I'm a fatalist. I gradually became numbed to the whole thing and just walked woodenly into the office every day to take my medicine or out to the airplane to talk to clients and have them say goodbye. One of our most harrowing meetings was with Ford Motor. They have this routine where they put you in a dark room and have a prepared slide show reviewing your record. And a guy drones on in a monotone about the particulars in your portfolio and then a slide flashes on the screen, showing where you come in: "outstanding," "good," "satisfactory" or "unsatisfactory."

So he went through our portfolio for the past two years, and at the end the slide went up, and it said, "*un*satisfactory." Then they did the whole thing for one year: "*un*satisfactory." Then for six months and for three months: "*un*satisfactory." And Mike [Michael Shanahan, now president of the Capital Group] leaned over to me and said: "All they're going to do is fire us, for crissake. Why don't they just call us in L.A.?" But they didn't fire us. In fact, Ford is one of the longest and best clients we have. Still, after that meeting we got on the plane in Detroit, and we staggered off in California so drunk that we left our car and took a cab home.

Another good client was Inland Steel, where we dealt with then-treasurer Bob Greenebaum—a really nice guy and very supportive. One day he indicated that he couldn't support us to his committee anymore, and I said, "What about this as a last chance? I'll pull the guy off the portfolio and manage it myself, and I just know I can get it turned around." His finance committee said okay, so I got all the research people together and said, "I want every one of your guys to come up with your one or two really red-hot ideas."

We turned over the portfolio about three quarters as a result of this meeting. And, lo and behold, the portfolio took off like a rocket ship for about 90 days. And then the wings fell off. I now think that if you take good research people and ask for a stock that will do it *right now*, you end up with a missile whose power is gone, and all it's got left is momentum and soon it will crash. That was when Greenebaum called up and said: "Only an idiot would try to catch a falling anvil, Kirby. Send the money back."

Our nadir was June 30, 1973. At that moment we had one account, the Kettering Foundation, for whom we had underperformed the market by 32 percentage points in 18 months. That doesn't get you into the bottom percentile; it gets you into the bottom *decile* of the bottom percentile. One benefit of your numbers getting that bad that fast is that some clients say: "There's no way we're going to fire them now. We'll only ever get back to where we started if we keep the yo-yos and hope they keep their crazy portfolios." By that time we had long since given up our Mohawk Data and

Recognition Equipment and were buying the cheap stocks, which were Exxon and Du Pont and AT&T. Everyone else owned Xerox, Avon and Polaroid.

The issue became the two-tier market, so when an *Institutional Investor* reporter asked me what we were going to do, since it looked as if, continuing on our present path, we might be going out of business, I said: "Well, yeah, maybe we are. But I can tell you, the one thing we are not going to do is fade back into our own end zone and throw a Hail Mary pass, hoping that somebody's going to catch it and save our bacon. Sooner or later people aren't going to pay 80 times earnings for a Polaroid while they pay six times for International Paper. And if we've got any clients left when that happens, they'll be okay."

Nineteen seventy-three and 1974 made everybody in the world say, "We've got way too much of our pension fund in common stocks. Nobody told us they could go down 45 percent in 24 months." And so the business began to mature. Standards of prudence began to develop, and the business grew because of the market and an enormous ongoing flow of money out of bonds. We had a chance to flesh out as an organization.

Still, I wonder if this is really a *profession*. You probably need 10 years to distinguish skill from luck, and we've only had about 15, and the market's been going up most of the time since the wild, wonderful rally of 1975. As far as I'm concerned, there's really only one thing we need to do to be more professional, and that's focus longer term. It seems to me that most of the guys who made what Barton Biggs calls "a unit"—100 million bucks—invested in a few well-chosen companies and stayed there. The investment business is one of committing your clients' capital to quality growing companies and leaving it there until the company changes or gets grossly overvalued. You ought to have to disclose whether you're in that business or the screwing-around business.

The basic question facing us is whether it's possible for a superior investment manager to underperform the market for three years in a row. The assumption widely held is no. And yet, if you look at the records, it's not only possible, it's inevitable. If you focus on a meaningful time horizon—10 or 15 years—every manager runs into a three-year-plus air pocket somewhere. If there's a logical explanation for why the world doesn't see things the way I do, I think it's because the whole thing is so damn new.

Money managers have created their own nightmare by saying, "Boy, look at the February we had." They call about March 3. And this creates an awesomely short-term focus on the client's part. You could have a really great 10-year record, but about the time you underperform the S&P three percentage points two years in a row, the client begins asking: "What's wrong with you guys? Lost your touch? Taking too much vacation?"

The thing I find deplorable is money managers' telling prospects, "We can produce a 600- to 800-basis-point advantage," and the prospects' buying it. It's nuts. Look at the audited, real-life, for-sure records of older mutual funds. (We can't use those of money managers because they're on the honor system, unaudited.) I had the research guys whip up a list of mutual funds that have been around 30 years or more. There are 71 equity funds that qualify, and only 22 of the 71 have beaten the S&P 500: That's less than one third. Templeton is off the charts, but if you take the next five, they have beaten the S&P by a little less than 200 basis points on average. So the client gets a one-in-three shot of beating the average, and if he hires someone in the top 10 percent, he's not going to beat it by much more than 200 basis points, no matter what.

So what do we tell our prospects? Naturally, I wouldn't bring this up if I couldn't say the following: Nos. 3, 4, and 5 on that mutual fund list were from the Capital Group.

But could we point to the same results in the trust company? No. When my ship comes in, I'm going to fund a study of the relative performance of mutual funds and comparable pension funds. The guys who manage mutual funds spend roughly 100 percent of their time focusing on investment decisions. If a pension manager is lucky, and few of us are, he spends 50 percent of his time on the portfolio and the rest talking to the clients. That's a problem in itself, but the nature of the conversations makes it worse. Because the client focuses on the 3-W list: What Went Wrong? Our Ford position was the classic example of all times. We started buying in the low 40s at the end of 1979 and were still buying down around 16, 17 at the end of 1981. We must have owned six to seven million shares of the stock; it was in every client's portfolio. It takes maybe six quarters to build up a mistake of that magnitude. Every time it goes down, the client says: "You bought more Ford? What is wrong with you?" And you say to yourself: "I could solve this problem really easily—namely, write a sell ticket. He'll never ask me that question again." It's like canceling an appointment with your dentist for a root canal.

But it's not the right thing to do for the client. Remember the Kettering Foundation, for whom we underperformed the market 32 percentage points in 18 months? It only took two-and-a-half years more to where, over the life of the account, they were ahead of the market. One of my favorite sayings is that a sick portfolio is like a sidewalk burn: If you keep picking at it, it will never heal.

And someday a broad awareness among institutions is going to develop. And they're going to stop hoping to beat the averages by the 600 or 800 basis points that marketing people are promising them, and they're going to stop paying 1 percent fees based on that hope. I think fewer and fewer people are going to hire active managers.

I read someplace that there are now 5,000 registered money managers, and of the 5,000, 4,000 of them must have made a million dollars apiece last year. (I don't think anyone in our shop has ever made a million in a year.)

And when you look back at the whole 20 years, the overwhelming feeling that hits me is: Never have so many people made so much money by achieving so little.

We've contributed a negative result in the aggregate, and we've been paid like Croesus for it. You'd think, in due course, retribution or regression to the mean would reel us all in and, of the 5,000 firms now in business, 4,500 would go off and do something else.

Dean LeBaron

CARY REICH

Dean LeBaron makes things happen. His firm, Batterymarch, became one of the industry's primary innovators: early and deep in computer applications; early and deep in indexing; early and deep in automated trading; early and large as an investor in third-world markets, etc., etc., etc.

Talk about his business acumen . . . makes LeBaron visibly uncomfortable. Call him an investment theoretician. Call him a contrarian. But, please, don't call him a *businessman*.

"I tend not to think of Batterymarch as a business," says LeBaron. "I have no business plan, no budget. I'm not known for being methodical. And our investment styles don't seem very businesslike. Buying bankrupt companies is not a businesslike approach. And because of our computerized trading system, we never get a broker referral. Is that very businesslike? Probably not. And take the general atmosphere of openness here; I'm not sure that's businesslike. Most other managers would not want their clients and competitors sitting around their office. We do it, but it doesn't make good business sense. And voting against corporate boards on antitakeover measures probably isn't good business either."

Nevertheless, it is as a business creation that Batterymarch truly stands out. No investment management firm runs as much money with as few investment professionals: twelve, to be exact, including LeBaron. No firm of its size makes do with as thin a supporting cast: The Batterymarch staff numbers 35, including those investment professionals, all working on one floor of the Federal Reserve building in downtown

Excerpted from *Institutional Investor 19* (August 1985), pp. 106–107, 109. This copyrighted material is reprinted with permission from: **Institutional Investor, Inc.**, 488 Madison Avenue, New York, NY 10022.

Boston. Because Batterymarch eschews stock picking in favor of broad, strategic themes, it has no need for a corps of analysts. Because all trading is done by computer, it employs no traders. Because Batterymarch does not make sales calls, relying instead on its reputation to attract new clients, it has no need for salesmen. As a result, Batterymarch's average revenue per employee is a staggering $880,000, undoubtedly the highest in the business.

What's more, Batterymarch has achieved all this by being a perfect organizational expression of its creator's twin passions: contrariness and computers. By concentrating on broad groups of out-of-favor stocks, such as near-bankrupt companies and depressed growth stocks, Batterymarch has both carved out a niche for itself and reaped substantial gains for its clients when the market wheel inevitably turned. And by having its portfolio managers concentrate on formulating and refining those broad themes—all the stock screening and selection is done by computer, once the theme's general characteristics are cranked in—Batterymarch has mastered the art of running a huge asset base with minimal staff. . . .

Batterymarch, in short, is a near-ideal fulfillment of the vision LeBaron had ten years ago, when he remarked, "My idea of the future money management organization is a few senior people and one big machine." And the atmosphere of the place is totally in keeping with its founder's style: quiet, informal, more like a college library in midsummer than a bustling investment firm. Since LeBaron once observed that "all the really interesting conversations in an office occur in the corridors or in the men's room," he has fashioned an office layout that, in effect, is one big corridor. All the portfolio managers, including LeBaron, sit in cubicles open to whoever passes by. Throughout the day, small clusters of people gather, chat, peer at one another's computer terminals and then go their separate ways; this is about as close as Batterymarch ever gets to actually having meetings. LeBaron dips in and out of cubicles and conversations as the spirit moves him, describing himself as "a roving meddler." Much of the time, the only sound to be heard is the soft clatter of a computer keyboard. Once in a while, a phone actually rings.

LeBaron revels in the silence, taking particular pride in showing off the "trading room," which consists of a single computer terminal on a desk in the middle of the office. He loves to point out that the vice president in charge of trading goes out jogging each day between 3:00 and 4:00 P.M. and that she also covers about a dozen accounts in her copious spare time.

Aside from the tranquility and the cubicles, the other distinctive feature of the Batterymarch office is the microcomputer on each desk. What's distinctive about the micros is that they come in all sorts of shapes, sizes and brand names. "Anything they feel comfortable with, they can have," says LeBaron. "Sure, it's inefficient. It means you need more memory, and the programs don't work as smoothly. But this way, everyone does it their own way." Computers, in fact, are the one exception to

LeBaron's rule of running a low-overhead shop; he believes in ordering first and then figuring out what to do with the stuff later. The result is a room full of equipment he and his colleagues used briefly and then discarded.

Peter Lynch

JOHN TRAIN

Peter Lynch became a celebrity when his disciplined, relentless pursuit of investment performance made Fidelity's Magellan Fund one of the business' all-time success stories. As if to mock himself and his extraordinary self-discipline and extraordinary commitment to detailed knowledge, this professional has also written two popular books strongly suggesting that amateur individual investors can beat the pros. He retired from active investing for Fidelity in 1991, but continues as a leader of the organization.

How can it be that a single individual, virtually without a staff, and managing an enormous mass of capital . . . greatly outperforms a large, able organization—the best that the governing body of an old and famous institution can assemble—handling only a fraction as much money? . . .

The chief reason is that a supremely capable individual—and Peter Lynch is one—easily outmaneuvers a large committee. . . . Wellington, who never lost a battle, also never held councils of war; Napoleon liked to say that one general was enough for an army. In other words, the trick in these two competitive games, investment and war, is to find the ablest chief available and, under philosophical guidance, give him his head. If he is not the ablest chief available, change him. But don't expect an assemblage of less able men to outmaneuver him. . . . Peter Lynch has two research assistants—one to collect Wall Street news and attend company presentations, and the other to call companies and go to research meetings. When asked if he mightn't like another, he responds vaguely: Perhaps . . . someday . . . you spend so much time talking to them. . . .

It also helps to be rather free with the emoluments. Peter Lynch is a hired hand, but he knows what he is worth, and his employer, Fidelity Management, pays him several million dollars a year. . . .

Selected excerpts from pp. 192–198, 203, 207, 221–223, from *The New Money Masters* by John Train. Reprinted by permission of HarperCollins Publishers, Inc. ©1989 John Train.

How so? Well, Peter Lynch essentially created the Magellan Fund. Since he took charge in 1977, it has become the largest mutual fund in history, $12 billion in assets at its peak in August 1987, and $8.4 billion at March 31, 1988. It has over a million shareholders, and incidentally pays Fidelity, its managers, $60 million a year in management fees and as much as several hundred million in sales commissions. . . .

This investment prodigy is the son of a professor of mathematics at Boston College, who later moved to the John Hancock Company. . . . He attended high school in Newton, Massachusetts. Summers he worked as a caddy, which is where he began hearing about the stock market. Businessmen out golfing exchange investment ideas, and some businessmen are very well informed.

Young Peter sank $1,250 of his savings in one of the stocks he heard about, Flying Tiger Line, a way of riding the explosive growth of the Pacific countries as well as the development of air freight. He bought in at $10. Flying Tiger went up and up. Peter sold some to get his money back, and then sold more in dribbles all the way up. The last went in 1989 when the company was taken over by Federal Express. By the time he had cashed in most of his stock he had made enough money to pay for his graduate study at the Wharton School of Finance in Philadelphia.

First, however, came college. Here a second golf-derived bonanza came his way: Boston College had a $300 partial scholarship intended precisely for caddies, which Peter won. Later the Goddess of Golf smiled upon him yet again: In 1966, waiting to start in at Wharton, he got a summer job at Fidelity. There were 75 applicants, but Peter was the one who had caddied for D. George Sullivan, the president of the company. He joined the ROTC at college, and on emerging from Wharton spent the required two years in the Army. He was sent not to Vietnam but ("lucky even then," he says) to South Korea. In 1969, after being discharged, he was offered a permanent job at Fidelity, starting as a metals analyst, and has worked there ever since. He has now become so successful that he can no longer squeeze in time for golf.

In 1974, after a few years in analytical jobs, Lynch became Fidelity's director of research, while continuing to cover the chemical, packaging, steel, aluminum, and textile industries. . . .

In analyst meetings, he urges his colleagues not to tear down each other's ideas—"Don't rip up my Volvo idea," as he says—but rather to explain why their own ideas are good ones

In 1977, after eight years as a permanent employee at Fidelity, Lynch, now 33, was put in charge of a little fund that Fidelity had around, Magellan. Originally intended for foreign securities—whence the nod to the eponymous Portuguese navigator—Magellan had been started in 1963; two years later it was hit by the Interest Equalization Tax, intended to support the dollar by discouraging U.S. investment abroad, and was forced to reorient itself toward domestic securities. In 1976 it absorbed Essex Fund, with $14 million. When Lynch took over it had only $22 million in it, concentrated in relatively few holdings, and was an almost invisible part of the Fidelity empire.

• • •

Lynch's cardinal advantage over the legion of his competitors, in addition to his basic talent, is the enormous dedication he brings to the task. Lynch tries harder. Indeed, one finds it exhausting just to think about his routine. In 20 years of marriage he has taken two proper vacations. "I went to Japan and just saw companies for five days and met Carolyn in Hong Kong. So we had Friday, Saturday, and Sunday in Hong Kong. Then I saw companies Monday, Tuesday, and Wednesday in Hong Kong. Then we went up into China for two or three days. Then, I saw companies in Bangkok. Then, we saw a little bit of Bangkok. Then, I flew to England and I saw companies for three, four days there. It was a fabulous time." Not every wife's conception of "a fabulous time"! A stockbroker who accompanied him for some days mentions that in a country where things barely get going at ten o'clock in the morning Lynch insisted on starting to see companies at eight, and was quite grumpy that none could be found to talk to him at six! When at the end of the day the idea of dinner was raised, Lynch begged off: "I gotta read four annual reports by tomorrow." This broker said he had never seen someone so well prepared for company visits. . . .

He is off to the office by car pool at 6:15 in the morning—reading all the way—and back by 7:15 at night in a Fidelity car (after eighteen years traveling by bus), still reading. He gets two or three feet of reports and recommendations every day, which are neatly piled on a table at one side of his office until he gets to them. Every lunch he spends talking to a company. He also comes in on Saturdays to look through his stack of reports, but only reads in detail about 5 percent of what is there. He may also read for a few hours on Sunday mornings before attending mass with his family.

• • •

One can think of Peter Lynch as a dark-suited mobile strainer, processing hundreds and hundreds of bits of information a day. Some of it arrives passively, like the krill scooped up by the whale; much of it, though, is deliberately hunted out. Brokers fall in the first category: Lynch hears from some 200 of them. He might receive several dozen brokers' telephone calls on an average day.

Ordinarily, Lynch doesn't accept calls directly. Callers have learned to leave concise messages with his secretary or one of his two traders. He may return one call for every ten he receives, but he will initiate calls on subjects of concern to him. Either way, he exhorts the person at the end of the line to compress his message to a minute and a half and actually starts a kitchen timer when the conversation begins. After 90 seconds, *brrringg!* Or he will just end the conversation: "Sorry, I got another call comin' in." Pretty soon the callers get the point about brevity. Even in that short time, he will quite often ask some key questions several times, perhaps in different ways, like a cross-examiner.

• • •

Lynch's most solid investment information comes from company visits. After so many years in a big investing institution, he has gotten to know hundreds upon hundreds of well-placed executives in the business world who desire nothing more than to be obliging to institutional stockholders, their most important owners. What's more, you learn how to interpret what you hear. Some company presidents promise more than they can deliver, some are always overcautious, some are honest and reliable. Knowing which is which gives the professional an inestimable advantage. And visit them he does, 40 or 50 a month, 500 or 600 a year.

• • •

Lynch's endless quest, his endless searching among companies, is directed above all toward the *obvious winner, based on changes in the key variable.* As he goes back repeatedly to a given company or industry, he spots changes. Business has been dreadful for a year. Then it's not quite so bad. "Even when a company just moves up from doing mediocre business to doing fair business, you can make money." . . . So he starts to buy, not just the top company in the group, as T. Rowe Price would, or what seems like the most attractive bargain, as Warren Buffett would, but, like James Rogers, the entire group, *in toto:* quite possibly dozens of companies. Then, as they start to move, he may winnow the list down to a favorite few. . . .

Lynch's emphasis [is] on the *obvious* winner. Lynch claims that if other investors made as many calls as he did, they, too, would spot the changes in company fortunes that he does, and would almost always recognize the same buying opportunities. "You have to stay tuned," he often says. . . .

Lynch is a bit over six feet tall, slim and athletic looking, with silver hair over a pale, finely modeled, almost spiritual face that is faintly suggestive of a much handsomer Andy Warhol. He is pleasantly rather than elegantly turned out. . . .

He speaks rapidly and profusely, using a colloquial, even somewhat adolescent, choice of words, "So I say to myself, gee, what'm I do'n?" In talking, he waves one or both of his hands, sometimes with his glasses in them, smiling faintly. . . .

Lynch describes himself as typically Irish and gabby—when not working, of course. In response to questions, he will start to answer, launch into a digression, and then babble on about what is in his mind, realizing eventually that he has gone off the point. Asked about an eventual career evolution, he says he might like to teach someday, and one can readily believe it. . . .

Quite surprising, in my experience of notable investors, is Lynch's balanced, calm, modest, and unassuming approach to his profession and to life—except, of course, for his phenomenally intense preoccupation with his work.

• • •

Lynch's office approaches the ultimate in clutter. Against a window run two yards of reports in a horizontal parade, and in front of them vertical stacks of the reports that have come in during the week, arranged by categories. Manila files litter the floor. Inches of paper blanket his desk, and I counted some 60 yellow legal pads peeking out here and there from the debris. The writing on the top sheet of each pad covers a concern of the moment: companies that fill some particular criterion, such as interesting insider buying; questions to ask the officer of a company when he calls back; notes that need to be expanded . . . whatever requires attention. . . . I suppose the point is that he can put his finger on what he wants quickly enough, and he knows roughly where in the jumble everything is lurking. Perhaps we have here the difference between artificial order—the garden of a French château, for example—and working order, such as a jungle, which looks chaotic to the passerby, but makes sense to God or a naturalist.

Even the walls of the office are a muddle; giant pictures of his children (slightly askew), prints, posters, framed share certificates. Almost hidden among the papers is a single beige telephone, flanked by a row of framed family photographs, and, like an alp rising behind foothills, a computer terminal on a side table.

In his office his conversations with colleagues are terse in the extreme. From time to time a head appears around the door and emits a squirt transmission of a few dozen syllables. Lynch will reply with a grunt or two; the head vanishes. The conversations are like the soundtracks of old speeded-up movies of the 1920s.

• • •

Lynch has a brusque, commonsense contempt for many if not most of the formulas that are peddled as shortcuts to stock-market success. . . .

There is, however, one exception: catching the turn. That maneuver attracts Lynch strongly. He wants to make a partial investment a bit ahead of the turn in the fortunes of a company, and then build up his holding as the turn actually occurs.

Lynch gives little weight to a company's dividend policy. In his own language, "I can't say that dividends are something I feature."

"A horrible fallacy," said Lynch, "is buying a stock simply because it has gone down, what is called bottom fishing. If the market thought that

Federated Fido was worth $50 six months ago, and it's $20 today, then it must be a bargain! But that was true when it was at $40 and then at $30, and it may well be true when the stock goes down to $10. You have to have a clear conception of the true value and work only off that, not off the stock's recent performance history."

• • •

"I spend about 15 minutes a year on economic analysis," he says. "The way you lose money in the stock market is to start off with an economic picture. I also spend 15 minutes a year on where the stock market is going. All these great, heady, thinking deals kill you."

He finds that worries based on economic predictions are particularly useless. . . .

Lynch notices that people always ask him about the outlook for the economy and the stock market and other such large and general questions. But nobody can give those answers. . . .

"The GNP six months out is just malarkey. How is the sneaker industry doing? That's real economics."

John B. Neff

JOHN TRAIN

John Neff is the professional investor's professional investor—partly because his investment performance was outstanding for over a quarter century and partly because he earned those fine results by talent, self-discipline, and hard, hard work. No investor ever managed so large a mutual fund for as long and so very well.

John Neff, of Berwyn, Pennsylvania . . . is little known outside the investment community because he is modest, gray, and unspectacular. He looks and acts not at all the Wall Street hotshot, but the Midwestern executive: nice house a little way out of town; wife of over 30 years; modest, unfashionable, and slightly messy clothes; no magnificent paneled office, just the disorderly, paper-strewn den one expects of a college department head. He doesn't get into the newspapers, least of all the gossip columns. Main Line society has never heard of him. And yet, he is one of the most eminent

Selected excerpts from Chapter 7 from *The New Money Masters* by John Train. Copyright © 1989 by John Train. Reprinted by permission of HarperCollins Publishers, Inc.

financial figures in the country. Indeed, in several polls he has . . . been the choice of money managers to manage their own money.

Neff has run the Windsor Fund for 24 years. Through 1988 it had a compound annual return of 14.3 percent versus the S&P's 9.4 percent over the same period. For the last 20 years he has also run Gemini Fund, a closed-end dual-purpose investment company. It, too, has grown at about twice the rate of the market. Finally, over the more than ten-year period he has run Qualified Dividend Portfolio One it has yet again approximately doubled the performance of the market. Year in, year out he is likely to be among the top 5 percent in performance of all funds. So it's no accident. Even more surprising, he keeps up this performance even though he now runs a huge amount of capital. . . .

Neff is a "value" man: He only buys when a stock is too cheap and acting badly at that moment in the market; and he infallibly sells when, by his criteria, it is too expensive, again always when it is acting strongly in the market. He buys stocks that are dull, or to use his own terms, "misunderstood and woebegone," and sells when the market has gotten the point and has bid them up to fair value, or over fair value. In this he is a classic contrarian.

Where Neff differs from his peers is in his *insistence on income. Neff claims that the market usually overpays for the prospect of growth,* but growth stocks have two drawbacks: First, they suffer from high mortality—that is, often the growth doesn't continue long enough after it has been recognized—and second, *you can often get a better total return from a slower-growth company that is paying a high dividend right now.* . . .

The future dean of the "growth and income" school was born in Wauseon, Ohio, outside Toledo, in the Depression year 1931. His parents were divorced in 1934. His mother then remarried, to an oil entrepreneur who moved the family all over Michigan and eventually to Texas. Neff attended high school in Corpus Christi. He held outside jobs all the way through school and, having little interest in his classes, received indifferent grades. After graduating he took a variety of factory jobs, including one in a company that made jukeboxes. Meanwhile his own father had prospered in the automobile- and industrial-equipment-supply business, and persuaded Neff to join him. Neff found that experience extremely instructive. His father, he says, taught him the importance of paying great attention to the price you pay.

Neff then spent two years in the Navy, where he learned to be an aviation electronics technician. On receiving his discharge, he resolved to finish his education, and so enrolled in the University of Toledo, studying industrial marketing. His interest was fully aroused, and he graduated summa cum laude. Two of his courses were corporate finance and investment, and he realized he had found his métier, having previously thought that finance was a world reserved for Ivy Leaguers. While still at the University of Toledo, he married his wife, Lilli Tulac, a native Toledoan. The head of Toledo's Department of Finance at that time was Sidney

Robbins, an extremely able student of investments, who in fact was given the important job of updating Graham and Dodd's famous *Security Analysis*. So from the first Neff was exposed to the value theory of investment . . . Later he attended night school at Case Western Reserve to earn a master's degree in banking and finance.

Neff hitchhiked to New York during his Christmas vacation of 1954 to see if he could get a job as a stockbroker. He was told by Bache that his voice didn't carry enough authority, and that until it did, they would only take him as a security analyst. Lilli didn't like New York in any event, so Neff did indeed become a securities analyst, but with Cleveland's National City Bank, where he stayed for eight and a half years.

In time he became head of research for the bank's Trust Department. However, as a Graham and Dodd disciple he believed that the best investments were the least understood, and thus often found himself at odds with the Trust Committee, which preferred big-name stocks that would reassure the customers, even if they didn't make them money.

After Cleveland, in 1963, Neff joined Wellington Management in Philadelphia. . . .

• • •

Neff has an earnest, broad, humorous face, with a large chin and a wide, up-curling mouth that reveals a sequence of expressions. His high forehead is surmounted by silver hair, and he wears metal eyeglasses perched on a small nose. He speaks with a gravelly Midwestern voice. A pen is stuck in the pocket of his white shirt. He wears argyle socks. . . .

Neff shares two characteristics with many other great investors: He was poor as a boy, and he is a compulsive worker now. He works 60 to 70 hours a week, including 15 hours each weekend. In the office he concentrates virtually without interruption and drives his staff extremely hard. He is tough and harsh when he feels that a job has not been properly done. On the other hand, he invites staff to participate in his decisions, which they like.

• • •

Neff is considered an outstanding securities analyst. Although in recent years he has not himself ordinarily made company visits, he talks to companies at length. After almost 35 years' experience in his profession, Neff has already bought or studied a high proportion of the companies that he is considering for purchase at any time. In other words, it is often a question of updating his knowledge, rather than starting from scratch.

He is constantly looking at industry groups that are unpopular in the market. He confines his research to stocks with particularly low price-earnings ratios, and, ordinarily, unusually high yields. And, in fact, over the many years that Neff has run Windsor Fund, the average price-earnings ratio of his portfolio has been around a third below that of the general market, while it has on average yielded 2 percent more.

He has described himself as a "low-P/E shooter." However, unlike Benjamin Graham, he is concerned with the underlying nature of the company. He wants a *good* company at a low price.

Leon Levy and Jack Nash

ALISON LEIGH COWAN

Leon Levy and Jack Nash are highly regarded by their peers on Wall Street partly for the magnitude of their success, but primarily for the *way* they have achieved their objectives: originality, audacity, and patient persistence. For business, Odyssey Partners was their chosen vehicle. For fun, Levy finances the excavation at Ashkelon near Tel Aviv, the largest funding ever from a single private patron. Typical.

When Jack Nash and Leon Levy left Oppenheimer & Company, the Wall Street firm, to start their own investment boutique in 1982, they named it Odyssey Partners after the Greek tale. "After all," Mr. Levy said, "the Odyssey is nothing but a journey fraught with opportunity and peril."

The partners have seen more of the former than the latter in the last six years. Between Mr. Nash's ability to cut deals and Mr. Levy's quirky but shrewd hunches about the economy, the two have parlayed about $50 million that they cleared from the 1982 sale of Oppenheimer into hundreds of millions of dollars. . . .

On a day-to-day basis, Odyssey's partners trade a portfolio of stocks and bonds. But they are better known for surfacing in takeover skirmishes, including, most recently, the battle for J.P. Stevens & Company. For the moment, Odyssey has edged out a competing bid from West Point-Pepperell Inc. with a friendly offer of $1.14 billion in cash for the textile giant.

They may soon have another takeover fight on their hands. Last Thursday, Odyssey disclosed it had approached UNC Inc., an aerospace company, about doing a leveraged buyout with management. Odyssey's proposal was rebuffed. . . .

Mr. Levy, who is 62 years old, and Mr. Nash, 58, shun publicity. They rarely grant interviews, and their names are omitted from the portal of their Madison Avenue office. "You've never seen people operate less on ego." . . .

Their reputation, on the other hand, looms large on Wall Street for being early in spotting the rewards of leveraged buyouts, in which buyers borrow heavily against a company's assets to finance the purchase. And at a time when others are rediscovering the virtues of small companies with low overheads and hands-on management, Mr. Nash and Mr. Levy now look like trend-setters. . . .

The longtime duo . . . make money the hard way: slowly.

Odyssey rarely receives dividends. Unlike . . . other leveraged buyout groups . . . it refuses investment banking fees for fashioning deals. And the partnership still holds some of its earliest investments long after they have gone public.

Including Odyssey's days as an Oppenheimer unit, the limited partnership has averaged a 24 percent compounded rate of return over the years. Since 1982, its returns have been much higher, according to one insider. But . . . Nash and . . . Levy realize these high returns will be tough to sustain as the portfolio swells. Currently, they have $500 million in liquid, marketable securities and their less-liquid stakes in some 50 companies are worth about $350 million. . . .

The partners have few hard rules and are not squeamish about betting on companies that others find confusing, including private concerns and companies in distress.

For instance, Mr. Levy's premonition that railroads, which haul coal, would rebound along with the coal industry led Odyssey in 1983 to buy a large stake in the Chicago Milwaukee Corporation, the parent of a bankrupt railroad. The company was then valued at less than $25 million. But following the sale of the railroad, timberland and some real estate, the company now sits on $400 million in cash and still has a few assets.

Another hunch led the partners to Gundle Environmental Systems Inc., a maker of heavy-duty liners for waste sites whose owners had hired Oppenheimer in 1986 to sell the company. Gundle had always considered itself a plastics company, rather than the recession-proof, environmental protection gold mine that Mr. Young saw it to be. Mr. Nash clinched the deal when he came up with the $30 million asking price in cash. . . .

Others in their shoes might have taken profits a few months later when Gundle went public and issued new shares at $8 apiece, a price that valued the company's equity at $36 million. But Odyssey's partners sat tight. Today, the stock is trading at about $20, and Odyssey's 50 percent stake is worth $45 million.

"The best investments require a great deal of zitsfleysh," said Mr. Nash, using a Yiddish expression for patience. Paying taxes every time the portfolio turns over only leaves the partnership with less money to reinvest, he said. . . .

To be sure, Odyssey has made mistakes. The firm stumbled after it bought a 1.2 percent stake in Trans World, whose holdings included an airline, hotels and a real estate broker. Odyssey proposed that a spinoff of the unrelated parts would fetch at least twice the going price for the unfocused whole. Trans World's management won the ensuing fight.

Some of the takeover business . . . say Odyssey was simply ahead of its time. . . . Institutional investors at the time were much more reluctant to oppose management. "If they had done it a few years later, they would have won." . . .

"We were a little naive," Mr. Levy said, who regrets not accumulating more Trans World shares first. . . .

Still, Odyssey's successes have far outnumbered its defeats, others in the takeover business say. Both Mr. Nash and Mr. Levy had already made their marks—and money—at Oppenheimer. Mr. Levy, as chairman of Oppenheimer's group of mutual funds, and Mr. Nash, as chairman of the parent company, adroitly navigated the firm, which catered to institutional investors, through several periods of retrenchment and pushed it into the lucrative retail trade.

As the firm became larger, Mr. Levy missed his research and Mr. Nash his deals. They also saw that Oppenheimer, to do deals for its own account, would need more capital.

In 1982, Oppenheimer's brokerage and mutual fund businesses, along with the name, were sold to Mercantile House . . . of London for $162.5 million. . . .

The remaining deal-making unit was renamed Odyssey. In some ways, this venture bears a strong resemblance to the place where the two City College graduates met 37 years ago: Oppenheimer's cramped eight-man shop on 25 Broad Street. . . .

Max Oppenheimer, who had been a broker at Hirsch & Company, formed his own firm in 1950 and recruited Mr. Levy, a Hirsch factotum, as research director.

Though barred from a securities analysis course in college because of his poor grades, Mr. Levy clearly had the knack. A year after he graduated, he bought shares in Pacific Western Oil and Jefferson Lake Sulfur, two companies whose insiders were feverishly buying shares.

A student of psychology in college, Mr. Levy assumed that management knew something. "Events are not that predictable, but people are," he said. He was right, made plenty of money and a year later was teaching the course that had turned him away.

Mr. Nash, a German refugee who spoke no English when he arrived in America at the age of 12, started as an Oppenheimer trainee in 1951 and returned in 1954 after a brief stint in his father's textile business. Within five years, he was running the show. . . .

The partnership made sense. The affable, but forgetful, Mr. Levy—known for once leaving his wife Shelby behind at a black-tie dinner—hatched the ideas. Executing them was left to the disciplined Mr. Nash.

As their moves on Stevens and UNC show, Odyssey's partners still have strong ambitions.

Stephen Robert, chairman of Oppenheimer Group Inc. and a limited partner in Odyssey, remembers that when J. Paul Getty died, Mr. Nash and Mr. Levy calculated how much the oil billionaire's net worth had appreciated each year since 1933: 17.7 percent. "And he became the richest man in the world." . . .

Barton Biggs

JULIA ROHRER

Barton Biggs is acknowledged to be one of the best writers and thinkers on Wall Street. He spearheaded Morgan Stanley's development of a strong research department and a large asset management business. These dual responsibilities entailed simultaneously having offices in separate buildings on opposite sides of 49th Street, a fact that confused some people but seemed merely to excite his sense of humor. In the decade that followed this admiring piece, it became clear that Biggs had fully succeeded in his attempt "to be a global investment strategist."

The missive seemed to lack the dash and wit that usually characterize the weekly commentaries written by Barton Biggs, Morgan Stanley & Co.'s managing director and chief investment strategist. But it still packed a wallop. Stressing his firm's view that investing is becoming an increasingly global profession, Biggs disclosed that Morgan Stanley intends to establish a separate foreign research department, to be at least partly in place by the end of the year. Not only that, he wrote, the firm will have investment strategy and research units in such key markets as Tokyo, London and Australia.

But the big news came in the fourth paragraph: Biggs, the engineer of Morgan Stanley's original research building (*Institutional Investor*, June 1974), will be heading the international effort himself. He'll be focusing on "asset allocation, international events and the relative attractiveness of the world's markets," he wrote. And though Byron Wien, formerly a partner at Century Capital Associates, will take over his strategy role for

Excerpted from *Institutional Investor 19* (June 1985), pp. 131–46. This copyrighted material is reprinted with permission from: **Institutional Investor, Inc.**, 488 Madison Avenue, New York, NY 10022.

the U.S., Biggs added, "I am going to attempt to be a global investment strategist."

• • •

Behind a reserved, seemingly even-tempered manner—he has been described as looking as if he stepped out of a John Cheever novel—Biggs is a highly motivated, keenly disciplined, competitive individual, with a distinct style and way of doing things. Speculation about his ability to be successful as a global strategist leans heavily in his favor. And a good part of the reason is that since going to Wall Street in 1961 as an analyst for E. F. Hutton & Co., Biggs has had a most impressive success record.

He came to his role of portfolio strategist relatively late in life, however, because his early ambition was to be a writer. And after graduating from Yale in 1955 (with a degree in English) and spending three years as a lieutenant in the Marine Corps, he became a $25-a-week copy boy for the *Washington Star*. He left the *Star* to teach ninth-grade English and devote more time to writing. But "after 100 rejection letters," he says, "I realized I had miscalculated."

Biggs then entered business school at the University of Virginia and pursued a career more in line with family tradition. (His father, the late William Biggs, was chief investment officer at Bank of New York and would have been considered a front-runner for the secretary of Treasury spot had Hubert Humphrey won the 1968 presidential election. Biggs's brother, Jeremy, is an executive vice president at Fiduciary Trust Co.) He was No. 1 in his class the first year and was promptly recruited by E. F. Hutton. Biggs finished up his MBA at New York University and became the personal assistant to then-chairman Sylvan Coleman.

At Hutton he also ran a paper portfolio for A. W. Jones & Co., the hedge fund—where he met Jones's partner, Richard Radcliffe. And in 1965 Biggs and Radcliffe joined forces to start Wall Street's third hedge fund, Fairfield Partners. After raising an initial $10 million from a diverse group of investors, including Laurence Tisch, chairman of Loews, Fairfield had nearly $50 million under management by 1970. Fairfield also began running an international fund, which was marketed by Morgan Stanley.

The connection eventually led to Biggs being asked—in 1973, at the age of 40—to become the first partner to join Morgan Stanley from the outside. His franchise was to build an institutional research department, and just 14 months after Biggs joined the firm, Morgan Stanley ranked seventh on the 1974 All-American Research Team. According to Richard Fisher, Morgan Stanley's chief executive officer, there's no doubt where the credit belongs. "He built the department entirely on his own," Fisher says.

• • •

Biggs contends that running a research department isn't so hard. "Basically," he explains, "you're dealing with very smart, creative people. Our style is to give them a fair amount of discretion. We let all of them say what they want so long as it is noted that it is their opinion and not the firm's." As a result, analysts often disagree in print with Biggs, who over the years has written the lead commentary in Morgan Stanley's weekly research publication. . . .

This willingness to tolerate differences of opinion stems from Biggs's belief that "group think" is of little value. Nor are committee judgments, "when the members' striving for unanimity overrides their motivation to realistically appraise alternative(s)," as he wrote in one of his commentaries last year, quoting Yale psychologist Irving Janis. At the same time, his laissez-faire management style may also stem from the fact that "he really does not like to manage," as an associate puts it. "He is really quite shy." He is so reserved, reports Dennis Sherva, head of equity research at Morgan Stanley, who has worked with Biggs for eight years, that "I have never seen him get angry."

Biggs's reserve is probably one reason—his duties as chairman of Morgan Stanley Asset Management being another—he is less active than other Wall Street portfolio strategists in "pressing the flesh" and getting out to visit clients. In addition, he shuns small talk and playing the role of toastmaster. For example, on a two-week trip to Australia, during which he and a number of institutional investors were wined and dined by Australian finance VIPs, "not once did Biggs ever give a toast," recalls one member of the group. Even at the most elaborate, small dinners, this source continues, Biggs seemed reluctant to show enthusiasm for a host's hospitality.

That may seem unusual for a man considered by many to be Wall Street's best writer, for his wit, intellect and productivity. . . . But he does some of his most important work in private. Almost every Sunday over the past 12 years, Biggs has gone into his den at home to write an investment or research commentary for publication the next day.

• • •

Underlying his impressive longer-term record have been some astute market calls. In 1980, for example, when other Wall Street pundits were talking about an "embedded" inflation rate of about 7 or 8 percent, Biggs's knowledge of supply-side economics and his interpretation of the impact of supply-side politics, among other things, led him to draw a scenario for disinflation. He advised clients to get out of oils within two weeks of a 10-year peak in oil stocks. "It was one of the best calls I have ever seen," says research chief Sherva. More recently, in the spring of 1983, when technology stocks were still being touted, Biggs wisely cautioned his clients on that group.

It is Biggs's belief that by far the biggest part of performance depends on the big asset allocation decisions; as a result, he has emphasized those decisions over individual stock selection in his strategy pieces on the U.S. market. For his global product, he will also be supplying broad asset allocation guidelines among industries as well as broad stock/cash/bond ratio-type assessments; the only difference is that he will be looking at securities and countries around the world.

In fact, Biggs maintains that being a global strategist "won't be that different" from what he's been doing all along. As he explains it: "You want to have a knowledge base, and you want to talk to people and follow events, read the *Financial Times* and so on. Then all of a sudden things begin to fall into place. Then you get the feeling a particular market is attractive, and you have the knowledge base, the analysts and the specialists who can tell you what in that market is the right thing to do."

Julian Robertson

GARY WEISS

Julian Robertson absorbed a heavy performance hit in 1987, yet produced an after-fee total return for the decade that was $4\frac{1}{2}$ *times* the S&P's 342 percent gain for the period. One experienced observer declared him to be "the best money manager in the world right now" when this profile was written in 1990. He may well have been. In 2000, he closed down.

Tiger . . . 47.

So reads the lobby directory at 101 Park Avenue. The Manhattan white pages are more helpful—Tiger Management—and it gives a phone number as well as an address. The public manifestations of Julian Robertson are like that—sparse. An SEC filing here. A paragraph in the financial press there. Fame has not come to Julian Robertson. Fortune, yes. But not fame.

Up on the 47th floor you don't see a mackerel-striped carnivore, but rather a quiet group of desks, neatly and democratically pushed together. Beyond a wall of glass, curved like the bridge of an ocean liner, the canyons of Lower Manhattan are three miles ahead.

Excerpted from *Assets* (November/December 1990), pp. 31–36. © 1990 Time Inc. Reprinted by permission.

It's August 9, 1990, and the visibility is splendid. With a little squinting and a lot of imagination, you can practically see the analysts, money managers, and traders pacing their cubicles, wild-eyed. Saddam Hussein has been pouring troops into Kuwait for seven bloodcurdling days, and the world's financial markets are is disarray. Over the past week, the Dow Jones industrial average has fallen more than 100 points. But the damage has been even worse abroad, especially in the Japanese and European markets that had risen to new heights only a few months before. Global investing had been all the rage. Now, it seems that there is nothing to do but rage.

Julian Robertson is a global investor, with $942 million deployed across the planet, but he is unfazed by the chaos in the world markets. He is talking about his favorite subject—stocks. It is a subject that, at the moment, would cause most money managers to curl into a fetal position. Even before the massacre of the preceding week, the Standard & Poor's 500-stock index was up a paltry 2.6 percent for the year. At this point, his flagship Tiger limited partnership has gained by a figure resembling the S&P—except that the decimal point has been moved to the right. Unbeknownst to all but a handful of rather happy people, the money in Tiger has gained not 2.6 percent, but 26.7 percent. Most money managers would burst a blood vessel from sheer joy if they'd done half as well.

The 58-year-old Robertson is proud of his record, all right, but it seems that something more important is gnawing at him. "Stocks that have been good to us this year?" he says in a slow, North Carolina drawl. He names a couple and then pauses, lost in thought. "Hey Ed," he calls to an associate seated not far away. "We talked to a guy today who says that Chase [Manhattan] is the thing we ought to be short. . . . It might be interesting to look at Chase." His colleague is noncommittal. Yes, he is familiar with Chase, and he begins to expound upon it. Robertson, amiably, cuts him short. "I want to tell you this: If you don't short some of those banks . . ." He grins, mischievously.

The rest is (for want of a better word) history. On August 9, Chase stock was changing hands at $19. The Street was cautious but hardly bearish. Two days earlier, one prominent analyst had reaffirmed the "attractive" rating of another prominent bank holding company, Chemical. But in a matter of weeks, as news of the ill tidings afflicting banks in general and Chase in particular spread across the financial pages, money-center bank stocks were in a free-fall. And none fell further or faster than Chase—which collapsed to $11 a share, a loss of 42 percent of its market value, by the end of September.

As financial crisis go, this one ran true to form from the investment standpoint: By the time the full dimensions of the banking fiasco became obvious, the stocks were already in the cellar. It was too late. For most investors, the decline and fall of the banks was a short-selling opportunity lost unless you had a crystal ball. Or were Julian Robertson.

Foresight. Flexibility. A global perspective—with the ability to go short as well as long anywhere on the planet. For Robertson, there is simply no other way. "Some may think it ambitious that we are determined to be global investors," Robertson noted in a letter to his partners in June. "We think any other approach would be shortsighted."

Globalism for Robertson is more than just buying a few overseas stocks to dress up his portfolios. It means judging every investment opportunity, foreign and domestic, from a global point of view. It also means applying the venturesome yet risk-averse hedge fund approach to world investment. It has meant riding the upward crest of German stocks when they were rising mightily after the collapse of the Berlin Wall—and selling short as they peaked, profiting from their decline. It has meant escaping unscathed from the downfall of the Japanese market through long-term "put" options, purchased when the market was still healthy.

It's an approach that is laced with a strong dose of humility. . . . Robertson does not pretend to know when any market—domestic or foreign—has peaked or bottomed. He buys (or sells short) stocks on their fundamental virtues (or lack thereof). Robertson then seeks, in the time-honored manner of hedge funds, to guard against future market collapses by short-selling, and by using foreign and domestic index "put" options that gain dramatically in value when the market falls. He casts a wide net for investment ideas: His network of contacts ranges far beyond the usual Wall Street coterie of analysts and investment bankers to include other money managers and the partners in his hedge funds. Above all, he uses a strict selling discipline to limit his losses. In the wake of the invasion of Kuwait, to cite one notable example, he swiftly dumped in excess of $100 million in Japanese currency and bonds that he had purchased only a few days before.

If there's a formula for investment success, especially in these uncertain times, that's it in a nutshell. And there is no more successful practitioner of adroit global investing than the occupant of the suite of offices with the view at 101 Park. "For my money," Morgan Stanley's worldwide strategy director Barton Biggs recently observed, Robertson is "the best money manager in the world right now." . . .

Robertson's numbers have a touch of magic, but there's no legerdemain to his approach to money management. He's an old-timer on Wall Street who apprenticed as a stockbroker at Kidder Peabody back in the 1950s. In many respects, he is still an old-fashioned, unexciting "fundamental" stock-picker. As a hedge fund manager, he has the freedom to do anything—to go long or sell short, to use options and take positions in currencies, and to use leverage, buying stocks on margin, to get more bang for the buck. But, Robertson insists, he invests for the long term. He is not a market-timing, cycle-following, in-an-out trader. . . .

In selecting stocks, in the United States or abroad, the Robertson approach is deceptively simple. Stock-picking wizards are like that—they make it look easy. "We try to learn a lot about [the companies], we try to talk to their competitors, their managements," says Robertson. "We're conveniently located, so some of the small companies we're involved with—and some of the larger ones, too—are perfectly willing to come by here. The underwriters are kind enough, when they're having secondary stock offerings, to bring the managements by here." Indeed, a visit to Robertson's office of any length is inevitably interrupted, at least once, by a call from a CEO.

A simple credo, but the trick is to do it right. . . .

In making stock selections, Robertson is more of a manager than an auteur. "I'm normally the trigger-puller here," is how he puts it. Robertson relies heavily on a youthful, handpicked team of analysts, a roster that includes two Wall Street "names": Timothy Schilt, founder and portfolio manager of the Japan Fund while at Merrill Lynch, and Arnold Snider, formerly a star pharmaceuticals analyst and ex-chairman of the stock selection committee at Kidder. While Robertson makes the final decisions on all stock picks, his managerial style is bottom-up, collegial. . . .

Another contrast with the Street norm is that Robertson is not afraid to tear himself away from the office. He is an avid skier and tennis player, owning a home in Locust Valley on Long Island's swanky North Shore and a vacation condominium in Sun Valley, Idaho. And he vacations six to eight weeks a year—although he admits to being on the phone with the office every day, even if it means getting up at six in the morning. (Nobody's perfect.)

At this point in the profile of a successful man, it is customary to point out the subject's humble origins. Actually, Robertson's were stolidly middle-class. He was born and raised in Salisbury, a small town in North Carolina, on the main road between Charlotte and Winston-Salem. In the 1930s, Salisbury was a "sort of typical Small Town U.S.A.," Robertson says, and he was a sort of typical small-town kid. "I loved to fish, but I never did much hunting, like a lot of boys did down our way," he recalls. Why not? "I'm kind of careless, and I really don't think it would be a good idea for me to hunt," he confesses. "I might shoot somebody or shoot myself in the foot."

Julian Sr., still active at 90, ran a textile mill for the Erlanger family of New York City. One of his pastimes was stocks. He was an active investor after the Crash of 1929, when the Erlangers, convinced that the market would recover, loaned him money to invest. The elder Julian passed on his fascination with investments to his children, perusing financial statements with them. "I still remember the first time I ever heard of stocks," says Robertson. "My parents went away on a trip, and a great-aunt stayed with me. She showed me in the paper a company called United Corp., which was traded on the Big Board and selling for about $1.25. And I realized that I could even save up enough money to buy the shares. I watched it. Sort of gradually stimulated my interest." He was six at the time.

After graduating from the University of North Carolina with a degree in business administration and serving in the Navy, he joined Kidder Peabody as a sales trainee in 1957. He later became a broker—and a successful one at that. "I was just an honest slob who told them not to trade all the time," says Robertson. "These people were 'market players,' and I showed them that that was not the thing to do." He toiled successfully as a stockbroker until 1974, when he moved to Webster Management, Kidder's money management subsidiary.

George Soros

ANISE WALLACE

George Soros produced a truly phenomenal fund management record. When the amounts under management were relatively small, as when this 1981 profile was written, a frequent question was, "Yes, but can he keep it up with more and more money to invest?" Over the next 15 years, he showed emphatically that he could. Those few who hadn't heard of him then certainly have heard of him now.

When the name George Soros is mentioned to professional money managers, their responses tend to echo the remark once made by Ilie Nastase about Bjorn Borg: "We're playing tennis and he's playing something else." As Borg is to tennis, Jack Nicklaus is to golf and Fred Astaire is to tap dancing, so is George Soros to money management. "I don't know of anyone who is as good," says Robert Wilson, who is no slouch at running a hedge fund of his own. "George is the all-star."

The word "star" is not, of course, something one often hears to describe money managers these days. The difficult markets of the 1970s littered the corners of oblivion with the bygone champions of money management and produced little in the way of new heroes. Yet, since 1969, George Soros has earned an estimable reputation as the money manager's money manager. Assets in his Curaçao-based Quantum Fund have grown from $12 million in 1974 to more than $381 million at the end of last year. In a dozen years of running money for such clients as Pierson,

Excerpted from *Institutional Investor* (June 1981), pp. 39–43. This copyrighted material is reprinted with permission from: **Institutional Investor, Inc.**, 488 Madison Avenue, New York, NY 10022.

Heldring & Pierson in Amsterdam and Banque Rothschild in Paris, Soros has never had a down year; last year the fund was up a staggering 102 percent. . . . And in the process, observers estimate, Soros has turned his fee income into a personal fortune worth $100 million.

For all his personal and professional success, however, Soros has remained something of a mystery man, a Howard Hughes of investments. Aside from his occasional—and uncharacteristic—appearances in *Barron's* annual forecast panel, few on Wall Street or in the financial community at large know much about the reclusive fund manager. Yet few *haven't* heard of his record. "He has everyone in awe of him," says the sales head of a major Wall Street firm. "Even people who have never met him are in awe of him, just from his reputation."

The object of these breathless phrases is an energetic, fast-talking, blue-eyed Hungarian, a globe-trotter and a truly global investor, who jumps among international markets and currencies. And adding to the mystery surrounding his record is the fact that no one is ever quite sure where Soros is making a move or how long he stays with an investment. As manager of offshore funds, he is not required to register with the Securities and Exchange Commission. He avoids Wall Street professionals. And those in the business who *do* know him personally admit that they have never felt particularly close to the man. As for fame, it's widely agreed that he can happily do without it. "He doesn't like publicity or need it," says a Paris-based money manager. "I don't think he wants recognition." Indeed, in a rare interview for this article, which he had long ducked, Soros said in his thickly accented voice: "You're dealing with a market. You should be anonymous."

For someone who has been so successful, Soros goes to great lengths to downplay his record, report those who deal with him. "Most money managers tell you how smart they are and how much their accounts are up for the quarter," says Barton Biggs, partner in charge of research and money management at Morgan Stanley. "To hear George talk, you'd think he was always *losing* money. He always tells you how early or how late he was."

• • •

Humility is as rare a commodity on Wall Street as customers' yachts. But then George Soros shares little with Wall Street—he's in it, but not *of* it. Soros ignores Street research and has antagonized the major block-trading houses with what many consider an abrasive and arrogant manner. Other observers, however, attribute such criticism to plain jealousy; they say that Soros, to date, has simply been able to outfox the most cunning Wall Street traders. "Fundamentally, traders are in competition with Soros," explains the executive vice president of one Wall Street firm that deals with his fund. And the head of trading for a major Wall Street block firm tacitly confirms this. "If you buy something from Soros, you'd better run for cover," this trader says. "He's too smart for us."

Soros is exceedingly businesslike and doesn't waste time on small talk or with those from whom he can't derive some benefit. He is usually polite but distant, and one can almost see his mind racing from one idea to another. . . . A demanding employer and business associate, he is also universally described as fair and willing to admit his mistakes. Those who know him on a more personal basis refer to him as "charming but distant."

The pattern of Soros' success can, in part, be traced to his youth. A Hungarian Jew born in 1930, he and his family stayed two steps ahead of the Gestapo during World War II. They often spent weeks in friends' attics or basements, never knowing if they would be there for hours, days or weeks. "I'm sure that has something to do with the fact that George feels there is no safe haven in the world," contends one business associate.

After the war, Soros left Hungary for Paris at age 17 and never returned. He gravitated to England in part, he says, because he has always been an anglophile. . . . He wound up attending the London School of Economics and wanted to stay on as a professor, but his grades simply weren't good enough. He then worked for a London investment firm and came to the United States in 1956. After a few years at F. M. Mayer & Co. and Wertheim & Co., he joined Arnhold and S. Bleichroeder as an analyst in 1963. . . .

Soros' Eastern European background fit in perfectly with this old-world firm and its clients. He speaks four languages (English, Hungarian, French and German) in addition to a smattering of Italian and Esperanto. . . . In 1969, Soros began running Bleichroeder's Double Eagle Fund, an offshore fund for international clients. Like many offshore funds, it was run out of Curaçao, where the tax rates on dividend and interest income are lower than in the United States and where funds are not subject to U.S. tax and securities laws. Many of the clients of these funds are wealthy Europeans, Arabs and South Americans (the minimum investment in the Quantum Fund is $100,000) and tracing the money is, at best, difficult. . . .

During the early days of the fund, Soros and his partner James Rogers, a Yale graduate from a small town in Alabama, scored heavily not only in the U.S. market but also overseas—and by taking large short positions.

• • •

By 1973, Soros had decided he wanted to be his own boss, so he and Rogers left Bleichroeder to set up Soros Fund Management in an office overlooking New York's Central Park. This combination of a Hungarian Jew and an analyst from the backwoods of Alabama then proceeded to turn out what just may be the best record ever in money management. While the large institutions were on the verge of seeing half the value of their holdings wiped out in the next two years, Soros and Rogers were prepared for the growth-stock debacle. They had made a big play in smokestack stocks along with other issues and the fund recorded gains of 8.4 percent and 17.5 percent in the debilitating years of 1973 and 1974. Meanwhile, they also bet against the large institutions and shorted such favorites as Tropicana, Disney and Polaroid. The fund earned more than $1 million by shorting one stock alone—Avon at $120. As Soros told the *Wall Street Journal* one year later: "We start with the assumption that the stock market is always wrong, so that if you copy everybody else on Wall Street you're doomed to do poorly."

Soros is hard pressed to explain what exactly is involved in his decision-making process. He eschews professional economic analysis and decides interest-rate trends by "reading the newspapers." When pressed to explain how he decides on his investment themes or concepts, he only says: "Basically something clicks. When you have a certain view of the world, you are sensitive to certain possibilities that are triggered off by certain kinds of change." . . .

Soros himself admits that he is more interested in the fundamental changes that occur within markets. "I'm not terribly interested in playing a game by certain rules," he explains. "I'm much more interested in looking for changes in the rules of the game or, if possible, even changes in the way the changes in the rules of the game occur. When I identify something like that, then I really like to move in."

In late 1977 and early 1978, for example, Soros and Rogers decided to move in on technology and defense stocks. Although Soros, in characteristic fashion, moans that he was late getting into technology, most Wall Street veterans remember that few on the Street were even *looking* at technology and defense-related issues at the time. "They were dead," says Morgan Stanley's Biggs. "Remember, you had Jimmy Carter as President talking about human rights. George was talking about those stocks 18 months before the Street was."

• • •

Spotting such trends early helped, of course, but there was more to it than that. When Soros decides to move he concentrates his bets and swings in with conviction. Based upon the extremely large positions it took, the fund's performance soared in 1979 and 1980. . . .

But performance in U.S. stocks is only a part of it. Last year, for example, he sold short the British pound at the top, and Soros also made two major moves into British gilts. These bonds, which can be purchased for only a fraction of their full value, are the perfect kind of speculative vehicle for someone like Soros, observers say. The bonds were in huge demand at the time, and Soros, with the help of a British broker, rounded up an extraordinary number of them. While Soros refuses to disclose how big his play in gilts was, one source close to the firm says that by leveraging his position to the hilt he purchased almost $1 billion of the bonds—and earned about $100 million on the move.

Obviously, Soros has made his mistakes, too. Two recent examples include his November 1980 move into energy stocks and his year-end move into long bonds. After reportedly losing about 10 percent in his energy position, Soros got out of the energy stocks—before they fell another 30 to 40 percent. He also claims now that he has retreated from his long bond position. "A recent mistake," is all he will say when asked for an explanation. But his ability to get out before the bottom collapses is also indicative of his success, say those who have watched him work. . . . This investment style means that Soros is often early into a theme or concept. When asked if it ever makes him nervous, he said no, "I'm much more nervous when I'm late."

Soros is able to cut his losses early, sources say, because he frequently changes his mind and doesn't let his ego get involved. . . .

If he does have a weakness at selling, most people attribute it to Soros' isolation from the other players on Wall Street. For example, like Bob Wilson, he shorted Resorts International when the Street was pushing the gambling stocks to unthinkable highs in 1978 and 1979. Soros was caught in that bind, says one who watched his situation, because "he had no idea what Wall Street was doing." Unlike Wilson, who shorted the stock and then went on a six-month vacation before the stock took off, Soros changed his mind, went long and made a small profit. "You see, you never know when a concept becomes public property and how far it might carry. So generally I don't know when to sell," he says.

• • •

Inevitably, Soros' phenomenal record of growth also raises the nagging question of whether he can continue his past successes. After all, in the old days, with $20 million under management, he could take large positions in smaller, more illiquid stocks. But now, with the fund at $381 million, he will have to look in other places and be forced either to trade the fund more actively or to cover larger companies. In such circumstances, no one is quite sure whether Soros will be able to sustain his record, and almost everyone agrees that it will be more difficult for him to do so—even Soros himself. "Running a big portfolio is a new challenge," Soros admits. "It is a problem and I don't know how we will succeed in coping with it. Time will tell."

Philip Carret

JOHN TRAIN

Phil Carret started in finance as a writer for Clarence Barron, after deciding that he wouldn't be an industrial chemist and wear a tacky celluloid collar all his life. He subsequently had a long love affair with investing and only in his mid-90s began "taking Saturdays off." He continued the affair past his 100th birthday.

Phil Carret (pronounced "Carray") must be the most experienced investment man around: Having entered the field in the early 1920s, he can boast some 67 years of immersion in the hurly-burly of the market. At 91, he still arrives at his office early every morning. With his two sons, a granddaughter, and a small staff, he runs over $225 million in mostly private portfolios. . . . In his tenth decade, he seems perfectly unimpaired in faculties. He has a large, generous face with deep lines. He chuckles often and radiates benevolence.

His office is in an old art-deco office building on New York's Forty-second Street, just across from the south entrance of Grand Central Station. On the front of his desk perches a sign saying "A cluttered desk is a sign of genius." "Look at this!" he says, grinning fondly. "My wife gave it to me."

• • •

Carret started the Pioneer Fund in May 1928. It had about 25 stockholders: members of his family and a few friends. He ran it for over half a century, until he retired as its manager. During that 55 year period, Pioneer's compound annual total return was 13 percent. (It is 15 percent if you start at the Depression bottom.) That means that an original shareholder who had put in $10,000 and reinvested all his income would at the end have been able to withdraw over $8 million when Carret left. (He would also have been jarred by a 50-percent drop in the early 1930s.) Thirteen percent is not a remarkable performance figure today, but it meant a great deal when inflation was low. In any event, the lesson is that over long periods compound interest works miracles.

• • •

Selected excerpts from pp. 50–51, 54, 57–60 from *The New Money Masters* by John Train. Copyright © 1989 by John Train. Reprinted by permission of HarperCollins Publishers, Inc.

"I like over-the-counter stocks. And yet I'm more conservative than most people. Most people think that 'conservative' means General Electric, IBM, et cetera. But I've always been in offbeat stuff. They're less subject to manipulation than New York Stock Exchange companies, and are less affected by crowd psychology. . . .

"I'm a collector of odd little outfits. I have a few shares of something called Natural Bridge Company of Virginia. The highway goes right over the Natural Bridge, so if you want to see the bridge itself you have to go down into the valley, from where you can look up at it. The company owns the land under the bridge. They have a restaurant and a motel. People go and stay for a day or two. Someday the state of Virginia will have a profligate administration that will buy the company for more than its market price. In the meantime, I don't mind waiting."

· · ·

". . . Business principles are just that, principles. One deviates from sound principles at his peril. Some people are smart enough to do it—to dart in and out, for instance—but they are few and far between. I saw a study that set forth the average life of a margin-account trader. It turned out to be two to three years. One customer had lasted for 13 years before he lost all his money, but he'd started with several million."

On the subject of principles, here are Carret's 12 investment precepts . . . :

1. Never hold fewer than ten different securities covering five different fields of business.
2. At least once in six months reappraise every security held.
3. Keep at least half the total fund in income-producing securities.
4. Consider yield the least important factor in analyzing any stock.
5. Be quick to take losses, reluctant to take profits.
6. Never put more than 25 percent of a given fund into securities about which detailed information is not readily and regularly available.
7. Avoid "inside information" as you would the plague.
8. Seek facts diligently; advice never.
9. Ignore mechanical formulas for valuing securities.
10. When stocks are high, money rates rising, business prosperous, at least half a given fund should be placed in short-term bonds.
11. Borrow money sparingly and only when stocks are low, money rates low or falling, and business depressed.

12. Set aside a moderate proportion of available funds for the purchase of long-term options on stocks of promising companies whenever available.

• • •

Carret has viewed every total eclipse in recent years—11 of them—and goes to any lengths, including one trip up the Amazon, to see one. But other than this distraction, which does not take much time, he admits to no outside interests or hobbies.

"Every individual human being is unique," says Carret, continuing, "I guess I'm more unique than most."

A person of evident frankness and honesty, Carret does not hesitate to express and act on his opinions, which are often strongly held. Some people do not care for this traditional New England downright manner; others find it praiseworthy. A friend described him as being at peace with himself: a strong, solid character, with no inner misgivings.

MOVERS AND SHAKERS

Saul P. Steinberg

CHRIS WELLES

Saul Steinberg later expanded his fortune and extended the scope of his presence primarily through the Reliance Group. However, he will probably be most remembered as the boy wonder chairman of Leasco Data Processing—and for his breath-taking takeover threat against Chemical Bank. The phenomenon is explained in this article.

Saul Steinberg, who is 29 years old, very successful, and chairman of Leasco Data Processing Equipment Corp., is talking about his house, where he lives with his wife, an NYU art history major, and his three children.

"It's a modern palatial mansion just like that of any other successful kid of 29, you know—27 rooms, a tennis court, two saunas, six or seven servants, a couple of chauffeurs. Hey, go out and get a copy of *House and Garden* because my bedroom is on the cover. Big deal. I collect art, too. Picasso, Kandinsky, everybody. It's a much fancier place than I ever thought I'd have. I guess I was a little embarrassed when I bought it, but I've learned to live with the burden of my wealth. You gotta understand, a lot of things have happened very quickly."

Things have been happening very quickly indeed for Saul P. Steinberg, who looks somewhat like an overgrown, aging, former 11-year-old world chess champion. He has suddenly become the reigning boy wonder of programs, models, projections, profiles, integrations, simulations, strictures, systems and, above all, computers. He has accomplished the not exactly routine feat of elevating a company from assets of $7.9 million in 1965 to nearly $1 billion in 1968. From a couple of offices in a Brooklyn loft, Leasco has become the world's largest independent computer services organization, with 8,500 employees operating in 50 countries. Steinberg's own stake has gone from $25,000 to $60 million, not counting $20 million worth of investments in other companies.

Even as recently as a year ago, Leasco could be conveniently lumped together with the other conventional computer leasing companies. "We do a lot more now," Steinberg thunders, his arms making ferocious sweeps through the air. "You gotta understand that just leasing computers is only 15 percent of our sales now, okay? We don't only tell a company what

Excerpted from *Investment Banking and Corporate Financing* (Spring 1969), pp. 46, 48–50, 83–84. This copyrighted material is reprinted with permission from: **Institutional Investor, Inc.**, 488 Madison Avenue, New York, NY 10022.

computer they need. We design the system, the program, run the whole show. We produce the sales models for them, the projections, the inventory reporting, everything. They don't have to get involved, okay? That's because we bring the *brainware and the hardware together.*"

• • •

He enjoys the exciting theatrics, which he often uses to sew up acquisitions, but, says a Wall Streeter who has dealt with him, "he has an enormous ability to put what really is into perspective. He never lets a corporate ideal get into the way of reality. Saul and his staff are meticulous and thorough in anticipating problems. They are truly excellent chess players." Not, of course, always. His idea of acquiring the Chemical Bank and its $8.5 billion in assets earlier this year was not too well thought out. When first reports appeared in the press, Chemical chairman William S. Renchard said he would resist Leasco with all the means at his disposal "which may turn out to be considerable." They did indeed. The New York banking community possesses considerable financial influence, and during the following weeks it was not too subtly suggested to Steinberg that if he should try such a takeover, Leasco future growth, even its current business, might be, shall we say, somewhat stunted. Steinberg quickly backed down.

Saul Steinberg's initial $25,000 investment in his *deus ex machina* was a present from his father, who ran a small Brooklyn rubber manufacturing plant named Ideal Rubber Products. He had grown up in Brooklyn and had obtained the idea of going into computer leasing when his instructor at the Wharton School of Finance and Commerce at the University of Pennsylvania (class of 1959) asked him to write his senior thesis on "The Decline and Fall of IBM."

"My instructor was sure IBM was some kind of fandangle," says Steinberg, "and he wanted me to go out and prove it. I was the kind of student who was prepared to believe anything was bad, so I accepted the assignment. But after I had gotten into it and done a lot of research, I discovered that it was the instructor who was really the fandangle. IBM, on the other hand, was an incredible, fantastic, brilliantly conceived company with a very rosy future. But when I told him this, he wouldn't believe me. He wouldn't even look at my research. So I ended up having to write on another subject which I don't even remember."

Steinberg's research had also convinced him that there was a lot of money to be made in computers—from the start Saul was much more impressed by their ability to produce dollar bills than punch cards. He saw that IBM was charging a 50 percent premium on rentals which gave the lessee the privilege of returning the machine before the end of the lease, and decided he could sign up clients for uncancellable long-term leases at reduced rates. In 1961, when he was 22, he established the Ideal Leasing Co. in 200 square feet of dismal cement floor space in a loft in one of

Brooklyn's slum sections. Though "IBM didn't appear too anxious to co-operate with us," he and his partner, Hank Sweetbaum, his roommate from Wharton and now executive vice president of Leasco, were welcomed at other computer manufacturers like Honeywell and RCA, who were so anxious to get sales on their machines that they introduced Steinberg to many of his customers.

• • •

Expanding a computer-leasing business and building up a software and consulting capability can require, of course, much more cash (though leasing does throw off useful amounts of depreciation and tax credits) than can be obtained in stock offerings. Thus, like his colleagues in similar money-hungry companies, Steinberg established Leasco as a debt-free holding company and went fishing in that great, deep, still pool of green known as the insurance industry. Early last year he became interested in the Reliance Insurance Company, a conservative, 150-year-old fire, life, and casualty company in Philadelphia, with assets of $700 million (three times Leasco's) and revenues of $330 million (six times Leasco's).

• • •

"I tell you, this is a company where things are really happening," he cried recently, his words caroming off his office's overstuffed couches and chairs, polished bookcases, and plush, drawn drapes. "We've got a billion dollar company here, headed by somebody who is only 29 years old. Isn't that the essence of the American system? But that's our problem. People want to know: is it for real? They just can't believe it.

"But it's all *true*," he went on, his voice rising. "Not every company has 3,000 professionals. Not every company is doing exotic work for the U.S. government. Not every company is a consultant for the World Bank. Not every company. . . ."

A secretary rushed in with a glass of water and a pill. "My *vitamin!*" he announced. "I was wondering why I was running down."

William Zeckendorf

E. J. KAHN JR.

Bill Zeckendorf took real estate finance—and promotion—to new heights. He enjoyed his role greatly, did exciting projects—but failed. This breathlessly "gee whiz" profile was written in 1951, when Zeckendorf was in his prime and flying high. Some people suspect it was satire, not reporting, and they may be correct in that assessment.

In 1942, when William Zeckendorf, a splendid example of how a determined young man can get ahead even in the Age of the Income Tax, became executive vice-president and general overseer of the New York real-estate firm of Webb & Knapp, Inc., the concern's liabilities exceeded its assets by $137 thousand. Today, Webb & Knapp has a liquidating value conservatively estimated at $20 million, and Zeckendorf, as its president and sole owner, is, at the age of 46, probably sitting as pretty as anyone this side of a Texas oil field. (He may be sitting prettier, since he also has an interest in some gushing acreage in Oklahoma.) Until shortly before he joined Webb & Knapp, Zeckendorf, who has earned considerable renown since then as the assembler of the site on which the United Nations' headquarters stands and as the originator of a number of sweeping proposals to alter the skylines of New York and other cities, was a run-of-the-mill real-estate broker, of little repute even among real-estate men and so far from prosperous that at one point his home telephone was cut off because he couldn't pay the bill. At present . . . he can readily foot his phone bills, despite their being even more disproportionate to the norm than Zeckendorf, who usually weighs around 250 pounds, is himself.

Zeckendorf's one enforced absence from the telephone made his heart grow excessively fond of it. At his office, he refuses to let any of his three secretaries intercept the calls that come in for him; instead, deftly juggling three instruments, he deals directly with his switchboard operators. Now and then, the operators have half a dozen long-distance calls that he has put in stacked up for him, like planes awaiting a chance to land at an overburdened airport. The phone in Zeckendorf's penthouse apartment, at Seventy-second Street and Madison Avenue, where he lives with his second wife (his first, by whom he had two children, divorced him in 1934), has three extensions, and since they are attached to 15-foot cords, he is almost never out of reach of one or another of them. He has a phone in his car—a Chrysler limousine—to tide him over while in traffic. His romance with the telephone becomes most passionate when he is out of town. He goes abroad four or five times a year, and no matter where he is, unless he's hopelessly out of reach of a phone, he calls his office at least once every weekday. He sometimes talks to as many as eight of his associates in succession, remaining contentedly hooked up for an hour or two at a stretch. During a four-week trip to Europe last year, his bill for conferring electronically with his colleagues came to $2,700. Early this year, he and his wife spent three days in Rome, where, because he was bedded by influenza, she limited him to just one call to his office. He stayed on the phone long enough to run up a $300 charge, and felt much better for it.

Zeckendorf is practically always in a hurry. "Time is the most precious asset I have," he likes to say. He is usually pressed for it.

• • •

In the main, Zeckendorf has proved to be a highly efficient operator under the capitalistic system. Not long ago, he received a testimonial to his ability when a Hollywood producer suggested that they go into partnership on a business venture of some grandiose nature, involving both movies and real estate. The movie man, asked why he had made this proposal, replied, "Well, I've always been successful, but I never seem to be able to hang on to any of my money. I thought maybe with Zeckendorf as a partner I could." Zeckendorf's reputation for being a tenacious fellow with a dollar is based on shrewdness rather than on frugality. He is not a stingy man. Two years ago, a builder who had a $14 million structure half completed suddenly ran uncomfortably low on cash. "I tried practically every big bank and insurance company in the country and got nowhere," he said the other day. "All at once, I thought, Why not try Zeckendorf? I called him, and he said to come right over. I doubt whether he knew much about my situation, but in less than five minutes he had lent me a million dollars. That's the way Bill Zeckendorf works." Zeckendorf believes that more people would work the way he does if it were not for a lamentable tendency on the part of many supposedly big operators to be scared of large sums of money. "Any businessman can tell you that two and two make four," he says, "but even though he knows equally well that two million and two million make four million, the mere magnitude of the figures deters him from looking at them squarely. Instead, he trembles with fright." Zeckendorf remains conspicuously unruffled in the presence of large figures. A while ago, a broker dropped in at his office to inquire if a certain building Webb & Knapp owned was for sale. "Everything here is for sale," said Zeckendorf, employing a phrase he is fond of. The broker then said he had a client who would pay three and half million for it. "I wouldn't take a penny less than three seven-fifty," said Zeckendorf, who often dispenses with inconsequential ciphers. The broker said he had hoped Zeckendorf would be content with a slightly smaller profit on the property. "What makes you think you know what I paid for it?" asked Zeckendorf slyly. The broker said he had reason to believe that he knew, and, upon being challenged, said, politely dropping into Zeckendorf's idiom, "Three three three five." Zeckendorf smiled fleetingly and enigmatically, but with just enough warmth to convince the broker that he was correct. "Three seven-fifty, take it or leave it," Zeckendorf then said, as if he realized he couldn't hope to get that sum but was going to make one last stab at it. The broker said he'd have to see how his client felt about it, and departed. "You know," Zeckendorf later told a friend who had been in his office during this interchange, he was nearly right on his guess, except that he was a trifle high. I'd have let him have it for three and a half if I hadn't had a hunch that he didn't really have a client and was just fishing for information." A few weeks afterward, Zeckendorf, to whom luck sometimes seems as gracious a handmaiden as wiliness, sold the building, through another broker, for just short of four.

Zeckendorf dotes on deals that involve large sums of money, preferably at least a million dollars, but his favorites are those that, regardless of size, give him a chance to indulge his penchant for ingenious financial arrangements. Several years ago, he was particularly pleased when, after buying for $85 thousand an East Side house that had been converted into apartments, he managed to sell it to one of its tenants for a $150 thousand. The tenant, a widow, had been paying six thousand dollars a year rent. Zeckendorf chivalrously pointed out to her that she was living on investments and that, assuming she was getting 4 percent on her capital, she had to tie up $150 thousand of it to pay her rent. "Why not put the identical sum into the building, live rent-free, and collect rent from the other tenants?" he urged her. The lady was persuaded of the soundness of this reasoning and bought the building. Zeckendorf was almost equally delighted with one deal that didn't come off. After having talked a big corporation into accepting a block of good—but unspecified—bonds with a face value of a million and a half dollars as part payment for a building he was about to buy from it, he roguishly produced the stipulated equity in the form of the corporation's own bonds, which were then worth sixty cents on the dollar. A spokesman for the corporation stiffly declined this offer. "You mean to say you don't consider your own bonds any good?" asked Zeckendorf. "Far too good for you," the corporation's man replied lamely. On still another occasion, Zeckendorf acquired a million-dollar property without committing a dollar of his own, and, indeed, profited handsomely on the transaction. Knowing that a certain store, which owned the premises it occupied, needed cash badly, he offered to pay a million for the property and give the store a 30-year lease at what he was able to convince its owners was the preposterously low rental of $67 thousand a year. Putting up the property as collateral, Zeckendorf then borrowed the million from a bank at 4 percent, or $40 thousand a year, and thus came out $27 thousand a year ahead on the exchange. "It was a good deal in another respect, too," he told a friend cheerfully, "because the store isn't doing very well and will probably go broke in 10 years. Then I can put in a new tenant, at a higher rental."

In the course of one of many discussions that other real-estate men have held about Zeckendorf, Charles F. Noyes, who has been in the trade for 53 years, was moved to remark, "Bill's just terrific. There's no one in the business as colorful and spectacular as he is. He's the fastest man in town." Zeckendorf himself occasionally ponders the motives that drive him at such a speedy pace. "I think men run fastest when they run on account of fright," he said in an atypically reflective moment, while sniffing an aged brandy on the terrace of his four-room penthouse—a terrace that, incidentally, has been subdivided for dining, dog-walking, and shuffleboard, and that adorns a building owned by his wife, to whom he affectionately makes a present of whatever premises they have an apartment in. "Some men run because of ego, some because of avarice, and some because of love, but the man who runs because of fright runs the fastest. I've experienced real economic fright, and that's why I run so fast. I think I have very little avarice as such—I have the lowest regard for money simply as money—but my basic interest is in security, a desire to defend myself from the degradation that a lack of money can bring." For over a year, he has been on the point of moving to the penthouse of another building he owns—a four-story penthouse. He has hesitated to make the switch, though the quadruplex quarters are vacant, because he is not convinced that he is yet ready for such diggings. "I always like to play for the highest stakes," he says, "but I have a phobia about living beyond my means. Not that I've ever lived within them, but I mean living beyond them in an ostentatious way. It's almost a superstition with me; I have a fear of failure. I think it would be inappropriate for me to live on a four-story scale until I feel secure enough to do it comfortably. I'll make the change when I'm satisfied that it would be more ludicrous for me to go on living where I am than to move to a more spacious place."

Roland Rowland

_____

TOM BOWER

Tiny Rowland became a British subject at age 22, changing both his name and his nationality. Investigated by government agencies more often then any other British businessman, once denounced by a Prime Minister as being an example of the ". . . unpleasant and unacceptable face of capitalism," and a man who regarded the paying of bribes as an investment in people, he also accumulated a sizeable fortune while developing Lonrho into a global commercial empire employing more than 100,000 people. Beginning in 1991 Lonrho, caught between the burden of its huge debts and the chilling effect on earnings of slumping commodity prices, fell on hard times. Late in 1993, at age 76, Rowland lost control of the company he invented—to the German businessman he had brought in to fix the mess. This brief, revealing story launched a recent biography.

Torrential rain drenched the runway, obliterating the Nigerian lunchtime light. From the doorway of the VIP terminal at Lagos's Ikeja airport, Maurice Hynett peered through the mist as the Gulfstream jet skidded across the tarmac. Two employees, breathing heavily, awaited the signal. As the steps lumbered down from the aircraft, Hynett nodded and the three men raced forward with umbrellas to welcome their boss.

Smiling, suntanned and dressed immaculately, Roland (Tiny) Rowland emerged with perfect bearing from the doorway. Sheltered from the driving rain, he was escorted towards the venerable building. Uniformed officials, representatives of the military dictatorship, watched motionless as the personality glided past. None considered demanding a passport or a visa. Nor did Rowland anticipate the request. In Tiny's world, the Gulfstream was the passport.

Waiting outside was a fleet of flagged Mercedes limousines. Six motor cycle outriders were impatiently revving their engines. The style suited Rowland's aspirations. This was not a business trip, rather it was a mission, a factor in his unremitting agenda. A visit by the chief executive of Lonrho to the president of Nigeria—a meeting of heads of state. In Rowland's mind, running a country and a company were similar tasks and both were best undertaken by dictators.

Reprinted from *Tiny Rowland: A Rebel Tycoon* (London: Heinemann, 1993), Preface, pp. 1–7, by permission of The Random House Group Ltd. and Curtis Brown on behalf of Tom Bower. © 1993 Tom Bower.

As the convoy sped towards town, Rowland uttered a few words reassuring Hynett, a Lonrho trouble-shooter, that he remained "the blue-eyed boy." The meeting with General Yacuba (Jack) Gowon, Nigeria's president, had been arranged with panache and promises by another Lonrho fixer, Tony Lumley-Frank. Rowland required a reprieve from potential disaster. Six months earlier, the Organisation of African States had outlawed any further relationship with Lonrho. Rowland would beseech the general to terminate the humiliation.

Rowland's accommodation, the state guest house, was a good omen. But first, there was a formal dinner. Hynett knew that his employer would savour the frisson on his return to Lonrho's shabby offices in London's Cheapside the following day: "Interesting dinner in Lagos last night." The image was cultivated and nurtured.

The prospect of that evening caused the occupant of the third car driving from the airport some unease. Larry Bickerton, based in Nigeria for 26 years, was the manager of a trading company which Lonrho, in a phenomenal burst of activity, had just acquired. Amid the greetings at the airport, Bickerton had been studiously ignored by Lonrho's chief executive. The reason would become apparent twelve hours later.

Once ensconced in the guest house, Hynett outlined the arrangements. Dinner for 50 guests had been arranged in Quo Vadis, Mike Segrani's fashionable restaurant in the penthouse of a downtown towerblock. "It's discreet," disclosed Hynett. "The Nigerians are not keen that the press should discover you're here." The emphasis upon secrecy, as Hynett knew, appealed to Rowland, who equated stealth with power and influence. Publicity for the lone gun was to be avoided except on his own controlled terms. Anything written at that time, in April 1975, was invariably antagonistic. Although among Africans it was different. They displayed respect and friendship.

As Hynett explained, at least five ministers had accepted invitations and the other guests were senior civil servants, military procurement officers and a clutch of influential chiefs. "The wheelers and dealers who are Lonrho's boys," as Hynett described them to Rowland. "All the political leading lights will be there and the soft underbelly from whom we're earning." Nigeria, as Rowland knew, was probably the most unscrupulous nation on the continent. "Both Nigerian and European food will be served," continued Hynett.

Rowland was delighted. Unlike other businessmen, Rowland saw marvelous opportunities in black Africa despite its total gross national product being less than tiny Holland's. Under his control, Lonrho's pre-tax profits had soared in the past 14 years from £100,000 to £63 million. Over the next 14 years, the pre-tax profits would rise, he believed, beyond his critics' dreams. Convinced that he would build a Goliath equal to Harry Oppenheimer's Anglo American, he genuinely loved Africa and the Africans loved

Tiny. Even his critics would be pushed to allege that he had harmed any African country.

Rowland's performance that night was immaculate, confirmation to Hynett of the prevalent narcissism in his character. With grace, charm and wit, the 58-year-old tycoon treated individual guests in his uniquely self-deprecating style. Seeming or pretending to know everyone, he encouraged his guests to be in his presence and they felt rewarded by the experience.

To Rowland, oil-rich Nigeria was a special challenge. The potential earnings for his trading conglomerate were enormous, although the sheer scale of corruption was daunting and, from his experience in West Africa, provided few guarantees. Within the past year, Maurice Hynett had attempted to overcome that particular hurdle. Those to be "kept sweet" had been dispatched to London to collect a brown envelope from "Accounts." Within Cheapside, they were considered "seeds well sown."

Paying bribes did not trouble Rowland although Hynett recalls, "Tiny didn't want to talk too much about it." For Rowland, they were "special payments" or "an investment in people." Even his critics would attest that Rowland is not personally corrupt. "Every man has his price," he would say. "The definition of an honest man is when his price is too high." Dispensing money simply ensured Lonrho's continuing success. The perennial question was whether a corporation which paid bribes could be intrinsically honest. In London, where Rowland had surrounded himself with many nonentities, the answer among City practitioners seemed negative. Even Rowland noticed that his subordinates in Cheapside lacked his competence and brilliance but he ignored that each had been personally selected by himself.

Incompetence at headquarters in Africa, however, could not be tolerated. The management of Lonrho's 39 subsidiaries employing over 100,000 people producing or trading a bewildering assortment of merchandise from sugar to newspapers, platinum to beer, and motor cars to gold comprised diligent professionals, specially chosen to produce profits without supervision. Rowland, the deal maker, was not a manager. Nothing was bought without Rowland asking, "Who will run it?" and Rowland prided himself on not visiting the assets he owned.

Larry Bickerton was not a Lonrho type, although Rowland would be pressed to define the typical Lonrho employee. The type was generally defined by negatives rather than virtues. Bickerton epitomised Rowland's antipathies. "I can't abide their culture," Rowland told Hynett, "the old colonial English, drinking G and T at the club bar, who wear shorts and knee-length white socks." But even Hynett had not anticipated the drama which would unfold at one o'clock that morning.

Everyone agreed that the dinner had been a jolly affair. As the last guest staggered into the lift and headed home, Rowland, half-sitting on the back of a chair, beckoned Hynett, Bickerton and two others. With the debris of the dinner strewn across the horse-shoe table, the four gathered around the man whose activities two years earlier had been castigated by an English prime minister as an example of "the unpleasant and unacceptable face of capitalism."

Rowland's topic was Bickerton, an amiable and decent man who understood Nigeria and was liked by everyone. Gently rocking the chair back and forward, speaking in a monotone, polite voice, Rowland accused Bickerton of running an amateur, low-profit and unaggressive show. "I want a new image here. I want someone who will get under the skin of the local people." Inexorably, the hapless manager was deflated, denigrated and finally demolished. Bickerton was ordered to return to Britain. "But my children are at school here," he spluttered. "There are schools in England," smiled Rowland.

"Crushed, he was simply crushed," recalled Hynett, who during his 13 years' service in the Royal Navy and the SAS had never witnessed similar cruelty. "Rowland's mocking voice didn't rise by a decibel. The moving chair was the only sign of tension." Amid the human devastation, Rowland's calm was a deadly virtue. Lumley-Frank was similarly struck. "I have a tremendous regard for Tiny but he behaved like an absolute bastard. We were flabbergasted that he could be so brutal to a man." Bickerton shed tears.

The manager's emotions did not appear to trouble Rowland. Hypersensitive about real or imagined slights to himself, he was not worried about humiliating and manipulating employees—paradoxical in a man who proclaimed the importance of loyalty among members of the "Lonrho family." To his victims, his protestations of fidelity sat uneasily with his evident skill in identifying and playing upon weaknesses. Like God, he had passed judgment.

Even his oldest colleagues could only speculate that the source of his vitriol dated back to the 1940s when, as a suspected Nazi sympathiser, he had been interned by the British government. Having buried that legacy, he was later pursued for avoiding payment of taxes. Twenty-five years afterwards, he was outlawed as a pariah by the City. Like a woman, Tiny wanted to be admired and, by the same token, loathed his critics, distrusted their motives and would offer no concessions in the countless vendettas he has waged to secure their total destruction. Invariably, Rowland would complain that he was the victim of prejudice, a conspiracy or dishonesty. Others would remark that, so often, Rowland was himself the initiator or even the aggressor. In Lagos, it was very clear that Bickerton was an object of his displeasure, against which Rowland could prove the righteousness of his case and assert his indomitable ambition to rule.

Bickerton's sentence, seemingly endless in passing, lasted just ten minutes. Quietly and separately everyone left the restaurant. In the guest house, Rowland was satisfied with the first part of his itinerary. He was not a philanthropist and Lonrho was not a charity. He desired money and power. Others might allege that he was running an expensive hobby which had proved profitable for himself and not for his shareholders, but they misunderstood.

Britain, his adopted country, penalised rather than praised initiative and wealth creation. He had to fight for himself and for Lonrho. To most, his agenda was self-aggrandisement, a trait which was particularly disliked amongst the British ruling classes, the very people whose admiration he sought.

In Africa it was different. The stigma attached to him by governments in London disappeared when he crossed the Sahara. Welcomed by governments, he was treated as a hero. Hence his visit that morning to General Gowon, Nigeria's president, would be like a meeting of the Titans.

It was not accidental that Rowland's fortune was not earned in the democracies of Europe but on a continent ruled by a mixture of murderers, corrupt military officers and their puppets.

Intoxicated by the power which Europeans wield in Africa, Rowland delighted in straddling the continent, flying from London to discuss war, peace and money with an assortment of presidents, many of whom had become old friends. Proving himself and occasionally deluding himself that he was a maker and shaker of African governments compensated for the devastating opprobrium he has suffered in Britain. The subtleties of Westminster-style government held little appeal for a man who flourished when dealing with like-minded benevolent dictators. "A one-eyed king in the land of the blind," is the judgment of an African and former Lonrho director. "He deals with some Africans as if they are corrupt or gullible."

The events in Dodan Barracks the following morning when Rowland called on General Gowon suggest the contrary. Earlier that year, Rowland had maneuvered Lonrho into bidding for an exclusive contract to supply oil to the whole of black Africa. The audacious ploy had exploded and Rowland needed a mediator to repair the damage. Gowon, an unusually honest leader, seemed willing to assist. Their meeting was planned to last 45 minutes. At its best, Rowland's performance with his targets is unsurpassable. The charm, the wit, the notable absence of any condescension, the seduction, the evidence of his affection for Africa and his intelligence persuaded the president to extend their conversation for two hours. Cynics would say that Gowon was simply grateful that a white man had flown especially from Europe to see him. But eyewitnesses would confirm the importance of Rowland's network of contacts, developed since 1948, across the continent. "A player in my league," was the highest compliment Rowland could pay in his continuing quest to contact the rich and the influential.

Rowland emerged satisfied from the president's office. Standing in the hall was Daniel Gowon. Rowland noticed that the foot of the president's younger brother was deformed, the result of polio in childhood. "I know a doctor in New York who can fix that," said Rowland. The remark seemed to be forgotten in the ensuing conversation. Two months later, Daniel Gowon telephoned Lumley-Frank, the Lonrho fixer in Lagos. "Tiny's a marvelous person," he sang from a New York hospital. "He sent a plane ticket and everything's fixed."

Paying for Daniel Gowon was generous. Two weeks after Rowland's visit to Lagos, the president was removed in a coup. The same night, Rowland dictated a telex for Hynett: "Why on earth do you waste my time and introduce me to a load of has-beens?" Hynett laughed. Tiny had a wonderful sense of humour. He also had a brutal temper. Hynett would witness both.

For Rowland's life is a story of paradoxes: a man who surrounds himself in mystery and refuses an entry in *Who's Who*, but who yearns for publicity and an everlasting legacy. His is a life of a simultaneous battle within himself and against his adopted country. His rebellion is against history, political reality and, he says, corruption. The course of his revolt, its successes and failures, is a reflection upon Britain over the past 50 years.

James Goldsmith

OTTO FRIEDRICH

Energetic and skillful in the pursuit and financing of corporate takeovers, James Goldsmith had more fun than most, achieved considerable success in business, and pioneered "maison à quatre." Sitting at the peak of a global empire, he made a large fortune—and no few enemies as well.

Luck, be a lady tonight. When Jimmy Goldsmith's first son was about to be born, in 1959, he insisted on getting a private room at the best clinic in Paris, even though he didn't have any money to pay for it. Then he went to the Travellers Club on the Champs Elysées and found a rich man whom he could entice into a game of backgammon. "He finally got me out of the clinic," says Ginette Goldsmith, whom Goldsmith married four years later, "with his winnings from that game of backgammon."

Their son Manes is 28 now, working in Mexico City for the Mexican national football team, and Jimmy Goldsmith, officially Sir James Goldsmith, is not exactly penniless anymore. His net worth is estimated to be more than $1.2 billion, including holdings ranging from the Grand Union grocery chain to a publishing house in Paris to some oil wells in Guatemala to about 2.5 million acres of rich timberland in Washington, Oregon and Louisiana. And because he liquidated most of his French and British holdings in recent months—"I've got my bundle," he likes to say in these [1987] postcrash days—he has $300 million in cash and short term securities. That success not only makes him a potentially major predator in today's markets but gives him the freedom to lecture the world on his views.

Goldsmith also still has Ginette, after a fashion. Now 51 and divorced since 1978, she lives in one wing of Goldsmith's Tudor-style Paris mansion, originally built for the brother of King Louis XIV. In the other wing of the same estate, across a courtyard bright with impatiens, lives Goldsmith's companion, Laure Boulday de la Meurthe, 36, a slim beauty with waist-length hair, and their four-year-old-daughter Charlotte. De la Meurthe is the editor of a monthly style section in L'Express, the weekly newsmagazine that Goldsmith controls. There is also Goldsmith's legal wife Lady Annabel, who lives in a Georgian mansion outside London where Goldsmith spends a few months every year. Asked how he manages to keep three ménages (there are seven children in all) in such a state of contented coexistence, Goldsmith said, "Money helps."

Goldsmith not only likes making lots of money, he likes spending lots of money. "I don't understand people like Warren Buffett," he says of the parsimonious Nebraskan financier, "who pride themselves on living in their first home and driving a used Chevy to work, despite being billionaires." Aside from Goldsmith's Paris home and his town houses in New York and London—all filled with antique furniture, paintings, statues, silk hangings—he has just acquired a 16,000-acre hideaway on northwestern Mexico's Gulf of California. "It's the most beautiful place I've ever seen," he says. "It's got the sea, mountains, rivers, lakes. Most of the land is being turned into an ecological reserve, so we can bring back the animals that have always lived in that forest. But I'm building a house there, and I'll be able to give a house to each of my children."

Goldsmith is eating quail as he speaks, washing it down with a vintage claret. He is entertaining a visitor at Laurent, an elegant one-star restaurant off the Champs Elysées. He happens to own the place. He bought it on impulse more than 10 years ago, after a late-night party there.

"My roots and my heart are in France," he says as he lights a Monte Cristo. But though he holds citizenship in both Britain and France, he doesn't want their official honors and no longer has any interest in being Sir James. "I wouldn't accept that title today," he says, "nor any other decoration from a government, such as the French Legion of Honor. I want to be free. I guess that's what having money really means to me."

This is not a tale of rags to riches. The Goldschmidts, like their neighbors and relatives the Rothschilds, had been prosperous merchant bankers in Frankfurt since the 16th century. When Jimmy's grandfather Adolph came to London in 1895, he came as a millionaire and bought a mansion off Park Lane. Jimmy's father Frank, who changed his name to Goldsmith, went to Oxford, fought at Gallipoli, sat in Parliament, but found London's wartime anti-German emotions so painful that he moved to France, married a French wife and prospered in the hotel business. He lived in a world of yachts and limousines and casinos, and so did the son born in 1933, Jimmy. When he was six years old, according to a new biography by Geoffrey Wansell, *Tycoon*, a woman gave him a 1-franc coin. He put it in a slot machine and was inundated by a shower of coins.

By the time Jimmy went to Eton, he devoted much time and thought to playing the horses. At 16, he invested £10 in a three-horse parlay and collected £8,000. He decided that Eton was no longer worthy of his time. He bought himself a car and headed for Oxford, where although not enrolled as a student, he learned about chemin de fer and girls. When the subject of a career eventually came up, Jimmy served a brief stint in the Royal Artillery. He later went to Paris and joined his older brother Teddy in a tiny pharmaceutical business.

Jimmy at 20 was big and tall, 6 ft. 4 in., with bright blue eyes, and his pursuit of romance soon led him to Maria Isabella Patiño, 18. She was the beautiful daughter of Bolivian tin millionaire Don Antenor Patiño, who had brought her to Paris to meet a prospective husband. Instead, she met and fell in love with Jimmy Goldsmith—not exactly the sort of son-in-law Patiño had in mind. "Young man, we come from an old Catholic family," said Don Antenor when Jimmy went to ask his consent for the marriage.

"Perfect, we come from an old Jewish family," said Jimmy.

"It is not our habit to marry Jews," said Don Antenor.

"It is not our habit to marry Indians," said Jimmy.

Don Antenor shipped his daughter off to North Africa with a chaperone. Jimmy chartered a plane and pursued her. The Patiño ménage doubled back to Paris. Jimmy found her there and persuaded her to elope with him to Scotland, where no parental consent was needed after the age of 18. Don Antenor chased the fugitives to Edinburgh and hired detectives to find them. By now reporters were also in hot pursuit of the couple they continually referred to as the playboy and the heiress. The fugitives hid in various friends' houses for the three weeks required to establish Scottish residence, then got married. Don Antenor went to court to have the marriage annulled, but lost. "They can expect no financial assistance from me," said Don Antenor as he disinherited his defiant daughter.

She was by now pregnant, but just before the birth, she suffered a massive cerebral hemorrhage. Shortly after the baby was delivered by Cesarean section, she died, at 18, having known Jimmy less than a year. The grief-stricken widower went on a short trip to West Africa, and when he returned, he found the Patiño family had kidnapped the baby, claiming Jimmy was an unfit father. He went to court and got the baby back.

Despite Goldsmith's youthful reputation as a scapegrace playboy, there are other patterns here: a determination to do exactly as he pleased, an insistence on living well, a readiness to fight anyone who opposed his wishes, a willingness to take risks, a confidence that more money could always be found. Such patterns, combined with shrewdness and luck, make a success in business all but inevitable. His pharmaceutical business grew rapidly, too rapidly. At one point, he was on the verge of bankruptcy, then discovered on the day that his notes came due that the Paris banks had all gone on strike, thus giving him time to raise more money.

He invaded Britain in 1957, gained control of the British food company Bovril in 1971, reorganized it, moved on to the United States in 1973, acquired the ailing Grand Union chain for $62 million, reorganized it, launched a raid on Diamond International, began eyeing St. Regis, the Continental Group, Colgate-Palmolive, Crown Zellerbach, Goodyear Tire & Rubber, Pan Am. He operated through a network of Panamanian and Caribbean holding companies, all ultimately controlled by an organization called the Bruneria Foundation, headquartered in Liechtenstein and entirely owned by Goldsmith and his family.

"People in America were willing to work much harder than in Britain," Goldsmith says, rubbing a lemon-size piece of amber as he paces up and down in an almost bare penthouse office, which overlooks the Arc de Triomphe in Paris. "Most people forget America's strength is not its culture but its ideology, and that ideology is freedom."

Goldsmith's takeover strategy was simple. His targets were almost invariably old companies that had strayed from their original purpose through diversification, acquired too many senior managers, and were selling at a good deal below their breakup value. He would break them up, sell off the odds and ends, streamline the core and move on to the next project. Goodyear, which Goldsmith tried to acquire last year, provides a good example. The company's original purpose, he told a congressional committee, "was to build better tires, cheaper, and sell them harder," but it diversified into oil and gas, started building an expensive pipeline, dropped $214 million and was losing tire sales to the South Koreans. Goodyear survived only with the help of favorable legislation, and when the battle was over Akron's mayor expressed local sentiments by saying, "We kicked that slimy bastard out." But Goldsmith ended with a profit of $93 million, and Goodyear adopted many of his ideas for a return to profitability.

Goldsmith can be ruthless in his pursuit of profits. "There is a lot of internal rage in Jimmy," says John Train, a New York financier who knows him well, and Goldsmith himself acknowledges. "When I fight, I fight with a knife." Yet he is rather different from the standard buccaneer. When Ivan Boesky moved uptown from Wall Street in 1985, he rented a suite of offices in the same building that housed Goldsmith's New York headquarters, 630 Fifth Avenue, and then asked for a meeting. "He spent most of his time telling me about all the contributions he was making to charity," Goldsmith recalls. "That put me off right there." He refused to have any further business or social contact with Boesky, and when Boesky subsequently admitted to insider stock trading, Goldsmith remarked of his neighbor, "Boesky crawled out of a drain."

Carl Icahn

MARK STEVENS

Carl Icahn, progressing from bluff to greenmail to terror, built a personal fortune approaching $1 billion during the 1980s, by investing in—and sometimes taking over—undervalued companies. His start and some glimpses of his persona are described in this chapter from a recent biography.

In the summer of 1979, Carl Icahn, then a relatively obscure Wall Street figure with a hole-in-the-wall brokerage firm and a knack for making money in the options business, traveled to Miami to visit his mother Bella and his uncle, Elliot Schnall. In the course of a dinner with Uncle Elliot, a successful businessman who had been an Icahn role model all of his life, Carl made a startling announcement. He was going to start a new business: investing in, and taking over, undervalued companies.

To Schnall, a dashing social butterfly who had parlayed the sale of a looseleaf company into an idle-rich lifestyle with homes in Palm Beach and Southampton, the idea of young Carl running off half-cocked into a risky new adventure was positively frightening.

"When Carl told me he was going after undervalued companies, I said, 'What! Why the hell don't you stick to Wall Street—stick to what you know? You don't want to get involved in running companies. I've been involved in running two companies, and I can tell you you don't need that headache.'"

To Schnall, and to almost everyone else in America in the relatively innocent 1970s, the reason you bought a company was to run it and build it and someday will it to your heirs. So when Carl asked Schnall to invest in his first move on an undervalued company—the Ohio-based Tappan

Company—the same uncle who had earlier loaned Carl $400,000 for a seat on the New York Stock Exchange, balked. Schnall rejected Carl's overtures, saying, "To hell with that, I'm not moving to Ohio." The way Schnall saw it, "If you went after a company, you had to live there."

Undaunted, Icahn pressed on, repeating what would become one of the key buzzwords of the 1980s: "Undervalued. Undervalued. Undervalued." Still he made no headway with his prospective backer, who could only view a takeover in terms of traditional corporate ownership.

"I said to Carl, 'What the hell are you going to do with Tappan anyway? You don't know a damn thing about stoves. In fact, I know more than you because I owned one and those Tappan stoves are lousy.'

"When Carl said I was 'missing it,' I fired right back at him saying, 'I'm not. Tappan's just a lousy stove.'

"But to Carl, what the company made was basically irrelevant. I didn't understand that at the time."

Determined to get another perspective on the matter, Schnall contacted a friend who had played a key role in creating acquisition strategies for the high-flying conglomerate Litton Industries. Recalling that Litton had considered buying Tappan, Elliot recognized that the company's due diligence could now prove invaluable to Carl. As it turned out the former Litton executive had some pointed advice for the budding takeover artist.

"Tappan's a lousy company," he told Schnall. "Tell your nephew to stick to Wall Street or he'll lose his shirt."

When the dutiful uncle delivered what he hoped and believed would be the coup de grace to Carl's wild scheme, he found instead that the warning carried no weight at all. Carl's response to the Litton caveat: "What the hell do they know?"

As it turned out, not very much. Soon after, Icahn would launch a battle for control of Tappan, intimidating management to the point that a white knight would be called in to rescue the beleaguered appliance maker from the clutches of a hostile takeover. But Carl would prove to be the big winner, netting a $2.7 million profit as Tappan's shares were acquired for a premium over Icahn's purchase price.

For Uncle Elliot, it was a lesson he would never forget.

"Carl was still a young man, and in a single deal that took place over a period of months, he was able to make about $3 million." Schnall says, "At the time, all I could think of was that it takes smart guys twelve lifetimes to make that kind of money.

"I was awed by it."

But to Icahn, the Tappan experience simply validated his theory about corporate management. Soon after, he would see an even more desperate management give him his first taste of greenmail. At the time, Icahn had built a position in a company, then traded over-the-counter, to the point that he owned a substantial block of the outstanding stock. As a major shareholder concerned with his investment, Icahn informed management that he wanted to see significant changes in the way the company did business. In response, senior management agreed, reluctantly, to grant Icahn an audience.

On the appointed day, Icahn appeared at the company's executive offices, where he was promptly ushered into a meeting with the CEO and his top lieutenants. In this closed-door session, Icahn presented his litany of complaints about how the company was run along with a punchlist of improvements he believed would spike up sales and profits. Although Icahn never said so directly (at this stage of the game he was still testing his limited power), there was a veiled threat that if changes weren't made, the company's most outspoken shareholder would seek a controlling interest.

Listening to Icahn's monologue in utter silence, the CEO and his team allowed the brash gadfly to make his galling presentation, and then asked him to wait in a reception area while management conferred with an investment banker who had sat in on the session at the company's request. Convinced that he had made a forceful case for reconfiguring the business, Icahn paced like an expectant father, waiting for what he hoped would be a favorable response to his plan. When the investment banker returned, Carl greeted him enthusiastically. "What do they think? What do they think?"

What Icahn was about to hear shocked him. The conversation went like this:

Investment banker: "You know, Carl, they don't like you at all."

Icahn: "That's funny, I thought I was making headway."

Investment banker: "No, you're a bad judge of character. They just don't like you, Carl. Let me tell you what we're going to do to you. We know you're a tough guy and what have you, but here's what we're going to do to you.

"I don't like to threaten you, but we are going to begin by smearing your name. We've got three PR firms. We've got the best three PR firms in New York. Starting tomorrow, we are going to start smearing your name . . . and we know you may not be scared of that. But you know they are going to start calling you a racketeer, and maybe your wife doesn't like being with a racketeer when she goes out to a restaurant. It's not well thought of. Maybe your friends will sort of smirk, so think about that one. But after you are smeared in all the newspapers, think about the next step. If you keep buying stock, then we are going to dilute the hell out of you. That is what we plan to do. We are going to issue an awful lot of stock here to all the people, all our friends, and you keep buying stock but it's like we're printing up stock in the basement.

"It's like the old days with the robber barons, you know. Vanderbilt was buying stock with the other guys in the basement printing it up. Fisk or Gould was printing it up and selling it to him. That's what we are going to do. We are just going to print up stock and we are going to give it out all over the place . . . Now that's what we're going to do and we have a few other things we haven't told you about."

Just as Icahn thought he had run headlong into an unyielding adversary, a carrot replaced the stick.

"Now on the other side of the coin," the investment banker continued, "here is what we are willing to offer you: a $10 million profit if you will go away. And I'll tell you another thing. I've got a list of ten other companies in my pocket that I suggest you go after. That's my offer."

Then he said, "Hey, look, Carl, do you want twenty-four hours?"

For an options trader who had learned full well the importance of taking profits when they materialized before his eyes, there was little to think about.

Icahn said, "I don't want twenty-four hours, I'll take the deal right now." . . .

This was more than a financial coup for a bright and ambitious young man. It was a lesson, an epiphany, that would enable Icahn to terrorize America's corporate establishment for a decade, amassing one of the nation's great fortunes in the process.

Today, Icahn Enterprises—encompassing securities brokerage, rail car leasing, real estate, interests in an airline, junk-bond trading, and thoroughbred breeding—is headquartered in a compound of modern, low-rise buildings in Mt. Kisco, New York, just minutes from the chairman's 120-acre estate. His personal office, a replica of an English duke's drawing room enlarged to the size of a cricket field, is adorned with exquisite oriental rugs and a rich inventory of antiques. Everything about the setting smacks of wealth and power. A stairway leads to a book-lined balcony that wraps around the office and a personal elevator to the side of Icahn's massive desk whisks the king to his private dining room one level below. Here he dines majestically, overlooking an environment of ponds and rock gardens created to please his eye and soothe his mind.

An elegant conference room, where Icahn is known to preside over marathon negotiating sessions that stretch deep into the night, reeks of subdued power. Twelve beige tufted-leather chairs surround a large conference table. At the boss's end, a telephone console is at his fingertips, as is a remote-control wand for opening and closing the power window shades that lie behind long green drapes. Inset in a mahogany-paneled wall is an oil portrait of *Bold Ruler: Horse of the Year 1957*. Icahn, himself a horse breeder through his company FoxField Thoroughbreds, is the proud owner of Meadow Star, a champion filly. . . .

Icahn is a creature of the telephone, speaking on one line while a control panel's blinking red lights remind him of the lawyers, investment bankers, and assorted seekers of his time who are lined up in holding patterns waiting to give him news of ailing airlines, casinos that can be bought on the cheap, undervalued companies waiting to be picked off like so many fish in a barrel.

He talks in a rambling, New York street style, heaped with schmaltz and laced with heavy doses of "screw them," "fuck him," and "tell them to go to hell." Eyes closed, one hand snaking through his thinning hair, he is completely absorbed in the conversation, planning and strategizing as he engages in the intellectual wrestling match that is his forte. Totally self-reliant, he is a master negotiator. He believes no one, expects the worst of people, distrusts his allies and adversaries alike, and makes no pretense at intimacy.

"If you want a friend on Wall Street," he has said, "get a dog."

Although he is surrounded by high-priced executives and sycophants, only one person—long-time deal analyst and alter ego Alfred Kingsley—truly has Icahn's ear. From the earliest days of the Icahn juggernaut, Kingsley has been by his side, identifying takeover patsys, planning tactics, presenting the opportunities and the caveats for the boss's review. Blessed with a brilliant financial mind and a gift for seeing through corporate financial statements to find diamonds in the rough, he is a backroom numbers cruncher whose insights come to full flower in Icahn's skillful hands. . . .

Icahn's steely assessment of his own financial tactics can be summed up by an exchange he had with Federal Judge Gerald L. Geottel in the course of a 1984 legal proceeding over alleged improprieties over the purchase and sale of Saxon Industries stock. Explaining his stock market philosophy, Icahn said: "If the price is right, we are going to sell. I think that's true of everything you have, except maybe your kids and possibly your wife."

When a shocked judge responded by asking "Possibly?" Icahn confirmed that he had heard right. "Possibly," Icahn repeated, adding the caveat, "Don't tell my wife." . . .

"Carl is the kind of person who follows his own instincts and formulates his own ideas," remarked attorney Theodore Altman, who represented Icahn in his raids on Dan River, Phillips Petroleum, and Simplicity Pattern. "We could line up all the recognized experts in the world on how to do something and Carl will say, 'Let's look at it a different way.'

"He is determined to pursue his own instincts."

So extraordinary are those instincts that investment banker Brian Freeman once said: "If he lives long enough, Carl will have all the money in the world."

In recent years, however, even Icahn supporters have come to believe that his determination to squeeze his adversaries beyond ordinary limits will blow up in his face, leading ultimately to his undoing.

Albert and Paul Reichmann

<hr/>

PETER C. NEWMAN

Albert and Paul Reichmann settled in Canada a decade after fleeing the consequences of World War II via Tangiers. In the ensuing years, they built a mighty fortune in real estate based on Olympia & York— before falling on hard times and then rebuilding their position. This sketch gives us the flavor of their several commitments, at a time when nobody questioned either their genius or their survival.

Some of their best friends may be Wasps, but the Reichmann brothers— those mysterious, impassioned boys from Tangier who have become Canada's triumphant Acquisitors—live in a world unto themselves made deliberately inaccessible to outsiders.

Their climb from financial obscurity has been breath-taking.

They arrived during the mid-1950s and spent their first 20 years on this side of the Atlantic as modestly successful builders. Then as if by sleight-of-hand, within the past half-decade they blossomed forth like the stars of a speeded-up time-lapse movie. They have become the world's largest developers, with international assets estimated at more than $7 billion, growing at nearly a billion dollars every six months. That places them in the same league as the Eatons, except that the Reichmanns' personal cash flow (about $7 million a day) is much larger. Their company, Olympia & York, ranks substantially ahead of any of its U.S. competitors.

Through the sheer volume of their accomplishments, the Reichmanns have reached that enviable plateau where they have unlimited access to bank credit and other forms of financing, so that almost anything they want to accomplish becomes possible. Seymour Friedland, an associate editor of the *Financial Times of Canada*, calculated that by the summer of 1981 the family's borrowing power hovered near $10 billion.

The deal that took them into world-scale competition was their 1977 purchase (for $50 million down) of eight of New York City's largest office buildings, now worth at least $1.5 billion. Apart from the 50 million square feet of office space they own in Canada, the United States, and Europe, the brothers seem to be acquiring companies as if they were weekly lottery tickets.

<hr/>

Excerpted from *The Canadian Establishment, Volume 2—The Acquisitors* (Toronto, Ontario: McClelland and Stewart, 1981), Chapter 4, pp. 199-204, 208-210, by permission of McClelland and Stewart Limited. ©1981 by Peter C. Newman.

It was during their purchase of the Walker block that the brothers' lack of humour best demonstrated itself. Wilder, who ranks as a prince of the Canadian Establishment's inner circle, had heard rumours that the Reichmanns were buying up large blocks of his stock.

When Wilder, who operates from the forty-second floor of the Reichmann-owned First Canadian Place, finally received a call from Albert in May 1981 that he wanted to come visiting from his thirty-second-floor office for a brief chat, the Walker president knew what to expect. But as Reichmann walked into his office, wearing his black homburg, Wilder thought he'd try to put the developer at ease with a touch of fun. "Have you come to collect the rent, Mr. Reichmann?" he inquired with mock concern.

Instead of smiling, Reichmann was plainly taken aback. "No," he said. "I checked before I came, and it's fully paid." . . . .

The brothers cultivate an air of mystery and intrigue. They employ bodyguards, seldom grant interviews, and never answer telephones. "Olympia & York is a family concern and there is no need for tacky directors or shareholders . . . or joint decision-making," commented Garth Turner, business editor of the *Toronto Sun*. "The Reichmanns are private, tidy people. They run a private, tidy business. They have also learned you just do what you want to do, and don't waste time issuing press releases or trying to sway public opinion. That way, you get rich."

For most of a decade, newspapers and magazines had to represent the three brothers with a dated 1965 shot taken by a *Globe and Mail* photographer. When Albert appeared unexpectedly at the Oakdale Golf and Country Club in the summer of 1981 during a reception for the chief of the Israeli air staff, whose presence had attracted a clutch of press photographers, he spotted the cameramen and patiently hid behind a column for most of two hours, finally walking out of the room backward to avoid their lenses.

The brothers belong to no clubs, don't list themselves in who's who publications, don't head charity drives—in fact, they seem to perform none of the social obligations or token niceties that foster most businessmen's reputations. Yet they are widely praised and admired.

Jack Poole, who heads Vancouver's Daon Development, considers the Reichmanns "the primo developers in the world. They're great people to do business with—the finest example of prudent risk-taking and quality workmanship in the industry." On the investment side, Andy Sarlos, who heads Toronto's HCI Holdings, calls them "the most honourable people you can do business with. They're creative yet not impulsive and can be entrusted with great amounts of money."

The occasional voice is raised against them, as a reminder that they aren't supermen. "They're not really very different from any other developers," says one Toronto financier, who prefers to remain anonymous. "Just because they wear beanies, go home at five o'clock on Friday evenings, and are always standing there looking devout doesn't mean that much. In most of their dealings they tend to be extremely legalistic and not as good as some of their competitors in observing the *spirit* of contracts and agreements." . . .

The brothers' insistence on wearing their *yarmulkehs* and their strict observance of the Sabbath are their most widely recognized characteristics. Albert doesn't like discussing his theological beliefs (or anything else) but maintains, "We've never lost a deal because of our religion."

All the brothers tend to dress in narrow-lapelled, double-breasted charcoal suits with white shirts and thin black ties. Albert is formal to the extreme.

Paul has the look of resigned intensity that sometimes characterizes the extremely religious and probably adheres most strictly (if that could be so) to the family's Orthodox faith. . . . . Unlike their less fervent brethren they recognize little separation between law and religion, no line of demarcation between Jewish customs and the secular, civil matters in their lives. While other Jews try to reconcile the laws of the Torah to the demands of modern life, Orthodox believers like the Reichmanns adjust their lives to the disciplines of strict adherence. Because their customs depart so radically from those of most Canadian businessmen (even most Reform Jews), the Reichmanns are automatically assumed to be enigmatic and involved in strange and profound rituals. In fact, they are following, as privately as possible, the precepts of their faith.

All their buildings have *mezuzahs* (tiny parchments with biblical verses on them) inconspicuously placed near the entrances. The Reichmanns eat food only from their own kosher kitchens, and on one occasion when Paul was opening an Olympia & York bank building in Cleveland, he brought along his lunch in a paper box, just in case he couldn't get properly prepared nourishment when he arrived.

The brothers live close to one another in north Toronto not far from the Shaarei Shomayim Synagogue on Glencairn Avenue but don't worship there because it uses electricity on Saturdays, and this is not Orthodox. They prefer the more austere Beth Jacob on Overbrook Place, and most of their philanthropy goes toward the Beth Jacob high school. They also subsidize 30 full-time scholars at a nearby graduate school for Talmudists.

One example of the exactness of their observance of religious dictates was a wedding celebration the Reichmanns sponsored for a niece at the Centennial Ballroom of Toronto's Inn on the Park on July 2, 1981. The hall, which holds nearly a thousand people, was full. Distant members of the family had flown in from Israel, Antwerp, London, Philadelphia, and New York, complete with nursemaids for their children, all of whom stayed at the Inn. The Toronto contingent of the Reichmanns was outfitted by Maggy Reeves, one of Canada's top fashion designers, who provided a total of 17 gowns—which meant that upwards of $50,000 went for dresses alone. The Reichmanns flew in a special hairdresser from New York to prepare their women's coifs.

As is often the case at Orthodox weddings, the room was divided down the middle by a green wooden fence to separate the men from the women. The women were served liqueurs from the bar; the men could drink whisky. The Reichmanns also flew in an orchestra from New York to play Chassidic music; the men danced with the men, the women with the women. The food, served on silver dishes belonging to the Reichmanns, was prepared by the only source the Reichmanns fully trust, the catering service of Beth Jacob Synagogue.

It was the wedding of a minor Reichmann, but each table was bedecked with flowers, among them bouquets of white roses that came into bloom as the evening progressed. Flowers that bloom on command: that's what presiding over assets of $7 billion can bring you.

• • •

The [First Canadian Place] project provided a case study of the Reichmanns' unusual operating methods. The building was erected on land already owned by their client, thus saving Olympia & York a great amount of carrying costs. Because Paul had noted that most North American tradesmen spend half their eight-hour shifts handling materials instead of performing their direct tasks, he devised new construction methods. By using such special systems in materials handling, Reichmann estimated that he saved 1.3 million man-hours of work.

The other part of the Reichmann operating formula is to cut head office overhead. The entire operation is run by 15 senior executives with mobile squads responsible for major projects. Decisions are reached quickly by either Paul or Albert. No one wastes time negotiating complicated contracts. The huge Shell Centre in Calgary was three-quarters completed before an actual contract was signed.

The Reichmanns' most spectacular single transaction was their 1977 purchase of eight New York skyscrapers from National Kinney Corporation for $350 million. It eventually turned out to be the buy of a lifetime, but in the autumn of 1977 the transaction had the odor of a bailout. New York City at the time was in such precarious fiscal health that it couldn't sell its bonds; corporate head offices were scrambling to get out of town, and emergency plans were drawn up for the greatest municipal bankruptcy in history.

The Reichmanns bought the Kinney buildings for $25 million less than the former owners had paid for them, and then picked up three others from Penn Central. The twelve-million-square-foot package, which included the head offices of such corporate leaders as International Telephone & Telegraph, Harper & Row, American Brands, and Sperry Rand, had been on the market for three years with no takers. The purchase turned the Reichmanns into the second-largest private landlords in Manhattan—next only to the Rockefellers.

Rents in the newly purchased buildings had fallen to between seven and thirteen dollars a square foot. By the summer of 1981, the same occupancies were bringing in as much as $70 a square foot (throwing off a cash flow estimated at more than $2 million a day), and the buildings themselves had tripled in value. Ronald Nicholson, a New York developer, summed up the deal by pointing out that "the Reichmanns bought those buildings like 20 minutes before the real estate market turned around. They had a great buy—whether they were brilliant or lucky or whatever, I don't know. Every sharp guy in New York had looked at those buildings and turned the deal down. I can't believe the Reichmanns were smart enough to anticipate what was going to happen. Rents went from 10 bucks a square foot to 20 overnight. Nobody could have anticipated that."

What Nicholson didn't realize was that even while carrying out his most daring coup, Albert Reichmann was being his usual ultra-careful self. Before making the final decision, he quietly visited New York and personally interviewed many of the buildings' tenants, including every one of the street-floor coffee shop concessionaires—who are *always* the most reliable sources about any building's advantages and liabilities.

Bruce Wasserstein

DEIRDRE FANNING

Bruce Wasserstein's aggressive approach to advising on acquisitions earned him prominence in the merger and acquisition boom of the 1980s. In addition to the nickname "Bid-'em-up Bruce," he established his own firm—after being deflected at First Boston.

When Bruce Wasserstein was a youngster, one of his idols was Zorro, the masked TV hero who often broke the laws of colonial California in the interests of a higher justice. Thus inspired, when sibling rivalries got out of hand, little Bruce would take the law of the Wasserstein household into his own hands. As sister Wendy tells it, Wasserstein would charge into the bedroom occupied by his sisters, dump all the clothes from their dressers

Excerpted from *Forbes* (August 7, 1989), pp. 58–61. Reprinted by permission of *Forbes Magazine*. © Forbes Inc., 1989.

and mark his initial B on their pajamas. His blade? A Magic Marker. His apparent message: Revenge strikes those who cross me.

Some three decades later Bruce Wasserstein is carving his initials on the U.S. business world. As with his old hero Zorro, Wasserstein's presence in a deal heartens his clients, strikes fear into their opponents.

At its elegant offices in midtown Manhattan one day in June, Wasserstein Perella & Co. was right in the middle of the five biggest deals of the moment. There was Time Inc.'s $13.4 billion bid for Warner Communications; McCaw Cellular Communications' $6.1 billion bid for LIN Broadcasting; Alfred Checchi's $3.6 billion offer for Northwest Airlines; Hanson Plc.'s $5.52 billion offer for Consolidated Gold Fields Plc.; and the $3.25 billion bid by Wasserstein's own firm for Britain's Gateway supermarket giant. Add up the deals and you find something like $32 billion on the table. All at one time and all riding on Wasserstein's expertise.

The Delaware chancery court's mid-July decision in favor of the Time-Warner merger is yet another victory for Wasserstein Perella.

What makes this unprepossessing 41-year-old with the scuffed shoes and rumpled shirts so formidable? What makes him stand out in a business crowded with some of the smartest, most aggressive people in the country? What enables his Johnny-come-lately outfit, Wasserstein Perella—born only 18 months ago—to outdo some of the oldest names on Wall Street?

The answer, in good part, to those questions is a carefully cultivated image, which now precedes Bruce Wasserstein in corporate boardrooms around the country and which, as Wasserstein himself readily admits, has become his firm's most powerful selling point.

"I would never want to be on the other side of Bruce Wasserstein," shudders Vernon Loucks Jr., chairman of Baxter International, the Deerfield, Illinois-based health care outfit. Get Zorro on your side and you're safe. Cross him and you may be in trouble. Never mind that this Zorro fails to cut a dashing figure; his stock in trade is intellect, not physical daring.

In building this imposing image as a powerful friend and a dangerous enemy, Wasserstein has been positively brilliant in manipulating newspaper reporters. He will volunteer tidbits of information that can distinguish the reporters' stories; he does so in the confident and rarely disappointed expectation that the grateful reporter will at least mention Wasserstein's name. Not only mention his name but see that his or her story, if not wholly favorable to Wasserstein, at least gets his viewpoint across. Wasserstein is not alone among the big merger players in knowing how to use the media, but he has few peers in skill at the game.

Wasserstein's self-confidence in dealing with the media was no doubt developed through his experience as a college newspaper reporter at the University of Michigan and, for a summer in 1969, as a *Forbes* reporter/researcher. At an early age, then, this bright young man took the measure of many of the corporate mighty and concluded: I'm as smart as they are. He also learned what reporters wanted and needed.

Thus, where many dealmakers distrust the media and others are contemptuous, Wasserstein is shrewdly cooperative and accessible to reporters. This virtually guarantees him valuable exposure and at least ensures that his point of view won't be neglected.

From the moment Wasserstein was named co-head of First Boston's mergers and acquisitions department in 1979, he began polishing his image for brilliance and toughness and using that image to get business. Today, of course, he plies his trade at Wasserstein Perella, the outfit he founded with his First Boston mentor-turned-sidekick, Joseph Perella. Started with just around $100 million in capital, the firm today is worth perhaps $500 million.

Lately accolades about Wasserstein have spilled from the business press to general interest magazines like *Newsweek*, which last month featured an article headlined "The Wizards of 'Wasserella.'"

Bruce Wasserstein has always been something of a wizard. Born in Brooklyn, New York to an affluent textile manufacturer and his wife, Wasserstein was a precocious child. He was, at an early age, an avid chess player. When he was 11, attending the prestigious Ethical Culture School in Brooklyn, he handed in a paper on the stock market. "His teachers were always complaining that he wasn't paying attention in class," recalls his father, Morris Wasserstein. "But his mind was constantly working, and he always ended up with the good marks." Typical: Bruce Wasserstein knew he could excel without working as hard as the other kids.

Keeping up in the Wasserstein family was no small feat: Of Bruce's three sisters, one, Wendy, 38, is the Pulitzer Prize-winning author of the current Broadway hit *The Heidi Chronicles*, while another sister, Sandra Meyer, was recently appointed head of corporate affairs at Citicorp. The third sister, Georgette, is married to a doctor in Vermont.

The Wassersteins are fiercely supportive of one another's achievements. In Bruce Wasserstein's office, an entire wall is covered with Wendy memorabilia: framed *Playbill* posters from her plays and the program from her Pulitzer Prize ceremony. Wasserstein himself has sat on the board of directors of Playwrights Horizons, the New York City group that nurtured Wendy's career. He is one of the institution's biggest individual financial backers.

The young Wassersteins are almost a family conglomerate of accomplishment, a conglomerate where considerable synergy prevails.

Bruce Wasserstein himself combines disarming charm with a barely concealed arrogance. He got on the fast track early, entering the University of Michigan at age 16 and going on to Harvard three years later for a joint degree in law and business. In 1973 he began work as an associate at the blue-chip Wall Street law firm Cravath, Swaine & Moore, where he was a protégé of the formidable senior partner Samuel Butler. He was hired away in 1977 by Perella, then the head of First Boston's mergers and acquisitions department.

From being Perella's helper, Wasserstein soon outdid Perella in dealmaking savvy and image building. Perella, as affable as Wasserstein is intense, seemed to settle comfortably into the role of face man for his former subordinate. While their firm bears both names, no one, inside or out, doubts who runs the deals. Wasserstein does.

Such drive and braininess as Wasserstein commands inevitably breed a certain amount of contempt for lesser folk, and Wasserstein's detractors see clear evidence of his arrogance in what everyone who knows him calls his "Dare To Be Great" speech. This, both friends and foes aver, is his hallmark.

The speech—or rather the message—comes in varying lengths and versions. It is usually delivered when a client shows signs of being nervous about overpaying for an acquisition. Leaning earnestly across the table toward his client, Wasserstein begins to talk quietly, yet forcefully. "If you want to be a global player in this industry, you are going to have to pay a price," he declares—or words to that effect. "You must step up and pay the price, or you'll lose it all to your competitor."

At such moments, Wasserstein is more salesman for a deal than he is the wise, cautious counselor. Little wonder his detractors—and even some of his admirers—have come to call him "Bid-'em-up Bruce."

In a business that depends heavily on corporate egos and pride, Wasserstein's brand of psychological bullying often pays off in closing deals. How many customers have the strength of character to worry about mere numbers when a famous investment banker, endowed with charisma by the media, dares them to be great! . . .

Wasserstein's personality, his ambitions and his tactics are fascinating, but they are not the real issue. Something much bigger is at stake. . . . Certainly some of today's takeovers make sense, but even a good deal is a bad deal if the price isn't right. . . .

To the extent that the deal brokers encourage clients to up the ante, they will bear some of the responsibility for the inevitable damage to investors and to the financial system. By then, of course, Wasserstein and the other deal brokers will have long since banked their fees.

Scarsdale Fats

'ADAM SMITH'

> While Scarsdale Fats had a real name—Bob Brimberg—he was as huge,
> brilliant, aggressive and quick as he appeared to be in his featured role
> in 'Adam Smith's' rollicking 1969 book, *The Money Game*. This sketch,
> and the book itself, neatly capture the pace and attitudes that produced
> what came to be called "performance investing."

With all that money in so relatively few hands, it was inevitable that someone would get the hands together on an informal basis, just as a pleasant,
tension-relieving gesture. The gentleman who is the Madame de Staël of
the institutional investment business is called Scarsdale Fats, and he really
does exist. He exists, he gives lunches, and everybody comes. Lunch on
Wall Street is working time, and what started at Scarsdale's informally has
developed to such a point that the lunch guests bone up beforehand and
take notes.

On any given day, the lunch guests at Scarsdale's are likely to represent
a couple of billion dollars in managed money. Now, when you handle this
kind of money, you are, believe me, welcome almost everywhere. You could
eat at any place on Wall Street, free, in private dining rooms where the
paneling has been flown over from busted merchant banks in the City of
London, where the silver is hallmarked with the house mark, the house
being Lehman Brothers or Eastman Dillon or Loeb Rhoades or even the
places that fly their own flags over the Street. Over in the other private
dining rooms the waiters move on cat feet and dishes never clatter and the
cigars are pre-Castro Uppmanns out of the firm humidor, and through
the pleasant masculine Havana haze after lunch you can feel, as the voices
murmur about pieces of empire, $100 million here, $200 million there,
that all's right with the world, if there's trouble anywhere we send a gun-
boat and give the beggars a good thrashing.

So why are they here at Scarsdale Fats', these guys with all the money?
Here there is no French chef, no house silver, no paneling, no carpeting,
no noiseless, perfectly uniformed corps of waiters. The chairs are metal
folding chairs, the tables are plastic, there is a big bowl of pickles on the
table, the napkins are paper, and if this is the private dining room of a

New York Stock Exchange firm, Wall Street is not what it used to be. If the trend catches on, Robert Lehman will look at the empty seats in his dining room and think the chef has been putting flour in the gravy, and John Loeb will be sitting in *his* like Stella Dallas wondering if everybody somehow got the date wrong, not that either of them is going to get any poorer.

And here is Scarsdale himself. As far as I know it was a couple of the Boston institutions that hung the nickname on him, which shows that Boston institutions are not as stuffy as they used to be. In the old days they wouldn't talk to anybody who didn't have a Groton nasal drip, and now they'll talk to just about anybody they think will make them some money. Anyway, here is Scarsdale, pressing the hors d'oeuvres on his guests with mother love, eat, eat. He has already wolfed down about a third of the deviled eggs himself, so the guests better be quick on the draw. Obviously he stepped over, not on, the scale his partners keep beside his desk to save his life. One of his enthusiasts describes him as "glob-shaped." Minnesota Fats is an ectomorph and Sydney Greenstreet would blow away in the Scarsdale Fats ratio! All Scarsdale will say is that he is comfortably over two hundred pounds. Let's say he is pyknic. Look it up.

Scarsdale introduces the guests. There is a guy who handles the trust accounts from a Very Big Bank. And a second Very Big Bank. And two guys from Very Big Funds. A young gunslinger type from a performance fund. A hedge fund-er and a man from one of the statistical reporting services. The effort of introducing everybody makes Scarsdale so nudgy he washes down the hors d'oeuvres will a roll and butter.

And why are they here? Because Scarsdale asked them. Let him tell: "I had to do it to compete. What have I got? Nothing. Those hot young research analysts at Donaldson Lufkin can write hundred-page reports. Bache can field a thousand salesmen. The white-shoe firms can fly the Old St. Wasp flags. So I thought: Who has money? The funds. Be nice. Ask them to lunch." To corned-beef sandwiches, to meatballs? "Everywhere else these guys go, somebody is trying to promote them, to sell them something. Not me, I have no opinions."

So what Scarsdale did was to call, say, Wellington, and say that Keystone and the Chemical were coming to lunch, and then he called, say, Keystone and said the others were coming, and then he called, perhaps, the Chemical and pretty soon there he was, Perle Mesta. Two more things helped. One was the rules: Everything is off the record, informal, no names, no sandbagging. You don't want to say what you're buying, fine, but don't say you're selling what you're buying or Scarsdale will come and lean on you himself and then no more meatballs forever.

The other thing is Scarsdale himself, the way he runs the lunch with no nonsense, as if he were Lawrence Spivak and there were only 30 minutes minus commercials to extract the truth.

Now look at it another way. You are 32 years old and you are a portfolio manager making $25,000 a year. All you have to do is handle $250 million and make sure it does better than anybody else handling a portfolio anywhere. You get two phone calls, lunch invitations, one from the old firm with Wedgwood plates in the private dining room and one from Scarsdale. You already know what stocks the Wedgwood-plates-dining-room people are selling. At Scarsdale's you can find out—maybe, because there is a certain poker-game aspect—what some of your compatriots are up to, and nobody will try to sell you. Certainly not Scarsdale; he prides himself on not knowing anything, even though his corned-beef sandwiches are buying the best research in the country. All you have to do is stay friends. Maybe—it's not required—you give him a little order sometime, a thousand Telephone, just to help pay for lunch. Where do you go?

"Awright, everybody siddown," Scarsdale says. He calls on the man from the Very Big Bank. What's gonna happen, and what are they buying?

The man from the Very Big Bank starts talking about the gross national product and productivity and other verbal smoke-screen items and Scarsdale cuts him down.

"You had seven hundred million in cash last week. You still got it?"

"We spent fifty million," admits the man from the Very Big Bank. "We bought some utilities, at the bottom, before they went up last week."

"Of course before they went up," Scarsdale says. "Anything else?"

"This bear market isn't over yet," says the man from the Very Big Bank. "You fellas—you young fellas under 40—you haven't seen a real bear market. You don't know what it is."

"Did you buy anything else? Come on, come on," Scarsdale says.

"Nothing else," says the Big Bank man, but nobody is leaning forward to hear because most of the other guests are under 40 and they don't know what a real bear market is. They've just seen the market go down $100 billion and their best holdings have melted and if this isn't a real bear market they don't want to know about the real one. Maybe next time the Chinese will have ICBMs.

"All right," Scarsdale Fats says. "Give the man over there some meatballs," he tells the waitress. Scarsdale Fats strikes like an adder at the meatballs as they go by and manages to spear two before the bank man falls gratefully on his portion. Then he butters up another roll to refuel. He turns on one of the fund men.

"Charley X was here for lunch Tuesday," he says, mentioning a rival fund manager. "He says this market is like it was in fifty-seven-fifty-eight. He says he bought stocks at the bottom."

"He bought at every bottom this year," says the fund man, "and every bottom was lower than the last. I'm surprised he has any chips left."

"Where is the market going?" says Scarsdale.

"We've seen the lows," the fund man says. There is a collective *ah-h-h* from the assembled guests. Candor. Commitment. The market turns around and drops through 744 on the Dow, this guy has committed himself wrong, but he's definitely committed himself.

"What three stocks do you like?" Scarsdale says.

"We nibbled at a few airlines," the fund man says.

"The airlines have had it; we're selling our airlines. Look at the strike settlement. Look at equipment delays. You can have them," says a counterpart fund manager across the table.

"So go sell your airlines," the first fund man says. The guests are warming up, and the lunch is turning into a success. "We think the growth stocks will move up 30 percent or 40 percent from here, the true ones will double, and the others will drop away and disappear."

"What growth stocks? What growth stocks?" says Scarsdale. Scarsdale does not even know it, he is being such a good moderator, but at the moment he is eating all the remaining rolls in the roll dish.

"I bought some Polaroid, down around the lows, maybe at 125," says the fund man. There is another collective *ah-h-h*. Nine other slide-rule brains are working away: Even if he says he bought it at 125, maybe he bought it at 135. If he bought it at 135, and the earnings go up, he's not going to turn around and sell it. Strongly held Polaroid at 135. *Ah-h-h.*

"What earnings next year for Polaroid?" says Scarsdale. "Four dollars? Four-fifty? Five?"

"What's the difference?" the fund man says.

"Good," Scarsdale says. "What else? What other stocks? What else?"

"Well-I-I," says the fund man, "I may have bought some Fairchild at the lows. I think I bought some at 96."

"Fairchild never sold at 96!" hollers the second bank man. "The low was 97."

"No sandbagging!" Scarsdale cries.

"Maybe it was 98," the fund man says. "I recall buying a lot at 98."

"Fairchild is falling apart," says the man from the hedge fund. With a hedge fund, you can go short. "Fairchild has lost control of its inventories. The Street doesn't know it yet, but Fairchild's fourth quarter is going to be disappointing."

"I don't care," says the fund man.

"Next year could be *extremely* disappointing," the hedge fund man says.

"I don't care," says the fund man.

Now the lunch has really warmed up. Maybe the hedge fund is short the Fairchild the other fund is long. Gunfight at the Broad Street Corral. Or maybe the hedge fund man isn't short the Fairchild—he hasn't said he was—maybe he is just making growling noises to make people *think* he is short the Fairchild. When the Rothschilds got the word about the battle of

Waterloo—in the movie it was by carrier pigeon—they didn't rush down and buy British consols, the government bonds. They rushed in and *sold*, and then, in the panic, they bought.

"What else? What else?" cries Scarsdale.

"The market is going up," the fund man says. "I don't know for how long, and I may change my mind. Maybe next spring. But, for the moment, up."

"Good!" says Scarsdale. "Give the man some meatballs! Give him some salad! Where are all the rolls?" Scarsdale cries to the waitress.

Lunch is over and Scarsdale is back at this desk. Two of the guests didn't eat their cheese cake and the empty plates are now on Scarsdale's desk, plundered, a few crumbs stirring after the pounce. Scarsdale is on the phone keeping his other institutional managers wired in, trusting there will be orders and other profitable fallout. He has his notebook open.

"Larry X was here to lunch today and he thinks we've seen the lows and he is buying some airlines. Joe Y was here and he thinks we have another leg to go on the downside and he isn't buying. Harry thinks Joe's figures on capital spending are $10 billion too low. Here are the airlines Harry likes. . . ."

At the next desk, Scarsdale's secretary is lining up some senators for a dinner Scarsdale is giving. The legends are already starting. Scarsdale is supposed to have introduced Neddy Johnson, the junior Johnson of Fidelity, to a senator and to have said, "This man controls two billion dollars." And the senator says, "So what, we spend that in half an hour." Senators! Next thing you know, there will be a tablecloth in Scarsdale's dining room, and the pickle bowl will be gone, the silver will have a leopard's head and the mark SF, everybody will turn stuffy again, and we'll all have to figure out somewhere else to go.

Alfred W. Jones

CAROL J. LOOMIS

Alfred Winslow Jones, who may have invented the hedge fund, established A.W. Jones & Co. as a leading presence in the performance market
of the 1960s. He was, even then, perceived as much as a scholar in the
Street as a Street-wise scholar. This article is also of interest for what it
reveals about broker-manager relationships in the years when "the
story"—and who got it first—often determined a manager's short-term
performance.

There are reasons to believe that the best professional manager of investors' money these days is a quiet-spoken . . . man named Alfred
Winslow Jones. . . . Few businessmen have heard of him, although some
with long memories may remember his articles in *Fortune;* he was a staff
writer in the early 1940s. In any case, his performance in the stock market in recent years has made him one of the wonders of Wall Street—and
made millionaires of several of his investors. On investments left with
him during the five years ended last May 31 (when he closed his 1965 fiscal year), Jones made 325 percent. Fidelity Trend Fund, which had the
best record of any mutual fund during those years, made "only" 225 percent. For the *ten*-year period ended in May, Jones made 670 percent;
Dreyfus Fund, the leader among mutual funds that were in business all
during that decade, had a 358 percent gain.

The vehicle through which Jones operates is not a mutual fund but
a limited partnership. Jones runs two such partnerships, and they have
slightly different investment objectives. In each case, however, the underlying investment strategy is the same: the fund's capital is both leveraged
and "hedged." The leverage arises from the fact that the fund margins itself to the hilt; the hedge is provided by short positions—there are always
some in the fund's portfolio.

• • •

For most of his life Jones, who is now 65, was more interested in sociology
and in writing than he was in the stock market. In 1938 he set out to get
his Ph.D. in sociology at Columbia University. While working toward the
degree, he served as director of Columbia's Institute for Applied Social

Analysis and undertook for it a major project on class distinctions in the United States. The project became the basis for his doctoral thesis, which was published under the title *Life, Liberty, and Property* (two years ago it was reprinted by Octagon Books, Inc.). *Fortune* asked Jones to condense the book into an article (February 1941) and hired him as a writer. Over the next five years (part of it spent with *Time*) he wrote articles on such non-financial subjects as Atlantic convoys, farm cooperatives, and boys' prep schools. He left Time Inc. in 1946, but in March, 1949, he was back in the pages of *Fortune* with a freelance article, "Fashions in Forecasting," which reported on various "technical" approaches to the stock market.

His research for this story convinced him that he could make a living in the stock market, and early in 1949 he and four friends formed A. W. Jones & Co. as a general partnership. Their initial capital was $100,000, of which Jones himself put up $40,000. In its first year the partnership's gain on its capital came to a satisfactory 17.3 percent, but this was only a suggestion of things to come. Not quite all the original capital has been left in the partnership, but if it had been it would today be worth $4,920,789 (before any allowance for the partners' taxes).

In the early years Jones was experimenting with a number of investment approaches, including the "hedge" idea, which was essentially his own. Increasingly, he began to concentrate on refining and employing this new technique.

• • •

In effect, the hedge concept puts Jones in a position to make money on both rising and falling stocks, and also partially shelters him if he misjudges the general trend of the market. He assumes that a prudent investor wants to protect part of his capital from such misjudgments. Most investors would build their defenses around cash reserves or bonds, but Jones protects himself by selling short.

To those investors who regard short selling with suspicion, Jones would simply say that he is using "speculative techniques for conservative ends." . . .

His problem, therefore, is to buy stocks that will rise more than the general market, and sell stocks short that will rise less than the averages (or will actually fall). If he succeeds in this effort, his rewards are multiplied because he is employing, not just a portion of his capital, but 150 percent of it. The main advantage of the hedge concept, then, is that the investor's short position enables him to operate on the long side with maximum aggressiveness.

Jones's record in forecasting the direction of the market seems to have been only fair. In the early part of 1962 he had his investors in a high risk position. . . . As the market declined, he gradually increased his short position, but not as quickly as he should have. His losses that spring were heavy, and his investors ended up with a small loss for the fiscal year (this is the only losing year in Jones's history). After the break, furthermore, he turned bearish and so did not at first benefit from the market's recovery.

• • •

Despite these miscalculations about the direction of the market, Jones's selections of individual stocks have generally been brilliant. . . .

Any hedge-fund operator will explain that although the hedge concept is essential—"I need it to sleep nights," says one of them—the real secret of his success is his ability to get good information about stocks and to be able to act on it quickly. The partnership form of organization is helpful in both respects. . . .

Jones and the other general partners are to receive as compensation 20 percent of any realized profits (after deduction of realized losses) made on the limited partners' money. This arrangement is common to all the hedge funds, and the idea was not original with Jones. Benjamin Graham, for one, had once run a limited partnership along the same lines.

• • •

In total, including the gains he has made so far this fiscal year, Jones is managing close to $70 million of capital. Even with the borrowed money added in, this makes his operation no bigger than a medium-sized mutual fund.

But the weight Jones swings on Wall Street is many times magnified by the fact that, like all hedge-fund operators, he is a prodigious producer of commissions. Since short sales can never result in anything but short-term gains or losses, the hedge operator moves in and out of them freely. Similarly when he has losses on the short sales, he also finds it easier to take offsetting short-term gains on long positions. In general, the hedge funds have a high portfolio turnover.

• • •

One big reason the hedge funds find it natural to move in and out of stocks a lot is that, far more than most other funds, they have a special ability to get a flow of good, fresh ideas about stocks from brokers—and get them early.

• • •

The Jones organization is set up so that decisions about purchases and sales can be made immediately, without committee consultation. There are five portfolio managers, all general partners, each of whom has discretion over a percentage of the partnership capital; in addition, several outside "advisers," one of them an investment counselor, the rest brokerage-house analysts or salesmen, have been given blocks of capital to manage. Either Jones or his No. 2 man, Donald Woodward, sees each order before it is executed, but they interfere only when it seems to them that the partnership is getting overloaded with a given stock—e.g., if several of the portfolio managers are being sold on the stock at the same time—or is maneuvering itself into an undesirable "risk" position.

The portfolio managers will tell you that, given the long-term trend of the market upward, their most difficult job is picking good short sales. Wall Street's analysts typically concentrate on discovering bullish corporate situations, and only rarely have promising shorts to bring to Jones. As a result, he and the other hedge-fund managers normally consider themselves lucky to break even on their short portfolios. . . .

Recently Jones has devoted more and more time to traveling and to philanthropic projects, many of them financed by his own Foundation for Voluntary Service. He has made some field trips for the Peace Corps, and his foundation is currently supporting the activities in this country for five young social workers from India, as a sort of "Reverse Peace Corps." He is also thinking of writing another book—on what to do about poverty in the United States.

Gerald Tsai

CHRIS WELLES

Jerry Tsai courted personal publicity while at Fidelity and converted the resulting fame as a portfolio manager into fortune by launching the Manhattan Fund at a most propitious moment. Then, despite dreadful performance numbers, he converted the management company into a major stake in CNA. Seemingly on the ropes when this profile was published, he would later parlay G. Tsai & Co. into control of the venerable American Can Company, recreate it as Primerica, and sell that to Commercial Credit after acquiring Smith Barney. While Tsai may not have done well for others, he certainly did well for himself.

When people on Wall Street talk about Jerry Tsai, it is with that special contemplative, faraway tone used to pronounce final judgments on deposed statesmen and bankrupt empire builders, men who in their era flourished mightily but, when the times changed, inexorably faded from view. Briefly, with a few slow nods of the head, they display some reverence, a little pity, perhaps a touch of cynicism, and then go back about their business.

Excerpted from *Institutional Investor* 3 (June 1969), pp. 57–58, 60, 64. This copyrighted material is reprinted with permission from: **Institutional Investor, Inc.**, 488 Madison Avenue, New York, NY 10022.

Indeed, it does sometimes seem that the era in which Jerry Tsai thrived has had its day. Growth was his style and his success and it thrust him into the limelight as he bought and traded the great growth companies. But as that vogue began to fade, and other money managers adapted to change, Tsai continued to stick to his guns.

Yet, there was a time in the heyday of glamor stocks when some people believed Jerry Tsai possessed mystical powers from the Orient (he was born in Shanghai) which somehow allowed him to perceive the future.

. . .

The popular press quickly converged on Tsai, elevated him to the status of a genius and ruminated at length on what might lie behind his "inscrutable" countenance. (Westerners habitually label "inscrutable" anything from the Orient which they cannot instantly understand.) As recently as last May, *Newsweek* impassionedly referred to Tsai as "something of a mystery man" who "radiates total cool . . . from the manicured tips of his fingers to the burnished black tops of his slip-on shoes" and remarked with awe about his "blank, impassive—friends actually call it 'inscrutable'—gaze."

Then last year, without warning, Jerry Tsai collapsed, as the era of the big glamor stocks abruptly ended. While the Dow Jones Industrial Average was up 5 percent, and many other performance mutual funds were up 30 and 40 percent, Tsai's Manhattan Fund, which he had started to loud fanfare in 1966 after leaving Fidelity, was actually *down* 7 percent, the worst record of any of the 310 funds in the Arthur Lipper survey. Superman had been confronted with a giant hunk of Kryptonite. Billy Batson, gagged, had been unable to shout SHAZAM! and switch into Captain Marvel. SpiderMan had lost his radioactivity. The star had fallen.

As the year went on, Wall Streeters smirked, mocked, snorted and scoffed. "Jerry must have left all his brains up at Fidelity," they said chortling. The press went searching for a new star. Later people all but forgot about him. Jerry Tsai and the Manhattan Fund were still in business, of course, but reporters no longer besieged his shiny, rosewood-paneled office with the goatskin-covered bar cabinet. Tsai is buying! was no longer whispered in board-rooms. Portfolio managers, analysts and brokers no longer tied up his telephone in hopes of obtaining a tiny hint of which way he intended to move next.

. . .

Tsai has not been wasting time despairing about his fall from grace, however. He recently pulled off a business coup that few, if any, other fund managers can match. As Fred Alger explains it, "Jerry has now taken things one step further into the future. First he created enough of an image as a performance man to get enormous assets under his management. Now he has translated that into extraordinary capital values for himself." Last August,

Tsai sold his Tsai Management & Research Corp. to CNA Financial Corp., a big Chicago-based insurance holding company that is diversifying into many financial fields. Tsai, at 40, who 10 years ago was an unknown, relatively impecunious securities analyst, now owns CNA stock worth about $35 million.

And while growing hordes of fund managers are scrabbling like hungry mongrels to beat each other out in the performance sweepstakes, Tsai has all but withdrawn from running the Manhattan Fund and embarked on a whole new career developing non-insurance acquisitions for CNA.

It should be understood that Tsai is really quite unlike the image the press built for him. He is eminently scrutable. His principal talent is not so much picking stocks as it is a very Western flair for corporate maneuvering. He has an abiding, also very Western, ambition to expand and control any organization for which he is a part.

• • •

"My mother is a very smart lady," he says. "She was always buying and selling real estate, gold bars, stocks, even cotton." One reason he and his sister rooted for her was because whenever these transactions turned out well, they received extra allowances. On her advice, Jerry from the time he was 11 would exchange his Chinese allowance for American dollars to protect his savings from the ruinous inflation besetting China at the time. "Even a movie ticket got to cost twelve thousand dollars," he recalls. "Every three months we would turn in our old currency for a new issue." Very early in his life, Jerry began developing a strong desire to make it big on the fabled American Wall Street. "What more exciting thing is there for a man?" he asks, shrugging his shoulders. He applied to and was accepted by Wesleyan College in Middletown, Connecticut and in 1947, at the age of 17, he arrived in the United States for the first time.

Soon after he transferred to Boston University where he majored in economics, began trading in the stock market, and graduated in 1949. Only two months later he picked up his MA. After a year at a Providence textile company, he returned to Boston University to work on an MBA; however he soon became impatient to move on to Wall Street and got himself hired by Bache as a securities analyst. A year later, a friend at Scudder, Stevens arranged an interview with Edward C. Johnson, the fabled "Mr. Johnson" of Fidelity Management and Research in Boston. . . . Johnson thought about Tsai for a month, then hired him as an analyst. This was in 1952. Tsai swiftly assimilated the intricacies of money management, and within six years he was allowed, at the age of 29, to start the Fidelity Capital Fund, Fidelity's first public growth fund.

• • •

Tsai's Fidelity Capital and Jack Dreyfus' Fund are often given credit for being the main initiators of the modern performance fund idea. This requires two modifications. The basic growth philosophy of Fidelity Capital came from Mr. Johnson rather than Tsai. And Fidelity Trend, the other of Fidelity's two principal funds, actually outperformed Capital during much of Tsai's tour at the head of Capital. But Tsai personally received most of the public and professional acclaim for a number of reasons. One was his race, which created instant allure—the "inscrutable" legend. Another was the retiring, publicity-shy nature both of Mr. Johnson and his son, Ned, who ran Trend. Finally, there was the dramatic way in which Tsai operated.

Tsai's speciality was the big glamorous stocks such as Xerox and Polaroid which were generally considered to be too speculative for anyone but private traders. At a time when broad diversification was the prevailing philosophy, Tsai concentrated his portfolio in a small handful of these glamor issues. Though all respectable money managers bought on fundamentals, Tsai freely admitted he traded by the charts. He would establish positions with dramatic snatches of tens of thousands of shares. Then, watching the technical progress of his holdings very carefully, he would dump his positions with equal suddenness when a company developed tinges of weakness. "I never fight the tape," he said. His annual turnover generally exceeded 100 percent, an almost scandalous level then unparalleled among other institutions.

Many on Wall Street were entranced by such flashy maneuvering, but those forced to execute his orders were less thrilled. "Jerry used real bludgeon tactics in his trading," recalls a friend. "He would call up Bache, for example, and tell them he had 100,000 shares he wanted out of no more than two points under the market. If they screamed too loudly, Jerry would just give them his General Motors-type trades for the next month. He knew how to play his leverage." Tsai was almost "sadistic," says a former associate, in the way he cheerfully sent specialists on the floor of the exchanges into a state of near collapse.

The investment climate of the early 1960s was perfect for Tsai. As more and more institutions discovered the virtues of growth and performance, they went searching for the same glamor issues Tsai was buying. Tsai's reputation gave many of his portfolio maneuvers a certain self-fulfillment. His progress within the Fidelity organization, though, had run into a snag. By 1963, Tsai owned nearly 20 percent of Fidelity Management and Research (Mr. Johnson held 40 percent), and Tsai clearly expected that after an appropriate period of time he would be running the company. Indeed, those who were at Fidelity say his political activities, though less flashy, were just as adroit as those in the market. But it became more and more obvious that Tsai had a formidable competitor for the top job after Mr. Johnson retired: Ned, Mr. Johnson's son. In 1965 Tsai confronted Mr. Johnson with the issue: Was Ned or he to be the successor? Mr. Johnson replied that after all Ned was his son and that it was his intention that Ned eventually take over. As much as he admired Mr. Johnson, Tsai felt he had no other choice but to leave. "Fidelity is a family business and Mr. Johnson's wishes were very understandable," says Tsai. "But I wanted to be number one, not number two." Tsai sold his Fidelity stock back to the company at book—$2.2 million or 1.3 times earnings—and set out on his own.

• • •

As Tsai worked to organize the Manhattan Fund in the latter part of the year, the degree of public anticipation almost approached that of the Second Coming. Tsai had planned to sell around $25 million worth of shares, but on February 15, 1966, when what was regarded as the great new bandwagon to a new land of assured wealth was unveiled, a fantastic $270 million poured in as the public dashed to climb aboard. "We came out at just the right time," says Tsai. "The psychology was bullish, the stock market was doing great and people were in the mood to buy something new." The Manhattan Fund's inauguration was the height of Tsai's near deification, and it ironically coincided almost precisely with the all-time high of the Dow Jones Average.

Fred Alger

GILBERT EDMUND KAPLAN AND CHRIS WELLES

Fred Alger went east to Wall Street after a brief stint as a security analyst for Wells Fargo Bank. Segueing into rebirth as a fund manager, he quickly found fame as one of the quick-draw "gunslingers" prominent in the performance investing mania of the late 1960s. Unlike several of the era's other Freds—of which David Babson declared there were too many—this one survived and has remained active and successful to the present day. This brief profile was written many years ago, when Bernie Cornfeld's Fund of Funds was still a force to reckon with and an aura of cheap excitement (and no little awe) hovered over the Street's "personalities."

Fred Alger is a quiet, unassuming, thoughtful-looking man of 34 with tousled hair and glasses, who wears nondescript gray suits with fat suspenders and black shoes, who sits most of the day in a tiny office in downtown Manhattan, and who last year made $1 million. He has a battered wooden desk

---

Excerpted from *The Money Managers* by Gilbert Edmund Kaplan and Chris Welles, editors (New York, 1969), pp. 19–24. Copyright © 1969 by Institutional Investors System, Inc. Reprinted by permission of Random House, Inc.

covered with clutter, and a great view of the building's airshaft. Wall decoration consists of Scotch-taped messages. Five other associates and two secretaries are crowded into the premises. There are a few wooden folding-tables littered with paper cups. The rug has coffee stains. There is no stock ticker, no stock-quote machine, no broad tape—only a couple of well-worn slide rules and a blackboard.

Though Fred Alger doesn't look like a star, there is approximately $300 million whose disposition depends on what he happens to feel like at any particular moment. Security Equity Fund, for which Alger's company, Fred Alger & Company, Inc., is research consultant, has during the past four years chalked up an appreciation of over 260 percent, one of the best in the industry. An associated fund, Security Investment Fund, has outperformed the market every year, for the past six years, despite a high percentage of bonds.

Alger and his associates also advise two funds in Bernard Cornfeld's Fund of Funds complex called FOF Proprietary Fund Ltd., plus ten private corporate accounts. Alger says that, except for Security Investment, all of these accounts invest in similar stocks and have recorded similarly impressive records.

The Security funds are for Alger kind of loss-leaders, for the fees he receives managing them are quite low. But they are a public advertisement of his abilities. This advertisement has attracted other money involving fees much more interesting. The transformation of stardom into remuneration occurs when you get paid extra for performance. From his other accounts, Alger's companies get 1 percent of the assets (the amount of money in the fund) or, providing he beats the record of the Standard & Poor's 500 stock average, 10 percent (5 percent for FOF) of the total appreciation (how much his fund has gone up) whichever is larger. Thus the better he does, the more money he gets, and there is no upper limit.

Alger is paid this kind of money because in money management today there is a growing feeling that though good, solid, steady, diligent work may be adequate to achieve respectable results, for a heady performance record that leaves the Dow far behind, something more is needed. Talent, Feel, Knack, Sense, Touch. Either you has it or you doesn't.

Talent is not cheap. Men who are paid for simple brainpower are expendable. If they get sick or tired or fired, a replacement is always waiting. The assistant moves up. The bureaucracy inches on. But talent is a one-of-a-kind commodity. No one looks quite like Elizabeth Taylor. No one flashes his teeth quite like Paul Newman. Fred Alger, though possessed of much quiet self-confidence, modestly does not regard himself as the beneficiary of any miraculous gift. "It's not that we're any smarter," he says. "We just work at it, minute by minute, all day long." But he will agree that "if you want to draw the talent, you have to pay for it." Luring stars these days means dangling in front of them a piece of the action. . . .

Alger's hang-up is that he really doesn't care much about money. True, he has a nine-room Park Avenue apartment, but then he has a wife and three children under eight. His possessions and material desires are as bereft as his office walls. He is really oblivious to the outside world. Every day he plods through the same dull routine, including a subway ride to the office and a BLT sandwich and chocolate ice cream for lunch. His social life is almost nonexistent (a highlight is Wednesday night duplicate bridge). "I still get lost around New York," he says. "I don't think I could tell you the name of one play on Broadway." Excess personal income is all plowed back into Security Equity. He says he never makes investments for himself.

So if it isn't money, what is it? The thing that makes Fred run is: The Race; Winning; Number One; Beating the other funds. "I would rather be down 60 percent in a year and be number one than be up 60 percent and be number ten," he says. "It is perfectly all right to win by a nose." He likes the spectators to know who is winning. One of Bernard Cornfeld's incentive schemes is the monthly circulation of a performance ranking of all the funds in his empire. One month, due to a misprint, Alger's fund was listed as number two instead of number one. Alger immediately flew to Geneva to straighten things out. "We get a little upset if they don't have us right," he explains.

Thus Alger's strategy is dictated not by some higher standard of desirable gains, but by what the other funds are doing. The starting gun sounds January 1. For most of the time the idea, says Alger, is to "stay with the pack. After a while, it becomes clear which funds are in the lead and we get into the stocks that are making the move." This keeps Alger pretty much up front; his talent for market timing allows him to match the pace, though he is usually still just reacting to what the others do.

Chances to win the race come "during those five or six times a year when you have a chance to do something distinctive, to leave the pack, change your portfolio mix, and move ahead."

Jerry Kohlberg, Henry Kravis, and George Roberts

SARAH BARTLETT

KKR became a dominant firm in the dominant industry of the late 1980s—LBOs—and the personalities of its principals mattered greatly in its evolution toward becoming a Great Power. Jerry Kohlberg originated and financed the firm; his probity and philosophy caused him to leave it. The aspects of the personalities of Henry Kravis and his cousin George Roberts that resulted in the separation are captured in this article.

Gone were the days when KKR could circle around a company, carefully inspect its financial details, make an offer, and then negotiate a final price with management and directors that would be slightly higher than its original offer but not significantly so. Now, every time KKR bid on a company, two or three others would try to muscle in, too. KKR went from dictating its own terms to being just one of many bidders in an auction.

As anyone who has ever been to an auction knows, the person who has the most money and is willing to spend it wins. In the mid-1980s, thanks to its carefully cultivated ties to the public pension funds, no one had more money to invest as equity in companies than Kohlberg Kravis Roberts. . . .

George [Roberts] and Henry [Kravis] did have a choice. They did not have to throw themselves into the takeover frenzy with such abandon. There were, in fact, some people who felt it made more sense to hang back and wait for others to get carried away, make their inevitable mistakes, and be forced to retreat to the sidelines. Then, still armed with incredible firepower, they would be ready to come in for the kill. William Simon, former Treasury secretary, did just that. He dropped out of the LBO market altogether in 1986, complaining of too much competition and excessive prices, and only announced his return in 1991, after the frenzy had subsided. In the intervening years, he made a nice fortune bobbing in and out of the unstable market for savings and loan institutions. KKR's chief competitor, Teddy Forstmann, followed a similar strategy. He was frequently criticized in the business press for refusing to engage in bidding wars and, as a result, for not buying a company for two years. However, when the dust finally settled, his was one of the only large firms left standing. In 1990, Forstmann Little was able to acquire two major companies—General Instruments and Gulfstream Aerospace—with virtually no competition, and find the financing to complete the transactions—a major feat considering the banking industry's newfound wariness of highly leveraged transactions.

Everything about [Jerry] Kohlberg's behavior suggests that he, too, would have chosen this more conservative strategy. However, Kohlberg was still out of action, distracted by headaches and unable to work a full day. He kept trying to come in to the office, but he'd missed so much and was still feeling too drained and physically unwell that he would often have to leave around lunchtime. Left to their own devices, his two young stallions were inexorably drawn in the opposite direction.

Instinctively, these two men had spent their lives priming themselves to win. And they were not about to change now. Though they would later deny it, doing deals became much more important to them than doing *good* deals.

Winning had always been something of an obsession for George. Even his close friend Mike Wilsey is amused by how tenaciously George clings to victory, or at least the appearance of victory. George likes to make bets, not on horses or dogs, but casual bets with friends over obscure facts or predictions. He'll bet you that Saddam Hussein will be killed in a coup by such and such a date, or that the Mets will win the World Series. But if he's wrong, he will go to great lengths to reconstruct the bet in such a way that he still comes out the winner. If Saddam survives a coup attempt, he'll say that he had only predicted he would be attacked. Or if the Mets lose, it will be because a certain pitcher twisted his arm and George had only said they would win if he was on the mound, or some such modification designed to extricate him from having to admit that, heaven forbid, he had lost.

"He's lost bets with people, and even with me, and he manages to rationalize in his mind that he hasn't lost it. And he doesn't pay it," says Wilsey, unable to suppress a giggle at his friend's somewhat juvenile behavior. "If he lost the bet, his understanding of the bet will vary or the circumstances will vary, or he'll get back to me and I'll never hear from him. One sign of an intensely competitive person is that it's important to win, and betting is one indication of it."

George is always trying to find a way to manufacture a victory out of a defeat. John McLoughlin, his lawyer, remembers the frantic bidding war that KKR got into for Gulf Oil in 1984. The firm was still regarded as somewhat new to the game and perhaps a bit out of its league. After round-the-clock strategy sessions amidst intense competition with the other bidding group, Standard Oil of California, which was staying at the same hotel, George was finally asked to make his 20-minute presentation to the board. Afterward, he, McLoughlin, and the rest of the KKR team retired to a conference room in Gulf's Pittsburgh headquarters. Over the next several hours, Marty Siegel, their investment banker, played cards with some of his team from Kidder Peabody, while George and the rest sat and stewed. Finally, they received a call from the chairman of the board summoning them to his office. They figured the news would be bad, since the chairman had not indicated that they would be meeting with the special committee of directors on the board, as the winner almost certainly would do. The chairman made some remarks about how impressed the board had been with their presentation and the quality of their analysis, but in the end he said he was sorry but they had decided to sell the company to the other bidder.

The chairman finished by saying he was so impressed, he'd like to shake George's hand. George, never skipping a beat, grabbed the man's hand and immediately informed him that since the Federal Trade Commission would almost certainly force the new owner to shed some of the company's divisions to avoid antitrust violations, he'd like to put in a bid for those divisions right away. The chairman, his hand still being pumped by this intense young man, was completely taken aback. "He wins well, but he does hate to lose," says McLoughlin, laughing as he recalls the incident. "George spares no effort if a deal hangs in the balance. He never stops thinking."

Indeed, if you ask George what companies he's most proud of having helped grow, he'll tell you that what he really cares about is not so much the company's operations but the kick he gets from proving that a deal can get done when skeptics say it can't.

George prides himself on his persistence, on never giving up. He enjoys telling a story about KKR's purchase in 1983 of Golden West Broadcasters, which owned KTLA, a large independent television station in Los Angeles. A friend introduced him to the company, and after taking a close look, he decided KKR should buy it. Negotiations for the company ensued over the next several months.

Just when George thought he was close to completing the deal, he got a phone call from KTLA's top lawyer thanking him politely for his interest and hard work, but informing him that the company had decided instead to do a deal with Capital Cities, the media giant run by Tom Murphy.

George was incensed. "I said, 'You can't do that.' He said, 'What do you mean?' I said, 'Look we've invested a lot of time and effort and money in this.' I said, 'You can't sell it out unless you at least listen to me.' And he said, 'Okay, we owe you that.' And literally, Tom Murphy was down in L.A., ready to sign the deal with him. So we went down and I stayed there till eight o'clock that night, and we worked out a deal. We wound up making a deal to buy it for much better terms for them, the sellers, than we had originally [planned]," George says with a hearty laugh. "But we at least worked it out."

George left the meeting elated. It was one of those crisp fall days that can make any urban jungle seem so much more civilized. As he was walking to the garage to pick up his car, he decided the evening was so nice and his news so good that he would stop off at a pay phone and call his cousin

Henry. "I said, 'I've got good news and bad news for you.' He said 'What's that?' I said, 'Well, the good news is, we've got a deal to buy KTLA.' He said, 'That's great!' I said, 'The bad news is, we've just paid a record price for any single television station ever sold, and,' I said, 'the only asset we have is some antenna on top of a mountain, because they don't own anything else.'"

The two cousins laughed heartily at the seeming absurdity of it all. But after he hung up, George got to thinking. Not about how he had just thrown around a lot of somebody else's money for an asset that was hard to nail down, but about how different the outcome might have been if George had not been George. "What would have happened if I had said, 'Well, okay, we lost.' If I hadn't been incensed enough to insist on a meeting?" George thinks one reason KKR has been so successful is that he and Henry have always refused to back down in the face of long odds.

Winning is paramount, and George will work and work and work at it until he finds a way. His greatest asset is his ability to remember and manipulate numbers. Friends say he will sit through endless meetings and never take a note. But ask him 3 years later about the interest due on a particular 16-percent note, or the research budget for a particular product at one of the 17 companies KKR owns, and he will give you chapter and verse. Guests arriving at his home will often find George sitting alone in a room, staring out into space. He is not daydreaming, he is engaging in mental juggling: trying to figure out if he can take one figure from this column and move it to another, increase the equity, take out some debt, cut capital spending in this company and increase the marketing campaign, anything that will enable him to stretch the limits just that much further. "We're not afraid to go try something," says the indefatigable George. "We're not afraid to try to bite off, a lot of times, more than people think that we can chew."

Henry is no different. "I've always been the kind of person, as is George," he says, "that the word *can't* isn't even in our vocabulary. You know, I tell my children exactly the same thing. I say, 'Just take that out of your vocabulary, just forget about it.'" The more Henry thinks about it, the more wound up he gets. Suddenly, it's as though he's been transported into a meeting with other KKR executives. "'Don't tell me you can't do it, don't tell me the market's not big enough! We're going to figure out how to do that.' . . . We were prepared to push and be creative and create new securities and just take the attitude, 'don't take no for an answer.' Other firms may not have been that way. Look at what happened to Gibbons Green. They bought a few companies, and sort of, so what? Look at Clayton, Dubilier—yeah, they made some nice money, but sort of, so what?"

"We always took the attitude we want to be on the cutting edge," said Henry. "We were the *first* ones to do a tender offer of a public company as an LBO. We were the *first* ones to do a billion-dollar deal. When we bought

Houdaille in 1979 for $350 million, everyone said, 'You can't get that done.' . . . I say, 'I don't know till we try, but we're going to try, we're going to find it somehow.' We had senior bank debt, we had senior notes from an insurance company. We had senior subordinated, subordinated, junior subordinated, two classes of preferred stock, two classes of equity, and warrants. And if we could have thought of another class of security, we'd have come up with that one, too."

George and Henry approach life with totally different styles and personalities, but they both end up at the same place. "We'll go skiing and George will always go with the instructor," says Wilsey, who knows both men well. "He will ski the whole day, the whole time with the instructor. He'll never leave the instructor. He follows him. He does whatever he says. He's a great perfectionist. He's dedicated and he's a great learner. He'll take instruction. And he's controlled when he skis. Henry, on the other hand, goes like hell. It's very important to be pushing a little bit, pushing the limit. And George is very controlled. He wants to master it."

Wilsey saw the same patterns when they went fishing. "Everyone else went off and did their own thing. And George stuck with me and I taught him how to fish. He's very patient, trying to learn. Now I'm going to go fishing with Henry, and I'm sure Henry's going to charge off, and I'm sure it's going to be important to catch the most fish."

Henry wants to be the biggest, the best, the winner, and he will risk a lot to achieve it. George will study the problem to death, until he figures out how to dominate it. George would face far fewer challenges were it not for Henry's hell bent nature always putting the two on the line. But Henry might fall flat on his face if his cousin were not always standing there right behind him, rooted to the earth, ready with the sure, clever answer. Separately, the two might not have succeeded to nearly the same degree; together, they present a powerful, unified front. . . .

George's mother, Carolyn, thinks that "their relationship is one of the most unusual I have ever heard of or read about. It is almost unreal. . . ."

A better way to describe Henry and George's deep bond, their almost eerie intuitive closeness, says Wilsey, is that they are like twins.

With Jerry [Kohlberg] still out of commission, the "twins" [Kravis and Roberts] were left to figure out how to respond to the whirlwind of takeover fever that was starting to encircle them. Corporate raiders were becoming a commonplace phenomenon; names such as Ivan Boesky and Boone Pickens were dominating the headlines. More and more companies were being whispered about as takeover targets, and there were other leverage buyout groups out there with other people's money to fling about.

George and Henry had a choice, but they could not stop themselves from entering the fray.

BUSINESS BUILDERS

Longstreet Hinton

RON CHERNOW

Longstreet Hinton, born in Vicksburg, Mississippi, was head of the Morgan Bank's Trust Department, set the tone for the best of such organizations and was a principal progenitor of institutional investing.

After a dinner spent wearily sifting through names of potential chieftains [to manage Morgan's new trust department], George Whitney turned to a young associate, Longstreet Hinton, and said apologetically, "Street, I guess you're it." . . . It was then considered quite daring and unorthodox for a nonlawyer to run a trust department, which was always entangled in legal estate questions.

Street Hinton was from Vicksburg, Mississippi, and reminded everybody of a Southern cavalry general. He was tall and spare, ramrod straight, somewhat curmudgeonly, with a long face and prominent ears. His father had ended up as minister of Saint John's of Lattingtown in Locust Valley, the "millionaire's church" so dear to Jack Morgan. Hinton's formative experience was in settling Jack Morgan's estate. He drew upon the art expertise of Belle da Costa Greene. "She told me that Fifty-Seventh Street was the crookedest place in the world and not to trust anyone," recalled Hinton of his foray into the world of art dealers. . . . A tough customer, he quickly took control after the merger [of Morgan with the Guaranty Trust Co.], telling Bob Jones, head of the Guaranty Trust Department, "What makes you think you know how to run a trust department?" He reminded Jones that he had lost his largest account, Ford Motor, to J. P. Morgan. Hinton ran the combined show. . . .

Trust departments had been regarded as loss leaders. Hinton thought they should make money. Most trust managers were sober men with iron-gray hair who put money into government bonds and they weren't notable for their imagination. When the Morgan Trust Department made its first common-stock purchase, in 1949, it was thought so audacious that Hinton had to telephone Russell Leffingwell, on vacation in Lake George, New York, to clear the purchase. After 1950, changes in tax laws and collective bargaining prompted an explosion in pension funds, and much of this money gravitated to commercial banks. After General Motors designated Morgan as one of its pension-fund managers and allowed investment of up

Excerpted from *The House of Morgan* by Ron Chernow, Chapter 28, pp. 560–561, used by permission of Grove/Atlantic Inc. © 1990 by Ron Chernow.

to 50 percent in stocks, the business boomed. "What made us was the General Motors fund," said Hinton. "When we led the parade there, then everybody else wanted us." . . .

In the early 1960s, the Morgan Trust Department operated from a wood-paneled room with antique furniture, facing the New York Stock Exchange. Forty impeccably dressed managers in dark suits and black shoes sat in leather armchairs before glossy rolltop desks. Invoking Pierpont Morgan's philosophy, Hinton initiated the gospel of buy and hold. When a corporate director asked for a policy statement, he replied, "It's easy. We don't have one. We never sell stocks."

Hermann J. Abs

Hermann Abs gave key leadership and momentum to Deutsche Bank and to Germany's financial recovery after the Second World War. A man of many talents, he was the key negotiator with the Allies of Germany's war debt settlement as well as an influential advisor to Chancellor Konrad Adenauer. He was also a long-time friend and associate of Alfried Krupp. This description is from his obituary.

Hermann Josef Abs . . . personified both the triumphs and some of the problems of German business during the past 60 years.

During his post-war heyday as head of Deutsche Bank, the country's largest bank, Mr. Abs won renown as the quintessential German banker, using his network of directorships and influence to play a significant role in rebuilding the West German economy. A man whose mild appearance belied his capacity for hard work and occasional ruthlessness, Mr. Abs stood for many years at the centre of corporate Germany.

Aged only 36, he became a member of the Deutsche Bank management board in 1938—a position in which he stayed throughout the second world war. He remained Deutsche Bank's honorary chairman up to his death. Not least because of his war-time role, he ranked among the most controversial bankers of the century—as well as one of the most outstanding.

Abs was the chairman of Deutsche Bank's management board between 1957 and 1967, and headed the supervisory board for a subsequent decade until 1976. The influence of Deutsche Bank and the country's other big universal banks on Germany's corporate and financial life has

Excerpted from *Financial Times*, Tuesday, February 8, 1994. By permission of Financial Times.

been modified since Abs ceased to play an active role in Deutsche Bank's affairs. . . .

Deutsche Bank none the less retains a pivotal position in the German economy—a tribute to the capacity of Abs and his contemporaries to re-build the country's big banks after the war along the lines of traditions laid down when they were established in the 1870s.

One of Germany's post-war traditions is that Deutsche Bank has peri-odically attracted praise and vilification in roughly equal measure. Abs, once termed by David Rockefeller "the world's leading banker," was also labelled a "Richelieu": he was frequently exposed to criticism that he en-joyed too much power for Germany's own good. . . .

By allowing banks and industry to build up and extend long-term rela-tionships, the system that Abs helped restore after the war allowed West Germany for a long time to overcome short-term economic vicissitudes with greater success than most of its European trading partners. That sys-tem is now being put to a crucial test as a result of the trials of German unification.

Virtually throughout his career, Abs followed a steeply rising path. He was born into a comfortably-off Catholic family in Bonn on October 15, 1901. After a false start on a quickly abandoned university law course, he turned to banking. His apprenticeship took him to London, Paris, Amsterdam and the Americas.

In 1935, at the age of 34, he became a partner in a well-known Berlin private bank, Delbrück, Schickler & Co. Within three years he joined Deutsche Bank—at the time, a frontline institution, but not yet the biggest in Germany.

His more senior German colleagues recognised early Abs' capacity and judgment in international banking matters. One of his pre-war accom-plishments was to help represent Germany at negotiations to freeze the banks' foreign debts. In view of his intelligence, sardonicism and Catholic background, Abs was regarded with hostility by the more rabid members of the Nazi party. He was never a party member. But throughout the war he remained close to some of the technocrats running parts of the Nazi econ-omy. As a professional associate of Walter Funk, the Reichsbank president, he was a member until 1945 of the Reichsbank's advisory council.

In spring 1945, as the war neared an end in Berlin, Abs left the German capital bound for Hamburg in a Karstadt department store delivery lorry crammed with Deutsche Bank files. After a short-lived appointment as an adviser to the British military government, he was imprisoned by the Americans for three months and was proposed in 1948 as the first head of the Bank Deutscher Länder, the nascent federal bank and the forerunner of the Bundesbank. He turned the job down—above all, it seems, because the United States occupation authorities had made clear they would not have him.

Abs' ambivalent war-time activities remained controversial to his death. Unlike many Germans of his generation, Abs never claimed to have resisted Hitler. A man who was not imprisoned or hanged or shot by the Nazis cannot claim to have opposed Hitler, he once said. Deutsche Bank helped the Nazis confiscate Jewish property and assets in the late 1930s and 1940s as part of the Aryanisation laws. Abs had also been on the supervisory board of IG Farben, the conglomerate with a stake in the chemicals company that developed the Zyklon B gas used to kill millions of Jews in gas chambers.

After 1945, Abs helped some Jewish clients who had escaped the death camps to recover compensation from the Bonn government. . . .

In 1983, as a result of criticism of his pre-1945 activities, Abs suffered the ignominy of being put on a U.S. government watch-list of undesirable aliens, and was officially barred from entering the United States. However, this did not, according to the Deutsche Bank, prevent him from making periodic U.S. trips.

Abs' real post-war career began in 1953 when, in a milestone marking West Germany's reintegration into the community of nations, he negotiated the London agreement restructuring Germany's foreign indebtedness.

In a step which freed Germany from the burden of reparations that had blemished the survival chances of the Weimar Republic, Germany's debts were written down and allowed to be repaid between 1953 and 1983—an accord that became a model for many subsequent rescheduling agreements. Abs was also appointed head of Kreditanstalt für Wiederaufbau, the German reconstruction bank that channelled assistance from the Marshall Plan to West Germany's war-damaged economy.

Abs went on to head the southern German group of the three banks into which the allies had split Deutsche Bank. There he engineered the reunification of the three successors, becoming head of the reconstituted Deutsche Bank's executive board in 1957. During this time, Abs built up his close relationship with Konrad Adenauer, the first West German chancellor, in office between 1949 and 1963—a fellow Rhinelander, sharing Abs' mordant wit and his taste for power. Abs was once asked whether the rumour was true that the "old man" had once asked him to become foreign minister. Abs' oblique reply was: "When Adenauer really wanted something, he didn't ask you—he told you."

Abs' was fluent in three languages and had a working knowledge of three more. He spoke the clipped, sometimes slightly archaic English of a country squire—gentle in tone, acid in content. His capacity for work was legendary. He claimed that, for weeks on end, he could work every day— habitually at a stand-up desk—from 8 A.M. until midnight.

On top of this, he found time to collect French Impressionists and to head committees running Beethoven's birthplace in Bonn and Goethe's in Frankfurt.

If Abs' voice was conservative, it was also that of a classic banking pater-nalist. One of his recurring themes was that business must serve the com-munity. A much-repeated aphorism was that profits were no end in themselves; to conduct business for profit alone would be like living only to breathe. Society would tolerate private business only if it could prove that profits for the enterprise created benefits for society. . . .

By 1970, mindful of the requirement for durable European monetary arrangements, he was talking of the need for a European central bank.

His experience of the Third Reich explained part of Abs' caution over expanding Deutsche Bank into foreign countries. He believed that co-operation with foreign banks, rather than outright takeovers, marked the most appropriate course.

As memories of war receded and a new generation took over the helm, Deutsche Bank's policy became more adventurous.

The most dramatic international move came at the end of 1989 when Deutsche Bank bought the U.K.'s Morgan Grenfell for £950m, much in-creasing its clout in areas such as international mergers and acquisitions. The bank justified the move in the sort of understated terms much used by Abs: Deutsche Bank could learn much about investment banking from its new London subsidiary.

At the peak during the post-war period, Abs was a member of 24 super-visory boards in Germany—so many that a law was passed in 1965 limiting bankers' board appointments. . . .

In the 1960s, Abs teamed up with Professor Karl Schiller, the Social Democratic economics minister, to use his prestige and contacts to devise a network of warranties which saved the Krupp concern from almost cer-tain bankruptcy. He also helped to engineer the transaction in the 1970s by which Kuwait bought a stake in Daimler-Benz from the Flick family when it lost interest in controlling the star performer of German industry. In the post-Abs era even some Deutsche Bank directors have recognised that the traditional system may be a bit too cosy, forecasting that, eventu-ally, the banks will run down their shareholdings in industry. . . .

During his great days Abs was probably as popular as it is possible for any banker to be. Toward the end of his life, he did not, however, hold either politicians or the great majority of his compatriots in great regard. He believed the exaggerated demand for social welfare in West Germany's comfortable, consensus society was a severe hindrance to economic dy-namism. . . .

In his latter years, as the world hummed around him, Abs plainly did not enjoy having an inordinate amount of time on his hands. If he was faintly disdainful of modern Germans, and sometimes appeared slightly too pleased with himself, there was (to adapt a saying of Churchill) some excuse. He had a considerable amount to be pleased about.

George S. Moore

George Moore brought three things to Citibank: an aggressively innovative approach to business, a commitment to recruiting and empower-
ing talented young people, and internationalism—the hallmarks of that
organization over the past 50 years. The everyday problem for him was
where to get money to lend; whereas, for his successors, it is not the
availability, but the price of their raw material that keeps them awake
at night. This excerpt tells us how "the money position" came to dominate banking's post-World War II development.

Among our most serious banking problems during my time as president
and chairman was the need to find the money our customers wanted to
borrow. We were repeatedly squeezed. It was a new problem in my time at
the bank. In the 1930s, there had been a great shortage of borrowers; during the war the government had seen to it that there was plenty of money
around for the defense industries that had to be financed, and after the
war the banks were full of the government bonds the Federal Reserve System had helped them buy as part of the process by which we borrowed to
pay for the war. Even then, those of us working the districts were conscious of the importance of getting corporate customers to leave deposits
with the bank as well as borrow from it, and one of the measurements of
the success of a regional department or a special industries group was its
ability to increase the deposits credited to its customers.

An obvious way to increase the money the bank has for lending is to move
out geographically, adding new branches and new depositors. That was how
Bank of America, which was chartered to operate through the whole state of
California, became the biggest bank in the world in the 1960s and 1970s—
by opening more than a thousand branches. It is as far from northern California to the Mexican border as it is from Maine to Florida. The Bank of
America had a huge market at its doorstep and for years they were the only
California bank that exploited this huge potential. But we were restricted by
law, first to the five counties of New York City and then to those five plus
the immediately adjacent suburban counties, and before we could move into
those we had to jump hurdles at the Federal Reserve and the Comptroller's
office. We did the best we could—we opened 36 branches in Nassau and
Westchester Counties between 1960 and 1966, not to mention another 43
branches in the boroughs of New York City. But the yield in terms of lend-
able deposits was relatively small.

It was clear that if we couldn't get more money to lend, we were eventually going to be suffocated. We had constantly before us the lesson of [New York City's] First National Bank, which depended on a handful of giant customers for much of the money they had to lend. That was why First National Bank shrank in size during the boom years of the 1940s and 1950s, and had to come to us to merge. We had always looked for ways to give service for the money companies left with us. I remember Sheperd saying at a meeting as early as the mid-1950s, "We can't expect people to give us our inventory for nothing; we're going to have to pay for it." Thus for example, City Bank invented the "lock box," the system by which customers paid their bills to a post-office box that would be opened by the bank rather than by the company that had sent the bills, so the money could be credited to the company's account before the bookkeepers went through the process of canceling out the payer's indebtedness.

But companies still didn't want to leave a lot of money lying around idle, especially as the U.S. inflation rate in the 1950s lurched up toward 3 percent a year, high enough in people's minds in those days that Jack Kennedy ran against Richard Nixon in part with the challenge that the Eisenhower administration had weakened the country by failing to control inflation. And the Glass-Steagall law of 1933, written by congressmen who thought (wrongly) that banks had collapsed because they paid too much interest for demand deposits, prohibited us from paying anything at all for money that had been left in the bank for less than 30 days. Companies that would once have carried high balances in their checking accounts, then, began routinely to transfer the money out to short-term Treasury bills, or to the purchase of interest-bearing "commercial paper" issued by other large companies to meet their short-term borrowing needs. We had a double whammy: companies that used to leave spare cash in the bank were taking it out, and companies that had financed their short-term financial needs with bank loans were borrowing directly from our ex-depositors.

Banks had for years issued "certificates of deposit" for a given term—30, 60, 90 days, six months, one year. Those could pay interest under the law, and though the Federal Reserve System controlled the maximum we could pay, it usually kept that rate above the market rate for money. Corporate treasurers with money to hold for more than 30 days were usually, not always, willing to lend it to the banks by purchasing CDs rather than lend it directly to other corporations by purchasing commercial paper. Banks were considered safer. But the issuers of commercial paper had a gimmick. Informally—but anyone who didn't live up to these informal arrangements would be dead in the market in the future—they promised the buyer of the paper that if for any reason he needed cash while the paper was still outstanding, the issuer would buy it back for the face value. And we couldn't make such promises.

Sheperd and Wriston found a way around this problem. We would issue a *negotiable* certificate of deposit, which the owner could sell to someone else if he needed his funds sooner than he had expected. We tried this first in Europe, and it didn't work; Swiss Bank Corporation, which had bought our first negotiable CD for a million dollars, found that there was nobody ready to pay them for it when they wanted to sell. So when we introduced the plan to the United States, we very carefully arranged with Discount Corporation, where I was still on the board, that their traders would make a market in bank CDs parallel to the market they already made in Treasury bills and notes. Today this negotiable certificate of deposit is almost as important as straight checking-account deposits as a source of funds to the very big banks.

In the early days of our plan, we didn't need new capital for the bank, because Howard Sheperd, believing as old-fashioned bankers did that a bank can *never* have too much capital, had sold a lot of stock through rights issues in the early 1950s. This held down our earnings-per-share for the better part of a decade, but by 1963 the bank was growing so fast that our "capital ratio" was falling below what the examiners liked to see, and we went to market. The vehicle was a $200 million issue of convertible debentures (much more money than it would be today). The advantage of the convertible debenture was that interest rates on the bonds were lower (because there was also a play on the stock), and the dilution of our stockholders' equity would presumably be postponed until we had begun to earn enough on the new capital to pay it.

Our underwriter was First Boston. The terms were a coupon of $3\frac{3}{4}$ percent, with conversion to common shares at a price of $70 a share, about 20 percent above the then market price. But the day before the issue was to be brought to market, disaster struck, in the form of the foreign-exchange losses in our Brussels branch. Our lawyers and First Boston's lawyers agreed that this $8-million loss was "material" and would have to be reported. The issue had to be postponed and re-priced, to offer a sweeter 4 percent coupon and a lower conversion price of $66.75. Oddly, we probably wound up making money on this, because the higher coupon meant that holders of the debentures delayed converting them to stock somewhat longer than they otherwise would have done. Our dividends rose every year that I was president and chairman (and still do), but with the improved coupon on the bond (4 percent vs. $3\frac{3}{4}$ percent) it took an additional 18 months before the dividend on the stock into which the bond was convertible exceeded the interest we were paying on the bond. Because the 4 percent interest payment on the debenture was tax-deductible to the bank, while dividend payments are after taxes, our bottom line showed greater retained earnings than it would have showed if we'd been able to keep the original pricing of $3\frac{3}{4}$ percent and the bond had been converted earlier.

Then, as a last straw, on the morning of the day we were to go to our directors for approval of the new arrangements, James Coggeshall of First Boston arrived at my office at nine in the morning to tell me that two days after the scheduled sale day for our issue, his firm would be in the market selling bank bonds again. I was flabbergasted by his total unconcern about the obvious conflict, arising from the fact that the same customers of his firm would be interested in both issues and would seek advice on which to prefer. I told him that if he insisted on his "right" to manage both issues, we would exercise our "right" to remove his firm from the leadership of our syndicate, and proceed with the five firms now listed in the second "bracket." Moreover, I said I had to know by 10:00, because we had a board meeting. He excused himself, went to a conference room and made a phone call, and returned to say that his firm was dropping out of the Chase issue. The next day I had a call from George Woods, who had recently retired as chairman of First Boston, to apologize for his former firm's behavior.

While I waited for Coggeshall to change his mind, incidentally, I had a visit from André Meyer of Lazard Frères, who had scented something in the wind. He generously offered to underwrite the issue for us on what were really better terms than First Boston's, for First Boston had as usual included in its contract some protections for themselves. The obligation they were undertaking was to purchase and sell to the public that part of the convertible bonds issue not purchased by our existing stockholders (who had rights to buy first). So there would be some time between the day the issue first went on sale to stockholders and the day when they had to accept their commitment. Their contract, as is usual, provided for "escape clauses": if there were a major change in the condition of the bank, or in the economy, they didn't have to make their purchases. Meyer said he would waive that escape clause, agreeing that Lazard Frères would immediately put the money for their commitment into our account at the Federal Reserve, no questions asked. But when Coggeshall withdrew his previous suggestion that First Boston would do the Chase deal, too, I felt bound by our previous arrangements. Then, of course, Meyer and Lazard did the Chase deal. . . .

But we never got away from our funding problems, all the rest of my time at the bank. The one meeting I attended every day I was in New York was that of the money committee, and the most elaborate of our communications arrangements after headquarters was moved from 55 Wall Street to 399 Park Avenue was the closed-circuit television system that allowed midtown and Wall Street economists and market specialists to see each other during this mid-morning meeting, where we exchanged information about what our biggest customers were going to take from or pay into the bank that day, and what funds we would need to meet their demands and maintain our legally required reserves at the Fed. It was our policy that when the president or the chairman was out of New York, the other sent a letter at least every week, and more often twice a week, to describe what was happening at the bank. I have a stack of these letters, to me and from me, and there's scarcely one that doesn't express concern or relief about "the money position."

Although we had the negotiable CD in our armament, the Fed could determine whether or not we could use it. The top interest rate we could offer was subject to control by the Fed, without right of appeal. In 1966 and again in 1969, the Fed in effect stood us against the wall by keeping the rates we could offer below what the market was paying for commercial paper and even Treasury bills, which meant that the money simply ran out of the bank. To square our books on Wednesdays, when the Fed added up our reserve position for the week, we often had to borrow from the Fed itself, at the "discount window." This left us to a degree at the government's mercy, because the Fed insisted that access to the discount window was a privilege, not a right. What saved us was the availability of Eurodollars. There was no control over interest we could pay for funds abroad (it never would have occurred to anybody in the 1930s when the banking legislation was being written that an American bank would be borrowing dollars abroad). It cut into our profits to buy money abroad, but over the long run we would have been hurt worse if we had been unable to meet the needs of our good long-term borrowers.

Soon after my retirement, the Fed needed help from the banks to handle the crisis in the commercial-paper market that followed upon the collapse of Penn Central, and the compromise that was worked out established a category of large certificates of deposit—over $100,000—that would not be subject to interest-rate controls. Thereafter, Citibank never had to worry that money would actually be unobtainable. For my successors, the daily problem was not the availability but the price of money. You sleep a little better at night, but it may be even harder to make a living.

David Rockefeller

E. J. KAHN JR.

David Rockefeller was the youngest of five brothers and one sister. He continued to contribute and to achieve on a major scale in the many years after this article was written for *The New Yorker,* which omits his work with the Museum of Modern Art, Rockefeller University, the Trilateral Commission, New York City, and many other organizations devoted to social, artistic, and international purposes.

Before David Rockefeller decided to go to Russia last July for a conference on Soviet-American relations, he gave the trip a good deal of thought. There is nothing unusual about an ordinary American's visiting Russia nowadays, but, as Rockefeller realizes, he is not ordinary. Not only would he arrive bearing an emphatically capitalistic surname, the mere mention of which is supposed to suffuse Russians with wrath, but there was also the matter of his being the president of the Chase Manhattan Bank, a worldwide power structure with over $12 billion in assets and the kind of influence that that kind of money begets. Moreover, Rockefeller had heard hints that if he should get to the USSR he would probably be invited to confer with Premier Khrushchev, and there was no telling how explosively the Communist leader might react to a confrontation, on his home ground, with a notorious international banker. For a while, accordingly, Rockefeller wasn't sure he should go. While assessing its pros and cons, he told one acquaintance, "I wouldn't want to do anything disadvantageous to the country or the bank. I want to make sure I do what's appropriate."

"Appropriate" is a word that Rockefeller often uses. He does not mean by it that he is loath to do anything others might disapprove of; he means that he wants to do what it is proper and useful for someone to do who is endowed with his unique combination of vast personal and business resources, and who, because of these, is saddled with no less vast responsibilities. For any Rockefeller to do anything *in*appropriate, he feels, would reflect unfavorably, if not damagingly, on the entire clan, and would also raise doubts about that particular Rockefeller's ability to carry his fair share of the family's heavy joint burden. David Rockefeller was once fittingly presented to a dinner audience as "a man for whom life is an obligation, not a joy ride." And

Reprinted from *The New Yorker* (January 9, 1965), pp. 37–38, 40, 42, 46–47, 50, 52, 54–55. By permission; © 1965 E. J. Kahn Jr. Originally in *The New Yorker*. All rights reserved.

he himself, upon being asked not long ago how he and his wife went about helping their children adjust to their uncommon heritage, said "We've tried to teach them that they are fortunate but that along with their opportunities they'll have responsibilities. You can't expect to have the one without the other." Rockefeller has six children—two boys and four girls, the oldest 23 and the youngest 14. Some of his friends considered it a characteristically thoughtful touch on his part that, of the six, the one he elected to take to Russia with him was his second-oldest daughter, Neva, who is 20 and a junior at Radcliffe. The conference he attended was held in Leningrad, and her name, as it happens, is also that of the broad and handsome river that flows through the heart of the metropolis. Neva Rockefeller was actually named after her maternal grandmother, Neva Smith McGrath, but when Rockefeller arrived in Leningrad he could not resist letting the local citizenry leap to its own delighted, erroneous conclusion.

It was in Leningrad, on a Tuesday, that Rockefeller was told Khrushchev would like to see him the following afternoon at the Kremlin, in Moscow. Taking Neva with him, the banker went south by overnight train, and the next day participated with the Soviet leader in two and a half hours of what Rockefeller subsequently called "the most intensive conversation I've ever had with anyone." It was a far-ranging, if inconclusive, colloquy, covering, among other subjects, the capricious attitude of the Russians toward international copyright law, the failure of the Soviet Union to repay its wartime lend-lease obligations, and the possibility of increased trade between the two men's nations. Neither the Communist nor the capitalist arrived with any prepared memoranda; they talked off the cuff. (Khrushchev, who furnished an interpreter and some mineral water, acceded unhesitatingly to Rockefeller's request that Neva be permitted to take notes.) At one point, Rockefeller remarked that his mother had visited Russia in Czarist days— back in 1896, the year before she married John D. Rockefeller Jr. She had been travelling with her father, Senator Nelson Aldrich, of Rhode Island. That got Khrushchev going on what he called the inevitable evolutionary progress of the entire world toward Communism. Waving a hand toward the scribbling Neva, the Soviet leader told her father that sooner or later people everywhere would spontaneously embrace Communism. "Someday your daughter Neva will think as I do," the Russian said amiably. Neither Neva nor her father replied.

Rockefeller's concern about going to the USSR in the first place had been compounded by his awareness that although the Kremlin obviously knew who he was, there seemed to be some vagueness about this lower down the Party line. Two months earlier, he had had a letter from a Russian he'd met at a 1962 conference in the United States—a *Pravda* commentator who was also a deputy of the Supreme Soviet. In the course of plying Rockefeller with questions about the state of the American economy, this correspondent had inquired, "Is it true that you intend to enter politics, trying your chances in Ohio? If that is so, I wish you success." Whether the *Pravda* man had in mind Rockefeller's brother Nelson, the governor of New York and then still a contender for the Republican Presidential nomination, or his brother Winthrop, then the Republican gubernatorial nominee in Arkansas, was uncertain, but the mere question was unsettling to David Rockefeller, who has steadfastly shied away from active participation in politics since 1948, when he was an elector for Thomas E. Dewey. Many Americans have hoped that David Rockefeller *would* try his chances in politics. He has been publicly proposed for Mayor of New York, and several highly placed Republicans have privately indicated that they would be delighted to support him if he should ever indicate an interest in the presidency. Rockefeller is appreciative of such sentiments, but he is unswayed by them. For one thing, he is quite content with his present lot. "I can't imagine a more interesting job than mine, to tell you the honest truth," he said to a friend a few months ago. "The bank has dealings with everything. There is no field of activity it isn't involved in. It's a springboard for whatever interests one may have in any direction—a very good platform from which to participate in the economic advancement of the world."

Banking operations are so diverse that a very big bank, like the Chase, has a stake in nearly every legislative act. Nelson Rockefeller's political opponents periodically hint at dark conspiracies between the administration over which he presides and the bank over which his youngest brother presides. In 1963, for instance, when a bill to amend New York's liquor laws was under debate, one Albany legislator professed to [see] chicanery in a provision of the statute that would make it easier for department stores—some of which have big accounts with the Chase to sell whiskey. "Is this state being run by the governor or the Chase Bank?" the lawmaker demanded rhetorically. Up to the Goldwater stampede, it used to be customary at Republican National Convention time for disgruntled GOP conservatives to suggest that all Republican candidates were picked by the directors of the Chase Bank. The directors aren't quite as powerful as that, but the legend of their power has gained sufficient credence so that the most recent Republican candidate for governor of Illinois, Charles H. Percy, found it prudent to resign from the Chase board when he set out after the nomination. It is therefore hardly surprising if David Rockefeller goes out of his way to avoid partisan entanglement in his brother Nelson's legislative programs. "I've tried to be scrupulously careful not to give any substance to conflict-of-interest charges," David says. "I wouldn't want to do anything in the political field that seems inappropriate." He has been so scrupulous that not long ago one of his assistants at the bank complained, "I could get a lot more done in Albany when Averell Harriman was governor. . . ."

The *Christian Science Monitor* once described Rockefeller as "a businessman who is listened to all over the world." His prestige is substantial, and it is still growing. These days, New York City is the hub of the globe's money markets, and Rockefeller's voice, though he never raises it, is one of the most respected in the financial community. A downtown investment banker who is himself attentively listened to wherever he goes said the other day, "I can't believe that if a poll were taken today to ascertain who the outstanding person in Wall Street and banking circles is, there would be anybody who could compete with David. He is the best product that the capitalistic system has produced. . . ."

Rockefeller is familiar with most of the principal cities of most of the countries on earth. One he visited recently was Perth, in western Australia, from which he travelled 300 miles inland to inspect a 15-thousand-acre tract of pasture land that he had recently bought, with a partner, as a personal investment; he also inspected a million-and-a-half-acre tract nearby, on which the Chase International Investment Corporation, a subsidiary of the bank, had started a sheep-and-cattle-raising venture. The corporation is also involved in hotels in Puerto Rico and Liberia, a Brazilian ready-mix-concrete plant, a Nigerian cotton-textile mill, a Venezuelan paint factory, and a Turkish steel mill. Bank presidents have to keep hopping nowadays. Last year, the Chase opened branch banks in, among other spots, Bangkok, Singapore, and Hong Kong, and Rockefeller, a conscientious executive, has put in a ceremonial appearance at each unveiling. (The Chase had pulled out of Hong Kong in 1951, because the bank's management at the time was leery of getting mixed up, however indirectly, in trade with Communist China. While Rockefeller, who is of a less cautious managerial breed, was in Hong Kong last January, he made a speech saying that the United States might appropriately start to think about engaging in limited trade with China.)

The Chase has over 200 branch banks and representative offices around the world, and the resident officials of each one naturally want to make the most of it whenever a big frog from headquarters hops into their small outlying pond. The crowds that assemble to greet Rockefeller at airports—they include not only branch-bank managers but finance ministers, American ambassadors, reporters, photographers—are sometimes large enough to make bystanders wonder what movie star is approaching. (When Rockefeller visited St. Croix in the Virgin Islands, a few years ago, the leading hotel took a full page in the local newspaper for an ad headed "Welcome, David Rockefeller," and in the same issue he was further greeted by an editorial headed "Welcome!") His wife, Peggy, who is a woman of considerable charm and of a fairly acid wit, which nicely complements her husband's habitual blandness of manner, sometimes accompanies him on these jaunts. After one expedition to Pakistan and India, she remarked, "Wherever David goes, there always seem to be banks that want, more than anything else in the world, to feed him."

Rockefeller himself is undaunted by schedules that rarely leave him a free moment from eight in the morning until midnight. Inertia appalls him. A while ago, he was making a swing through the Middle East with . . . a Chase executive vice-president. . . . Upon concluding some business they had in Beirut, the two men said goodbyes all around and went to the airport, only to learn that because of a last-minute hitch their plane would depart three hours late. [His colleague], who had been trying gamely to match Rockefeller's whirlwind pace, was overjoyed at the prospect of even that respite, but Rockefeller would have none of it. "As soon as David learned of the delay, he rang up a couple of men in Beirut he hadn't had time to talk to. . . . They were some sort of experts on Middle Eastern politics. They hustled out to the airport and huddled with him in one of those special side lounges where airports put people like David and sheiks, and he dug for information right up to takeoff time. With David, there's never a moment of nothingness."

Whether Rockefeller is travelling on business or for pleasure, his motto is "*Carpe horam.*" He is so relentless an organizer that among friends who have taken trips with him he is known as "the cruise director. . . ."

Rockefeller rarely visits any country without paying at least a courtesy call—more often than not it is a business call—on its head of state. Such a gesture is expected of him, much as if he were a head of state himself. (*Pravda's* account of his seminar with Khrushchev, while it was constrained, accorded him a measure of coequality. "N. S. Khrushchev and D. Rockefeller had a frank discussion of questions that are of mutual interest," the paper said.). . .

When the chiefs of foreign countries visit the United States, they are likely to pay reciprocal calls on Rockefeller. Their schedules here are tight, as a rule, but they manage to make room for him. Sidney J. Weinberg, the senior potentate of Goldman, Sachs said not long ago, "David's always got an Emperor or Shah or some other damn person over here, and is always giving him lunches. If I went to all the lunches he gives for people like that, I'd never get any work done.." . .

Rockefeller. . . has a placid and kindly disposition. A friend of his of 25 years' standing . . . said that during that entire period he has never heard Rockefeller utter an unpleasant word or a petty one about anybody. It is hard to find anybody, moreover, who has a cross word to utter about Rockefeller. A Wall Street friend of his—André Meyer, the head of Lazard Frères—says, "There's nothing on earth I wouldn't do for David. It's not because he's a Rockefeller but because he's the kind of human being you *want* to do something for. I've never seen him mean. I've always seen him acting with poise and class, and greatness. In this financial jungle, you have all kinds of animals. He's the best."

These days, the survival of the fittest in that particular jungle depends as much on endurance as on equanimity. A rugged constitution is as essential for a peripatetic banker as for a touring golf pro or a campaigning politician. Rockefeller seems to be endowed with an almost unlimited reservoir of energy. His looks are deceptive. He has a smooth face, as round as a full moon, from which a needlelike nose projects sharply; in broad outline it is the kind of face a child might construct from an orange and a toothpick. He stands nearly six feet tall, weighs a 185 pounds, and, at first glance, seems a mite flabby. As a boy, he was. Ascending a pyramid on a trip to Egypt with his parents in 1928, he had to be helped by two Arab guides, one pulling and one pushing. Nowadays, he is solid. He never relaxes. When he appears to be getting tired, he refreshes himself by shifting his attention from one subject or one person to another. "Where he gets his strength from and why he keeps going as he does is hard to understand," his wife said. "I think it's simply because he loves work."

Rockefeller once told his eldest son, "Whatever you do, if you do it hard enough you'll enjoy it. The important thing is to work and work hard." At home, as abroad, he himself customarily operates at a non-stop clip for 16 hours a day. Friends who want to snare him for dinner have to start negotiations several months in advance. His interests are so diverse and his approach to them is so intense that they have to compete for his attention. In a curious way, his time has become more valuable than his money. He is able to make the most of his time by not having to worry much about the humdrum logistical aspects of life; chauffeured limousines and private airplanes are usually available to him, and once, when somebody asked one of his assistants how in the world Rockefeller ever kept track of his financial affairs, the man replied succinctly, "The Rockefellers can afford very good accounting." Even with all this help, however, his efficiency awes all those who know him.

"All the Rockefellers have been brought up to love humanity," a rival banker remarked recently. "David also likes people."

It is just as well that Rockefeller does like people—even, apparently, when they are making speeches at banquets or slapping backs at conventions—for a banker is expected to be accessible to all sorts of them, especially if they have accounts running into seven figures or more. Customer relations are of great importance in banking, and Rockefeller rates high among his peers as a practitioner of that unctuous art. "David will dine with insufferable bores and have lunch with almost *anybody*," the president of another big bank says admiringly. "He'll do things that you wouldn't ask an assistant vice-president to do." Rockefeller sees nothing unusual about his approachability. "It's one of the important tasks of bank officers to see customers," he says. "It would be a mistake not to make oneself available."

George S. Johnston

FRED BLEAKLEY

George Johnston guided the Scudder organization for over a quarter of a century, graciously moving it from a dispersed "partnership" of separate offices into an effective corporate whole. As a result, it not only enjoyed renewed growth and restored vitality, but also regained the better aspects of a true professional partnership. Along the way, clients never received other than first priority.

George S. Johnston, the burly and affable president of Scudder, Stevens and Clark, just may be the holder of one of the world's least enviable skiing records. It seems that on three of his first five visits to the slopes, in 1946, in 1948, and again in 1949, he wound up the day's exercise with his leg in a cast. "On my first try, some college friends took me to the top of a mountain," he recalls somewhat ruefully, "and 300 yards down the slope I met a tree. The next time, I ended up in a brook, and I seem to have conveniently blocked the third occasion out of my mind." Where lesser men might have called it quits, though, Johnston went on to become an accomplished skier; this spring, as he returned from a skiing vacation in the French Alps with two of his sons, he could even boast: "I haven't broken any more legs, either."

It goes without saying that George Johnston is an extraordinarily persistent man. And the quality is most apparent in his job at the helm of the world's largest investment counseling firm. During a time of turmoil for the industry, the counseling business, and Scudder itself, is being sorely tested. . . .

In any event, Johnston's reaction to the mergers and budding competition [in the industry] has been to introduce new services and push ahead with reorganization of his firm's structure. Scudder is a partnership, but five years ago Johnston urged a reorganization along corporate lines and with corporate titles. Thus as president, Johnston, who is 46, now is part of an eight-man management board.

• • •

Excerpted from *Institutional Investor* 5 (May 1971), pp. 41–42, 44, 65–68. This copyrighted material is reprinted with permission from: **Institutional Investor, Inc.**, 488 Madison Avenue, New York, NY 10022.

Johnston himself seems to have come right out of central casting for his role as president of Scudder. He by no means gives the impression of being a dynamo, yet in addition to his dogged persistence, those who know him also comment on his meticulous concern for detail, his foresight about the business and what is often described as a down-to-earth friendliness. In fact, conversations with him give one the feeling that Johnston is the man next door, pausing to chat while raking leaves. In appearance, he is something over six feet tall, has a ruddy complexion with a scattering of freckles, wears horn-rimmed glasses and dresses conservatively. His manner is subdued, and at times he strikes visitors as slightly absent-minded. For example, advised of a phone call from a client, he walks to his desk and buttons his coat before picking up the receiver. What he says, though, is pure and persuasive business—laced with the slightest trace of a Southern accent. This is understandable since Johnston was born and raised in Memphis, and this background has left its mark on the manner in which he deals with people. "It is almost impossible to get through a door behind George Johnston," says one colleague, who also reports that a note from Johnston to his cleaning lady about where to place a lamp is written with the same tact with which he would address the firm's largest client.

• • •

In management meetings Johnston will often start off a discussion by laying out two completely opposite—but thoroughly thought-out—sides of an argument. And he seems to be motivated by what he describes as a desire "to get things done completely and as correctly as possible. You're letting someone down if you don't. If you have a client and send him a report full of obvious errors that should have been caught, he'll lose confidence and respect in you."

• • •

After the war, Johnston returned to Yale, became a Phi Beta Kappa and earned a degree in economics—and thereafter came plenty of job offers. One he recalls was $2,000 a year—plus lunch—from U.S. Trust Co., but he decided to go with Scudder for "not a helluva lot more," he says.

He was assigned to the bond department under Sidney Homer and quickly was exposed to the intricacies of the business. . . . During that period, Johnston lived at the New York Boys' Club free, in return for working with the youngsters four nights a week. He now has four boys of his own, having married—his wife's name is Cynthia—the weekend before being recalled to the Korean War. When he returned again, Johnston decided—much to Homer's regret—to get a broader feel for the business by going into the investment counseling end. At this time, he also spent three years at night attending NYU's Graduate School of Business. By 1960, he was moving up rapidly at Scudder, and few were surprised when he succeeded to the top job in 1968.

• • •

These days Johnston is also wrestling with the major issues that confront the industry as a whole. One of special concern to Scudder is institutional membership [on the New York Stock Exchange], and the firm prodded the Investment Counsel Association to write William McChesney Martin stating the opposition's case. Johnston personally wrote Martin a similar letter in mid-March, and he also went on record as favoring more fully negotiated rates which, he says, would take away the pressure of firms such as his to become NYSE members and enter the brokerage business. "We would be lousy brokers," Johnston says flatly. Not only would such moves set up the potential for conflict of interest within his own shop, he says, but also major firms which are needed to position blocks would suffer. . . .

George Johnston, as one colleague puts it, "has the patience of a truck." And he has learned this can pay off, as a story related by a golfing buddy indicates. Jonathan Mason, who runs the Japan Fund, says that he was "perfectly awful" when he first took up the game, and at the National, most club members politely declined to have such a duffer in their foursome. But not Johnston; he patiently took Mason in tow and helped him to improve his game. It may sound apocryphal, but a year later the two men teamed up and walked off with the club championship.

Jonathan Bell Lovelace

CHARLES D. ELLIS

Jonathan Bell Lovelace, an exceptionally perceptive entrepreneur and an unusually modest man, founded and financed, through 20 long years of breakeven results, the organization his son would guide to world leadership in investment management: Capital Group Companies.

In 1929, even the most thoughtful observer would hardly have identified the modest 34-year-old former investment banker, then taking the train to Los Angeles with his wife and son, as the man who would soon launch the firm that, by the end of the century, would be widely recognized as one of the leading professional investment management organizations in the world. Jonathan Bell Lovelace had a rendezvous with Capital Research—and the emerging profession of investment management.

Lovelace grew up in southern Alabama, where his family was active in timber and railroading. He trained to become an architect in just two years' study at Alabama Polytechnic, and one year later had earned a master's degree, showing a special aptitude for mathematics. (He also managed a championship football team and developed an enduring interest in team sports.)

Enlisting in the Army for European duty in the World War, he encountered new concepts and technologies. He was in a group that pioneered the new field of anti-aircraft artillery, solving the vital, but very difficult task was learning how to hit fast-moving targets. Lovelace provided the necessary calculations and his was the first American artillery unit to shoot down a German plane. For many years, he kept a large chunk of wood from the fuselage as a souvenir.

Lovelace, who mustered out as a Captain, had met new people with interesting new ideas, including Edward MacCrone. Back home, MacCrone had split from a firm that was a predecessor of Merrill Lynch to form a small brokerage firm in Detroit—then the equivalent in industrial creativity to today's Silicon Valley—and urged Lovelace to get into the new and growing field of investments. He hoped Lovelace would become his firm's research "statistician" and assured him that such a position would be open if he were ever interested.

Noting that only one major building had been constructed in the state of Alabama during the year he graduated, Lovelace was resolved to leave architecture and make his future elsewhere. After the Great War, Lovelace had a brief stint in California where he and his brothers, Jay and Jim, bought a date ranch near Indio. But the war's end abruptly ended the sugar shortage that had contributed to the higher demand and price level of dates (and to the favorable environment for the Lovelace family's venture in date growing). By 1919, Lovelace decided to join his Army friend in his small stockbrokerage firm and move to Detroit.

Learning from visits to Scotland and a study of the Scottish unit trusts, Lovelace's new firm formed an investment company that very nearly became the first U.S. open-end mutual fund. However, before underwriting the new fund, Lovelace and MacCrone wanted to obtain at least some kind of regulatory "official approval" for their new idea. Their logical choice was to seek the blessing of Michigan's banking commissioner. But he felt the banks were already pressed by an excess of competition and turned them down, saying: "Gentlemen, this is a very interesting idea, but it will mean competition for our state's banks, so I decline to authorize it."

MacCrone's firm did quite well at organizing and sponsoring closed-end investment trusts—often concentrating on investments in a specific industry or region of the country—based on Lovelace's adaptation of the Scottish concept that individual investors would fare far better if they combined their investments, spread the risk, and retained professional investment management rather than buying individual (often speculative) stocks on margin through retail stock salesmen. In a strong market environment, Lovelace prospered; he became a Partner in E.C. MacCrone in 1924.

When Lovelace championed the idea of rigorous "field research," he and MacCrone had a series of disagreements over the allocation of time devoted to research. They finally agreed on a compromise: Research would be done Lovelace's way, but enough time must be allocated to provide coverage of the firm's new issue underwritings. Lovelace soon became a pioneer in investment research—and deeply convinced of its value and importance to sound investing.

By 1928, E.C. MacCrone was prospering, and most business executives anticipated a bright future. But based on his research into market price versus true investment value, Lovelace had become increasingly concerned about what he considered an excess of enthusiasm among investors. (One of Lovelace's calculations showed that the total market price of one bank's common shares equaled its total deposits, which in a bank, of course, are its *liabilities*.)

Lovelace became so bearish on the market that he sold off most of his stocks and bonds in the summer of 1929 and tried, unsuccessfully, to persuade his firm to become far more conservative.

Unable to convince his colleagues to adopt his cautious stance, Lovelace decided to withdraw from the stockbrokerage business. Modestly, Lovelace would later confess he had not liquidated everything: Responding to his partners' requests that he not visibly withdraw completely, he had left some of his capital in the firm.

He decided to move back to the then distant locale of Los Angeles. As usual when traveling to California, he took the train.

By 1931, Lovelace had established a small firm, Lovelace, Dennis & Renfrew—that was the nucleus of what later became Capital Research and Management Company—to develop the information needed for his activities as financial advisor to California companies and as expert witness on the issues surrounding companies struggling out of Depression-induced bankruptcy. Clients included Lockheed, Pacific Mutual Life, Capitol Records, where he was a founding director, and Walt Disney, where he served as a director and worked particularly closely with Roy Disney. If he couldn't work on *architectural* structures, joked Lovelace, he'd work on *financial* structures.

In 1933, he was asked to take over management of what remained of one of the investment trusts his Detroit stockbrokerage firm had sponsored before the Crash. With leverage in its capital structure, it had lost over 70% of its value during the market's collapse. When recapitalized as The Investment Company of America, it had assets of less than $5 million.

For the next 20 years, Capital Research operated, on average, at breakeven. Today, senior executives look back with gentle smiles and shaking heads at the economics that were an integral part of the serious pursuit of research. To save the time cost of travel to conduct research on companies far from California, the firm opened offices in New York City and Detroit in the late '30s. To control expenses, office-to-office telephone calls (for which the first three minutes incurred a rather high "connection" cost) were made in carefully planned and coordinated groups with each person standing in line and taking a turn to conduct his part of the pending business. The New York office was fitted out with old furniture and received S&P's loose-leaf "tear sheets" on public companies from the office in Los Angeles—but only after the new replacement "tear sheets" had been received by the main office. (If NYC was 3 hours ahead of LA, staffers joked, it was also about one *year* behind!) Most interoffice communication was done by mail: After all, 3¢ stamps beat long distance toll charges!

In addition to his cost-conscious manner and his commitment to bottom-up research, Lovelace believed in developing a culture of working with people you really liked and who shared a disciplined commitment to rationality in investing and integrity in serving investors.

A gentle man, Lovelace was "certainly not effusive" with praise and was exceptionally modest about his own contributions and achievements. "He was also slow to criticize," says Bob Kirby. "Everyone in the organization during his tenure felt that they had a lot of elbow room and were given ample time to perform before final judgments were made. I don't know how he accomplished it, but you always had the feeling that he was well aware of what you were doing and how you were doing, without any feeling that he was peeking over your shoulder. He understood that mistakes, even big ones, are an inherent part of this business and that you had to judge an individual, as you would a company, in a longer-term framework."

In 1953, Lovelace suffered a heart attack at age 58.* As everyone pitched in to share the management responsibilities, leadership devolved to others—and an important organizational development was launched at the suggestion of Lovelace's son and successor, Jon: the multiple counselor system of portfolio management. Lovelace and his colleagues were strongly opposed to a "committee" system because their own recent experience had shown committee decisions were all too often cautious compromises with risk aversion dominating creative thinking and social accommodation deflecting decisive action. They were equally opposed, also with experience, to the typical "solo" fund manager, recognizing that individuals could get off track or caught up with their own good or bad performance.

In contrast, the multiple counselor system divides the total fund into three or four or more separate parts, with each manager in authority over—and accountable for—the performance of his or her portion. The structure has been expanded to include a portion managed directly by the firm's

---

* He would live until 1979.

research analysts. Each counselor is expected and encouraged to act on his own strongest convictions. All transactions and investment performance are measured and reported frequently to all counselors, who are encouraged to help each other by sharing ideas and information, but are clearly expected to act independently and boldly. An investment committee watches over the process to ensure that it remains within the overall objective of a fund.

As a fund grows larger, it can be divided among more counselors to maintain each counselor's part of the total portfolio at a manageable size. Thus, the total fund can increase virtually indefinitely without size imposing heavy constraints on the counselors' individual investment effectiveness. Another benefit is that counselors are unlikely to get caught up in the "me-my-mine" syndrome that can lead to over-confidence at market peaks—or doldrums of discouragement at market lows.

Politically, Lovelace was a Jeffersonian Democrat. He allowed and encouraged young people with ideas to run with them. In 1955, he supported Coleman Morton's initiative to launch an early venture into international investing: International Resources Fund. In 1962, Ken Matheson-Gerst was encouraged to begin compiling the data on international investing that would develop into the standard international market index. In 1967, Howard Schow was encouraged to develop the firm's first domestic growth fund.

"Jon Lovelace Sr. was a very shy and private man, but he attracted many capable and powerful people because of his insights and because he was never afraid, as so many are, of smart people with ideas," explains Howard Schow. "His main love was to serve as an investment banker to real entrepreneurs. He was what the French call an 'accouché'—a midwife to ideas and the ventures that could bring them to life."

"When I started in 1965, JBL was already something of a legend/father figure, but the organization still reflected his personality," says Bob Kirby. "It is surprising that even though JBL has not been a part of the organization for the better part of two decades, the tone that he set still strongly exists. In a business where a lot of egoism exists, the organization still observes the tradition of egalitarianism and deference that was so much a part of JBL's persona."

"He was truly low-profile and unassuming," explains Kirby, "but his image of ultra conservatism was a bit of a fraud. He was a risk taker. Many innovations that were viewed as risky by some of the senior people in the 1950s and 1960s were implemented under JBL's sponsorship."

Lovelace believed deeply in the productivity of thorough, original research into investment values that others would have overlooked—research that would determine the actual worth of a company—followed by buying at reasonable prices relative to analyzed prospects. Looking at a company's numbers was never enough. Believing that management made the difference, he said, "The only difference between Chrysler Corporation and its predecessor was Walter Chrysler."

Combining careful research with a long-term view of valuation, Capital's portfolio turnover remains well below industry norms. "Lovelace believed in independent or contrary thinking. Combining this view with his genuine politeness, Lovelace often explained that it's important to be accommodating. When everyone wants to sell, you accommodate them and buy. When everyone wants to buy, you accommodate and sell to them."

In 1954, Lovelace established an international investment staff—at the urging of his son Jon—a full generation before such an idea would even start to become generally popular, to support the new International Resources Fund. In 1962, an overseas research office was opened in Geneva—partly to find international stocks to invest in, but largely to do the original research needed to evaluate American companies in a realistic international context. In the early 1960s, when most American institutions had no foreign investments, Investment Company of America had over 10% of its portfolio invested internationally.

While its main business would not actually be managing personal trusts, but pension trusts, the trust company's first client relationship began at the request of a wealthy individual investor who wanted Capital Research to act as his investment fiduciary. The firm soon became one of the largest managers of corporate and public pension funds.

With his innovative, creative approach to designing and building Capital Research, Jonathan Lovelace may have been exercising the talents and aspirations that nearly had him in architecture. When Lovelace's son Jon, himself a very private and modest man, was asked what he thought his father would say was his most significant accomplishment, he said he thought his father would demur that he hadn't done anything spectacular.

Others will hold that the Lovelaces, father and son, have nurtured a remarkably collegial organization of unusually gifted and highly dedicated professionals by both declining to take the spotlight within or outside the firm and by sharing generously the ownership value created and by exemplifying a quiet dedication to realizing the highest standards of professional service to investors.

David Fisher recalls a conversation from nearly a generation ago that made a lasting impression—partly in its thoughtful rigor on the *substance* of the topic under discussion; partly on the collegial style or tone of the discussion. Fisher was 28; Jonathan Lovelace was in his 70s. They had an appointment for luncheon. Lovelace wore a three-piece suit and a hat and deferentially called David "Mr. Fisher."

"What attracted you, Mr. Fisher, to this type of work?" enquired Lovelace after they were seated at their table.

Fisher ventured to explain his appreciation for the marvelous operating leverage that could come to a well-managed investment organization with relatively fixed costs if the market rose and new assets came in. Lovelace, whose career had shown he was clearly comfortable taking productive business risks, was concerned. Explaining that he doubted there was any real operating leverage cycle-to-cycle over the long term in investment management, Lovelace suggested that if there *appeared* to be any real leverage, he would think this was more likely an indicator that not enough was being invested in the organization's current and future *capabilities* to do its work really well. "Jonathan Lovelace's concern about investing enough in the future continues to be a hallmark of the organization today," explains Fisher.

With design innovations making seminal contributions, the tiny regional investment company Jonathan Bell Lovelace took over in what then must have seemed an unlikely area of the country would grow in assets managed to $1.1 billion in three funds supervised by 100 employees by 1967. By 1995, it would become an organization of 3,000 employees responsible for over $200 billion—and widely respected by professional investors as continuously one of the world's very best.

Arnold Bernhard

VARTANIG G. VARTAN

Arnold Bernhard, a pioneer in the application of statistics in Finance, invented Value Line and made it the best known information service available to investors. He built an investment data base, applied a constant discipline to its use, developed an organization around it, and led this organization from its inception in 1936 until his death in 1987. This obituary is from the *New York Times*.

For more than half a century, Mr. Bernhard presided over the company [Value Line Inc.] and its flagship publication, the Value Line Investment Survey, which each week ranks 1,700 stocks for their projected market performance. This computerized system is based mainly on historical price and earnings trends, and more than 134,000 subscribers pay $495 annually to receive it.

"The market, to a large degree, is a captive of its past as well as an anticipation of the future," Mr. Bernhard once said. . . .

His innovations in stock market forecasting flew in the face of Wall Street brokerage houses that preferred to stress corporate earnings predictions and other techniques. His approach also contradicted the "efficient market hypothesis," which holds that information is reflected in stock prices so quickly that no attempt to beat the market can succeed in the long run.

From the outset—the first issue of the investment survey was cranked out on a mimeograph machine in 1936—Mr. Bernhard sought to find a standard of value for stocks "that would not give way to emotionalism."

This approach reflected personal experience: in the 1929 crash his mother lost the insurance money left by his father. "I kept telling her to sell her Cities Service stock, but she refused," he recalled. The stock eventually fell to $3 a share, from $50.

Mr. Bernhard originally used a separate mathematical equation for each company. [Eventually], working with Samuel Eisenstadt, his chief statistician, he devised a single formula to apply to the entire spectrum of 1,700 stocks—in effect measuring one stock against all others. Its success placed the Value Line Investment Survey permanently on the map of the financial world.

But the system, like all others, is far from fool proof. It [once] took a beating on oil service stocks . . . because a high ranking based on historical performance neglected to take into account an impending glut in the global oil supply that was to decimate profits. [Later], . . . Value Line's rigid approach misjudged a difficult market environment.

Mr. Bernhard's company became a valuable training ground for hundreds of security analysts who, over the years, left his less-than-princely salaries to seek fame and fortune elsewhere. Some became money managers, and others founded brokerage firms. One of the best-known alumni is John S. R. Shad, who went on to become chairman of the Securities and Exchange Commission and is now Ambassador to the Netherlands.

Mr. Bernhard's reputation for discipline dominated corporate life at Value Line, where employees were required to sign in and out of the office. A tall, somewhat autocratic man with a clipped mustache, he turned a chilly shoulder to prospective heir apparents, thus causing a number of aspiring executives to leave. "I'm told there are big reunions of Value Line alumni, but I'm never invited," he told an interviewer. "I'm not as chummy a person as I'd like to be."

The line of succession finally became clear in April 1985 when his daughter, Jean Bernhard Buttner, now 53, was named president and chief operating officer. Value Line announced yesterday that she would assume the duties of chief executive officer. . . .

The Bernhard business empire often attracted suitors, reportedly including such corporate powerhouses as Dun & Bradstreet, American Express and Merrill Lynch. When they turned up at his door, Mr. Bernhard would listen to their offers, smile and raise his price. "The truth was that he really didn't want to sell," one colleague said. "Value Line and the ranking system were his consuming passion."

Instead of selling out to another company, Mr. Bernhard made Value Line a public company with an offering of some shares in May 1983; the family interests retained 81 percent of the common stock. In addition, Mr. Bernhard, who was listed in "The Forbes Four Hundred," a compilation of the richest Americans, kept much of his personal wealth invested in Value Line's group of mutual funds.

The son of immigrants—his father came from Germany and his mother from Rumania—Mr. Bernhard was born on December 2, 1901, in New York City. He grew up in Newark, Delaware, and Rutherford, New Jersey, and graduated from Williams College.

He went to Wall Street after a spell as a drama critic for *Time* magazine. He wrote a play, *Bull Market*, that never reached the stage. In later years, however, he helped finance several Broadway plays. . . .

While working briefly for Jesse Livermore, a legendary speculator, Mr. Bernhard wrote a report recommending copper stocks. Mr. Livermore, unpredictable as usual, promptly sold the stocks short.

Mr. Bernhard then moved to Moody's Investors Service, where he worked as an analyst and later as an account executive. But, after the Depression began, he lost his job in 1931.

That year he founded Arnold Bernhard & Company when some former clients asked him to continue managing their money. Today Value Line, in addition to issuing its various publications, serves as an investment adviser for its 14 mutual funds and also manages money for pension funds and other clients, with combined assets of about $7 billion. Arnold Bernhard & Company is now mainly a non-operating company that holds the family's controlling block of Value Line Inc. stock.

Edward C. Johnson II

GILBERT EDMUND KAPLAN AND CHRIS WELLES

Edward C. Johnson—the fabled "Mr. Johnson" of investment management folklore—pioneered a new approach to mutual fund investing. As the leader and source of inspiration to his portfolio managers, he caused his Fidelity Management to transform mutual funds from savings into investment vehicles. Then, he taught investors to demand performance as an investment goal.

The origin of performance as an investment concept traces back a little more than a quarter of a century ago, to the time when a quiet Boston lawyer named Edward C. Johnson II, acquired a small firm called Fidelity Management and Research and began to mold it into a rather special

Excerpted from *The Money Managers* (New York, 1969), by Gilbert Edmund Kaplan and Chris Welles, editors, pp. 95–99, 101–102. Copyright © 1969 by Institutional Investor Systems, Inc. Reprinted by permission of Random House, Inc.

place where money was managed in a way it had never been managed before. "Mister Johnson," as this dean of money managers is almost universally described, accomplished the revolution by creating an environment—unique then and unusual even now—where individuals could devise their own individual strategies toward the overall goal of achieving maximum gains.

The results of this experiment were great. Most significantly, Fidelity showed everyone that aggressive, intensive money management with emphasis on capital appreciation could produce consistent, superior gains without undue risk, and that satisfaction with a fixed, annual yield on one's investment was unrealistic and imprudent. Fidelity also produced a wide variety of other practices which have today become synonymous with investment professionalism: notably the use of charts and the courting of Wall Street analysts by acting on their information and paying for it rapidly with commission business. The key to its success was its avowed cultivation of the individual, which attracted and developed . . . legendary masters. . . . Above all, Fidelity seems to have acquired a quality larger than its success in investing other people's money. Old Fidelians, even those who no longer work there, speak of it with the lavish nostalgia usually reserved for places like Scott Fitzgerald's Princeton. They may have moved on (sigh) but that was where it all came alive.

If you ask what this enthusiasm rests upon, they invariably mention "freedom" and "individualism." But it is not simply that the funds under management are left to individual portfolio managers rather than a committee. Fidelity's freedom is something more extreme and more pervasive.

It all comes back, everyone agrees, to the man who took over the place 26 years ago. "Fidelity," says one Street chartist, "is the lengthened shadow of Mr. Johnson."

Mr. Johnson is spare, sprightly, and though he is 71 he possesses enormous but restrained energy and a boyish delight in ideas. One associate describes him as a "mild-mannered, Clark Kent-type of guy." Typically his conversation turns to fairly cosmic ideas, and he seems very much at home with them. When he talks he holds his hands out, as if catching a volley ball or measuring a fish. What he is doing is shaping concepts.

Mr. Johnson does not like to be pinned down. If you ask him how he runs the institution, for instance, he scurries away. "Oh, I don't run anything. It runs itself," he says. "I'm just an assistant." He describes Fidelity's recent activities as something with which he has only a tenuous connection. "The diversification of the management company is something I watch with fascination," he will say. When asked when he will retire from doing whatever it is he does there, he tosses the question away as if it were rather rude. "I have no idea when," he replies, then follows with a devastating piece of self-effacement. "The ideal is that when you appear in the death columns people will say, 'Oh, isn't he here any more?'"

This is not all false modesty. When you ask his employees what kind of influence he exerts, they describe it in the same way. "He has run the company by not showing himself, sort of like Buddha," says one Fidelity man. Perhaps Mr. Johnson, an ardent student of Eastern philosophy, thinks of himself a little that way too: ruling by what one of his favorite writers, Zen expert Alan W. Watts, calls "the law of reversed effort," whereby "nothing is more powerful and creative than emptiness."

Certainly he tries to leave those around him as empty as possible. The one who compares him to Buddha notes that "Mr. Johnson has instant recall on the stock market. He can tell you what the market did on June 2, 1936. Yet he never exerts pressure on you. He never says: 'This is what happened 10 years ago so now I think you should do this.' You have to go to him and ask him what he thinks of the current situation. Even then he may throw the question back at you."

From this, a picture of what freedom means at Fidelity begins to emerge. Mr. Johnson describes its purpose this way: "You want an environment where people can develop their talents to the greatest extent. How do you do that? It's just one word: attitude. You want the greatest degree of *laissez faire* without chaos. Children know you love them and that you're always there and otherwise you leave them alone and that's it. That's the way it is here, too, I think. What you want to get away from is an organization and create an organism. Separate cells working together in something completely natural and unplanned."

What is the raw material for this process? What kind of man excels in such an environment? Here, again, Mr. Johnson is so nebulous that the answers almost seem not to be answers. "We want a man with an instinctive sense of value, an artist," he says. "Investing is like any art. We don't want the theoretical man with a lot of words, the so-called intellectual. We like the young man who will come in and not have ideas that are too firm and counter to our own. This doesn't mean we don't want a high level of difference of opinion; we thrive on it. I love prima donnas. They blow off steam and then go off and do something artistic again."

With so little direction, how do you recognize the good people?

"The cruel end result is in the funds. With stocks, in the long run you will see."

How do you hold the people who survive this test?

You don't. "We start off with the assumption that when you get somebody good and he pays off in a big way it's difficult to hold him. When he goes off, believe it or not, this is a strengthening thing. Besides, a star is at his best on the way up. Somebody leaving to go after a glamorous future is the best possible incentive for the men here."

There is one element missing from Mr. Johnson's picture of the Fidelity environment, and that is the mechanism that creates this organism of individualistic artistic prima donnas. Is it just the warm happy bath of freedom in which they are swimming? Hardly, to hear Mr. Johnson speak. For when he talks about the process that develops people, he says things like "struggle and trouble bring out the most glorious flavors." Or "change is what matters. If you read Eric Hoffer the way I do, you realize that change is a painful and often soul-wrenching experience.." . .

How, then, does one learn at Fidelity? Where do the impulses come from?

Here comes that nebulousness again. "All this thing is pure contagion," says Mr. Johnson. "The great golfers were caddies who watched the good players." . . .

If you give the right man such exposure, Mr. Johnson believes, the result can be exciting. "I have a theory," he says, "that if a person has talent that's oriented in the general direction of the stock market, he and the market together will develop a personality beyond anything else he could have developed alone. So many things affect his work that finding out about them gives him a voraciousness for life. The free exchange of ideas, the intellectual equivalent of rubbing elbows, develops his talent to the greatest extent."

Edward C. Johnson III

DAN ROTTENBERG

Building on his father's foundation, Ned Johnson has made Fidelity not only one of the largest but also one of the most innovative financial service organizations in the world. This sketch provides background as well as insight.

Because Ned Johnson owns control of Fidelity, he can do with the company as he pleases—and he often does. When Johnson was unable to hail a cab on Boston's streets one day, he started his own private-car service. When one of his executives suggested buying a chain of art galleries, Johnson replied that the venture had about a 25 percent chance of success—then shrugged and added, "If you want to do it, go ahead." His idea of fun is to spend days immersing himself in a new computer system. Once he even assumed the starring role—as a high-net-worth Fidelity customer—in a video he showed

Excerpted from *Town & Country* (April 1992), pp. 159–160. © 1992. Reprinted by permission of the author.

during a speech to a marketing association. "It is obviously not what I am paid for," Johnson acknowledges. "But there has to be a certain amount of time for frivolity."

If Johnson's business philosophy sounds like a recipe for corporate disaster cooked up by a blue-blooded dilettante whose privileged background has insulated him from life's harsh realities, there's a good reason. Johnson inherited Fidelity from his father, an attorney who was descended from two generations of partners in C. F. Hovey & Company, Boston's premier dry-goods store; they in turn were descended from Yankee Brahmins who first set foot in America in 1635. And indeed, to most of his colleagues, Johnson does suggest some droll, day-dreaming character, like James Thurber's Walter Mitty.

But where Walter Mitty's daydreams never evolved beyond the realm of fantasy, most of Ned Johnson's wildest fantasies have come true. Since 1972, when he took over Fidelity from his fabled father—the mutual-fund pioneer E. C. Johnson II—the company has grown from a handful of mutual funds with $3 billion under management to a $160-billion international financial conglomerate that includes the nation's largest mutual-fund company and its second-largest discount brokerage firm. In the process of attracting more than 3 million customers, Fidelity has revolutionized the mutual-fund industry—and, by extension, has revolutionized Americans' savings and investment habits.

Thanks largely to Fidelity's service and marketing innovations—many of which sprang not from committees but directly from Ned Johnson's head—today more than half of America's households have money invested in a mutual fund (compared to a reported 3 percent at the peak of the so-called go-go 1960s). From 1980 to 1990, mutual funds expanded from a $100-billion industry to a $1-trillion industry—with Fidelity's constantly expanding family of funds accounting for nearly 15 percent of that total.

Thanks also to the Johnson family philosophy of "laissez faire without chaos," plus an assortment of bonuses, incentives and "phantom stock" arrangements, Fidelity has somehow managed to convince many of its 7,700 employees that they are not employees of a giant corporation at all but individual entrepreneurs. "When you walk in here, day one," recalls 31-year-old Andrew S. Offit, who manages three Fidelity funds, "they say, 'Here's your phone and here's your office and here's your secretary and here's your industry, and how you do your research is up to you. If you want to go to California tomorrow, then go. All we care is that you pick stocks that go up more often than they go down.'" . . .

Johnson can afford to indulge his instincts and his idiosyncrasies because, in spite of Fidelity's awesome size, it remains very much his company—and one of the few money-management firms left in private hands. Ned and his family control 45 percent of Fidelity's shares—with a value estimated at $1 billion—and 88 percent of the voting stock. The rest of the stock is held by some 300 key employees who must sell it back when they leave the company. It's an arrangement that enables Johnson, as he puts it, "to do all kinds of interesting things, instead of paying dividends"—one that gives him a latitude that most chief executives can only dream of.

Johnson's decision to launch a discount brokerage service in 1979, for example, was made over the objections of most of his senior managers. At other companies, a product like Fidelity's Magellan Fund—which produced no profits for 19 years after its creation in 1963—would have been junked as a failure; Johnson stuck with it, and today Magellan is the nation's largest equity mutual fund—with $19 billion in assets—and until 1989 was a portal through which Fidelity introduced investors to its dozens of other products.

Fidelity's growth under Johnson also serves as a reminder that, contrary to popular myth, inheritors often make very capable chief executives. . . . To be sure, some founding fathers bequeath nothing but inferiority complexes to their offspring. But others pass on the vision and self-confidence that produced their own success.

Johnson's father was such a parent—a gentle, professorial Bostonian, trained in the law and fascinated by Oriental philosophy and religion, who reinvented himself, becoming one of the patriarchs of the modern mutual-fund industry. Mr. Johnson, as Ned's father was known even to Ned himself, began dabbling in the stock market in the 1920s, after reading about the speculator Jesse Livermore. "Here was the picture of a world in which it was every man for himself, no favors asked or given," he later recalled. "You were what you were not because you were a friend of somebody, but for yourself."

It was while testing various trading theories in an effort to generate more money in stocks that Johnson became aware of mutual funds, a fledgling industry based on a then-novel concept: by pooling the assets of thousands of small investors, mutual funds offered ordinary people the twin benefits of professional management and portfolio diversification—benefits that had previously been available only to the rich. But Mr. Johnson perceived even greater possibilities in the concept. Before he came on the scene, investment management was largely a defensive profession, operated by cautious committees primarily dedicated to preserving capital. Mr. Johnson argued that so-called prudent management was actually imprudent in a surging economy; he believed that mutual funds could make money for their clients—as opposed to merely preserving it—if each fund were run by a single bright and aggressive manager armed with the freedom to follow his instincts and knowledge.

To test his theory, in 1943 he acquired the 13-year-old Fidelity Fund, and three years later he fired its investment adviser and began to manage the portfolio himself. Until the mid-1950s he personally managed Fidelity. By the 1960s his gunslinger approach to investing had developed a new species at Fidelity: the maverick go-go fund manager whose mission was to beat the market by as much as possible. And by the time Mr. Johnson turned Fidelity over to his only son, Ned, in 1972—casually remarking, "I think I've run the company long enough"—Fidelity's assets under management had multiplied 1,000 times, from the original $3 million in 1943 to $3 billion.

Mr. Johnson's quiet, introverted son Ned attracted little attention as a student at Milton Academy and Harvard, where he majored in social relations. He joined Fidelity in 1957, rising from analyst to fund manager within three years under the guidance of his youthful mentor Gerald Tsai, who was then already developing a cult-like following as one of the first of the performance-oriented money managers. They later became rivals to succeed Mr. Johnson, and Tsai—a personal favorite of Ned's father—left Fidelity in 1965 when he perceived, as he later put it, that "it's going to go to Johnson the fourth, the fifth, the sixth." But some observers note an often overlooked point: while Ned's name may have assured him of the succession in any case, in four out of the five years from 1960 to 1965 his Trend Fund outperformed Tsai's Capital Fund.

Ned took charge of Fidelity in the depths of the late-sixties stock market collapse and the OPEC oil crunch of 1973–1974, both of which frightened investors out of stocks and mutual funds alike. It was then that he came up with the first of his inspired gambles, seizing upon a new innovation called the money-market fund, which applied the mutual-fund principle to fixed securities like U.S. Treasury notes and thus enabled small investors to earn higher interest yields. These funds seemed an ideal parking place for the funds of stock-market refugees, except for one problem: the cumbersome process of redeeming shares. Ned's revolutionary solution: allow money-market-fund investors to write checks against their accounts, just as they would with a bank account.

"It did mean that money went out faster," he remembers reasoning. "But it also meant that if people felt confident that they could take money out quickly, they were maybe a little more inclined to put money in."

In this serendipitous manner Ned established a corporate pattern by which one new idea generates other innovations, and each innovation helps feed the others. After launching Fidelity's discount brokerage operation, Ned later went on to strengthen it, for example, by later soliciting business from Fidelity's existing mutual-fund customers; but today its 63 discount brokerage centers (which also offer other Fidelity products) attract 40 percent of Fidelity's new mutual-fund business. These investor centers have also produced 60 percent of the business of a more recent Fidelity innovation: a five-year-old insurance-annuity company that now sells nearly $300 million in annuities.

Where Mr. Johnson worshiped a single god—investment performance— his son has created an environment in which his personal holy trinity of technology, service and performance all feed each other. In the original mutual-fund concept, small investors sacrificed personal attention in order to get professional money management. But in the computer age, state-of-the-art work stations and software enable Fidelity's phone representatives to provide instant stock-market information and details about the client's account, even though the client and the representative are total strangers—a process Johnson calls "personal service on an impersonal basis." Eventually, Fidelity customers will be able to transact all sorts of business over phone and computer lines without human conversation at all, unless they prefer it.

Beneath Ned's strategy lies the sophisticated (if unspoken) perception that convenient, user-friendly services—more than investment performance—are the key to customer loyalty. Indeed, some observers say Ned's father would agree that performance, his original emphasis, is today carried too far, with endlessly complicated and often irrelevant statistical comparisons of mutual funds. . . .

"The most important thing of all," Johnson says, "is that the company is run well for the mutual-fund shareholders and for the people who work in the company. We believe that can best be done by keeping the business private. But, you know, who knows what will come along in the future?" To hear Ned Johnson, the uncertainty sounds like the sweetest part of his job.

John C. Bogle

BURTON G. MALKIEL

Jack Bogle's tenacious drive to reduce costs and his insistence on candor with fund shareholders have made Vanguard the low-cost producer in the mutual fund industry and a widely-admired, major success. Tongue in check, Burt Malkiel, a Vanguard director, told this story when introducing Bogle to the Newcomen Society.

Jack is abstemious in everything he does. Between cities, he flies coach rather than first class. In cities, he takes subways rather than cabs.

A true story will shed some light on Jack's personality in this regard. Once Jack had to stay at New York's expensive Plaza Hotel for a meeting. When his turn in the check-in line came, he informed the desk clerk that he wanted the cheapest room possible. The clerk suggested an economy single at $250, but Jack insisted that was way too high. After Jack rejected

Printed with permission of the Newcomen Society of the United States, Exton, PA.

a number of other suggestions, the exasperated clerk indicated sarcastically that there was a windowless former broom closet next to the elevator shaft for $89. Jack quickly said "I'll take it," and as the bewildered clerk was searching for a key, Jack turned to a gentleman waiting in line behind him and apologized for holding up the line. The gentleman, who turned out to be a Vanguard shareholder, said, "Oh that's perfectly okay. You're Mr. Bogle aren't you? Cheap? Right!"

Joseph K. Klingenstein

CHARLES D. ELLIS

J. K. Klingenstein, the remarkably handsome, dignified patriarch of Wertheim Co., was a generous philanthropist and a principal pillar of the wealthy Jewish community. He had originally planned to co-invest with Benjamin Graham in GEICO, the master's most successful holding—but decided that the $150,000 required to do so was too much.

Known as "JK" to everyone, including his sons, but addressed as "Mr. Klingenstein" in his presence, he consented in 1963 to give the benefit of his experience to a dozen trainees, fresh out of business school and full of excess confidence in their future and in their current capabilities.

The audience would last 30 minutes, because it was scheduled to begin at 11:30, and all knew that JK went to luncheon promptly at 12:00. Mr. Klingenstein gave . . . an overview of the history of the firm and a brief review of the economy and the market. He was well-informed and thoughtful, but all had hoped for something more tangible or specific.

"Well, gentlemen, what else would you like to discuss?"

"Mr. Klingenstein," began a brash question "you are rich. We all want to be rich too. What advice do you have for us?"

Calmly gazing back through his pince-nez, Joseph Klingenstein gave his simple answer: "Don't lose."

The meeting was over. All agreed that JK's answer had been as unimportant as the question had been impertinent. Perhaps that had been his intention—something of a lesson in business etiquette.

But ever since that day, the import and importance of JK's advice has become clearer and clearer.

T. J. Carlyle Gifford

CHARLES D. ELLIS

Carlyle Gifford, as both a businessman and an investor, built Baillie, Gifford & Co. from founding to preeminence in Scotland and joined Maynard Keynes and George Ross Goobey in early and timely enthusiasm for equities.

Carlyle Gifford came from Scotland to America in style. Joseph Kennedy, America's ambassador to the Court of St. James, made the travel arrangements. During the first month of his visit, he was the house guest of Thomas Lamont, Jack Morgan, Clarence Dillon, Robert Lovett, Frank Altschul, Sidney Weinberg, Robert Lehman, and Perry Hall. Pres Bush (whose son would be president 50 years later) took him to lunch at The Links Club. George Whitney "put him up" for a fortnight. He was a frequent visitor to the offices of Secretary of Treasury Robert Morganthau. He stayed largely in New York City at the River Club, University Club, and Racquet Club, where he played squash, tennis, and "real."

Gifford was a Very Important Person—not because he was, at home in Edinburgh, both managing partner of a leading law firm (Biggart, Baillie and Gifford) *and* a leading investment firm (Baillie, Gifford & Co.); not because he had made his own way and fortune (a sizable one); and not because he was a director of 22 British companies and 8 investment trusts; nor because he fitted in so readily as "one of our own kind" with the Wall Street Establishment; but because he was the largest single customer in history to present himself to American securities houses—ready, indeed determined, to transact a great deal of business—soon.

Gifford was entrusted by the British government with the formidable task of selling all the American shares and bonds of the British people—securities which the British government had requisitioned and purchased for cash at the market price on February 17, 1940, to preempt a forced, uncoordinated, potentially self-destructive wartime liquidation of a portfolio that represented not just 2 percent of all securities on the NYSE, but 25 full days of the then volume of trading. According to Beth Ann Ashfield of the NYSE, today the volume of selling to absorb fully that same number of trading days would total $250 *billion*.

Gifford had been invited in the closing months of 1939 by Montagu Norman, the governor of the Bank of England, to join a committee to advise H.M. Treasury on the "requisition and realization" of the British people's American securities. To supervise the transactions and attendant negotiations, he was posted to America where he stayed almost two years and executed his enormous selling with considerable skill.

Gifford was, like so many of the leading Scottish and English investors, no stranger to America. In 1937, after several weeks of touring America, he wrote a trenchant, long memorandum, reviewing money flows, examining production in farming and in each major manufacturing industry, explaining the policies and goals of Congress and the Federal Reserve Bank, discriminating between Roosevelt's skills as statesman versus politician, and commenting in detail on the business economics of Wall Street.

Baillie, Gifford & Co. became after the war, at least partly due to Gifford's leadership and convictions, the largest Scottish investment manager, a position it continues to hold. Up until his death in 1975, at 93, he was only "semi-retired."

Gifford was a strong and persuasive advocate of investing in equities and of investing in America and a deep believer in free markets, writing in 1945 to *The Times* to advocate that Britain's civil aviation industry be organized on the American model.

Never an easy man to be with or work for, Gifford was said to have a gift for spotting errors and for getting to the heart of problems and, according to the Scottish Investment Trust Centenery report, was "a man of such impeccable judgment that he found more than his share of fools who were not to be suffered gladly. Inevitably, he was an awesome figure to younger employees. While known by some to have a keen sense of humor, there were those who lived in fear of him. On board meeting days, staff were banned from the main staircase and confined to their rooms, no matter what personal need might arise." When a partner tried to mitigate an employee's offense by saying, "He meant well," Gifford snapped in reply: "I hope that is never said of me!"

Siegmund Warburg

RON CHERNOW

Siegmund Warburg fled Nazi Germany to become an extraordinarily successful (and controversial) City of London fixture. He led the development of Eurobonds, introduced aggressive merger and acquisition tactics to the United Kingdom, reestablished his family's name in banking, and built a great firm. He was also capable of remarkable acts of caring and kindness and engendered profound feelings of respect and affection.

In early May 1934, Siegmund had a heated debate with Uncle Max that summed up the excruciating choices faced by German Jews. Max had always been a fighter. . . . He told Siegmund that Nazism was a transitory sickness and accused him of running away from the problem. Siegmund said that by staying in Hamburg, Max was raising false hopes and misleading people who didn't have the Warburg money and resources to protect them. "Most of my family said, 'You are mad, you are crazy, you are defeatist,'" Siegmund recalled of his decision to leave. . . .

On May 31, 1934, Siegmund immigrated to London. Only 31, he carried many scars and postponed dreams into exile. He rejected joining Kuhn, Loeb, deciding he was too European to become a Yankee and probably knowing that he could more easily run his own show in London. . . .

Later on, Siegmund liked to portray himself as a threadbare immigrant who lost everything in Germany and started afresh in London. . . .

It doesn't detract from Siegmund's stunning achievement to state that he started life in London with signal advantages and a host of impressive connections. He and his family first lived in a mock-Georgian house in Westminster—not exactly a shabby part of town—and they had a butler and a cook. Siegmund called on Montagu Norman, governor of the Bank of England, and they discussed a good school for Siegmund's son, George. . . . The Rothschilds and other City worthies received Siegmund, not as a lone, obscure refugee, but as ambassador of the distinguished banking house of M. M. Warburg & Co. (After arriving in London, Siegmund remained a Warburg partner in Hamburg and Amsterdam, retaining personal liability

Excerpted from *The Warburgs: The Twentieth Century Odyssey of a Remarkable Jewish Family* (New York, 1993), pp. 413–415, 548, 559, 561, 610, 632–35, 638, 641–48, 651–54, 674–80, 682–83, 703 by permission of Random House, Inc.

there.) Submitting a naturalization petition in 1934, Siegmund was sponsored by the barons of British finance—the Rothschilds, the Hambros, the Barings, and Lord Bearsted of M. Samuel. New Trading's bills were countersigned by N. M. Rothschild, giving the nascent firm the finest interest rates. . . . Siegmund's most important contact was perhaps Paul Kohn-Speyer, the chairman of Brandeis, Goldschmidt, who had married Olga Warburg. Paul Kohn-Speyer provided Siegmund with small offices at his own headquarters on King William Street. He also took a small share in New Trading and financed many of Siegmund's early transactions.

Once Siegmund had recuperated from a bout of jaundice, the New Trading Company was launched with four people on October 3, 1934. Siegmund liked to suggest that the company was his sole creation, but the little firm was created as much *for* Siegmund as *by* him and formed part of a broader Warburg plan to follow clients abroad. It started with modest capital of 120,000 pounds. Half of the share capital was held by the Dutch International Corporation in Amsterdam, jointly owned by the Warburgs and the Fürstenbergs and with Edmund Stinnes participating. The very name "New Trading" betrayed its origins, since many Dutch and German banks were called trading companies in homage to their origins as overseas trading banks. To the more literal British, it seemed an odd and confusing name. In early 1935, Max told Hans Fürstenberg that the Warburgs would trim their investment in Dutch International, but boost their New Trading stake, citing Siegmund's intense work for the latter as making that move logical. . . .

In recounting his London start, Siegmund was wont to edit out his Hamburg relatives, as if he had sprung, full-blown, out of nowhere. It is hard to imagine that Siegmund could have assembled the distinguished London board without the Warburg and Fürstenberg money and connections. Nonetheless, the credit for building up the firm must go entirely to Siegmund. Despite the stigma of being an immigrant with a thick Swabian accent, he developed New Trading with a tremendous fighting spirit. . . .

One of Siegmund's secrets was that he never sought refuge in false pride. He was scrappy, opportunistic, and unorthodox in finding clients. Having seen the German banking collapse firsthand, he focused on fee-based business with limited risk.

Though Siegmund was always the star of the show, he needed his supporting cast of uncles. Many people would come to regard him as the foremost global banker of the late twentieth century, but he didn't excel in basic financial techniques. His genius never lay in crafting a deal, restructuring a balance sheet, or appraising shifting financial markets. He always had teams of minions to do that. Siegmund was the master salesman, long-term strategist, and reigning administrative deity rolled into one. If a maestro who couldn't play every instrument, he knew how to coax topflight performances from his team of virtuosi. He understood intuitively the fears and insecurities of his fellow refugees, making them feel special and important. They feared, honored, and respected him. A man of warmth and extraordinary charm, he could also be a ruthless autocrat who knew every managerial trick to inspire, terrify, cajole, goad, and manipulate his staff. He was, at once, a seductive and unsettling presence.

The nuts-and-bolts operation fell to Siegmund's chief executive, Henry Grunfeld, whom many would regard as the brains of the firm and the smartest banker in London. For almost 50 years, he and Siegmund were as inseparable as Siamese twins. Feeling he owed his worldly success to Siegmund, Grunfeld worshipped him. Siegmund found Grunfeld a bit dour and Prussian, but revered his talents. Henry was the technician who would execute his wishes without ever challenging his ultimate authority. They developed a telepathic sense of each other's thoughts. If Siegmund suddenly shifted gears with a client in mid-conversation, Grunfeld would pick up the signal and follow suit without a word being spoken between them.

While Siegmund attracted, indeed encouraged, a certain mystique, Grunfeld avoided the limelight and lacked the king-sized ego that usually goes with superior intelligence. He shunned the travel in which Siegmund gloried and led a private life. Before his death, Siegmund told him, "You couldn't have done it without me and I couldn't have done it without you."

• • •

As World War II ended, it became clear that fate had handed Siegmund a rare opportunity. The Holocaust had interrupted the preordained order of succession in the Warburg kingdom, allowing a new claimant to the throne. Not only had the Nazis swept away M. M. Warburg, but Max was now old and infirm, suffering from a bad heart and high blood sugar. If Siegmund acted swiftly, he could seize the Warburg name and initiative. For sheer brains and ambition, he had always felt, with justice, far superior to his Mittleweg relatives and he resented having to beg for scraps from Uncle Max's table. Now in his mid-forties, Siegmund was ready to start life anew. With the war over, a German name for a London firm was no longer an impediment.

Max automatically assumed that *he* would guide the postwar plans to refurbish the Warburg name. During the war, Eric periodically stopped in London and noted the awesome strides being made by Siegmund. . . . While in London in September 1944, Eric discovered that Siegmund planned to establish an Amsterdam pied-à-terre for New Trading after the war—without Eric or Max. This was a highly significant step, for the Warburgs regarded Amsterdam as the most strategic spot to spearhead their reentry into Europe. . . . When Eric asked him to elaborate on his plans, Siegmund grew tight-lipped. . . . To brake his cousin's expansion, Eric pleaded with Siegmund to consult them before undertaking any plans in places where the Warburgs had operated before the war.

Siegmund resented the insinuation that Max and Eric had some monopoly on the family name, which struck him as appalling hubris. No less proud of the Warburg name than they, he considered himself the best qualified to carry the banner forward and he didn't intend to take a back seat to Eric again. All along, Siegmund had felt sharply conflicted emotions toward Uncle Max, who had started out as beloved uncle and surrogate father, then become the domineering boss partial to his son. Now Siegmund increasingly disparaged Max as pompous and arrogant, and with an inflated sense of his wisdom. Toward Eric, Siegmund had never felt warmly, finding him charming and amusing, but also a lightweight snob who lacked courage, guts, and drive.

In Hamburg, Max had been a giant presence in the financial world. Siegmund a nonentity, a country cousin from the wrong side of the family. Now as he began to fathom the scope of Siegmund's ambitions, Max derided him as an upstart who had forgotten his place in the Warburg universe. . . .

On January 29, 1946, *The Times* of London ran a minute three-line notice on the bottom of page seven. It said in its entirety: "The name of the New Trading Company has been changed to S. G. Warburg and Company. Since its formation the firm has developed into a house of industrial and merchant bankers and it is felt that the original name is no longer appropriate. There will be no variation in the management and activities of the company. ". . . The little firm had 30 employees, with total share capital of just 233,000 pounds. The announcement in no way foreshadowed its prosperous future. Siegmund was always the first to say that he never dreamed it would become a leading London house.

• • •

Still fearing excessive reliance on banking, Siegmund steered S. G. Warburg & Co. into diverse businesses. With this in mind, he decided to create a holding company and bought a shell company called Central Wagon Company. When the Labour government nationalized the railroads, it stripped Central Wagon of its assets and this enabled Siegmund to use its stock exchange listing for his new holding company. The customary name would have been S. G. Warburg Holdings, but Siegmund again thought it tempting fate to put his name on a listed company with a banking component. The new vehicle was baptized Mercury Securities instead.

The common wisdom about Siegmund Warburg is that he ruled his firm not by ownership, but by sheer force of personality. In fact, before the Central Wagon deal was finalized, he formed another private holding company called Warburg Continuation. Endowed with slender capital, it took control of S. G. Warburg & Company by subscribing to a new class of shares that had voting rights, but not equity rights, over the operating company. Siegmund took 52 percent of Warburg Continuation and parceled it out in four equal pieces among himself, Eva [his wife], and their two children, with the remaining 48 percent divided among the directors. So it was something of an illusion that Mercury Securities controlled the Warburg bank. Without fuss or publicity, this arrangement lasted for 20 years.

• • •

Perhaps it was his disappointment with people that made Siegmund so passionate about books. Entranced by them from boyhood, he got an unadulterated joy from reading that he didn't get from business. . . . Even Siegmund conceded his love of books sometimes surpassed his interest in people: "And I find it even sometimes more interesting to meet other people in books than in person.." . .

Some cynics thought Siegmund's book talk a magnificent cover, a sure-fire sales pitch designed to lure clients seeking that coveted touch of "class." If so, it was a masterful strategy, for it allowed Siegmund to create a seamless unity between his banking career and his all-consuming hobby.

How could a man of infinite appointments have time for this stupendous personal culture? The answer is that Siegmund never wasted a second. In stores, he would point his umbrella at clothes and say, "I'll take three of those." When he bought glasses, the optometrist would bring frames to his office. Siegmund would try them on and not even bother to look at himself in the mirror. Though he helped to introduce commercial television in Britain, he scarcely ever watched it and didn't listen to radio or attend movies. He never traveled without a book; if he had a few minutes to spare in a taxi or airport, he would open a book and read. . . .

Siegmund reflected a cult of simplicity common among the intellectual heroes of his boyhood. He mocked the money-mad crowd. . . . For this banker, greed was the most shameful sin. He complained that many financial people had an "erotic relationship to money" and cited André Meyer as a prime offender. . . .

Siegmund's head seemed too large for his body, and the symbolism was appropriate, since he was an entirely cerebral person. He was so unmechanical that Eva filled his fountain pens.

Siegmund had an unerring eye for telltale details and was fascinated by the character clues hidden in neckties. . . . He learned more about clients from their clothing than their balance sheets. One day in the 1960s, he brought some German and American executives together to discuss a deal he had been pondering for some time. In the middle of lunch, Siegmund's mood changed and he suddenly, inexplicably, cooled off on the deal. At a later postmortem, his puzzled staff asked what had gone wrong. Apparently, the American chief executive had hiked up the sleeve of his suit, disclosing shirt cuffs with monogrammed initials. With gleeful derision, Siegmund asked, "Did you see the man's cuffs?" he thought it an appalling example of nouveau-riche vanity that forever altered his opinion of the man. . . .

In the 1950s, Siegmund started to use graphology to screen job applicants at S. G. Warburg & Co., hoping to weed out people who were depressed or devious and spot those who were especially creative and reliable. Graphology revealed things ordinarily concealed from view. But in postwar London, it seemed an arcane procedure that added to the image of S. G. Warburg as a very strange, alien firm. After applicants wrote a few lines in a fountain pen, their handwriting, age, and sex were passed along to a graphologist. This diagnostic tool was taken seriously at Warburg. In one case a person rejected at his first interview was called back and hired on the strength of his graphology test.

• • •

Siegmund Warburg's virtues and vices were closely allied. The qualities that made him a trying person—his perfectionism, hair-trigger temper, and high expectations—made him a matchless banker. To his adoring but fearful troops at 9—13, King William Street, he conveyed constant dissatisfaction, making people strive to perform better. They stretched themselves for Siegmund, believing they worked directly for him and taking pride in it. Like some omnipresent deity, he would telephone even lowly subordinates to offer profuse praise or scathing criticism. He read outgoing mail and pounced on errors. Subordinates felt this all-seeing man knew their innermost weaknesses.

This boss had a long list of pet grievances. He didn't like diminutives, abbreviations, or people who chatted with clients in the corridor. He was tough on smokers long before such militancy was fashionable. . . .

A marvelous actor, Siegmund would stage fake tantrums then slyly wink at his associates. . . . He adroitly used his temper to keep people nervous, off balance, uncomfortable, working at maximum capacity. One evening, wandering through the office at six-thirty, Siegmund was dismayed to find empty desks. The next morning he fired off a memo, expressing regret that people left so early. . . . Shrewd at office psychology, he would stop by certain departments at seven every evening, training people to linger. When London suffered a blackout in the early 1970s, the S. G. Warburg staff beavered on by candlelight.

People found Siegmund's persistent demands terrifying, joyous, outrageous, uplifting. Many wives resented that he had stolen their husbands. . . Siegmund taught his staff not just to advise but to listen to clients, to study and heed their needs. At other firms, if the person in charge of an account went on holiday, the account shut down. At Warburgs, somebody always returned the client's call. Siegmund demanded that incoming letters be answered the same day. With a punctilious regard for the amenities, he never failed to send birthday or condolence cards to clients.

In the early 1960s, the firm moved to a nondescript office building at 30, Gresham Street, posting no nameplate outside. Siegmund worried about overly rapid growth. . . . Despite its antique clocks and fine prints, the office displayed what Siegmund terms "dignified austerity."

This sense of economy extended to words. . . . He inveighed against "a diarrhea of words and constipation of ideas" and rivaled Hemingway in his passion for brevity.

The same systems that ensured top performance served as instruments of control. S. G. Warburg's success rested on a paradox: The firm was headed by a mostly benevolent tyrant who preached a teamwork ethic. Siegmund shunned the star system in favor of esprit de corps. The firm spent inordinate time keeping people informed. . . . At least two Warburg people were present at all client meetings. Despite this intense group culture, Siegmund saw the firm as his own personality writ large and would never yield his prerogatives on major issues of personnel, strategy, and client relations.

After Weimar Germany, Siegmund didn't want to be blindsided by unpleasant surprises and liked to map out contingencies in advance. . . . Before takeover contests, Siegmund set up offensive and defensive teams to simulate all permutations of battle. People had to know their fall-back positions if their strategy misfired. He insisted upon postmortems to avoid future repetition of errors. . . . Banking for Siegmund involved perpetual self-criticism. . . .

By 1957, Siegmund had crafted the splendid fighting machine that would soon dominate London finance, but he still had second-rate clients. . . .

To complete restoration of the Warburg name, Siegmund wanted to enter the front ranks of London merchant banks. To do so, he had to penetrate the august Accepting Houses Committee, whose 17 member firms stood at the summit of London finance. . . .

In 1957 a member bank came up for sale for the first time in 50 years. Although the least prestigious member, Seligman Brothers provided the entrance ticket Siegmund wanted. . . .

Siegmund insisted that the merged firm bear *his* name. After hesitating, the Seligmans agreed that the letterhead would read, "S. G. Warburg & Company (incorporating Seligman Brothers)." This merger with a member of the venerable Accepting Houses Committee was an astonishing milestone for a firm launched just a decade before. . . .

Once his bank absorbed Seligman Brothers, Siegmund was in a unique position. He now had establishment credentials. But in the dull, provincial City of the 1950s, he again faced condescension from insiders as he had in Hamburg, or at Kuhn, Loeb. People snickered at S. G. Warburg & Co. as "bond-washers" who made small profits by turning over securities that went X-dividend. Siegmund was again cast in the role of arriviste and enfant terrible. . . .

Siegmund's entire career seemed but a preamble to the British Aluminium battle [with Reynolds Metals, an American producer] that rocked

London in late 1958. This fight would spotlight his tactical daring, his scorn for the smug scions of inherited wealth, his courage to gamble all for the sake of ambition, and his refusal to compromise in matters of principle. At the end, the British Olympians would be forced to acknowledge him as a peer, a new Prince of the City. . . .

The Aluminium War was . . . a clash between those born to power and those who felt themselves entitled to more power based on superior drive and intelligence. . . .

By January 6, 1959, Reynolds/TI announced that it had achieved majority control of British Aluminium stock. Siegmund Warburg had defied the British establishment and won. It had been an article of faith that hostile takeovers didn't happen to major British firms. Siegmund had smashed that myth with one terrific blow.

This feat gave him worldwide fame. The 56-year-old sphinx emerged to appear in media photos. He didn't crow about his triumph but he clearly knew its significance. . . .

At first, he encountered tremendous ill-will in the City. People crossed the street when they saw him coming. . . .

Slowly people realized that they needed Siegmund Warburg and couldn't afford his wrath. . . .

The Aluminium War was a watershed for S. G. Warburg & Co., giving it an exalted place in corporate finance, as executives took notice of Siegmund's masterstroke. It was also a watershed for the City, which had come to prefer style and ceremony to competence and conviction. . . . Before Siegmund came along, mergers were negotiated on the backs of envelopes. Now merchant banks set up professional corporate finance teams to stop the Warburg juggernaut. Young turks at other merchant banks wanted to imitate Siegmund. In the coming decade, the entire City would take on the disciplined, fighting spirit of S. G. Warburg. Corporate battles would henceforth be fought in the open and not behind closed doors. One man had indeed made an amazing difference. . . .

During the 1960s, the firm seemed virtually invincible, whether on offense or defense. . . .

This winning aura attracted many clients. . . .

After the Aluminium War, a partner at a rival bank confided to Siegmund, "No company director whose shares are publicly quoted can sleep well from now on, because he must always wake up in the middle of the night and wonder who will make a raid on the company.." . . Siegmund, who hated inept entrenched managers, rejoiced at that remark.

• • •

Starting with his early days at M. M. Warburg & Co., Siegmund had specialized in international securities issues. In postwar London he had been hampered by capital controls. Now, in the early 1960s, Siegmund would help to rejuvenate London as a world financial center, lavishly repaying Britain for its hospitality. In creating the Euromarkets, Siegmund would again inject tremendous dynamism into a lethargic London scene.

The Euromarkets would give Siegmund a chance to reverse many earlier disappointments. After the war, he had vainly urged Britain to join the Common Market, lobbying Jean Monnet and Konrad Adenauer for a central British role. . . .

Now, through the private markets, he was about to accomplish something that would bring closer his vision of an integrated Europe. With the pending imposition of the Interest Equalization Tax in America, Siegmund consulted both the Bank of England and the Bundesbank about creating a new global market in London to supplant New York. This new market would issue Eurobonds, using three billion surplus dollars that had circulated in Europe since the war. . . .

In January 1963, S. G. Warburg and Deutsche Bank were ready to launch the inaugural Eurobond issue for the European Coal and Steel Community. When the ECSC decided to postpone the issue, Siegmund launched the market instead with a 15-million-dollar, six-year loan for the Autostrade Italiane, which built and maintained the Italian highways. . . . It was the first foreign industrial loan issued in London in a generation and in several ways was a landmark. To eliminate a 4 percent stamp tax on the transaction, Siegmund had the bonds listed in Luxembourg. This imaginative issue was therefore signed in Holland, under English law, for an Italian borrower, with the loan quoted in Luxembourg, and paid in American dollars. . . . It didn't sell particularly well—Italy wasn't a special favorite of investors—but for a self-styled world citizen who had inveighed against nationalism since Hitler, this new borderless world of finance was a refreshing tonic to the spirit. . . .

Most of Siegmund's colleagues believe that he fully deserved his title as Father of the Euromarkets. Siegmund created the essential concepts while Gert [Whitman, a Warburg partner closely identified with the Eurobond development] was the man of a million details. Even those who adhere to this view, however, believe that Siegmund grew envious of Gert and tried to erase his substantial contribution. Increasingly as the 1960s progressed, Siegmund seemed like a king who demanded absolute fealty from his liege lords and was quick to strike down those who overreached themselves. Gert Whitman was such a casualty.

• • •

Besides inventing the Euromarkets, Siegmund Warburg left another enduring monument: the firm of S. G. Warburg & Co. itself. No man was more slavishly devoted to his mistress. . . . Siegmund found it hard to let go of his creation and he would stage the longest retirement drama in modern business annals. The firm, which now had 250 employees, was an extension of his personality and he could no more cut himself off from it than he could amputate a limb.

Siegmund often referred to his semiretirement, which became a standing joke at Warburgs. He managed to keep three full-time secretaries busy. . . . In 1964, amid much fanfare, he yielded the chairmanship of Mercury Securities to Henry Grunfeld and became, at least on paper, a nonexecutive director. As he said that year, "Leaders of industry and commerce are often inclined not to step down before the decline of their powers becomes manifest, holding on too long to their positions and thus preventing the formation of a strong chain of successors." . . . Siegmund himself would be strikingly guilty of this sin and his 1964 "retirement" was more a matter of show than substance. . . .

In July 1966, undoubtedly in recognition of his services to [Harold] Wilson, Siegmund Warburg was knighted. At first, as an avowed foe of vanity, he hesitated to accept it and only did so when Henry Grunfeld told him the distinction would benefit the firm. He was stunned and delighted by the knighthood, which was actually very important to him, for it validated his decision to live in England and conferred some ultimate certificate of success. . . .

In January 1970, in yet another step in his protracted retirement pageant, Siegmund became president of S. G. Warburg & Co. and Mercury Securities and surrendered his directorships in both.

Ostensibly Siegmund had withdrawn to Blonay to give room to his successors. Yet his personality was no less forceful when filtered through a long-distance telephone. It was simply not in his nature to let his creation out of his grasp, and nobody at S. G. Warburg & Co. was particularly shocked that the sovereign continued to issue decrees in exile from his distant castle on Lake Geneva.

Henry Grunfeld

RICHARD LAMBERT

Henry Grunfeld grew up in Germany but became one of London's great merchant bankers while making crucial leadership contributions to the development of the S.G. Warburg Group. A partner of Siegmund Warburg, the two met only after each had fled the Nazis. At 89, he continued to come to the office daily. This report of a rare press interview appeared in 1987, just afer that year's global stock market crash.

Henry Grunfeld has seen it all before. A senior figure in the German steel industry in the late 1920s and early 1930s, he witnessed at first hand the collapse of the central European banking system and the devastating effects of deflationary policies around the world. One of the outstanding merchant bankers in London since the Second World War, he still works a full day at S.G. Warburg, the firm which he built with his late partner, Sir Siegmund Warburg.

Now at 83, in his first press interview, he remains optimistic. "I do not believe that we can have a repetition of what I went through in 1931 because the degree of co-operation between governments and central banks is totally different today. It just won't happen," he says firmly. This was Mr. Grunfeld's position before the recent stock market crash—and it remains his position today.

There is now an established network of support between countries and institutions, he says, of a kind which simply did not exist before. Of course, problems like Third World debt are a matter of great concern, but the fact that they have been recognised and brought out into the open by both banks and governments is a very helpful sign.

"Banks used not to work together in this way. An important German bank faced a run in 1931: I was on the advisory committee, and the board just did not understand what was happening to them. The then Reichsbank tried to persuade the other commercial banks to club together to lend support. They didn't. The next day, the bank had to close—and the others all followed shortly afterwards."

Why didn't they help out? "It was a matter of personal schadenfreude: they were delighted their rival was in trouble. Compare this with what

Excerpted from *Financial Times* (November 23, 1987), by permission of the *Financial Times*.

happened when Continental Illinois ran into difficulties a few years ago. Things really have changed."

This is not to say that Mr. Grunfeld rules out the possibility of further short-term upheavals, but rather that he can judge them through an unusually long perspective. "I have now been, for over 65 years, active in business, and I have seen such catastrophic upheavals, and still in the long term things did sort themselves out," he observes.

Mr. Grunfeld's current role at Warburg is, in the words of Sir David Scholey, the chairman, to act as a constitutional monarch: that is to be consulted, to encourage, and to warn. Another senior director puts it rather more vividly. "He is a one-man bomb disposal squad. He still reads all the papers, and he has an uncanny knack of spotting and dealing with—trouble."

The two founders of Warburg had much in common. They were both educated in the humanities and had similar intellectual interests. They were both brought up in traditional family firms in Germany—something which plays an important part in their story—and had important positions in their home country at an early age. And they were both forced to flee from the Nazis, only meeting each other for the first time after they had left Germany.

"But our temperaments were totally different, and so was our approach to business. We were in many respects complementary.

"It has been said that Siegmund Warburg was more of a romantic and I was more of a realist. That is too much of a generalisation. But he described me once as a 'hard taskmaster' and that perhaps meant that I was rather searching and critical in my judgment of propositions and also of personalities."

Or as Sir Siegmund once put it in one of his rare press interviews: "He is much more skeptical about people (than me) almost to the point of being very suspicious. If somebody is friendly and polite, I would often take the politeness as a reflection of kindness. But Grunfeld would wisely say the man in question might want something out of us."

Even today, Grunfeld is capable of putting the fear of God into junior employees who fail to live up to his exacting standards.

In business terms, the two were interchangeable. Both were actively engaged in the famous battle for British Aluminium in 1959, a deal which put Warburg on the map and changed the UK takeover business for ever. Elsewhere, Grunfeld was active in the newspaper industry, closely associated with Lord Thomson and Cecil King, and he played an important part in setting up Britain's commercial television companies. He remains the merchant bankers' merchant banker, regarded with something close to awe by some of the most senior people in the international capital markets.

The bank's style was—and to a considerable extent, still is—that of a discreet and very tightly run family business. "There never was any chain of command. Everyone could come direct to us. The internal communications system enabled every executive to keep himself informed of what was going on even if he was away," Grunfeld explains.

Not for Warburg the genteel City way of patching over disappointments. "If something went wrong, we would never try to say there was no point in crying over spilt milk. We would have a very thorough examination to find out what had really happened and how we could develop from this point."

That approach also applied to new business. "When we take out a proposition, we always consider what we would do if it doesn't go according to plan," he says. "The phrase: 'we will cross that bridge when we come to it' isn't heard here."

More than 50 years after coming to London, Grunfeld retains a strong German accent and a way of emphasising his words to make a point. And although the bank has changed enormously in scale, it still keeps, to a considerable extent, the original values of its two architects.

There is its famous tight-fistedness, for instance—or dignified austerity, as Grunfeld prefers to call it. There is its dislike of personality cults and of the ostentatious pursuit of money. As Grunfeld puts it: "The most overriding consideration was to do business in accordance with the highest standards. The money side would then follow. We would not accept propositions or clients with which we were not prepared to identify ourselves."

Then there is its occasionally eccentric approach to recruiting. As he often does, Grunfeld explains this with an anecdote: "Someone once said that hiring people is similar to buying a tie. You don't buy the tie when you need one. You buy the tie when you see one and like it. And you should do exactly the same with executives."

The bank has never been a trend follower. It led the way into the Euromarkets and largely avoided such trouble spots as tankers, property and Latin America. One current fad which Grunfeld regards with intense suspicion is the financing of leveraged buy-outs. "The disproportion of capital to indebtedness is frightening. The debt can only be dealt with either by the disposal of assets or by cash flow, which assumes that profits will continue not only to be the same but to grow. Now I have been long enough in business to know that this just isn't so." . . .

Grunfeld believes that there is still a considerable shake-out to come among City firms. "If I have a worry, it is that there are too many people trying to do the same thing and not doing it very well."

He thinks that the London market is over-capitalised, especially in the gilt-edged sector, and is pleased that one or two leading players have already decided to cut their losses, since he thinks that this will make it easier for others to come to the same decision. "As you know, prestige is one of the most expensive things in the world."

Prestige is not something which he values: indeed, even more than Sir Siegmund used to, he seems to have gone out of his way to avoid the public eye over the past 50 years.

The turning point in his philosophy came in 1934, when for no reason he was arrested by the Nazis and held in prison for 54 hours. Many members of his family were later killed, and he was able to escape mainly because he happened to be the Spanish consul in that part of Germany. Although he talks about the experience with understandable hesitation, he says it permanently shaped his views of what was important in life.

Aspects of today's financial climate do worry him: the complexity of financial instruments which are widely traded by people who don't understand them properly; the hunt for market share; the fact that so few people have lived through a prolonged bear market; and—he re-emphasises the point—the growth of leveraged buy-outs.

But he does not worry about a repeat of the 1930s. "I just don't believe governments won't stick together and keep control. I think we have learnt our lesson," he says. "I look back over 65 years and conclude that things could have turned out very, very much worse. I retain my optimism in this respect. In the end, common sense will prevail."

David Scholey

JUDI BEVAN

David Scholey had a mission as head of S.G. Warburg Group: to construct an integrated and global securities and investment firm that would also be the leading investment banker in the United Kingdom. He succeeded by sharing a vision of, and unceasingly pursuing, a collective enterprise of such encouraging stature, professional standards of service, and meritorious advancement that its success would appear virtually predestined. But, the firm was unable to keep up with the required pace of technology, management, and capital commitment and was, in the end, too large within Britain and too small beyond it.

Sir David Scholey . . . as architect and chairman of S G Warburg Group, London's most successful integrated securities house . . . is the most powerful investment banker in the land. . . .

Excerpted from *The Sunday Telegraph*, February 24, 1991. Copyright 1991 by Telegraph Group Limited, London.

But Scholey is no typical City grandee. He knows how to build his own kite, reads Milton and served a spell as a river policeman. He squandered a year at Christ Church, Oxford, helping, among other things, to run an illegal roulette game. . . . with Peter Wilmot Sitwell, Alick Rankin and IG Index's founder Stuart Wheeler.

"I always feel guilt I had the opportunity of three years at Oxford and I blew it," he says. . . .

Perhaps it is guilt which has fired him to work so hard ever since. "He never goes to bed," says Wilmot Sitwell, chairman of Warburg Securities. . . .

The office is a small, cozy affair with pleasant pictures and a couple of good pieces of furniture. There is just one photograph, standing alone in a carved wooden frame—that of Sir Siegmund Warburg.

Scholey is an old Yorkshire name emanating from Holland but his closeness to Sir Siegmund sometimes causes people to assume Scholey is Jewish. He looks puzzled. "I've always thought that actually I don't know whether I'm Jewish or not," he says. "Siegmund once said he considered me an honorary member of the Jewish community," his face lights up with affection, "it was one of the greatest compliments I've ever been paid.". . .

His interests range through literature, music, kite flying, scuba diving, gold art, big game hunting to the field sports of the traditional City gent. He takes a shoot in Devon a few times a year where he entertains in some style.

Yet he does not come across like a traditional City gent. A big cuddly bear of a man, Scholey is far from awesome to meet, appearing relaxed and full of witty one liners. . . .

"He is the least pompous man I know," says Sir Michael Richardson, a man not known for praising the opposition. In an article in *Institutional Investor* which named him Banker of the Year in 1987 Scholey himself wrote: "I have never thought of myself as a natural member of what people here and elsewhere refer to as the establishment."

And despite earning around £500,000 a year since 1986 his dress is muted and careful—dark suit, pale blue shirt, grey wool socks and traditional lace ups—not a sign of a flashy watch or monogrammed shirt.

Scholey commands respect among peers and clients for his judgment and analytical skills but his outstanding talent seems to be with people. . . .

He has the knack of making you feel valued and clever. There is a constant drip feed to the ego. "What an interesting question, what a penetrating remark," he says all through the interview. It is like sitting in front of a warm fire.

Like his mentor, he is obsessive about communication. . . . Scholey is master of the hand-written note, be it to mark celebration or tragedy.

He counts many captains of British industry among his friends. "He gives merchant banking a good name," says Sir Michael Angus of Unilever.

"If he tells you it's a rotten idea, then you know it's a rotten idea," says Bob Horton of BP. But he also spreads his net worldwide.

Sir Christopher Hogg of Courtaulds comments: "If you drop his name anywhere in Japan, Europe or the United States, people light up like pin tables."

But no-one underrates his metal. "He can be very tough with a smile on his face," says Rudolph Agnew who first met him in the army.

Scholey was born on July 28, 1935, in Chipstead, Surrey. "I had an extremely conventional outer suburban childhood," he declares and then lets drop he was sent away to prep school at four because of the war. "Actually it had a pretty traumatic effect," he admits. "It made it more difficult for me to leave home for the rest of my life."

He was close to his father Dudley, who was a non-family partner at Guinness Mahon. "He had strong values, although he didn't wear them on his sleeve." He went to Wellington College which he describes as non-elitist, with a strong military tradition and a good balance between intellectual and athletic achievement.

"I was pretty average at everything," he says. "What sports commentators call 'there or thereabouts.'" He took "A" levels in Latin, Greek and Ancient History. "I enjoyed classics but I became much more interested in English Literature."

He passed his Oxford entrance exam at a time when it was still easy to get in. But he opted to do national service first. He loved the army. "It was very broadening and deepening. It was a wonderful transition into the open world." He found it so useful he feels it is a pity Britain stopped national service. "People who served in the armed forces realize their responsibility is as much to the people who report to them, as it is to the people above them. The arrows go both ways." . . .

By the time he arrived at Oxford in 1955 there had been a shift upwards in standards. "So I was the last of the presumptuous undergraduates," he says. He had a pretty wild time by all accounts and at the end of the first year he realized it would be a waste of everyone's time taking the exams.

It sounds a rather painful period. "It was much more painful for my father," says Scholey. "But he never gave me a rocket."

He was sent off to an uncle in Lloyds who secured him a job as a filing clerk. He spent a year in Canada at an insurance broker. When he returned Guinness Mahon asked him to join. . . .

In 1965 Scholey was introduced to Sir Siegmund Warburg at a party and soon after joined the firm. He rose almost vertically to become deputy chairman in 1977 and then joint chairman in 1980.

He worked with two others in a room linked to Sir Siegmund's office on one side and to his partner Arthur Grunfeld's on the other. "It was known as either the nutcracker suite or the fall-out shelter."

Did he do the famous handwriting test? "Yes of course." Those who knew him then say he was more aggressive than he would care to remember.

Scholey's affability masks his ambition, fired relatively late. . . .

So what are the flaws in the great Scholey? He is notoriously late for meetings—"because he gives each one his total concentration," says a colleague. And he can be evasive, steering you away from delicate subjects.

And so we get back to Milton. *Paradise Lost* is quite relevant to the City, I suggest. He laughs quite a long time. "Yes," he says, "but he did write *Paradise Regained*, too."

Maurice (Hank) Greenberg

CARY REICH

Hank Greenberg drives his American International Group executives to excel in the business of seeking profits by accepting risk. In the process, he has made AIG not only very successful, but also one of the few truly exciting companies in the insurance industry. This profile was written 10 years after he took control of the company.

In 1956 J. Milburn Smith, then an executive vice president at Continental Casualty, heard that a promising young attorney in Continental's New York office was threatening to leave. To keep the attorney, Maurice (Hank) Greenberg, in the fold, Smith gave him a key job at Continental's Chicago headquarters. As Smith recalls, "He had a lot of ambition, and he was willing to pay any price to move ahead." But Hank Greenberg had two things going against him—he was unusually aggressive, and he was Jewish. And in the insurance industry, at least at the time, neither characteristic was exactly regarded as a stepping stone to success.

When Greenberg arrived in Chicago, Smith didn't waste any words telling the young man what he would be in for. "You know, Hank, you've made it awfully tough on yourself," advised Smith, who later became Continental Casualty's president. "You picked a Gentile business, and worse than that, you picked a Gentile company. You're too fast for them, and they're not going to like that, and they're going to throw all the ba-

Excerpted from *Institutional Investor 13* (September 1979), pp. 91–96. This copyrighted material is reprinted with permission from: **Institutional Investor, Inc.**, 488 Madison Avenue, New York, NY 10022.

nana peels in your path that they can. Be on the lookout for it, because it's going to happen."

Greenberg, however, hardly seemed shaken by the warning. Flashing what Smith calls "those real strong sparkly eyes," the young man shrugged it all off. "I don't mind that," said Greenberg. "I can handle them. I can handle *anybody.*"

In the quarter century since then, Hank Greenberg has risen to a pre-eminent position in the insurance industry, but he has remained every bit the cocky, defiant iconoclast that he was when Smith first met him. Indeed, the 54-year-old Greenberg has made a career out of thumbing his nose at all the encrusted business practices and conventional wisdom of the insurance business. Instead of tempering his aggressiveness to fit the tempo of most of the industry, he has worn his pushiness like a badge of honor, doing all the things insurance executives aren't supposed to do. He innovates. He bargains like a rug merchant. He hollers at his executives. And—possibly worst of all—he says nasty things about the rest of the business in his annual reports and shareholders meetings. "All I want in life," he has said on more than one occasion, "is an unfair advantage."

Greenberg's status as the insurance industry's most abrasive and controversial figure has not made him many friends. But it has gained him the grudging respect of even his severest critics and competitors. Throughout the industry, both in the U.S. and abroad, he is regarded as the one true genius the insurance business has produced in the last generation. As his former boss, Milburn Smith, puts it: "He's the No. 1 insurance executive in the world today. I know, because I know most of them. When you talk to him, you're talking to the best."

The canvas on which Greenberg lets all this talent flow is the American International Group, a company whose background and character are just as unorthodox as those of Greenberg, its chief executive. Founded in 1919 in Shanghai by Cornelius Vander Starr, a restless, entrepreneurial, former San Francisco ice cream parlor proprietor, AIG's predecessor companies established themselves throughout the globe long before they became a factor in the U.S. market. Today, while AIG is only the twelfth largest property-casualty insurer in the United States, its worldwide scope is unrivaled. AIG operates in more than 130 countries, through offices and local subsidiaries, and 58 percent of its pre-tax income comes from overseas; no other major American insurance company even approaches those figures. Because of Starr's emphasis on employing local people to manage his operations around the world, the AIG work force has a multinational flavor that few companies can match. Vestiges of its Oriental heritage still show. The fare in the executive dining room at AIG's New York headquarters is Chinese, prepared and served by a Chinese kitchen staff, and AIG's executive floor is watched over by a dour male Chinese receptionist named Wong.

When Starr died in December 1968, he left behind a profitable but helter-skelter patchwork of foreign and domestic ventures that often ran at cross-purposes of each other. As Starr's successor, Greenberg used a combination of organizational skill and iron will to tie all the pieces together into a coherent whole. . . .

By craftily juggling those pieces, Greenberg has produced a track record over the last ten years that, in the opinion of many analysts, is without equal in the insurance industry. From the time he took over, he consistently—and publicly—said he was aiming for at least 20 percent earnings growth each year, and not once in the past decade has he failed to achieve it (the compound annual earnings growth in the past decade was 24.2 percent). At the same time, Greenberg also made it clear he didn't want this earnings growth to come at the expense of underwriting profits, and he has achieved that, too. While the property-casualty industry suffered the worst underwriting losses in its history from 1974 through 1976, for instance, AIG went through that period posting substantial underwriting profits each year.

The consistency of Greenberg's results in a notoriously cyclical industry has left many observers shaking their heads in disbelief. Mutters one insurance consultant: "How is he so smart that he can never have a loss, even though he's writing an increasing volume of business every year?" Greenberg himself is well aware of the skepticism. "Every once in a while," he says, "somebody looks at AIG and says there must be some kind of a secret mechanism. Something I clutch in my hand. But it's not that way at all. It really isn't any single thing. It's a combination of many factors, many of which are unique and not capable of recreation."

There are those who say that the secret ingredient, if there is one, is Hank Greenberg, and the fact that he is simply smarter and quicker than his rivals at other companies. As one AIG executive points out: "If you ask the chairman of some other major insurer a nitty-gritty question he has to call an assistant in. Financial people and actuaries run the business. But Hank is an underwriter. He was a cracker-jack underwriter at Continental. There is nothing he likes better than getting in there and slugging it out over the terms of a reinsurance treaty."

Few—if any—executives in the business can equal Greenberg's intimidating presence, a presence marked by constant browbeating of his aides, temper tantrums and blunt, sometimes coarse, language. One former AIG executive says he always suspected "Greenberg had a Rolodex wheel with all our names on it, and he'd twirl it to find out who he'd be lighting into that week." This man says he especially dreaded the meetings Greenberg had with the presidents of the various AIG companies. "He'd always be ranting about someone or other. It got so nobody ever really wanted to go. And having lunch with Greenberg is no joy either; the acid is always pouring into your stomach." . . .

And no one in the insurance industry can match Greenberg's impeccable instinct for what makes the industry tick and how to make money out of it. A former AIG executive says it best: "Until you're exposed to Greenberg, a lot of us in the insurance business probably don't have the hard business sense you need to make money in this business. A lot of insurance people don't look at the business as a profit-and-loss type of thing: they look at it almost as a production problem, and oh, by the way, there's a bottom-line problem. And somehow or other, some *other* department is in charge of making a profit. But you learn with Greenberg that the two things go together—producing 20 percent growth and being in the black most of the time, too."

Greenberg, himself, is slightly more generous in appraising the competition. "I wouldn't say they're all a bunch of dummies," he remarks. "They're not. Obviously there are some people out there who do pretty well. This is a big industry, and you can't just say that everybody in it is *totally* lackluster." But when he is asked what his competitors do that impresses him, Greenberg giggles. "You're being unfair now," he protests.

• • •

AIG's competitors, for their parts, tend to blanch at comparisons between their operations and Greenberg's. The head of corporate planning for one of the biggest property-casualty companies contends that "AIG has always been a specialty company. There is always room for a few entrepreneurial types, but we just don't specialize. And you're certainly not going to suggest that we change our stripes and do what he has done." And a top official at Aetna stresses that "We're in the primary insurance business, the business of assuming risk. Greenberg is in the money business."

Indeed, much of the controversy that swirls around Greenberg centers on the accusation that he is not really in the insurance business at all—at least, not in the same way the other major insurers are. The basis for this contention is Greenberg's extensive use of gross lines underwriting. Rather than simply act as a net underwriter, as most insurers do, and take the entire underwriting position on its own books, AIG prefers to sell a substantial part of the position off to reinsurers. The practice has its roots in the fact that for much of its existence the Starr organization did not have any primary property-casualty companies of its own; the business generated by its worldwide underwriting arm, American International Underwriters, was simply passed on to an association of other companies. But even though AIG now does have its own sizable property-casualty ventures, the concept of passing on a good part of the risk continues. AIG, in fact, is probably the biggest source of reinsurance premiums in the world, distributing in excess of $1 billion a year to reinsurers. . . .

Greenberg says that as far as he is concerned the main attraction in gross lines business is that it puts him in the driver's seat. "If we were going to write large commercial and industrial risk, I did not want us to be in the position of following somebody else's underwriting, or taking somebody else's wash in," he says. By acting as a gross lines underwriter, control of the policy terms are firmly in his hands, not in the hands of a broker or another insurer. And Greenberg pointedly adds that "we have a pretty big net line in this organization compared to many companies bigger than us. We believe in what we're doing, and if we believe in it, we'll take a big line."

Nevertheless, Greenberg does often seem to be playing a different game than the rest of the industry. There is, for instance, the wild array of exotic coverages he offers—products that more staid insurers tremble even to think about. AIG will insure everything from communications satellites (the lift-off, not the orbit) to fireworks displays, from skydivers to tree surgeons. Only Lloyds of London can rival AIG's hammerlock on such areas as corporate directors and officers liability and kidnap and ransom insurance. AIG will even insure other insurance companies against punitive damage awards by courts.

As unpredictable as these products may be, Greenberg seems perfectly at ease with them. Quizzed once by a group of analysts about his penchant for offbeat products, Greenberg replied that "The history of our experience has shown that we're much better off writing so-called "risky business" than the nonrisky automobile and homeowners insurance, which I consider terrible—as a matter of fact it frightens me every time I think about it." Added Greenberg: "In kidnap and ransom insurance, all you read about are the kidnappings. There are an awful lot of people who aren't kidnapped who buy insurance."

Ironically enough, all these new products are, in fact, a stabilizing force for the company. . . . In the words of one industry Greenberg-watcher, "Greenberg is like a racetrack tout who has enough going in enough races that he's always got a winner."

The other great advantage of new and exotic lines is that the products are so new and exotic that no one has any idea what they should cost—except AIG. As Greenberg puts it: "To the creator goes the benefits." Indeed, Greenberg has always had an uncommonly keen eye for seller's markets. . . .

One of the best examples of Greenberg's nose for a bargain was his wrangling for AIG's headquarters building in downtown New York City. The building, a masterpiece of art deco architecture, had undergone a $19 million renovation just before its previous owner, the Cities Service Company, relocated to the greener pastures of Oklahoma in 1970. But when AIG made its first approach, Cities Service was in a bind; a number of major tenants, including Merrill Lynch and Marsh & McLennan, had just moved out, and Cities Service was faced with mounting property taxes. Greenberg offered $15 million for the 66-story building and land; Cities Service reportedly asked for $34 million. After nine months of dickering, AIG closed the deal—at $15 million.

Some of Greenberg's most hard-nosed bargaining, especially in his early years at the AIG helm, was with reinsurers. According to one ex-AIG executive, "There was a time when he was building the company when he would have taken every advantage he could of reinsurers. There was no way you could make a treaty with him and come out whole over time. His objective was to cut a deal where the reinsurer didn't have a possibility of making anything." This man recalls several lectures he received from Greenberg about dealing with one of the biggest reinsurers, General Reinsurance. "He had a preconceived idea that you could never get really favorable terms from General Re, because they want pretty favorable terms," the ex-AIG official says. "And he always felt that I should have moved those treaties to some other, less experienced market where I could make a better deal. But I felt we needed the support of General Re, so we regularly disagreed on that." Adds this executive: "I don't think Hank approaches it quite that ruthlessly today."

A top official at General Reinsurance claims that any reinsurer who thinks he has been taken advantage of by Greenberg only has himself to blame. "There are a lot of people who would say if you go into a meeting with Greenberg, you'd better keep your hands on your wallet, and that's true," the General Re executive says. "And if you're naive enough or not paying attention, yeah, you might get fleeced. But he doesn't present himself falsely to anybody. He makes it plain that these are gambling propositions without any precedents, and he's going to sit down and negotiate the best deal he can. And your job is to evaluate the risk, because he tends to get rid of all the risk he can. If you undervalue it, you're just doing it to yourself."

· · ·

Starting with a clean slate—the Starr group's domestic presence up to the early 1960s was virtually moribund—Greenberg built a radically different organization. . . .

When the overhaul was complete, Greenberg had transformed AIG domestically into a big-ticket commercial lines underwriter that, alone among the major insurers, catered almost exclusively to the needs of brokers.

But Greenberg's blueprints, as ingenious as they were, might well have gone nowhere had it not been for one more ingredient—Greenberg's galvanic personality. "The whole system thrives on friction," notes one former AIG executive. And the individual supplying much of that friction is Greenberg himself. Says one AIG executive, "He does it through encouragement, tongue-lashing, chastising. He never leaves you with the question 'What did he really mean by that?' " Greenberg is constantly talking about the need for a "sense of urgency" in his organization—"I don't like things to languish," he says—and makes it clear that anyone who doesn't share that "sense of urgency" had best find employment elsewhere.

"We're a performance-oriented company; we only try to get winners," he told an analyst group a year ago. "The weak don't find our climate very hospitable and the ones we do have are willing to pay the price of winning."

Sanford Weill

ROBERT LENZNER

Sandy Weill may or may not be ". . . at the pinnacle of American finance," as some admirers claim him to be. It is certain, however, that his career as an entrepreneur-manager began at Carter, Berlind, Weill and Leavitt, a very aggressive 1960s brokerage on the make. This he built through acquisitions and control into a major firm, sold it to American Express, lost out there in the grind of palace politics, and began again. This time, he moved farther faster, becoming rich in less than a decade and overflowing with awareness and ideas. Having gained control of the Travelers as a base, he acquired Smith Barney and then Solomon Brothers and then merged with Citicorp to form Citigroup.

Only days after Sandy Weill has completed the $1.1 billion acquisition of Shearson Lehman Brothers, the 60-year-old chairman of Primerica Corporation is ready to strike again. It is September, and the target this time is Travelers Corporation, the insurance giant in which Primerica already holds a minority stake.

The Travelers deal is classic Weill, uncovering financial gold where others see only wreckage. For nine months, since Primerica first bought into Travelers, he and his top lieutenants have been rummaging through the company's troubled real estate portfolio. Now they are convinced the depressed properties have sunk about as low as they can go, and might even rise a little as the commercial real-estate market recovers in the next few years. Weill first presses the timid Travelers managers to dump $630 million in properties he doesn't like and then forges ahead with the $4.1 billion purchase.

"Here I've bought one of the great financial brands," he says with an ebullience that was missing as recently as last winter, before he began his recent buyout binge. "There aren't many of them left." Accordingly—and not for the first time in his career—Weill is adopting a new corporate identity, dropping the obscure Primerica name in favor of Travelers and its trademark red umbrella. He wants it to become more familiar in American homes than Merrill Lynch's bull or Prudential's rock.

With the merger completed, Weill now stands astride a company with assets of $100 billion, about four times Primerica's size just six months ago. He has done it by combining a down-at-the-heels finance company (Commercial Credit Company) with a money-losing brokerage (Smith Barney), another securities firm that had once been on the brink of going broke (Shearson Lehman) and an insurance company no one else wanted any part of. (For good measure, he also stole his old friend and adviser, Robert Greenhill, from Morgan Stanley, giving his company an instant presence in investment banking.) In the process, Primerica's shares have almost quintupled since 1986, helping create what one media analyst, Michael Blumstein of Morgan Stanley, calls "a growing Sandy Weill cult" on Wall Street.

The payoff for Weill has been the accumulation of a personal fortune of nearly $200 million. Last year, through the exercise of stock options, he became the second-best-paid executive in America, earning more than $65 million. That's just on paper, though, since Weill has sworn a "blood oath" never to sell his 3.7 million shares.

And yet, despite his new wealth and power, you can still hear in Weill the need to prove that he's bigger and better than the Our Crowd financiers who once sniffed at him, or the WASP establishment that thought him too aggressive and drove him out of American Express. Weill exhibits all the symptoms of "bruised ego syndrome," says an admirer and large shareholder. "He is driven to achieve and achieve again to make up for the slights of the past."

After the Travelers merger, Weill crowed, "I'm now bigger than American Express," exaggerating a bit but revealing his basic frame of reference. It is Weill's stated ambition to build the greatest financial institution in the country; to tower over American Express, in particular, would thrill him. And he's getting there. Just as he swallowed up undervalued brokerages in the 1970's, he is poised to gobble up more insurance companies tarnished by the real-estate slump. "I expect a wave of consolidation in the insurance industry," he says. "There will be fewer players five years from now, which will create opportunities for us."

Some critics question whether Weill can continue to succeed in an ever-expanding empire that, at last count, will number a colossal 65,000 employees. "The greatest risk for Sandy is being both a deal maker and a manager on such a scale," warns Samuel L. Hayes 3d, a Harvard Business School professor. "He could trip up if he loses a tight focus over his portfolio of companies."

Weill angrily dismisses such concerns. "That's what I've been doing for years," he scoffs. "Making deals and running companies. If you have open communication, it can work."

What you see with Weill is what you get. There is no pretense, no slick facade. Heavyset and dark-complexioned, he always looks slightly uncomfortable in his Turnbull & Asser shirts. For an Ivy League graduate, he is sometimes surprisingly inarticulate and unsophisticated about events outside Wall Street, and occasionally obtuse about people. When talking about himself, he often prefaces his remarks by saying, "My wife tells me that I . . ." Friends say his deep insecurity and constant need for affirmation stem from his adolescence, when his father lost everything in business.

That experience has also made him, at times, endearingly cheap. "Do you want to hear something fantastic?" he asked recently. "I just got a hotel room in Hartford for $59.95." Every Christmas he carps about the cost of the company's party, and he often keeps budget meetings going for 12 hours while he chops out unessential expenses. "He thinks like a small businessman, even questioning expenses of $50," says his 37-year-old protégé, James Dimon, Primerica's president.

Weill and his sister, Helen, grew up in the Bensonhurst section of Brooklyn, then a pleasant middle-class neighborhood. His father, Max (called Mac), a Polish immigrant from a town near Warsaw, was an overbearing man who constantly needled and carped at his son, while rarely offering compliments. He was "a fairly successful" businessman, Weill says.

But his father shuttered a fledgling steel business while Weill was at Cornell University. Not long after that, his father left his mother for a younger woman. Impulsively, Weill left Cornell to try to patch up his parents' marriage, missing a crucial examination and the chance to get his degree. The family crisis threatened Weill's engagement to Joan Mosher, a Brooklyn College student. "My in-laws wanted to cancel the wedding," he says, because "my parents were getting divorced and I already was a failure."

Ultimately, Weill got his degree and the wedding went ahead. Over the years, Joan Weill has played a critical role in her husband's business dealings, particularly in her opinions of people he is considering hiring. "She is his human voice to the world," says Ann Bialkin, one of Joan's closest friends. "They complement each other because she takes care of relationships and he takes care of business."

Despite his Ivy League credentials, the young Weill was rejected by several major Wall Street firms before getting a start as a clerk at Bear, Stearns, then a small brokerage company. He made $150 a month, a miserly sum even for the mid-1950s, hustling quotes on stocks for the infamous senior partner, the late Salim (Cy) Lewis, who used to scream at him through a barred window.

He soon moved to a better-paying job at Burnham & Company, whose senior managing partner, I. W. (Tubby) Burnham 2d, became his mentor. "Sandy was the hardest-working guy we ever had," says Burnham. "I wanted to make him a partner but one of our partners opposed Sandy, because he looked down on Sandy's Eastern European origins. Otherwise, he would have ended up running the firm."

In 1960 Weill opened a small brokerage firm that was "run on the basis of whoever did the most business last month was going to be the guy that runs the firm next month," he says. Frank G. Zarb, who joined Weill in the 1960s and is today one of two Primerica vice chairmen, says: "It was always like a zoo. It could get crazy. Sandy was more emotional in the 1960s, and he'd blow at the slightest provocation."

Still, Weill understood a basic secret about Wall Street. The back office, where buy and sell orders are matched and customer records compiled by computers, is the "heartland" of a brokerage house, the place where costs can make or break the business. "He who controls the heartland controls the world," Weill says, echoing the military historian von Clausewitz.

When the disastrous bear market of 1973 and 1974 took hold, many firms were too inefficient to make money on the reduced numbers of stock trades. Like a tank commander closing in on the cavalry, Weill swallowed up one operation after another, smoothly integrating them into his efficient back-office systems. From 1969 to 1979, the firm grew from a single office in the General Motors building to 280 offices worldwide. Weill also cut costs brutally by eliminating hundreds of jobs each time, mostly from the acquired brokerage firms. "Nobody believed we would survive, but we went on surviving," he says.

As the stock market recovered in the late 1970s, Weill's firm—by now called Shearson Loeb Rhoades—became one of the most profitable retail securities firms, its shares rising almost a hundredfold. But Weill became extremely nervous when competitors like Bache and Dean Witter were taken over by giants like Prudential and Sears Roebuck. Seizing an opportunity to join the most prestigious partner available, he sold out to American Express for $930 million. He personally pocketed $30 million, making him solidly wealthy for the first time in his life.

He also became president of American Express, which provided something else he craved: the prestige of being a top officer of a brand-name international franchise. He was awed by the perquisites of the position, the chauffeured cars, the private jets. He began to drop the names of world leaders.

Selling to American Express, nevertheless, may well have been Weill's worst career decision.

Had he kept Shearson independent, he might have driven the firm past Merrill Lynch in the 1980s. Certainly, he should have kept the brokerage firm as his power base within American Express, a strategy his wife astutely recommended. Most of all, he should have realized he would be miserable playing second fiddle to the chairman of Amex, James D. Robinson 3d.

Today, Robinson, who was ousted as chairman of American Express in early 1993, generally describes Weill as "an inspirational leader, who made American Express more entrepreneurial. Sandy added a lot of value to the company, when he was here." However, Robinson still knows how to stick in the knife. "American Express was a club," Robinson explains. "You don't make waves." Translation: In the Waspy atmosphere of Amex, Weill's trademark emotional outbursts and blunt demands were not appreciated.

Weill rapidly grew frustrated with the lack of cooperation among top American Express officers. "It was policy and personality," Weill says. "In the end the trust was gone. There was not a good feeling." So in 1985 Weill resigned, clearing the way for Louis V. Gerstner Jr., for years his bitter rival and now the chairman of IBM., to become president.

The next 18 months were hell. He rented a suite of offices in the Seagram Building with his young assistant, Jamie Dimon, and looked for companies to buy. Weill, shaken by being out of work for the first time since 1955, was restless and unhappy without a company to give him an identity. "I didn't know how to handle it right," he says. "If I had to do it over again, I probably would have listened to my wife and gone on a trip to Australia, New Zealand or Africa."

The comeback that today puts Weill at the pinnacle of American finance began humbly enough in 1986, when he persuaded Control Data, the Minneapolis-based data-processing concern, to let him take over its poorly performing finance subsidiary, Commercial Credit. He put up only $6 million of his own money for a small equity position. The rest of the purchase price—$857 million—came from investors willing to bet on Weill's past track record as a turnaround artist.

Next, he lined up a talented new management team headed by Robert I. Lipp, then president of Chemical Bank. He sold off operations that made no financial or strategic sense, like automobile leasing and credit insurance. Then he concentrated on cutting costs and building up the mundane core business of making unsecured personal loans to households with incomes of $20,000 to $45,000. As he had thought all along—despite the rise in personal bankruptcies that turned off other investors—it was an excellent way to make scads of money. "It's part of the American ethic to pay money back," he says, "especially to loan offices in the middle of small communities."

It was all far removed from the rarefied world of American Express, but Weill says that suited him just fine. "I learned that how you get there isn't as important as where you're going." In fact, he still insists that turning around Commercial Credit was the most fun he's ever had in business. "It was like going to camp again. There were five or six of us. We'd get up in the morning and have breakfast together. We'd go to work together. We'd have dinner together. We went home together. We called our wives together. We just played five days a week."

Camp paid off big time. Weill multiplied Commercial Credit's profits almost eight times in six years, from a measly $25 million to $193 million. In 1988, he got a chance to return to his first love—the stock-brokerage business. He offered $1.54 billion, mostly in Commercial Credit stock, for Primerica Corporation, the former American Can Company, which owned Smith Barney.

At Commercial Credit, a major factor in the turnaround was an entrepreneurial style in which branch managers were treated as owners. Managers who exceeded goals got fat bonuses, and those making as little as $25,000 got stock options for the first time.

If there is one key to Weill's success, it is this ability to combine wily investing talents with entrepreneurial management. One moment, he is an obsessive stock-market junkie, constantly popping up from his seat to check stock quotes on a computer terminal and claiming to detect instant "trends" in the price gyrations of some 30 banks, insurance companies and securities firms. Every uptick in Primerica shares is another shot of affirmation that makes him more animated.

The next moment he is the restless hands-on manager who wanders around his office suite to check on daily insurance sales, the number of transactions handled by Smith Barney or new loans put on the books of Commercial Credit.

The challenge for Weill is to run his huge new Primerica as a small private partnership. Lipp, Zarb's counterpart as Primerica's vice chairman, thinks he can. "Sandy is antibureaucratic," he says. "He hates committee meetings, organizational charts and long memos. We are all happy refugees from the mindset of large public companies." Weill is famous for never writing memos or drawing up organization charts.

He is famous as well for his temper tantrums, which have cooled only slightly with the passage of years. He often "rants and raves," says Dimon. "But when he finds out that he's wrong, which is about half the time, he apologizes and the incident is forgotten."

Weill also makes plenty of mistakes in his choice of personnel. He is loyal to a fault and can't fire anyone personally, relying on others to do the dirty work. And Weill's tightfistedness triggered criticism last year when he canceled the life insurance policies and raised the charges for health benefits for 1,600 Primerica retirees. He did so, he says, only after negotiations on a compromise broke down, and because he felt Primerica should not sacrifice the interests of its shareholders to finance what he says were unrealistic retirement benefits. He was furious when the *New York Observer*, a weekly paper owned by one of his former partners, Arthur Carter, charged that "Mr. Weill and his executives at Primerica are a disgrace to the business community." Although he lost the public relations battle, he still has not backed down.

Buying back Shearson from American Express earlier this year was Weill's crowning triumph. It made him the first Wall Street entrepreneur to build two major securities firms almost from scratch and use the second to buy back the first. And he exacted sweet revenge, dominating negotiations with the company that had unceremoniously dumped him a decade before. Weill paid only $1.15 billion, just book value, for what he believes is the most advanced data processing system on Wall Street, a nearly 400-office branch network, an 8,500-member sales force, a

$57 billion money-management operation and two modern office build-ings carried on Amex's books for $600 million. As a final insult to his for-mer company, he says he hopes to induce Shearson's customers to give up their American Express cards in favor of Primerica's bank credit card.

Though Weill can't quite believe how far he has come, he does not lack for the trappings of success. He lives in several elegant homes, including a penthouse off Fifth Avenue, a 14-acre estate in Greenwich, Connecticut where the orchards and formal gardens are cared for by a resident horticul-turist, and for weekend getaways, a simply furnished but huge "camp" on Saranac Lake, where wealthy German Jewish families choose to spend part of each summer. Every time concertgoers enter Carnegie Hall, they are greeted by evidence of his first major largesse, a concert hall in his name, paid for in part by his $2.5 million gift.

Will success spoil Sandy Weill? Is he in danger of succumbing to the fatal hubris that inflicts newly crowned kings of Wall Street? Weill chuck-les at the idea, saying his wife would never let him. "We have the kind of relationship where my balloon gets pricked and I come right down to earth very fast."

For now, Wall Street is willing to give Weill the benefit of just about any doubt. "Sandy does have a colossal ego," says an executive with one of Primerica's largest institutional investors. "But he hires people with egos that can stand up to his own."

James D. Wolfensohn

CAROL LEONARD

James Wolfensohn, an attractive, talented, and aspiring immigrant from Australia, has made a quietly substantial mark in both corporate finance and the arts. This profile tells us something of his background and career. Having sold his firm to Bankers Trust, he now chairs the World Bank.

When the Reichmann brothers realised that the future of their Olympia & York empire could be in jeopardy if the complex restructuring of its $12 billion debt was not a success, they . . . summoned James D. Wolfensohn.

Excerpted from *The Times* (April 25, 1993), p. 12. Reprinted with permission. Copyright Carol Leonard/Times Newspapers Limited, London 25 April, 1993.

When Willie Purves, the hardhitting boss of Hong Kong and Shanghai Bank, finally launched his £3.1 billion bid for Midland Bank, he too wanted one man by his side: James D. Wolfensohn.

In New York, where Wolfensohn's "bespoke" corporate finance business—fee income $75 million—is based, his clients read like a *Who's Who* of the most blue chip of American corporations. . . . He was once the protégé of Lord Richardson of Duntisbourne, a former Governor of the Bank of England and now chairman of Morgan Stanley International. In the sixties, Richardson, according to City legend, earmarked Wolfensohn to be his successor as chairman of J. Henry Schroder Wagg, the merchant bank. He had spotted him when he was head of corporate finance at Darling & Co, an Australian bank, and brought him to London. Wolfensohn made it as far as chief executive and deputy chairman, but the Schroder establishment closed ranks and blocked his path to the top.

For although Wolfensohn, now 58, might have acquired establishment status—he is chairman and chief executive of Washington's John F. Kennedy Center for the Performing Arts and a past chairman of the Carnegie Hall—he was certainly not born with it. The acquisition of that status has, like many an immigrant before him, been his life's work. He was born into a lower middle class Jewish family in Sydney, his parents immigrants from London. His father was a "modestly successful" business consultant and home was a small suburban flat. He attended state schools, Sydney University, and then became a lawyer with a local firm.

"No, there wasn't much money, but my parents were anxious to support me in every way they could," Wolfensohn recalls. "My father was very intellectual, and determined that I should finish my education since his was interrupted by the war. My mother was tremendously interested in the arts. She could paint and sing."

Wolfensohn was "pudgy, a very fat little boy. I was indulged by my parents, spoilt probably, and I ate far too much chocolate." Despite the picture he paints—of a rotund child giving passionate renditions of *Buttercup*—he made it into the 1956 Australian Olympic fencing team and went to university at 15, two years before his peers. "I was so out of it, socially and emotionally, that I failed everything in the first year. When I left, the vice-chancellor said I was the laziest person to go through the university." It was not until several years later, when an American anti-trust lawyer, on an assignment in Sydney, admonished Wolfensohn over his ignorance of balance sheets with the taunt that he should go to Harvard, that he unleashed his extraordinary drive. Wolfensohn filled in the application form that night and, six months later, he was in Boston.

"I didn't have any money to get there so I hitch-hiked a ride on an air force plane." He cold-called the minister for air and talked his way on to a London-bound Hastings jet. An uncle paid his onward fare to America. Once there, he worked his way through Harvard by running its laundry.

"Money doesn't matter at all now, but it was terribly important in the beginning because I wanted to get a base. I always wanted to have $100,000 because I knew that then no one could ever hurt me. I wanted the kids to have $100,000 too and that, for many years, was my goal. It was a sort of magical figure in my head. I have been very lucky—I've made a few dollars more than that."

Wolfensohn refuses to disclose his net worth. Sources in London, however, recall that after Schroders, he joined Salomon Brothers in New York, developed its fledgling corporate finance division and then left, in 1981, to launch his own firm. As he departed, he declared his intention to cash in his $4 million equity stake. A timely reverse takeover by Philbro increased the value of his holding to $14 million. Wolfensohn finally had the secure base he so desired. Since then, he has increased his fortune considerably.

His firm, James D. Wolfensohn Inc, employs 45 professionals, including partners Paul Volcker, the former Federal Reserve chairman, and Steve Miller, Olympia & York's special adviser. He has created an organisation that offers what he calls "an in-house investment banking service" to its clients, "advising them on strategy, financing, mergers and acquisitions and then implementing them, but not getting into the financing itself". He has also launched a joint venture with Fuji Bank of Japan to bridge the gap between Japanese and American companies and he is now launching a similar joint venture with Lord Rothschild—J. Rothschild, Wolfensohn & Co—to concentrate on "mergers and acquisitions and financial strategy in the EC and eastern Europe".

Bruno Schroder, a friend since Harvard, says: "He is totally unpompous, and he can slip into any level of society." Schroder quotes two lines from Rudyard Kipling's poem If: "If you can talk with crowds and keep your virtue, Or walk with kings—nor lose the common touch." He adds: "That whole poem is Jim." . . .

Wolfensohn explains that he became an American citizen 12 years ago, when he was short-listed to be president of the World Bank; that he is more likely to vote Democrat than Republican and that his one unfulfilled ambition is to be a concert cellist. . . .

When it comes to religion, Wolfensohn says he is "traditionally Jewish— I observe holidays and try to keep a traditional life at home." Yet because of his dual career, in business and the arts, he can have little time for domestic life. He spends two days and three nights a week in Washington, running the Kennedy Center. The rest of the week he is in New York, or travelling abroad. . . .

He says his wife and children want him to slow down or to take a six-month sabbatical. More objective observers, however, scoff at this suggestion. Andrew Knight says: "He's been saying that for years, each time he gets to the top of the next mountain. I don't know what drives him. I suppose it's recognition." . . .

"I think I've got it in perspective now, I think I've actually found where I am," he says slowly. "A lot of the insecurities that goaded me in the beginning have gone. I wanted to do these things in my own way, to prove something to myself."

Despite, or because of, those insecurities, Wolfensohn is clear that his immigrant status helped. "I am an immigrant and that is very important. As an immigrant you have to create an ambience around yourself. It also means, however, that you are not bound into any pre-ordained style. If you are poured into something, with a pre-ordained requirement to go into a family firm, or a certain profession, then that freedom is denied. That is why I feel so privileged."

Henry Crown

STEWART ALSOP

Henry Crown once owned the Empire State Building outright. His building materials company brought him more than $100 million in preferred stock when it was merged into General Dynamics in 1959. The quintessential self-made man, he was fired from his first job for fumbling a shipping order. "Money itself isn't the primary factor in what one does. A person does things for the sake of accomplishing something. Money generally follows." This admiring profile deftly captures a unique personality.

In 1919, with borrowed capital of $10,000, Henry Crown, the 23-year-old son of Jewish immigrants from Lithuania, started his Material Service Corporation. That year the company sold $218,000 worth of sand and gravel to Chicago's builders and made a profit of $7,000. By 1959, when Crown merged M.S.C. with General Dynamics, the company was doing over $100 million worth of business a year, and Crown received for his interest well over that sum in preferred stock. Meanwhile, Henry Crown had acquired coal mines, railroad holdings and important real-estate interests—including for a time, sole ownership of the Empire State Building, the largest hunk of steel and concrete ever owned by one man.

When Henry Crown started his Material Service Corporation, the building-supply business was one of the roughest, toughest, most politics-ridden businesses in Chicago, a rough, tough, politics-ridden city. Today Colonel Crown (he was a Corps of Engineers colonel in the Chicago area in

Reprinted from *The Saturday Evening Post*, © 1965.

the war) is anything but rough and tough. He is the very archetype of the great capitalist and entrepreneur—urbane, articulate, well dressed, and remarkably well preserved at the age of 69; the owner of a name respected in the most exalted financial circles; a great benefactor (unlike most of the new big rich, who are in the main a tight-fisted lot); and the founder of a vast fortune which his sons have been trained to carry on. If the United States were the British Isles, Henry Crown would certainly be Sir Henry, or possibly even Lord Evanston.

With some men it is easy to see through the wrinkles and the years to the boy who was father of the man. With Henry Crown it is very difficult. But once in a while it is possible to catch a small glimpse of the young, penniless, brilliant, obsessively hard-driving immigrants' son who left school in the eighth grade to fight and scheme and talk and work his way to enormous wealth.

There is, for example, Henry Crown's remarkable memory, which approaches total recall. He uses his memory as a defensive weapon. Asked a question he does not want to answer, he will embark on a recital so voluminous, so detailed, so filled with unfamiliar names, dates and figures that his questioner is left utterly bemused. He will repeat verbatim conversations which took place 30 years ago, and he will recall the month, the day and even the hour at which they took place (though he is sometimes vague about the year). When his questioner is visibly goggle-eyed, he will make a small gesture with his right hand, and use a favorite phrase: "To cut through." Then he will change the subject. This extraordinary grasp of facts and figures—and the way he uses it—bespeaks the sharp intelligence which kept Henry Crown, in his salad days in the sand-and-gravel business, always a jump ahead of his competition.

Or there is an occasional small anecdote which gives a glimpse of the drive behind the relaxed and urbane manner. For example, there is the story about the banquet honoring a man Henry Crown had hired as a vice president. At the banquet the new man was presented with a resplendent golf bag. When Crown was called upon to speak, his comment was brief: "It looks like a nice golf bag. But working for me, I'm afraid he'll only be able to use it between one and five A.M."

Or there is the tone of Crown's voice when he tells how close he came to disaster when he merged his Material Service Corporation into General Dynamics. The vast General Dynamics Corporation thereafter nearly went bankrupt. If that had happened, Crown says, "I would have been associated with the biggest failure in history." The horror and hatred of failure are audible in his voice.

Since those awful days General Dynamics has been snatched back from the edge of the abyss, in part, through the efforts of Henry Crown, and the Crown fortune and the Crown reputation are presumably secure. The Crown fortune provides Henry Crown with various gratifications.

He is proud, for example, that in making himself rich he has also made other people prosperous. Thanks to a retirement plan he established long ago for his employees, a former sand-and-gravel salesman is now worth half a million dollars, and a former water boy in one of his quarries is worth $362,000.

He enjoys his charities too. He is especially proud of a scheme he has thought up to teach the young and aspiring how to handle capital. He has established a fund of $8,000 at a number of colleges, the money to be invested each year by the members of the senior economics class. If the investments are profitable, the members of the class share the surplus, the $8,000 fund remaining intact for the next class.

He also enjoys some of the visible signs of wealth, notably his chauffeur-driven Rolls-Royce—his wife bought it for him when he remarked that a Rolls seemed better for has bad back than any other car—and the elaborately decorated swimming pool in the basement of his house. But Henry Crown is by no means a conspicuous consumer. His house is a vaguely Tudor, red-brick pile, built in 1929, in a middle-middle neighborhood in Evanston, a not very distinguished Chicago suburb. Some of the houses in the same block would hardly fetch $25,000, even at today's inflated prices.

There are a couple of nice pieces in the house, but most of the furniture is just good department-store stuff, covered in plastic to protect the material. A balcony overlooking the big living room is set aside to commemorate the Empire State Building period, when he and Mrs. Crown, a nice, plump, rather shy lady, used to welcome such visitors as Queen Elizabeth, Fidel Castro and Nikita Khrushchev to their wholly owned skyscraper. Otherwise, except for the swimming pool and the gold-plated faucets in the downstairs bathroom, the house might be the residence of a successful dentist.

It is obvious to a visitor, in short, that Henry Crown, although he likes to be comfortable, has no obsessive interest in the objects that money will buy. It seems a good guess that his great fortune is far less important to him than the reputation that goes with it—that to this now elderly man, who once was a penniless, embattled under-educated offspring of immigrants, the real reward of great wealth is the respect, even awe, which the name of Col. Henry Crown now inspires in many prosperous and important persons.

Albert H. Gordon

CHARLES D. ELLIS

Al Gordon helped put together the deal that saved a fast-failing Kidder, Peabody in 1931 and then rebuilt the firm and led it for more than half a century until 1986 (when control was acquired by General Electric), during an era when it was still possible for one person to lift and personify a whole organization.

Al Gordon was born in Scituate, Massachusetts, in 1901 into the prosperous family of A. F. Gordon, a leather dealer and prominent Boston Catholic who taught the importance of always putting the customer's interest first and repeated such aphorisms as "Money is to be used, not abused" and "Never trade for the last dollar." Young Gordon's schooling was classic Boston: Roxbury Latin, Harvard College, and Harvard Business School (even before the campus was built in 1925). With a remarkably active, life-long interest in learning, he was a wide-ranging reader of history, biography, and novels (including most of Trollope's 47 long novels) and served his schools quietly and substantially: 50 years as Trustee of Roxbury Latin and for many years an Overseer at Harvard—plus 30 years as Trustee at Memorial Sloan-Kettering.

An early lesson in the importance of self-confidence and taking initiative came Gordon's way in a Roxbury Latin baseball game against Noble and Greenough. With runners on base and two out in the ninth inning, the coach asked: "Gordon, if I put you in, can you hit the ball?" Saying "I think so," Gordon reached for a bat only to hear: "Go back and sit down. I want someone who *knows* he can do it!" Says Gordon, "From that time on, I have always been 'sure'."

Having been "in the middle" as a student at Roxbury Latin, young Gordon decided to aim higher at Harvard College and Harvard Business School, where he graduated near the top of his class. On his father's advice that "the pot boils faster in New York City!" he took a job at Goldman Sachs as an analyst, but soon transferred into commercial paper, one of the firm's main lines of business.

In an attempt to improve his effectiveness in selling commercial paper, Gordon took home a dozen files for weekend review. As Gordon recalls,

---

This profile relies often on a delightful short biography by S. Melvin Rines: *Al Gordon of Kidder, Peabody*, published in 1999 (Howland & Co.), and patient critique by Geoff Worden. Al Gordon's initial reaction to the biography was typical of the man: "I'll have nothing to do with it! Not my style. Too self promoting." Fortunately, for once, Gordon relented.

these were "unimportant files, no one had ever taken them out of the file drawers before. No one would ever want them in the future." Over the weekend, Gordon pored through one file after another, placing them on the floor when done. Monday morning, Gordon went to work, leaving the files on the apartment floor, where the cleaning woman found them and, assuming they were just trash, disposed of them. Obliged to report to Senior Partner Walter Sachs—or be reported by the bookkeeper—Gordon explained what had happened, including the files being worthless and unneeded. Mr. Sachs rose up out of his chair and came down thumping his fist on his desk four times! "Well," he shouted, "that proves what I've told others—one high-school graduate is worth three or four from the Business School!" And that was it. Nothing more was said.

Meanwhile, Al Gordon's great opportunity was unfolding at an ailing Kidder, Peabody.[1] In the early 1900s, Kidder, Peabody was the leading financier of AT&T,[2] inviting into its syndicate both J.P. Morgan and Kuhn Loeb. In turn, Kidder, Peabody was invited by Morgan to have a key role in underwriting U.S. Steel. The firm also joined in underwriting loans to foreign governments, including Japan, Italy, Argentina, and Great Britain, where it had in 1878 established a relationship with England's most powerful private bank, Baring Brothers.[3] While J.P. Morgan dominated corporate finance in New York City, Kidder, Peabody led the industry in Boston, the nation's other money center.

As common stocks gained popularity and more companies paid regular dividends, some of Wall Street's innovative firms moved beyond railroads and utilities to underwrite new kinds of companies, such as retailers and manufacturers of consumer products. But Kidder, Peabody (under Robert Winsor, an aging and quite conservative autocrat, who was senior partner from 1894 to 1930) did not and would not adapt to the "new ways" in underwriting and saw soliciting new business as unseemly and beneath the firm's dignity.[4] As a result, Kidder, Peabody's participations in important underwritings fell steadily.

Worse, a series of troubles pounded at the weakening firm. Kidder, Peabody's New York office suffered large underwriting losses in the late

---

[1] The Kidder, Peabody name was first used in 1865. The predecessor firm was JE Thayer & Brother, which traced itself back to 1824 and was described in 1857 by the *Boston Evening Transcript* as "a banking house second to none in the country."

[2] To attract investors, the firm hired 40 young women to write letters by hand to every family with a telephone, advising them to buy AT&T shares.

[3] Thomas Baring became a Kidder, Peabody partner in 1886. Barings named Kidder its exclusive American agent, a relationship that would last more than a century.

[4] Winsor suffered personal travails, too. He devoted considerable time to caring for his invalid wife and was deeply hurt by a prolonged lawsuit (which he ultimately won on appeal to reverse a prior conviction) accusing Winsor and three other bankers of defrauding Willett Sears & Co. of its corporate interests in 20 New England companies. Unfavorable newspaper coverage was extensive over several years.

1920s. Then the bankruptcy of Caldwell & Co. of Nashville, Tennessee, a regional municipal bond house that Kidder, Peabody had financed, caused a serious loss.[5] Scarce equity capital, critical to the operation of an investment banking firm, was reduced further when two partners retired and another partner died, resulting in their equity capital being withdrawn. Then the falling stock market took its toll. The public valuations of the investment trusts the firm had organized—and in which it held large positions—were invested in illiquid stocks that plummeted in price with the 1929 crash. Finally, the government of Italy's very large demand deposit was suddenly withdrawn. These specific blows—combined with the underlying weakness of the firm's rigid management being far too conservative and an overall lack of organizational vitality—caused the once-illustrious firm to become virtually bankrupt.

A beleaguered Kidder, Peabody anxiously sought help from J.P. Morgan's George Whitney. (He had once clerked at Kidder in New York before joining Morgan.) Having arranged an earlier $15 million refinancing, Whitney soon realized that Kidder, Peabody's capital assets were even more seriously impaired than previously estimated and that operating losses were getting worse. However, Whitney still believed Kidder, Peabody could be salvaged; realistically, its best assets were its name and its reputation with clients.

Whitney asked Edwin Webster of Stone & Webster, the engineering firm, to consider a rescue. Webster declined, but saw an opportunity for his son Edwin, Jr., who would be joined by his Harvard classmate, Albert Gordon, and Webster's brother-in-law, Chandler Hovey.[6] A serious horseback riding accident abruptly sidelined young Webster, but Gordon and Hovey went ahead on what would come to be recognized as favorable terms.[7] One of their first decisions was to move headquarters to New York City, where Gordon was the active partner (with Hovey in charge in Boston). The new Kidder, Peabody opened for business on March 17, 1931, St. Patrick's Day, determined to regain its standing in the industry by building its own capability to distribute securities in underwritings. Later that year, Kissel, Kinnicutt & Co., stockbrokers, was acquired and G. Herman Kinnicutt, a former Morgan employee, took over routine office management, freeing Gordon to concentrate on the search for new business. "To the extent that I am handicapped in building up my outside

---

[5] Vincent P. Carosso, *More Than a Century of Investment Banking* (New York: McGraw-Hill, 1979), p. 68.

[6] A plan to include E. V. R. Thayer of Chicago did not work out, because Thayer wanted his own name added to the firm's.

[7] Webster, Hovey, and Gordon agreed to pay Kidder, Peabody's former partners (now organized as Devonstreet & Co.) 25 percent of net earnings to a total of $2 million, and to pay the old firm's creditors (organized as Commonwealth Corp.) 10 percent of net earnings for 5 years. Even these obligations were subsequently greatly reduced.

relations," Gordon explained, "we must of course expect to have our syndicate profits cut down."[8]

The senior Webster not only provided most of the capital needed to keep the firm functioning, but also used his Stone & Webster connections with the nation's gas and electric utilities to get business for the firm. But it was Gordon who made the greatest contribution to Kidder, Peabody's revival. He "picked up a firm in shambles and built it up from scratch," one of the firm's employees recalled later. Gordon not only was the principal recruiter of new business, he was also the chief policymaker; his energy and drive were felt throughout the firm.

Gordon hired another young man named Walter Moffit, whose father-in-law headed Ralston Purina. Goldman Sachs handled Ralston Purina's commercial paper, and when it came time for Ralston to do a public offering, Walter Sachs assumed that Goldman Sachs would manage the offering. When, instead, Kidder Peabody obtained the business, Sachs called Gordon to ask to co-manage the deal 50–50. By now, Gordon had become friends with Walter Sachs and spoke with his Kidder partners about cutting Goldman Sachs into the deal. They were incredulous! "Why should we cut Goldman in on our profits?" Gordon listened attentively and then called Walter Sachs, "You have 25 percent."

After World War II, Gordon gave renewed emphasis on building distribution, and Kidder, Peabody acquired the securities subsidiaries of several banks. By 1948, Kidder, Peabody had 18 offices, extending as far west as Minneapolis, and Gordon could observe, "In my opinion, we have had an unrivaled *esprit de corps* because of our policy of putting the customer first, our cohesive team play—and because we have never taken ourselves too seriously."[9]

Kidder, Peabody built underwriting business where it could—for the most part, with smaller companies and utilities not already "taken" by the major investment banking firms. The focus on smaller companies fit well with Gordon's often-remarkable persistence in arranging a match between companies and investors.

"I never believed in telling people what they should do. In talking to our clients, Kidder tells them what they *can* do. We give them a list of ideas and tell them, for example, 'We'll give you the pros and cons, and you make up your mind.' This doesn't mean, however, that we don't try to steer our clients in original directions. For example, years ago we suggested to a client that he have us go directly to the institutions for the sale

---

[8] See note 5, p. 78.

[9] See note 8. Gordon enjoyed good jokes, including those on himself. On a visit to a small, remote town in Ireland, he went to buy a newspaper. "Today's or yesterday's?" asked the aged newsmonger. "Today's, of course!" answered Gordon—only to receive the laconic reply: "Ah well, for that y'll hav' t' come back on the morrow."

of securities rather than have his company go through the laborious preparation of a registration statement for a public offering. The result was what we believe to have been the first private placement."[10]

Kidder, Peabody developed private placement debt financing into an important specialty that was particularly well suited to its concentration on smaller companies that might not be able to raise capital through public offerings.

Gordon's resourcefulness was demonstrated in the first post-war financing of a Japanese corporation in America, a $5 million private placement for Sumitomo Metal Industries.

Placing the issue was very difficult. As Gordon was struggling to line up buyers, he happened to notice that the Pope had just appointed a Japanese cardinal for Japan. As a Catholic, Gordon promptly called the bond buyer for the Knights of Columbus to say, "If Japan is good enough to merit a cardinal, the largest steel company in that country should be a good enough credit for the Knights of Columbus." Gordon got an order for $1 million— the first and only investment the Knights of Columbus made in Japan for many years.[11] This keystone order put the whole deal over the top.

Gordon was always competitive and tenacious in searching out new business and earned a reputation as an aggressive pricer of securities offerings, asserting, "The secret of correct pricing is direct contact with the market, not to be dependent on other houses for the information you need, but to develop your own through your own sources." Gordon used "good pricing" to break into relationships a Kidder, Peabody trademark.[12] "In competitive bidding," Gordon laughs, "I had a simple method: I would listen to our syndicate manager's proposed bid, and the numbers and rationale supporting it; then I would add 10 basis points and recommend we submit that bid. My reasoning was simple: The other bidders were probably looking at the same numbers as our syndicate manager, so a slightly higher bid should win." And more often than not, it did.[13]

Still, Gordon could and would make exceptions for "human" reasons. When Kidder, Peabody fought for and won the coveted position as lead manager for a McCrory offering, George Leness (a future CEO of Merrill Lynch and a running pal of Gordon's) rushed over to say, "You may not know it, Al, but McCrory was the very first stock offering Charlie Merrill ever managed. It has long been considered 'his' account, and it would be a severe blow to him if Kidder were suddenly put ahead of Merrill Lynch." To which Gordon replied, "Tough luck. That's the way the ball bounces."

---

[10] Excerpted from *Euromoney*, June 1994; and *Institutional Investor*, July 1987.
[11] The Sumitomo financing led to a far larger Japanese financing: Kidder, Peabody's financing for a 4,000-mile cable under the Pacific Ocean. *The Hero's Farewell*, Jeffrey Sonnenfeld, pp. 160–161.
[12] See note 5, p. 94.
[13] S. Melvin Rines, *Al Gordon of Kidder, Peabody*, p. 90.

But Leness persisted, "But this situation is different. It may be that he'll be so distressed that it might kill him!" Al Gordon replied, "George, if you tell me that if we insist on having Kidder's name ahead of Merrill Lynch, it could kill him, we will give way." Leness thought for a moment, "Yes, Al, I do think it could kill him." Gordon gave way—and tough as he was, this was not the only time concern for individuals at other firms dominated.[14]

After more than 50 years with the firm, Gordon was still happy to continue as an institutional symbol and general goodwill ambassador—and to negotiate deals. He worked a full day well into his mid-eighties. Equally anxious that his presence never be resented by younger people, he sold back much of his ownership to the firm, retaining only about 15 percent by the time of the sale to General Electric. He was the last of the fabled Titans of Wall Street who had led their firms through the Depression, World War II, and the postwar years.

Even as a major figure on Wall Street and a generous benefactor of his beloved institutions, Al Gordon continued to be "careful" with money in the "use it up, patch it up, make it do, do without" custom of Bostonians. "I have one Chevette automobile. And my wife never had a fur coat and didn't want one. I'd much rather have an austere lifestyle: traveling in a truck, for example, from the Straits of Magellan to the Bolivian border. You can't spend a hell of a lot of money doing that."[15] Gordon traveled economy class on his frequent trips to Europe.[16] (This once caused a senior colleague who heard Gordon being paged at Heathrow to rush back to the counter to change his ticket from First Class to Economy to avert Gordon's spotting him sitting in First. Taking his newly acquired and relatively cramped coach seat for the long flight, he watched and waited for Gordon to arrive; he never did. Later, he heard that Gordon had taken an earlier flight; he was being paged because he'd left a package with his name on it at the London terminal.)[17]

Always an independent thinker, Gordon did not subject himself to foolish consistency. He kept an attractive home in New York City and also maintained a permanent suite at London's Grosvenor House Hotel—where he slept the night before running the London Marathon at the age of 82—and again at 83. Approaching 100,[18] Gordon goes to his office every day, works out twice a week, plays golf, travels widely, and still buys growth stocks, saying, "There is so much to do, so much to look forward to!"

---

[14] See note 13, p. 73. Gordon is a persistent health advocate, urging associates to be runners and offering $500 rewards in the 1960s to those who would quit smoking for at least six months.

[15] Cary Reich and Gilbert E. Kaplan, *Institutional Investor*, July 1987.

[16] The last time I saw Al Gordon was in the subway station at Grand Central, saving cab fare.

[17] S. Melvin Rines, *Al Gordon of Kidder, Peabody*, p. 133.

[18] His 100th birthday July 2001.

John L. Loeb

T. A. WISE

John Loeb made his firm, Carl M. Loeb, Rhoades & Co., one of the leaders on Wall Street in the post-war period. He was a man endowed not only with immense presence but also a remarkable sense of timing. For example, he completed sale of the firm's major Cuban sugar holdings the day before Fidel Castro took over. This glimpse shows us how the firm and its master appeared 30 years after its founding.

What goes on [at Carl M. Loeb, Rhoades & Co.] largely reflects the talent, instincts, and personality of one man, John Langeloth Loeb, 60. John Loeb founded the firm with his father in 1931 and has always been its dominant force. Few men claim to know him well. Those who do discern a prevailing warmth, charm, and quiet good humor. From even a slight distance, however, he appears to be "the aristocrat of autocrats," courteous, quiet-spoken, attentive in one mood, yet glacial, enigmatic, acid in the next—with the moods subject to change sharply and swiftly.

He can, as business requires, exercise enduring patience, but here too he is beyond prediction. In prolonged discussions, even his close associates cannot determine his position until he has voiced it. "He will listen attentively to a proposition, nodding his head all the while, and then say no," says one who has sat across from him frequently. This is particularly discouraging to suitors who have just completed a long, involved presentation and cannot for the life of them begin to know on which of many points he might be willing to bargain or negotiate. Once a deal is set, though, it is set in concrete so far as he is concerned, and he expects others to stand by it. On one occasion Loeb spearheaded negotiations on an important underwriting for a major corporation, a good customer. All the essential details had been worked out to everybody's apparent satisfaction. When the moment came for signing the papers the corporate president, well known for turning tough and negative in negotiations, began to seek additional concessions. Loeb turned abruptly to his colleagues and suggested that they go back to their offices to handle the work piling up. Tempers blazed and pulses pounded, but John Loeb walked out. It was a ticklish affair and Loeb, Rhoades fully expected to lose its relationship with the corporation. But, as Loeb knew, the corporation *did* need the money, and soon was ready to sign on the basis of the original terms.

The qualities that give John Loeb such confident control are an almost uncanny sense of timing and an ability to pick talented and often diverse types to operate in the several areas of the business. Like many big banking partnerships, Loeb, Rhoades takes care to educate the proper number of relatives and sons-in-law who may inherit partnership interests. But with this duty served, John Loeb chooses his prospective partners not so much for the capital they can bring in as for the talents they will be able to apply to the company's affairs. If the types are diverse in outlook, so much the better.

• • •

John Loeb continues to have his way. He made that clear recently at the close of a luncheon in the private dining room, when, surrounded by his partners, he outlined the firm's working philosophy:

> Since father and I founded our firm, really to look after our own affairs, we've sought to build a sound investment-banking and brokerage business. If we ran our business on a strict cost-accounting basis, some phases of it might not turn out profitable. But you can't measure this investment business that way. It's the whole mix that makes us what we are. But if we didn't get any fun out of it and if what we do is to be constantly suspect, it would be easier to shut up and go back to the job of investing our own money.

Gustave Levy

GIL KAPLAN

Gus Levy, one of those remarkable leaders who made Goldman Sachs Goldman Sachs, was born in New Orleans but was only at home in New York. His associations and fund-raising activities were legion. He held every position in Wall Street there was to hold. Yet, he was at work well before 8 o'clock each morning and thought of his success as being "a miracle." Here is a glimpse of the dedication he gave—and expected.

Let's talk about Goldman Sachs. People who work at the firm say the pressure you place on them is fantastic.

Well, we do demand a full day. But I think we've got as low a turnover as any place in the Street—certainly in key personnel.

Excerpted from *Institutional Investor* (Nov. 1973) pp. 35–36. This copyrighted material is reprinted with permission from: **Institutional Investor, Inc.,** 488 Madison Avenue, New York, NY 10022.

We think the secret of the business is not only to be bright but to be consistent. And the only way to be consistent is to make your calls and do your job and be constantly on the doorstep of your current and prospective customers. But I think we are a pretty happy firm and I've never heard of anybody complain of overwork here.

Yet it's been said that your firm has one of the highest divorce rates in Wall Street.

I don't know about that. But it is true that someone who works here is married to Goldman Sachs as well as his wife. We have a real spirit. We love to do business. We get a kick out of it and it's fun. And while none of us wants to deprive a guy of a family life and a home, we want to make Goldman Sachs a close second to his wife and family. A very close second.

John C. Whitehead

CHARLES D. ELLIS

John Whitehead, both self-made and patrician, brought the strategic planning and disciplined management to Goldman Sachs that enabled the firm to rise to global leadership based on his transforming vision of a differently structured investment banking organization that compelled the whole industry to conform to his concept and strive to keep up with Goldman Sachs' disciplined, unrelenting implementation.

When Ford Motor's common stock first came to market in 1956, in a sale by the Ford Foundation, the resulting initial public offering of $650 million of the world's premier privately-owned corporation was the largest ever. The offering would also be a triumph for Goldman Sachs—and would help advance the career of a young man who would later lead in decisively changing the basic structure of Wall Street. Looking behind the curtain that had protected the privacy of a very large corporation and of a famous family captured the nation's imagination. The man in the street now could own part of Henry Ford's amazing corporate empire.

Ford had been an exciting post-war, all-American comeback story. Returning from the Second World War, Henry Ford II found the family company in desperate need of strong management. He acted boldly and decisively, hiring Ernie Breech (with considerable incentive compensation) from Bendix to be Ford's CEO, while taking for himself, at 30 years of age, the top position as Chairman. Together, they hired the Whiz Kids from the Army Air Force; forced Harry Bennett and his goons off the shop floor, and piled into the rebuilding of Ford Motor Company. The public offering would be a symbol of the success of this important corporate rebuilding—and a vibrant adumbration of the career of John Whitehead.

Having grown up in Montclair, N.J., Whitehead worked his way through Haverford College; served in the Navy (participating in the invasions of Normandy, Southern France, Iwo Jima, and Okinawa); earned an MBA (with distinction) at Harvard Business School and joined Goldman Sachs.

"It was the only investment banking job offer I had. Candidly, I'd heard almost nothing about the firm. This was not really so surprising. In the Government's 1957 antitrust suit against the industry, we ranked only 19th on a list of the 20 defendants. Actually, I was relieved that Goldman Sachs was at least *included* as one of the defendants."

The Ford offering was not only the largest ever, it was very complex, taking more than two years of secret negotiations to get all the "interested" parties to agree on how much the Ford family should get for transferring part of their exclusive voting rights to the shares the Foundation wanted to sell. Under Henry Ford's will, the Foundation owned 95% of all Ford shares; but all voting power was held by the family's 5% block, and the NYSE would not accept the Foundation's stock for trading unless it had full voting power. Another party at interest was the Internal Revenue Service, which would need to rule that the benefits the Fords got were tax free. Sidney Weinberg [Goldman Sachs' chief] and Whitehead prepared some 50 reorganization plans over the two years. The final plan rewarded the Ford family with $60 million worth of additional stock—tax free. Under the final plan, the Ford family gave up its exclusive voting rights and had its equity interest in the company increased to almost 15%; the Foundation got sufficient voting rights to present its shares to the Exchange to be listed.

"Working for and with Weinberg, I had the day-to-day responsibility for the Ford equity offering. I was selected as a good #2: young, quiet—and not yet a partner. "Not long after the Ford equity issue, I found myself working on General Electric's $300 million bond offering. At the time, it was the largest industrial bond offering in history." "Those were exciting days."

Referring to a memorandum he'd written to advocate a change that would, over time, decisively accelerate Goldman Sachs' becoming the nation's preeminent investment bank—and lead to the restructuring of all major competitors and the investment banking industry—Whitehead explains he had cautiously held the memo in a desk drawer until *after* his formal admission to the Goldman partnership. Then copies of the memo were sent to all partners—which virtually assured its being discussed at their next meeting—proposing that Goldman Sachs learn from such successful clients as Ford, GE, and Sears and organize a Marketing Department. Pointing out, with deference to Weinberg's formidable success in bringing business to the firm, that if *ten* executives were each dedicated to seeking new business—and if each brought in only one fifth of what Mr. Weinberg brought in—they would collectively *double* the Managing Partner's remarkable success. In those days, distinguished investment banking firms did not solicit business. It was expected to come to them. So the idea of soliciting business with a team of people who did nothing else was something quite new and different. Weinberg didn't see the necessity of any such changes and was none too pleased that copies of the memorandum had been distributed.

At the next Partners' meeting, Whitehead presented the plan. Weinberg expressed reservations, but no formal vote was taken. "Since there was no vote, we had not voted 'No,' so I just went ahead," explains Whitehead. "So there'd be no incremental cost for the firm, the first step was to invite two of our regular commercial paper originators to add some of the firm's other products to what they would already be offering in their regular marketing territories. They were all for this enlarged opportunity. Soon, one of these fellows somehow got a mandate for a private placement with a fee of $25,000. Not much, even in those days, but it was recognized as business we'd have never had had except for their efforts. We sent a memorandum celebrating this wonderful accomplishment to all the partners, so everyone soon recognized that something was beginning to happen. We called it the New Business Department.

"Our fellows were used to filing call reports on the companies they visited. I read all of their call reports, often sending them back with notations like 'Did you try to offer them service ABC?' Or, 'Did you ask about XYZ?' Pretty soon the system began to work pretty well. "Prestige for this group would necessarily come later—with the results," observes Whitehead with his characteristic understatement. In truth, Whitehead's larger organizational achievement was to build up the stature, in the hard assessment of others, of the new business organization, later renamed Investment Banking Services or IBS. The first task was to build IBS into an organization that initiated, developed, and built business relationships with many, many corporations at a time when most of proudly-traditional Wall Street would not deign to solicit business. The second and simultaneous task was to patiently and persistently elevate the stature of IBS *within* the firm to equal the traditionally aristocratic Buying Department.

This equality in stature gave Goldman the ability to recruit and keep exceptionally talented and ambitious professionals in 'new business' for their full careers. In turn, these sales professionals were motivated by the knowledge that the product professionals they represented were also intensively specialized and therefore sure to be among the very best. This combined the strength of pure salesmen supported by pure product experts and gave

Goldman Sachs a truly "unfair" competitive advantage in the view of other Wall Street firms—and a steadily growing reputation for competence and commitment among its many corporate prospects and clients. No other firm would or could match it. Even competitors called it The Machine. By 1971, every one of the 4,000 U.S. corporations earning $1 million or more had an investment banker at Goldman Sachs specifically responsible for trying to do business with it. In the five years between 1979 and 1984, the firm probably added 500 new clients, literally doubling its clientele. Within a generation, every major firm on Wall Street would be obliged—by competitive realities—to adopt Whitehead's organizational concept.

Meanwhile, Whitehead was rising rapidly within Goldman and in the esteem of Sidney Weinberg, who ran the firm with absolute and unquestioned authority. Part of Whitehead's strength was a masterful and mastering blend of sociable charm with a clear-headed sense of organizational purpose, which others experienced in combination with an unrelenting, skillful pursuit of chosen objectives. Always soft spoken, seemingly never in a hurry, almost always smiling, with mellow good looks, Whitehead gives the impression he's coasting, almost loafing. Not so. He doesn't waste energy, gaining force and effect through the no-waves consistency of his commitment to a few long-range objectives and his steady, rational approach. He will calmly demand conformance: To assure completion of call reports and expense reports, Whitehead once simply instructed the office to hold onto monthly paychecks—partners included—until that person's call reports had been correctly filed. "He tells you clearly what he wants you to do; gives you the clear understanding you have no alternative and *must* do it; then proceeds to encourage you to believe you might very well be *able* to do it; and continues on to give you the feeling you might even *enjoy* doing it, particularly if you commit your every effort to be *sure* you'll succeed," explained partner Roy Smith, who played a key role in building the firm's international business. "It's really quite amazing."

Just before Gus Levy was made Goldman's Managing Partner, Sidney Weinberg, anticipating his own retirement, organized a Management Committee because, while admiring Levy's prodigious business-building capabilities and extraordinary capacity for work, he never fully trusted the instincts of a trader to be solely in command of the overall firm. And two years after it was established, John Whitehead and John Weinberg were made Management Committee members.

Whitehead gave more and more of his attention to things managerial; one was business planning. One day in late 1963, Levy, a forceful, deeply engaged front-line leader, cornered Whitehead in a hallway to bemoan the dreadful news that with all their hiring, they were now saddled with a huge annual overhead of $12 million. Levy was worrying aloud, "We'll have to

take in a million dollars every *month* just to break even!" Whitehead offered reassurance that—with some planning—this apparently awesome
cost could be met through normal and expected operations. For starters,
Whitehead said he would estimate the investment banking part of the firm
expected to do at least one private placement a month—and taking a pad of
paper, wrote down 12 x $50,000 to record the fees that might be expected
from this line of business. Then he added a line for commercial paper and
then another line for a third service and so on until he had accumulated $6
million in expected revenues from investment banking. And then he asked
Levy, who ran arbitrage and stockbrokerage, "And what would you expect
to do?" Responding to an implicit competitive challenge and quickly
catching onto the play of the game, Levy ventured an estimate of the commissions to be generated by each of his 25 largest stockbrokerage clients—
and then those likely to come from the next 50—and then something for
arbitrage. As each new item was put forward, Whitehead wrote it down on
the list. Then, noting that the total came to more than the previously
daunting $12 million, he had a rough P&L for the coming year and wrote
across the top "1964 Budget"—and the discipline of planning was on its
way to becoming a hallmark of the firm. The significance of this launching of professional planning is clarified by recalling an earlier Levy comment that his favorite kind of short-run planning covered the business to
be done *before* lunch, while longer range planning covered what was to be
done *after* lunch. This was a two-sided coin: On one side was the intense,
hands-on involvement in every aspect of the firm's operations that made
Levy such an effective player-leader. But on the other side was the potential risk and constraint on the firm's growth potential of "visual naviga-
tion." Whitehead knew that planning and managing Goldman's growth
would both release and concentrate the partners' energies on generating
that growth.

Another defining moment in Goldman Sachs' development came a
decade or more later—on a Sunday afternoon when Whitehead was at home
alone. Contemplating the growth of the firm as a whole, he had realized
that even with its remarkably low turnover of just 5%, steady business
growth was adding a 10% annual increase in staff. Taking the two together,
the addition of new people would be 15% every year. Realizing that this
pattern would accumulate in just three years to nearly half the firm's people being *new*, and thinking through the implications, Whitehead became
concerned that with the firm's getting larger and more diverse and adding
so many new people, the old "apprentice approach" to passing on the values
of the firm could soon be overwhelmed by volume. If the culture and the
values which had been and would be so very important to Goldman Sachs'
character, would not be assuredly passed on and instilled into its increasingly large and diverse new staff, the firm's character—and its future—
would be put at risk by its very own success and growth.

So, Whitehead brought together what he thought to be the previously unwritten core values of Goldman Sachs and wrote them out longhand. With minor changes by other partners, The Principles were then set in type and in due course sent to all employees—at their homes, as Whitehead explains, "So they and the members of their families could read them and enjoy reflecting with some pride on the nature of the firm with which they were associated." Then, in a follow through that is typical of Whitehead's persistence and thoroughness, each department head was encouraged to assemble all his area's employees for a reading of The Principles. An open discussion of what The Principles really meant in day-to-day working experiences was to follow and formal minutes of those discussions were to be prepared in some detail—and submitted by the department head to the Management Committee for review. As Whitehead genially observes, "They naturally took hold as the shared values that give the firm its special character."

In the mid-70s, an unsettled period for Wall Street, Whitehead was asked to explain Goldman Sachs' success. He said, "The main thing is the emphasis we have put over many years on recruiting the best people in all parts of the business. We spend an inordinate amount of time identifying and recruiting the best people. It's not something that pays off suddenly— you have to stick to it year after year. Eventually, you build a pool of very capable people that permits you to be a winner. If you have the best people, you'll be the best investment banking firm, and if you don't have the best people, there's no way you can be the best investment banking firm."

Reflecting on his own career experiences and how they influenced his concepts of management, Whitehead explains, "As a young professional, I felt there was simply not enough to do. You did what you were told to do; if no one told you to do anything, you had literally nothing to do. At home in the evening, just watching TV wasn't what I wanted. We were just serving time, not learning much and certainly not working at our capacity. John [Weinberg] and I were resolved to put much more responsibility to the young people in the firm."

Whitehead was aware of various career alternatives and received offers to join other firms, including J.H. Whitney & Co. when it was a very exciting new enterprise. "Goldman Sachs had no employee review process at that time, so if you were young and hopeful, you couldn't help wondering about your standing. When I told Mr. Weinberg about the offer, he told me in quite absolute terms that this was not to be. While I was in his office, he took the telephone, called Jock Whitney and spoke very directly, saying, 'Now, Jock, we need John Whitehead here. He's one of our best young men. I ask you now to withdraw your offer, Jock.' And that was the end of that!"

Three years into his rapidly rising career at Goldman Sachs, Whitehead was told—you weren't asked—by Sidney Weinberg that his son John would be coming to the firm for the summer months between his first and second years at Harvard Business School and that Whitehead should "show him the ropes." The two young men set their desks back-to-back so they could talk freely and exchange thoughts and ideas on virtually everything, day after day. "We found we thought alike on many, many things. We had the same hopes for Goldman Sachs. And we shared enormous respect and affection for—and frustrations with—Sidney Weinberg." A year later, John Weinberg joined the firm full-time and the person-to-person partnership with Whitehead that lasted for some 35 years began. The two men became general partners on the same day and held the same percentage of firm ownership throughout their careers.

Twenty-five years later, when Gus Levy died suddenly, the "Two Johns" as they were known within the firm, were well prepared. (Active and productive to the end, Levy had suffered a stroke during a Port Authority board meeting and died a few days later. Wisely, he had involved both men in major responsibilities as members of the Management Committee.) They met together over the weekend, and as close friends, agreed on a two-headed structure that was new to Wall Street. Rather than each taking full responsibility for one part of the firm, both would be co-heads of the whole firm. Their announcement memo said, "We hope you'll be glad to know . . . we'll serve together" and explained that any decision by one would be a final decision for both. After a few unwelcome experiences with partners seeking approval from the one who was *most* likely to agree, they advised all partners that they would do best by taking their proposals to the one Managing Partner *least* likely to agree.

"The managerial style changed . . . after Gus died and John Weinberg and I took over. We recognized that the big and very simple secret of whatever success Goldman Sachs had had was that it spent an inordinate amount of time attracting very outstanding people coming out of the leading business schools. There was a pool of tremendous talent that was basically underutilized at the time because responsibility hadn't been pushed down to them. So we did a lot of pushing down of responsibility, clarifying authority, departmentalizing, segmenting the business and creating profit centers all over the place.

"If we had tried to operate with the [former] style of single, dominant personalities, we never could have grown the way we did in the eight years that John and I were chairmen. It was only by spreading the responsibility and delegating authority that we were able to accomplish that."[1]

In 1985, after 38 years at Goldman Sachs, Whitehead was asked to become Deputy Secretary of State to George Shultz and served until early 1989. Since 1989, his corporate activities have been confined to AEA Investors where he "can see lots of old business friends roughly my own

---

[1] *Institutional Investor*, June, 1987, p. 28.

age" and most of his time is given to serving on the Boards of an impressive set of the nation's educational, artistic, international, and social institutions.

Recently identified[2] as "The Chairman of the Eastern Establishment"—itself identified as "fantastically concerned with the pursuit of what it defined as the good," Whitehead is described as "impeccably credentialed, but almost invisible. A silver-haired, genial man who emanates sober trustworthiness, which, rather than intellectual brilliance, is the key quality a Chairman is required to have. As all Establishment Chairmen must, he denied everything—that there *is* an Establishment or that he's in it—but the evidence is incontrovertible."

"EXCELLENCE" reads the sign on Whitehead's desk. He had it with him throughout his years at Goldman Sachs. He also had it on his desk at the State Department where many spoke French, and some asked: "Is it a Title—or a noun?"

John L. Weinberg

CHARLES D. ELLIS

Gregarious, shrewd and decisive, John Weinberg has no pretensions, very little patience with less than total commitment, a wonderfully irreverent sense of humor and the absolute confidence of untold numbers of ambitious peope within and without Goldman Sachs that he represents the heart and soul of the firm.

"I could talk for a week about him," says General Electric's Jack Welsh about John Weinberg in a 1984 *New York Times* article. "I'm really a fan. The thing that distinguishes John is that he's not just a dealmaker for a deal's sake. He's interested in what's right for both parties. He cares about his clients and his own people in as sensitive a way as anybody in business."

"You want people to feel good about themselves—and about the firm," says Weinberg, with the sincerely innocent assumption that what's so natural to him must surely be equally self-evident to others. "People want to be treated well and I don't see any reason not to. Goldman Sachs is a meritocracy. You get ahead here by your talents and hard work and we

[2] "Masters of an Old Game," Nicholas Lemann *Vanity Fair*, September 1994, p. 242.

try to treat everybody fairly." Consistently unpretentious and surprisingly approachable for a Wall Street lion who looks back across a 45-year career as a leading front-line investment banker and 14 years as Co-Chairman and Chairman of Goldman Sachs, Weinberg chuckles, "I'm here to help people. If they want somebody with gray hairs and scars, I'm the guy."

"The best work I do is anonymous," observes Weinberg. Since "retiring" in 1990, Weinberg has been a very busy man. He laughingly told *Forbes* in 1994 that he'd been bringing in more business in retirement than when he was fully active at the firm.

Weinberg combines a remarkable clarity of thinking and quick recall of names, dates, and other details with an almost instinctive awareness of what is right for each of the people involved in a situation, which enables him to move directly to a pragmatic resolution. As head of a hard-charging, fast growing, highly complex, and inter-linked firm of very talented, striving professionals, Weinberg was often called upon to resolve the inherent conflicts and disagreements to protect both of two goals other firms often found to be contradictory: cooperative teamwork and aggressive individual initiative. And it was important to do so quickly, decisively and with no lingering hard feelings. Weinberg's approach was simple and powerful. He'd lay out exactly how the problem would be resolved: "I'm going to decide this once and for all. Now, each of you should think very carefully about what you really want most to be in my final decision and then tell me the decision you'd like me to make, one you can—and will—live with. Make it just as fair as you can to the other people because they'll also be offering me *their* suggested final decision, and I'm going to pick *one*. That'll be it. Then we'll all get back to work."

With his disarming candor, people of all sorts readily trust Weinberg, which partly explains how he was able to contribute so substantially to the successful resolution of the once tense, potentially confrontal situation in which Seagram was the unwanted and by far the largest—potentially dominant—shareholder in DuPont, following DuPont's "white knight" acquisition of Conoco in 1981. In by far the largest such transaction ever effected, DuPont repurchased 156 million shares of its own common stock for an astounding $8.8 billion in 1995. Those closest to the deal would have appreciated the sophistication of the technique utilized in the execution: Using derivatives, the transaction qualified under IRS guidelines as an intercorporate dividend and so was taxable at just 7% rather than as a capital gain at a rate of 35%. In typical Weinberg fashion, he credits the attorneys at Simpson, Thatcher & Bartlett for doing an outstanding job in structuring the complex transaction and providing what he recognizes as "a lot of room for negotiating agreement." To appreciate Weinberg's performance, it helps to understand the background of the complex situation so decisively resolved. The Conoco bidding war began with Dome Petroleum's bid for no fewer than 14 million and no more than 22 million shares of Conoco at $65 a share. Dome was intending later to swap the acquired shares for Conoco's 52.9% interest in Hudson Bay Oil and Gas (another Canadian company), saving Conoco the capital gains tax it would incur in a cash purchase. However, Dome's offer was flawed and ultimately failed. Meanwhile, Seagram had $2.3 billion in cash it wanted to invest. Edgar Bronfman called in Weinberg, a long-time adviser to the Bronfmans and a director of Seagram. A tentative accord was soon set: Seagram would buy 35% of Conoco and agree to a standstill agreement. Soon thereafter, the situation was made much more complex by DuPont's purchase of Conoco—which made Seagram by far the largest, but clearly unwanted, investor in DuPont. Again, Weinberg would be the principal negotiator, this time with DuPont's senior management.

Like every successful dealmaker, Weinberg always looks for the "bond in common" and often finds it on a very personal level. The outward appearance of DuPont's very British CEO, Edward Jefferson, was stiff and aloof—far removed from John Weinberg's gregarious informality. But Weinberg learned that Jefferson had also served in combat and a friendly relationship quickly developed. Out of such common bonds develop the channels of communication that enable major transactions between distant and different organizations to be accomplished. As Weinberg explains so matter-of-factly, "Back in 1981, when the Bronfmans bought their position, we worked out the standstill agreement, including how many seats the group had on the Board and on each of the key committees. So we got to know everybody pretty well over the years." Weinberg adds that, while the high price DuPont paid for Conoco back in 1981 may have looked like the top dollar paid at the top of the oil market, "When run *by* Dupont *for* DuPont, it has been a big contributor." He does not mention that Goldman Sachs' policy of not representing a buyer in a hostile bid for a company had obliged him to resign from advising and to pass up an $11 million fee for managing Seagram's original "hostile" bid for Conoco (thereby demonstrating that the true test of a policy is willingly following it through even though it's costing you real money). Goldman Sachs was the only major investment banking house in New York City that did not take in millions from the Conoco fight as deal managers, arbitrageurs, or advisers. By the time the dust settled, Texaco, Mobil, Cities Service, as well as Seagram and DuPont, had all been involved in what was then the largest takeover in history.

Weinberg has long been much engaged in performing key roles in major transactions. For example, Manufacturers Hanover's purchase of CIT from RCA and Manufacturers' subsequent merger with Chemical Bank in 1991; GE's acquisition of RCA (Weinberg advised GE's CEO on negotiations with RCA's top brass); and U.S. Steel's purchase of Marathon Oil (then the second largest acquisition in American history).

When Sir James Goldsmith made his massive $21 billion raid on the United Kingdom's BAT [British American Tobacco]—the largest hostile bid in European history—an urgent call went out from CEO Patrick Sheehy in London to John Weinberg in New York (at least in part because Goldman Sachs, under Weinberg's direction, had three years previously defended Goodyear Tire and Rubber from a prior Goldsmith raid). Weinberg took the next flight to London to lead a successful defense of BAT, which helped establish Goldman Sachs as one of the principal investment banks to British industry.

In what must be an historical record, John Weinberg's 34 years of service as a Director of BF Goodrich and 26 years at National Dairy (today Kraft) extend his father's, Sidney Weinberg's, previous service of 32 years to each of these corporations. He continues to be one of the only investment bankers on the Business Council, the prestigious group organized by Sidney Weinberg at President Franklin Roosevelt's request. Weinberg keeps a plaque inherited from his father that enumerates the many setbacks suffered by Abraham Lincoln—on his way to becoming one of America's greatest Presidents—with the message that great success does not come without setbacks. Sidney Weinberg had made a point of taking his son to observe and meet business leaders. One cheery paternal invitation to "come for dinner and stay the night" was given without concern that the room and board would be proffered at J.P. Morgan's stately home in Washington, D.C.—being used during the Korean War by Sidney Weinberg and his two senior colleagues on the War Production Board, General Lucius D. Clay and Charles E. ("Electric Charlie") Wilson—or that the younger Weinberg was then a very junior officer in the Marines. John has described Sidney Weinberg as a demanding boss and a demanding father who once said, 'I don't care how far you go, but you damn well better try hard.'"

Weinberg clearly takes great pleasure in being effective and helping work things out. A recent example: Weinberg was an adviser to Eastman Kodak's Board of Directors and an adviser to the committee of the Board in charge of the search and selection of a new CEO for the company. He and Coca Cola CEO, Roberto Guizetta, had agreed that the right man to take the helm at Eastman Kodak was George Fisher of Motorola. They went to see Fisher together and, as planned, hit him with both barrels: First, a great American corporation was floundering and Fisher, with his leadership qualities and his understanding of technology, was uniquely qualified to be CEO and accomplish something of great importance for this major company and for America. Second, they laid out an incentive package that would make Fisher a wealthy man when he succeeded.

The two men were playing to win. But they were not making much progress and certainly were not getting to the close. During a lull, Weinberg was alone with Fisher, who said, "John, it's a great job and a wonderful offer. I know that. But I'm not going to accept it—even from Roberto and you—and I want to tell you why. My wife, Anne, has been wonderful to me, and I owe her the time and the fun she's clearly entitled to, but she would lose out on this if I took the job and embarked on a new major challenge at Eastman Kodak. I'm just not going to do that to Anne." Weinberg replied warmly, "That's wonderful, George, truly wonderful." Then asked gently, "Would you mind if I were to give Anne a call?" With Fisher's assent, Weinberg gets on the phone in a few minutes, explaining the Kodak opportunity and its importance and saying, "But, Anne, George won't take the job." Asked why, he explains with innocent appreciation, "Because he loves *you*." Anne Fisher asks for 24 hours. And well within the time limit, George Fisher is on the phone to John Weinberg. He and Anne have discussed it all and agreed he should move to Kodak. Once again, Weinberg has done his job.

Long-term relationships are particularly important to Weinberg, and he clearly feels most comfortable where the loyalty goes both ways and is equally strong. When it's not, he'll work hard to get it right—as illustrated by his work with General Electric. Weinberg explains, "My father had been a long time Director of GE, and we were all disappointed after his death that Goldman Sachs was not invited to continue the relationship as co-investment banker for GE, a traditional relationship the firm enjoyed. They turned to Morgan Stanley to serve as GE's lead investment banker. "I decided to see what could be done and made a point of showing up at GE's corporate offices in Fairfield, Connecticut, every month or so, meeting with people, particularly the new executives being brought into their senior group of managers. "I've always gotten along pretty well with regular working people, so one day, I'm there and it's pretty quiet, and one of the secretaries says to me, 'There's a new executive you should see,' and in another minute, she ushers me into the office of this guy I'd never heard of before: Jack Welsh.

"He'd never heard of me either, so he asks, 'What's on your mind?' and I have to say I really don't have anything particular on my mind and ask him what he's going to be responsible for at GE. He grins and makes a passing observation about the value of really doing your homework before calling on people and explains he's a Sector Executive for several business units, including GE Credit. "So I ask how Goldman Sachs can help, and he grins again, commenting about the importance of coming prepared with specific, documented proposals and action recommendations and asks, 'Don't you *ever* do *any* homework?' "We were actually getting along pretty well on a personal level," continues Weinberg, "and the next thing I know, he's saying how he hopes to become GE's CEO one day and asks me how Goldman Sachs can help him do a great job for the Corporation. We talked about various things and pretty soon things seem to come together for us both. "Over the next few years, we did a lot of work together because the steel industry needed a huge amount of investment in continuous casting equipment, and the IRS allowed a transfer of the Investment Tax Credit if you leased the equipment. Since the steel companies had little or no profits and few taxes against which to take the tax credit, we worked out a way for GE Credit to buy the equipment, take the tax credit and lease the equipment to the steel companies. Naturally, everybody was happy." At one time, these arrangements helped Welsh's GE Credit bring in a very significant percentage of GE's total reported earnings, enabling it to be the earnings engine for GE as a whole. "Over the years, Jack and I developed a good understanding and a lot of respect for each other. We've become great friends and see a lot of each other. He's an extraordinary human being."

In early 1976, recognizing that the Goldman Sachs partnership could become divided—with some partners wanting John Weinberg and some wanting John Whitehead to assume leadership—Gus Levy announced that he didn't want to choose between them and had decided to endorse "our usual formula for success in virtually all endeavors: teamwork." Both men were soon named acting Vice Chairman, and they also became co-executors of Gus Levy's will. When he passed away in late 1976, the eventual decision to "co-head" Goldman Sachs was as natural to "the two Johns" as it was unusual in Wall Street. The two friends simply continued the lunch-time analyses and planning discussions about the firm they'd had as young men at Scotty's Sandwich Shop near Goldman Sachs' headquarters and at their back-to-back desks in the converted squash court atop Goldman's New York headquarters on Pine Street about "what we were going to do when we headed Goldman Sachs." The announcement of Gus Levy's stroke to the firm stated that John Weinberg and John Whitehead would serve together as acting Co-Chairmen. Later, they announced they would serve together as Senior Partners and Co-Chairmen—not with each taking responsibility for half the firm as others might have done, but with both taking undivided responsibility for the firm as a whole. Weinberg reminisces, "During one summer between years at school, I had worked at McKinsey. It was my father's idea—and a good one. I got to know Marvin Bower, the Senior Partner of McKinsey, who knew a lot about the workings of organizations." When he heard that John and I had it in mind to serve as Co-Chairmen and Senior Partners, he said it would never work, and that when we had the whole firm really screwed up, he'd come down and help us un-screw it. But somehow it worked." "Though we [John Whitehead and himself] are very different kinds of people, we happen to be very simpatico," Weinberg once explained. "Our offices are close together. We communicate a lot. We really wear out the carpet between our offices. We have a very collegial approach to management of the firm." "We'd speak on the phone almost every day, and every Sunday evening, we'd talk about the agenda for the next day's Management Committee meeting and agree on what we needed to do." "I did mostly outside work with clients," says Weinberg, while his co-head, John Whitehead, "did a lot of the organizational work, as well as outside work with clients. John had vision. He was tough, too. He would tell people what to do, without messing around." Weinberg is at least as tough himself, particularly when protecting the firm's culture from the threat of emerging arrogance among young partners who would be told to "knock if off—or else."

Weinberg believes deeply in the concept of 'shared values': "It's the glue that holds the firm together—so we can all work together." Concerning the importance of esprit de corps, Weinberg acknowledges the link with the Marines. "Loyalty down; loyalty up. That's the key. Never leave any dead or wounded on the battlefield. And come on *hard*." "We are scrambling every day, talking to clients about what they need—and delivering it." An unabashed patriot of Goldman Sachs, he explains quite openly and naturally, "I really love this place."

Reflecting on Sumitomo's massive investment of $500 million in Goldman Sachs in 1987—a timely, surprising (particularly to competitors), and forceful solution to the firm's surging need for much more equity capital—Weinberg explains that Sumitomo was acting on the advice of McKinsey on how the enormous Japanese bank could most rapidly prepare itself to enter the investment banking business. "They were very nice people, but not particularly experienced with some of the ways of Wall Street. When their CEO came to see me, explaining rather proudly that to avoid causing any suspicion about what he might be up to, he'd come circuitously—by way of Los Angeles and then to Washington, D.C. and then had taken the shuttle to New York—I had to tell him that the shuttle was probably the single route most likely to have lots of reporters and other investment bankers on it!"

Weinberg grins cheerfully over the memories of such human foibles, as much as over the triumphant strategic impact of the action ultimately taken. In an industry where equity capital can be leveraged 50 times over by firms with high credit ratings, half a billion dollars of fresh money can be very powerful stuff. "At first, Sumitomo thought they wanted to have all sorts of trainees at the firm, but I explained that to protect their investment, it was important not to have the perception that Goldman Sachs was too close to the Sumitomo Group. So we limited it to one trainee at a time. And they would have no vote, just be a silent partner. Again, I explained it was to protect their investment. Of course, it was the best investment they ever made because they could fund the whole thing in the Euromarkets at a net cost to the bank of just 1 percent."

With characteristic understatement, Weinberg observes, "It's worked out very well for everyone." Weinberg has lots of close friends in Japan and notes, "I've been going there for 25 years," typically understating the reality that he's actually been going *twice* as long. But then, his first visit was as a Marine in the early stages of the Occupation.

His actively engaging, no pretenses manner leaves John Weinberg, a justly proud man, open to good-natured ribbing from his many friends—

sometimes in public, sometimes in private one-on-one fun. For example, when Jack Welsh called him to explain that he was just about to go into the GE Boardroom, and would come out as the new CEO—and that Goldman Sachs would be restored as the corporation's principal investment banker—Welsh began the conversation in a personally affectionate way that anyone on Wall Street would die for: "You're not pretty," he said. "You're not a rocket scientist." "But . . . you're oh so very lucky!"

Robert H. B. Baldwin

RON CHERNOW

Bob Baldwin, once he got the job as managing partner at Morgan Stanley, was relentless in pushing his vision of what the firm could and should be, leading its transition from a persona of quiet patrician competence to its present global and multiproduct prominence. Over the period that this successful transformation was taking place, its beneficiaries regarded him as a "driving leader." Later, when reform had run its course and a new image was in order, his presence was sometimes regarded as "an obstacle."

The Morgan Stanley partner who first saw the cracks in [the] immaculate world of loyal bankers and loyal clients was Robert H.B. Baldwin, a protégé of Perry Hall, who had retired in 1961. Baldwin was a man who sharply polarized opinion and was later seen as either the savior or the ruination of the firm. For better or worse, he would sweep away the cobwebs and drag Morgan Stanley into the modern era. At a place of proper gentlemen, Baldwin had a high energy level, fanatic drive, and a tremendous desire to manage people. Tall and athletic with cold piercing eyes and a brusque, humorless manner, he was the opposite of the archetypal Morgan man. His partners found him cold and awkward, a man who had trouble relaxing or making small talk, and he seemed misplaced in Wall Street's most elegant firm. Yet that was perhaps an advantage, for he wasn't shy about assuming power, as were the gentlemen.

Opinion divides on the question of Baldwin's intelligence. He had an outstanding academic record: a triple threat in sports at Princeton—football, baseball, and basketball—he also received a *summa cum laude* degree

Excerpted from *The House of Morgan* by Ron Chernow, Chapter 29, pp. 582–584, by permission of Grove/Atlantic, Inc. ©1990 Ron Chernow.

in economics. Yet his intelligence wasn't subtle or reflective but obsessive and suggestive of an implacable will. In his office, he had a needlepoint pillow on which was stitched, "The harder I work, the luckier I get." At a notably discreet firm, Baldwin would abruptly inform people that they were overweight or smoking too much. Entertaining clients, he would suddenly launch into extended monologues on his own achievements.

Bob Baldwin would develop into a classic hell-on-wheels boss who would dominate Morgan Stanley for years, making life memorably miserable for his subordinates. "He could be a real bastard in the supercilious way that he would exercise his power with subordinates," said one ex-partner. "And he sometimes made a terrible fool of himself in the process of trying to be a big wheel." Said another: "He lacks humility, he's self-centered and insecure and quite humorless. You don't want to have a drink with Bob Baldwin." Yet he was also honest and forgiving. More to the point, he was extremely perceptive about the strategic direction of investment banking.

Baldwin was relentless in pushing an idea. He once harangued legislators during testimony in Washington, then harangued his companion in a cab; when his companion got off, he harangued the driver. His hero was no dreamy poet or thinker, but Admiral Chester Nimitz. When his son was at Phillips Exeter Academy in the early 1970s, Baldwin, an unabashed defense hawk, addressed the student body on "the other side of the military-industrial society that was in such disrepute." . . .

Baldwin was maddened by what he called the white-shoe thing—the notion that Morgan Stanley partners were inept stuffed shirts who succeeded because of blood ties and social contacts. "My grandfather was a conductor on the Pennsylvania Railroad," he pleaded. "My yacht is a 13-foot Sunfish." Or: "I get wild when they talk about that white-shoe thing. Why are we number one? Because we are nice people? Because we play golf? I stand on our record.". . . [T]his discomfort with a sedate past sparked revolt among younger partners and enabled Baldwin to push for sweeping changes in the firm's *modus operandi*.

Baldwin was also perceptive about Morgan Stanley's defects in the mid-1960s. It was poorly managed and becoming too big for the old consensual style. There were no budgets, no planning, and no modern management—just endless collegial discussions. Bookkeeping was still done by clerks on high stools, who copied entries into leather-bound ledgers on tilt-top tables. All the while, the firm was growing and bursting in its small headquarters. In 1967, it vacated its cramped offices at 2 Wall Street. It was still unthinkable that Morgan Stanley would lack a Wall Street address. Harry Morgan was afraid that if the firm had a Broadway address, London friends might think him a theatrical producer. He was only reconciled to a new office building at 140 Broadway because it was the former Guaranty Trust address.

During the 1960s, Baldwin made repeated efforts to run the firm but was rebuffed. Stymied by his slow advancement, he went down to Washington from 1965 to 1967 and served as under secretary of the navy. In these years, Baldwin was always promoting schemes to proselytize for the war on college campuses. Partners who found him pushy hoped he wouldn't return. When he did, they again spurned his demand to take charge of daily operations, and he again decided to leave.

He nearly escaped to the giant Hartford Insurance Company. Felix Rohatyn of Lazard Frères was playing matchmaker between ITT chairman Harold Geneen and the Hartford board. As Hartford's investment banker, Baldwin frostily rejected an overture from Rohatyn. The Hartford board decided to bring in Baldwin as a one-man "white knight" to ward off ITT's advances. In December 1968, Baldwin was set to become Hartford's chief executive when Geneen, enraged by reports of his move, launched a hostile tender and forced Baldwin to retreat back to Morgan Stanley. Now it was a no-exit situation: Baldwin and Morgan Stanley had to come to terms. With his enormous frustration and bottled-up energy, Baldwin resumed his campaign to shake up the firm and in 1969 got it to call a rare planning session. Outvoted, he later conceded it was a "god-damned disaster." What saved him was partly a generational change. As older, Depression-era partners retired, they were slowly being replaced by a new group recruited in the early 1960s. In 1970, the firm's 28 partners admitted six young men . . . known as the "irreverent group of six," and eventually they would tip the power balance toward Baldwin, giving him the votes to launch change. But at first, they wanted the nice, tight, rich Morgan Stanley of old.

Alan C. (Ace) Greenberg

BARBARA HETIER

Ace Greenberg grew up in Kansas, but always knew he belonged on Wall Street. As successor to founder Cy Lewis, he built Bear Stearns into a major and highly profitable firm—his way. Strict, blunt, and very disciplined, he abhors fuzzy thinking. "When people are wrong," he once said, "we feel they are not entitled to have any opinion. That's how we do it. There's no give on that." To keep costs down, he also turns out lights in empty offices and saves paper clips.

"Watch, I do miracles," says Alan "Ace" Greenberg, chief executive of Bear Stearns, as he shuffles the deck for his favorite card trick, the Snowshoe

Reprinted from *Fortune* (August 1987). © 1987 Time Inc. All rights reserved.

Sandwich. Greenberg's magic isn't confined to drawing-room legerde-main. Almost single-handedly he took the decidedly unsedate securities firm into risk arbitrage in a big, and profitable, way, earning for himself a reputation as a trader who cuts his losses ruthlessly. In the nearly nine years that he has served as CEO, Bear Stearns has moved deeper into re-tail brokerage, seen its net income soar—it jumped by half in 1986, to $131 million—and found a comfortable niche as one of the three or four most profitable investment banks on Wall Street. Greenberg has reaped the rewards. Under a compensation plan installed when the firm went public late in 1985, Bear Stearns' stunning performance earned its chief executive a bonus of $4 million—for just the first *six months* of the firm's existence as a public company.

"Too much," he says—for an investment banker, an admission little short of miraculous. Greenberg elaborates: "We went to the board and said, 'This plan is too good for us.'" So the directors promptly reduced the cut that he and his fellow managing directors were taking down as bonus, from 40 per-cent to 25 percent of annual pretax income above $200 million. "I'm not going to stand out like a sore thumb compared to the heads of other firms!" vows Greenberg. "Maybe I'm worth more—and maybe I'm not." . . .

He has also laid down a rule at Bear Stearns that each managing director must donate 4 percent of his salary and bonus to charity. "He's extremely generous," says Laurence Tisch, past CEO of CBS, of his longtime friend. "Is it an acquired or an inherited taste? Either way, he's a very decent guy."

And notoriously down to earth. While most investment banks compete madly for Ivy League MBAs, Greenberg searches for what he calls PSDs: people who are poor, smart, and have a deep desire to become rich. "He's the most unpretentious, unaffected man," gushes an employee who works closely with him. "He doesn't have any of the trappings of the typical chief executive. No private planes, no limos, no frills, period." At a recent lun-cheon with a visitor in the company's private dining room, he ordered a hot dog; as he walked back to his office, he stopped in an unoccupied room to shut off the lights.

Greenberg comes into his own in the trading room, where he rubs el-bows with the other regular guys on a daily basis. "Anything going on?" he booms, walking in. He typically doesn't wait for an answer. After punch-ing a few keys on his computer, he once again is wired in to the market. His conventional executive office sits just off the trading floor, remarkably uncluttered because Greenberg is rarely in it. He prefers to orchestrate the day's action from a raised dais on the trading floor. "They tell me it's un-usual," he says. "But I don't know why. Maybe that's why I make more money than the competition."

On the days when he can break from the office early, he heads for the Regency Whist Club on Manhattan's East Side. A nationally ranked bridge player, Greenberg plays with "a bunch of professional thieves," a bunch known to include Larry Tisch and Milton Petrie, the head of Petrie apparel stores. Says Petrie: "He's an excellent player, but he takes all my money away. The stakes are pretty high. But I can't say how high—the SEC might get after us." Divorced some ten years ago, the 59-year-old Greenberg says he goes out every night. "I work very hard during the day. I walk out of here and don't give it another thought." Were does he go? "It depends on what she likes."

Greenberg has spent his entire career at Bear Stearns. "I always wanted to work on Wall Street," the native of Wichita, Kansas, says. "I read about it and saw movies. I just liked the idea of dealing with little pieces of paper." He began work at the firm—putting pins in maps to show the locations of oil wells—soon after graduating from the University of Missouri in 1949. The nickname Ace, Greenberg claims, has nothing to do with his talent for cards. On the Missouri campus in the years just after World War II, men outnumbered women four to one. An older student advised Greenberg on dating: "You know, Greenberg, you're not a bad-looking guy, but you're not going to do very well on this campus with a name like Alan Greenberg." The nonplused freshman asked for a suggestion. "How about Ace Gainsborough?" came the reply. The Ace part stuck, understandably.

Pete Peterson and Lewis Glucksman

KEN AULETTA

When Pete Peterson and Lew Glucksman, both proud men from humble beginnings, came into conflict at Lehman Brothers each represented one side of a house divided. In the circumstances, perhaps their head-on collision was inevitable. Here we are introduced to the seething tensions building up within the firm. You can *feel* the inevitable explosion about to occur.

The story begins on July 12, 1983. John B. Carter, president and chief executive officer of the Equitable Life Assurance Society of the United States, the nation's third-largest life insurer, had invited Pete Peterson to lunch in . . . Equitable's headquarters. . . . Peterson invited Glucksman to join him. This was not done grudgingly. On a professional level

Reprinted from *Greed and Glory on Wall Street: The Fall of the House of Lehman* (New York: Random House, 1986), pp. 5–18, with permission from Random House, Inc. © 1986 by Ken Auletta.

Peterson knew he needed Glucksman. For three years, Glucksman had managed the day-to-day business of the firm; all of the departments reported to him, and his knowledge of Lehman's affairs was vast. Moreover, Peterson had an agenda for the lunch and he wanted Glucksman's cooperation to carry it out. And on a personal level Peterson enjoyed taking credit for producing what he called a "new," a tamer Lew Glucksman. It was undeniably true that after almost 21 years at Lehman, Glucksman had become a calmer, less volcanic executive; he had shed about 70 pounds and improved a wardrobe once dominated by light suits and wide ties.

In a private partnership like Lehman, the wealth of the firm was owned by the partners, who variously claimed from 500 to 4,500 shares of common stock apiece. Together with the preferred stock, the average partner's equity totaled $2.3 million in the fall of 1983. Partners were paid salaries ranging from $100,000 to $150,000 [plus] bonuses ranging from $200,000 to $1.6 million, and a 3 percent dividend on the value of their preferred stock, of which the senior partners owned the majority. In a good year, a fairly senior partner made pre-tax income equal to a salary of about $2 million. . . .

Peterson drove his executives hard before each business meeting, demanding detailed information. . . . He insisted on strategy sessions, detailed memoranda, marketing plans. The Equitable luncheon was no different.

Instead of serving simply as an intermediary or risking its capital to accommodate important clients, Peterson was pushing his partners to risk more of their own capital on new business ventures, on leveraged buy-outs, in real estate ventures where there might be no ceiling on earnings.

From Lehman's standpoint, the luncheon was designed to educate Lehman and, Peterson hoped, point toward a joint business venture of some kind with Equitable.

The tension between Glucksman and Peterson was hinted at by the fact that they were chauffeured uptown separately.

"If I could avoid being with Peterson, I'd avoid being with Peterson," explained Glucksman. "I couldn't stand the monologues."

During cocktails, Glucksman and Peterson exchanged perfunctory greetings and mingled with the other seven guests at opposite ends of a bar area just outside the executive dining room. Glucksman began to seethe almost as soon as they entered . . . his co-CEO was invited to sit beside John B. Carter, at one of two places at the head of the rectangular table, while Glucksman was seated toward the far end of the table, to the right but not alongside chairman Robert F. Froehlke, who sat alone facing Carter and Peterson. Across from Glucksman, and to his right, sat two Equitable vice presidents. Glucksman later said he felt as if he were confined to the bleachers.

Then came "the speech," as Glucksman derisively described a typical Peterson presentation. *Oh, how he had come to detest that speech!* He knew it was coming when Peterson began to drop names.

While Glucksman stewed, Peterson launched another pet speech, this one about how he was pushing merchant banking at Lehman. He remembers Peterson proclaiming, "Leveraged buy-outs" . . . "are the way to go." Peterson invoked the name of former Treasury Secretary William E. Simon. In 1982, Simon's Wesray Corporation put up a few million dollars to purchase Gibson Greeting Cards from RCA in a large leveraged buy-out. The bulk of the purchase price—$80 million—was paid when Gibson borrowed money against its own assets to pay RCA. A year later, in May 1983, Gibson made a public stock offering in which Simon pocketed over $80 million in profit on the Gibson stock he sold and retained stock valued at about $50 million.

"Pete at this particular time was obsessed with the amount of money William Simon made selling Gibson," says Glucksman. "And he couldn't stop talking about it." Since Peterson was a member of the RCA board that approved the sale to Simon, since Lehman Brothers represented RCA, and since Simon then went on to embarrass RCA by making such colossal profits, Glucksman was humiliated that Peterson would even mention Simon to Equitable. . . . "We had never done a leverage deal," says Glucksman, "and the problem was that we looked like amateurs." . . .

Belatedly, Peterson tried to include Glucksman in the conversation. Several times he asked, "Lew, what do you think?" Glucksman seized on the questions as opportunities to silence Peterson and plunged into embarrassing monologues on how investment banking had changed or how Lehman recruited young associates. "It was almost like a canned speech," recalls one participant. "He really shut Peterson down. His speech really made no more sense than Pete's speech in the context of why Lehman was there . . . Lew was trying to demonstrate that he was in charge."

When he returned to Lehman later that afternoon, Sheldon Gordon, who had shared Glucksman's limousine, told Glucksman he was "embarrassed" . . . by Peterson's half-hour speech and by the way Peterson "hogged" the limelight. When J. Tomilson Hill returned to his office he told partners of the "crazy scene" he had witnessed. Those he told wondered how long the eight-week-old co-CEO marriage between Peterson and Glucksman would last. Besides, partners remembered that when the co-CEO announcement was made eight weeks before, Glucksman had smiled for his partners and the press and proclaimed that he was gratified. What many partners didn't know was that blunt-talking Lew Glucksman was acting. The resentments of an adult lifetime were percolating within him.

• • •

Lew Glucksman had spent a lifetime accumulating resentments. The son of middle-class Hungarian Jews, he constantly inveighed against the "Our Crowd" Jews in banking—symbolized in his mind by the Lehman family.

He thought of them as WASP's, not as fellow Jews. "All my life I resented it," Glucksman says, referring to the bigotry that he felt kept a heel to the throat of East European Jews and other minorities on Wall Street.

In his mind, Glucksman linked those who blackballed him to those who tried to fire him from Lehman in 1973 when his trading department lost $7 million. When he was angry he sometimes compared these partners to Germans who looked away while Jews were deported in cattle cars. Although Peterson was the son of Greek immigrants and was raised in unpretentious Kearney, Nebraska, his ties to the establishment and his patronizing manner made him one of *them* in Glucksman's eyes. He thought Peterson was too much the Washington "insider," . . . behaving as if investment banking still hinged on old-school relationships rather than market-responsive transactions . . . and as if corporations had not hired their own skilled financial vice presidents, who nowadays often coolly selected investment banks on a deal-by-deal basis.

More and more, Glucksman knew, investment banking earnings depended on whether your firm, in competition with other firms, was selected to perform a specific function or transaction rather than carrying on a long-term relationship with a stable group of clients. The institutional clients Glucksman had cultivated—the pension and mutual funds, insurance companies . . . and the investment banks that traded huge blocks of stock—now dominated the stock market. Among them, they accounted for 90 percent of all trading volume on the Big Board.

Unavoidably, tensions arose between "traders" and "bankers," two groups of people performing different functions. Essentially, a trader . . . must make quick, firm decisions, often by consulting a jumble of numbers on a cathoderay tube during and after hurried phone calls.

Bankers, on the other hand, usually have a longer horizon . . . [investing] several years in cultivating a relationship before it turns into a client. . . .

Glucksman knew Wall Street had changed. He knew that the giant firms and money managers who served as custodians of other people's money now strove to prove that they could maximize the return on their investments. Volatility, not stability, became the normal market environment—in 1983 alone, 30 billion shares or 60 percent of all outstanding stock changed hands. Among the traders who dominated the market, Lew Glucksman was one of the best. . . .

It gnawed at Glucksman that despite this rise of trading activity on the Street and at Lehman, despite the new importance of commercial paper and equities—trading and sales functions for which he had long been responsible at Lehman—he felt traders were still being treated shabbily. The old-line banking division at Lehman was producing a declining share of profits—only about a third of the firm's profits in 1982 and 1983—yet bankers still held 60 percent of Lehman stock, still allowed the trading departments only 35 of the firm's 77 partnerships. And bankers still had their own man, Peter G. Peterson, on top.

Glucksman was not like *them*. He arrived at his desk before six . . . proudly wore an inexpensive Seiko watch with a shiny steel band, almost always ate lunch at his desk on the trading floor instead of in Lehman's elegant 43rd-floor partners' dining room. . . . His office etiquette was democratic—he conversed with secretaries and clerks, and employees were free to drop in and see him. Instead of a windowed suite of offices overlooking the tip of Manhattan and New York harbor, as Peterson enjoyed, his private quarters off the trading floor were windowless and cramped, with seats for five people to squeeze around his fake green-leather-top desk.

On the trading floor, Glucksman was in the process of covering all the windows, so that the entire focus of the vast room would be turned inward, so that the hundreds of analysts and clerks huddled before their Telerate and Quotron screens would have nothing to distract them.

"He's a very mercurial, highly emotional man," observes former Lehman board member George A. Wiegers. . . . Another partner, who had been an ally, calls Lew "a slob. We always used to joke about whether Lew would get through a meal without spilling food on his suit."

That is one dimension of Lew Glucksman. Another is offered by Florence Worrel, his former secretary, who recalls how he worried about the children of employees, and how he helped them get into private schools, offered personal loans, and once dispatched his driver to take her daughter to Harvard.

Says partner James S. Boshart III, . . . "He was a very tough man, a very emotional man, a very smart man, a very caring man. A lot of this talk of him being tough was an act. . . . He felt that the man who ran the trading floor should be feared. The real Lew Glucksman had difficulty telling people difficult things."

Of Glucksman, Peterson says, "Lew built commercial paper into an $18 to $20 billion business. Even his more ardent critics will tell you that he was one of the best in the business at credit analysis."

In style or personality, Glucksman and Peterson were opposites. Peterson with his thatch of jet-black hair, his clear-framed eyeglasses, deliberate manner, trim figure and deep voice, conveys authority. He is an earnest man, whose tie is rarely loosened. Although Peterson can display a dry, self-deprecating wit, particularly before an audience, he usually appears solemn. . . .

Unlike Glucksman, Peterson immerses himself in public issues and the world outside. He sits on the boards of six blue-chip corporations, is treasurer of the Council on Foreign Relations and serves as a trustee of the Japan Society and the Museum of Modern Art.

At the firm, Peterson was Mr. Outside; Glucksman was Mr. Inside. Peterson cared more about the public weal and status, Glucksman about power. Peterson accepted and enjoyed an ambassadorial role . . . and . . . had an extensive social life outside of Lehman. He enjoyed attending an art or theater opening, an elaborate East Side dinner party. His talented third wife, Joan Ganz Cooney, president and founder of the Children's Television Workshop, which produces *Sesame Street*, had ushered him into New York's literary world. . . .

Glucksman's life, on the other hand, rotated around Lehman. Those Glucksman considered his closest personal friends were usually those he did business with. Rarely did he see them outside the business day. . . . Unlike Pete and Joan Peterson, Lew and Inez Glucksman rarely entertained. In fact, they were no longer close to each other. She was a part-time editor for a publishing company and had been a full-time mother of two grown daughters. At the end of a long day, Lew Glucksman would often scoop up some memos or a tool catalogue so he could contemplate furniture to build or repair, and he would have his driver wait outside as he dined alone in a Chinatown restaurant. When he got away, it was usually for lonely pursuits—skippering one of his boats, fishing, cabinetry.

If Peterson is the prototype of a smooth corporate titan, the earthy, volatile Glucksman was the opposite—a "jungle fighter." A fellow board member observes: "Glucksman's flaw was that there was an angry pig inside the man. He wasn't after money. He was after power, complete control." But Glucksman didn't perceive himself this way. What he dreamed of doing for Lehman was what Gustave Levy . . . or John Gutfreund had done . . .—build a muscular, modern investment bank.

Glucksman's urge for power was fueled by resentments. He came to resent Peterson's preferences for memos rather than meetings; he often complained about the way Peterson kept people waiting while he juggled telephone calls, about the wall of secretaries guarding access to him, about his condescending manner. "Ride out to the airport with me, Lew," he would command. Peterson, who always worried about his own weight, would say, "Meet my fat friend Lew."

Peterson's appeal owes more to his stature, his contacts, his considerable intelligence and the aggressive homework he does rather than to his charm or magnetism. His ability to recruit new business staggered even his detractors. . . . But the attention Peterson lavished on clients was rarely turned toward his partners, much less to those who worked in the trenches. One of his Lehman admirers, partner Steven Bershad, says, "He would set his mind on something and see nothing else. He would walk down the hall with a stack of letters and read the mail while going out to a meeting and write replies and just throw them over his shoulder, assuming someone would be there to pick it up." "He can be described as 'frank' or as 'cruel,' depending on your point of view," observes partner Robert S. Rubin, who thought him "cruel."

Glucksman thought Peterson was self-centered, haughty, uncaring. "I knew the man 10 years but I never had a personal conversation with him," says Glucksman. In fact, the Equitable lunch reminded him of another incident. As if the bone were still stuck in his throat, Glucksman becomes livid when he recalls how Peterson treated him "like a flunky" at a mid-seventies meeting with client David Rockefeller at the Chase Manhattan Bank. . . .

What is relevant is that this and other wounds still pained Lew Glucksman. It irritated him when Peterson said, as he still does, that "I didn't have a detailed grasp of that part of our business that was increasingly important—trading, futures, brokerage, commodities." This angered Glucksman because these trading functions were then generating two-thirds of Lehman's profits. And now that trading was getting its day in the sun, he feared that Peterson was angling within a few years to sell the firm for a substantial premium over the current share price.

Glucksman knew, and the partners knew, that for several years now he, not Pete Peterson, had been managing the day-to-day business, had chaired the operations committee, which Peterson did not even serve on. Meanwhile, Peterson focused on a core group of clients, on bringing in new business, on strategic planning and marketing. Ever since Glucksman was made chief operating officer in 1980, Peterson had been delegating more and more responsibility to him; by 1983, the chairman worked directly only with a handful of Lehman partners. . . . Despite his growing isolation from the board as well as the rank and file at Lehman, Peterson rightly believed it was he who set the strategic framework for the firm's success and who acted as a rudder for Glucksman, an opinion shared by many partners, though not by Lew Glucksman. "Over the last five years, Peterson didn't play an active role in the management of the business," says Glucksman. "I brought him up to date. We played a charade with him"—pretending he was in charge. It annoyed Glucksman that to the outside world Peterson got all the credit for successes Glucksman came to feel were his. "I got sick and tired of Pete always saying the same thing," says Glucksman. "Pete was a guy totally obsessed with the world hearing the name Pete Peterson."

Donald Regan

BERNARD WEINRAUB

> At a certain moment about 30 years ago, Don Regan decided that Merrill
> Lynch should be the leading institutional brokerage firm as well as the
> biggest retail broker—*and* a leading bond dealer, asset manager, and un-
> derwriter. More than this, he and his colleagues made it happen. He
> then went into the government, first as Secretary of the Treasury and
> later as Chief of Staff to President Ronald Reagan.

As a 27-year old Marine major swaggering back from five campaigns, including Gaudalcanal and Okinawa, Don Regan decided that too much life
had already passed him by to take the time to finish Harvard law school.
So in 1946 he looked around for companies with training programs. He
found two in New York, Mobil and Merrill Lynch. Not quite sure why even
today, he headed for Wall Street and hit it more or less like a whole platoon
of leathernecks running full tilt.

He made partner in 1954 at the age of 35, the youngest ever at the time,
and took over the big Philadelphia office. In the late 1950s, Merrill Lynch
wanted its young hotshot back in New York as head of the administrative
division. Regan thought that sounded dull, so he agreed on the condition
that he be allowed to set up a long-range planning department, an idea
that was still rare in industry and practically unthinkable on Wall Street.
"The securities business by 1960 was doing exactly what it had done since
World War I," Regan says, and his head was already swimming with ideas
about how to change it.

There had been one major exception to the industry's torpor—the innovative burst of Charles Merrill that created the firm in 1940. Merrill
reached a vast market of ordinary citizens by using the chain-store concept. But Charlie Merrill died in 1956, and by the time Regan began to
have some voice in the firm, it was rolling along as it always had, still the
nation's biggest brokerage, and growing, but not trying anything new.

Regan argued that Merrill's formula ought to be taken one simple step
further: the chain store should become a supermarket of every conceivable
financial service. Even before he reached the top he was forceful enough to
prod Merrill Lynch's leaders toward such new fields as mutual funds and
overseas banking. Annual revenues were $473 million when he became chief

---

executive in 1971, and by the time he left for Washington to become President Reagan's Secretary of the Treasury, they had topped $3 billion.

While still stressing Merrill Lynch's little-guy business, Regan moved aggressively into the institutional market and investment banking, where the firm now rivals Salomon Brothers and First Boston for first place. Then he veered onto bankers' turf with Merrill Lynch's Cash Management Account, through which customers can write checks against the value of their portfolios. In 1978, he started a program to assemble a national system of real-estate brokers, reasoning that even people who never invest in stocks or bonds buy houses.

What Regan did at Merrill Lynch would alone win him a place in Wall Street history. But in the process he also overturned most of the industry's traditions of the last 200 years. He saw Wall Street as a bastion of capitalism that was itself afraid of unfettered market forces, "Go back and read the Buttonwood Agreement in 1792 [which established the securities business in New York]. It set up a cartel." He was the first broker to come out against fixed commissions. Regan fought for the right to go public, and Merrill Lynch was among the first on the Street to do so. Wall Streeters called him a maverick, a term he detests. A maverick, he will tell you, wanders away. Don Regan believes he got out ahead of the herd and led it.

Regan showed little of that pugnaciousness at Cambridge Latin School and Harvard, where he preferred the library and the debating team to the athletic field. "I paid a great deal of attention to what I was being taught," he says. The Marine Corps was a pivotal experience. It gave him a salty style and a sense of how to organize an enterprise that's "precise as to who's going to do what." Most of all, he thinks, his tour through the Pacific taught him the courage to "do what I wanted to do."

Michel David-Weill

ROBERT TEITELMAN

Michel David-Weill's family took over management of Lazard Frères when the founding Lazard Brothers left no heirs. The last family member to rule the firm, he successfully revitalized three more-or-less independent Lazard houses into one of the few merchant banks that is both highly profitable and truly international. Owning one of the world's finest private collections of paintings and with a family fortune near $1 billion, he describes himself as "very attached" to the private banking tradition. This sketch gives us a good look at the man and his philosophy.

Trademark Cuban cigar in hand, Michel David-Weill pads across the off-white carpeting and rustles through a clutter of books on the credenza behind his desk. With a grunt of triumph, he returns, waving a dark-green volume: the directory of New York Stock Exchange firms, circa 1920. He settles himself, and hunches over the dog-eared pages. "Some great names have disappeared," he murmurs in his thickly French-accented English. "Bache . . . Belmont . . . Dominick & Dominick . . . Eastman Dillon . . . Hornblower Weeks . . . Lee Higginson. . . . These were names I knew." He squints through half-moon glasses. "Ah, and there we are: Lazard Frères. And there is my grandfather's name, David Weill.

"You know, it is very amusing," he says, snapping the book shut. "When people say you can now be assured of the future, I say, 'How can anyone be assured after they look at this book?' "

David-Weill talks on, but his warning hangs over the conversation. The short, pudgy banker is the largest shareholder and dominant partner of the three houses of Lazard: Lazard Frères & Co. in New York, Lazard Brothers & Co. in London and Lazard Frères et Cie. in Paris. Lazard has been around for well over a century now, and David-Weill, 60, is one of the wealthiest bankers in the world. And yet in the past decade or so, many observers have repeatedly predicted that traditional investment banking houses such as Lazard would be consigned at best to a diminished role, at worst to oblivion.

David-Weill dismisses those arguments—"Size is not as important in finance as it is in commerce," he observes, calmly obliterating one of the truisms of the age—while acknowledging the fragility of financial life. In

doing so he articulates a view that is both deeply traditional in its core beliefs and a radical break with conventional financial wisdom. David-Weill
was early to recognize the logic of globalization and the Lazard houses'
potential advantages. During the past decade he and Lazard have been engaged in a long-term strategic experiment that no one in finance has yet
managed to complete successfully: combining culturally distinct entities
into a true multinational firm. In Lazard's case it meant not only overhauling an aging three-ring circus but also making sure the eclectic
troupe performed in tandem. All the three houses really shared was a common name, a common genesis and parts of a common culture—and a
shareholder named David-Weill.

It is, in microcosm, as grand an experiment as the construction of the
European Community—and just as perilous. It demands a long view, a deft
feel for three different cultures and the willingness to gamble on a particular view of the world. It also requires someone who has the stature, and
the raw power, to pull the threads tying the three houses together. In Paris
partners refer to David-Weill's "legitimacy," a phrase that sums up the curious and nearly indefinable amalgam of traits that includes, but does not
demand, the correct bloodlines. "Only David-Weill currently has legitimacy," says Jean-Claude Haas, a Paris partner and a managing director in
London. "If he were not around, I suppose someone else—or some others—might have to emerge." New York general partner Robert Agostinelli
offers a blunter American formulation: "Michel *is* Lazard."

Legitimacy is not a problem today at Lazard; but what if David-Weill
should disappear tomorrow? The Lazard houses of course would survive,
though the global coordination process might be put at risk. Younger partners in particular talk as if globalization is no longer reversible and argue
that simple self-interest would guarantee future cooperation. London
chairman David Verey emphasizes the sheer number of people who now
have a stake in making coordination function properly.

Meanwhile, David-Weill continues to nudge the process forward. He
recently set up a coordinating committee—manned by Jean-Marie Messier
from Lazard Paris, John Dear from Lazard Brothers and Kenneth Jacobs
from New York—that will attempt to mediate serious conflicts. "But of
course there will always be some conflicts I ultimately will have to resolve," he adds.

David-Weill's role, however, in all three houses is far more subtle, far
more essential, than just convincing his partners to speak to one another.
"Michel is the balance wheel," admits New York senior partner Felix
Rohatyn, who of all the partners may have the closest working relationship
with David-Weill. "He makes it all work." Adds managing director Marcus Agius in London: "What is so interesting is how many people turn to
him for advice. He's got all this experience in his genes."

• • •

To outsiders the Lazard culture can be baffling. On the one hand Lazard boasts of having some of the most egocentric, individualistic investment bankers around, most trained at other firms—Lazard does not recruit new MBAs, and there is no such thing as a standard "Lazard banker." On the other hand partners chant the Lazard party line, a set of precepts synonymous with David-Weill's business philosophy. Partners particularly repeat a catechism that defines the firm according to David-Weill. One: Don't use much capital ("If you give a banker capital," goes a favorite David-Weill nostrum, "he'll only lose it."). Two: Keep lines of communication short. Three: Pursue a core business of advising major companies; everything else must support that. Four: The goal is to make money, but to do so—given precepts one, two and three—requires long-term relationships with clients.

Generally, Lazard partners speak of David-Weill as if he were more patriarch than boss. He does not rule like his New York predecessor, André Meyer, they say, he presides. He disdains memos and strictures, even at the risk of a certain chaos. He diffuses his business philosophy through conversation; he expects his partners to draw conclusions from the first principles he outlines. Adrian Evans, a Lazard Brothers managing director who came to the merchant bank only two years ago, describes David-Weill, as "a proprietor"—another phrase redolent of an earlier age. "He'll ask you if he could have a five-minute conversation; says Evans. "You sit down and discover that 45 minutes have passed and he's talking to you about his life, his views, and you're telling him quite intimate things. It's quite subtle."

He will occasionally flash very sharp claws. In 1977, when David-Weill was faced with reversing the decline of the New York house—not only was Meyer dying but Meyer's protégé, Rohatyn, was off saving the city of New York—David Weill moved aggressively. First, he snatched four senior bankers away from the old Lehman Brothers, a partnership that had long had intimate ties to Lazard. Then he forced seven Lazard partners into retirement. "He only rarely puts his foot down," says one Lazard partner. "But when he does he really gets your attention."

Such unilateral action is not normally his style. "We do not like to make revolutions," he says. "When you have to do that, it means you have somehow failed. We favor evolution."

David-Weill did not invent his business philosophy, he inherited it. His great-grandfather, Alexander Weill, gained control of Lazard in the 1880s from his cousins, the Lazard brothers, who had founded the firm 35 years earlier in San Francisco. Weill went on to build a small but powerful merchant bank with branches in New York, London and Paris.

During World War II young Michel and his sister were forced to hide out from the Germans; their father, Pierre David-Weill, fled to Lazard New York, then under the control of André Meyer. The war gave Michel a taste of what it was like for a seemingly solid world to come apart, an experience he shares with two of the most senior partners of the firm. As a young man in Austria, Rohatyn fled the Nazis with gold coins stuffed in toothpaste tubes. And Antoine Bernheim, the formidable senior partner in Paris, spent the war in hiding, only to discover that both parents had been killed at Auschwitz.

After the war the David-Weill family, led by his father, rebuilt the Paris house, and Michel earned a degree from the Institut d'Etudes Politiques before taking up a partnership in Paris in 1961. After spending time in New york working with Meyer, he returned to Paris, taking over when his father died in 1975. When Meyer fell ill in 1977, David-Weill assumed control in New York as well.

David-Weill's considerable outward charm masks a powerful ambition and drive for control. He swings regularly back and forth across the Atlantic on the Concorde: three weeks in New York, one in London, two in Paris. Like Meyer, he is never far from a phone; he encourages both partners and clients to call him. He occupies a place not at the apex of a Lazard pyramid, but at the hub of a wheel, with direct links to partners in all three houses.

One result: He can appear to be ubiquitous, aware not only of deals taking place in all three houses, but of problems and conflicts. It gives him great power and contributes to a sense of his omnipotence, to his mystique. "You go to see him to talk about a problem, and he often seems to already know about it," marvels one New York partner. "That's because he's probably talked to four other people. His information is amazing."

He directly controls two key levers of power at Lazard: compensation and recruitment. The finite nature of a partnership pie—"There is no inflation on 100 percent, so the currency is fixed," he says cheerfully—provides a constant spur to competition and a means of encouraging coordination. So seriously does he consider compensation that deliberations in New York now begin in mid-summer and end in December. This is not just an exercise in toting up fees, though rainmaking is clearly important. Part of David-Weill's power, and skill, lies in his ability to factor in qualitative judgments.

Second, by controlling recruiting—another skill that, like compensation, depends heavily on intuition and insight—he can continually reshape the partnership. However, when he makes a mistake—and he has—he can isolate it by slashing the partnership share, particularly in New York. "We are all the time looking for the relatively exceptional. It is not easy, because in our way of life it is important to get statesmanlike qualities."

• • •

Lazard is a throwback to an age when investment bankers—Bobby Lehman, André Meyer, Siegmund Warburg—dominated finance through their network of relationships. The long-term issue for Lazard is whether there will always be a demand for the kind of advice it sells—and this is advice that transcends M&A—or whether corporate finance will be commoditized and packaged at trading desks. And, in the end . . . the underlying question of the clash of traders and bankers is really a political, not a financial, issue.

Does society function better, or more equitably, with bankers in the van or traders? With a thick web of ties and historic relationship or with many atomistic units, endlessly competing? David-Weill is betting on the former; much of the rest of the industry believes the latter.

Meanwhile, David-Weill continues his endless Atlantic shuttle and his endless conversations. "Michel works far harder than he needs to and should," says Verey. "He's not doing that just for the fun of it. He's very eager to ensure that Lazard as a philosophy and as a collection of people remains important and to be reckoned with." David-Weill chooses to emphasize the tasks not done—those, indeed, that can never be completed. "The process will never be finished," he says, deep in an armchair at Lazard Brothers in London, a photograph of his father and grandfather over one shoulder. "The world changes, and we must be continually changing with it. But certain things, certain ideas, do not change."

He smiles the smile of a Sun King, or at least a constitutional monarch, exerting that force of personality—part genes, part intelligence, all Gallic charm—that is the essential David-Weill. He does not act like an anachronism. "He is special," admits Haas, who had just begun to work at Lazard in Paris when young Michel first arrived. "He has this ability that few people have to really think, to keep his mind on a problem for some time. He also lives with certain facts of life that most of us push aside—death, evil, disaster. Because he is reconciled to these facts of life, some people think he is indifferent or cynical. That is not the case at all; I think his secret is that he simply does not try to conceal them. He accepts those things and moves on."

William Salomon

MARTIN MAYER

Billy Salomon, the strikingly gracious and attractive son of Percy Salomon, one of the original Salomon Brothers—presided over the transformation of the firm into one of the world's financial powerhouses. Later, as he saw others capitalize on the value of the firm by selling out, he commented on the transaction, on the culture he had developed, and on the successor [John Gutfreund] he had chosen, saying: "I would have thought more recognition might have been given to those who built the firm."

Reprinted with permission of Simon & Schuster from *Nightmare on Wall Street* by Martin Mayer. Copyright © 1993 by Martin Mayer.

On a table by the oak door to the partners' dining room was an elongated black-bound ledger book called "the boards" in which was recorded, in handwriting, the firm's positions as of the close of business the day before: its inventory of municipal and government bonds and notes, commercial paper, corporate bonds, bankers' acceptances, and the like. At the back of the ledger—called "the back of the book"—was a list of the firm's own investments, held for long-term price appreciation and income rather than trading profit. The ledger noted the price at which each position had been acquired, both in the trading accounts and in the investment accounts, and the price for which it had sold in the previous day's final transaction—the "market price." Every so often someone entering the partners' dining room would pause at the doorway, open the "boards," and take a look at how the firm was doing. How the firm was doing was synonymous with how the partner was doing, because the rule was that the firm's investments were the partners' wealth. It was understood that apart from their homes, bank accounts, and insurance policies, partners in a trading house like Salomon did not have private interests separate from those of their firm.

In the early 1950s, Salomon's capital had touched $11.5 million, but in the mid-1950s, it went into decline. All earnings were divided among the partners at the end of each year, and they mostly spent what they made or put it into real estate rather than add to their investment in their firm. Partnership compensation was a mix of salary, bonus, and return on investment in the partnership itself. This was a privately held firm: no stockholders, no public reports of activity, profits or losses. In the early 1950s the average partner in the average year took home between $70,000 and $100,000 a year, which was an extremely good income. . . .

The leader of the firm in the 1950s was not, however, a pure example of the Salomon man. He spent a fair amount of time in his private office, beside the trading room, and he also maintained some private interests independent of the partnership. He was Rudolf Smutny, a tall man with a long face, a bald dome, a go-getter attitude, and a sarcastic manner. Smutny had come to Salomon Brothers out of the Marine Corps right after World War I; he also served a second time as a volunteer in World War II. He was an indefatigable salesman, often calling on the same bank two or three times a day, with a salesman's unquenchable optimism and high opinion of himself, including his capacities to analyze financial statements and to handle booze. When he made a sale in the trading room, he would bellow out, "I dood it, fellas." . . .

Flouting the unwritten Salomon rule, Smutny accepted election to the boards of Trailer Train, of Zeckendorf's Webb & Knapp, and of Associated Oil & Gas. Taking himself very seriously, he boosted his own share of the partnership income to 12½ percent, double that of partners much his senior, and began to abuse his expense account, charging his children's travel and entertainment (and in one instance, clothing) to the firm. His wife, who was also a formidable drinker—straight gin from eight-ounce glasses—sometimes abused other partners' wives on social occasions. . . .

The companies into which Smutny put the firm's capital did not pay dividends, and he made the earnings on the capital look better by purchasing short-term paper in Europe, where interest rates were higher but currency devaluations could devastate the dollar value of the paper. His domestic investments turned out to be mostly losers (Webb & Knapp wound up bankrupt, and although Trailer Train remained a Salomon client for more than two decades, it never provided much return on its stock.) Under Smutny's leadership Salomon's capital slid to only a little more than $7 million. . . . And many of the assets in the investment account were highly illiquid and hard to value. Among them, however, there was also one gigantic winner: Smutny's gamble in a little company called Haloid, which became Xerox after his successors sold Salomon's stake. If they had closed the business instead, distributed the Haloid shares among themselves and simply held on to them, the Salomon partners would have been richer than they ever became through their work.

· · ·

Among those who watched these developments in silence was the sole survivor of the original Salomon brothers, Percy, born in 1882 and long retired. He was a slim old man with thin shoulders but erect posture, who wore a high collar and spoke rarely. . . .

When he came in for lunch in the 1950s, which he did every so often, Percy rarely talked about business. But he did once, on a day in the fall of 1956, shortly after the firm closed the books on its October 1 to September 30 fiscal year. He stopped on his way out from lunch and cast his eyes at the ledger book on the table by the door. He took a minute reading the back of the book, then turned to the partners at the table, perhaps eight or nine of them, and said, "You fellows ought to be ashamed of yourselves, dealing in *shit* like this."

Among the partners present was Percy's son William, often "Bill" and more frequently "Billy," a salesman of no great attainments who had come to Salomon from prep school in 1933, having chosen to get married young rather than go to college. Someone who knew him at Horace Mann remembered him as charming, strikingly well dressed, with clothes from DePinna, and more or less vacant. His clients at Salomon tended to be those his father had serviced, and it was thought he had become a partner by reason of consanguinity rather than as a reward for accomplishment. He made the best paper airplanes in the trading room and was deadly with spitballs. Like his father, he was a gentleman, courteous to all. Small, rather delicate, with hair neatly parted on the left, he had not been heard to assert himself in the partnership. Percy, departing, let his eyes rest briefly on each of the other men in the room, including Billy, who had never heard his father use such language before.

. . .

Although a lot of people wanted Smutny out, discussions around the dining table revealed that the senior partners were not willing to take the lead in removing him. He was the firm's contact with several of its largest customers, and he had a habit of leadership nobody in the junta could claim. Truth to tell, they were all afraid of him—all except Billy Salomon, who talked things over in confidence with Leo Gottlieb of Cleary Gottlieb Steen & Hamilton, the firm's lawyers, and then patiently worked the partnership for almost six months, urging a meeting one morning before trading began, on a day when Smutny would be out of town. The stars came into the proper conjunction in April. At the meeting, after he and Ottens had described the financial condition of the firm and the losses on Smutny's pet projects, Billy demanded a vote to buy out Smutny's 12½ percent and dismiss him from the partnership. Levy and Holsten were not prepared to cast Smutny out, but Billy insisted. When Smutny returned from his trip, he found to his horror—for the firm was his whole life—that he had been expelled from Salomon. Charles Simon, who was there, gave the simple explanation: "Billy found he had bigger balls than he'd thought he had."

. . .

He turned again to Gottlieb, a shy man of rigid probity and rarely revealed brilliance (first in his class at the Sheffield School at Yale and then at Harvard Law School), who would continue to practice law well into his nineties. Gottlieb became a limited partner, investing half a million dollars of his own money, and wrote a new partnership agreement for Billy. . . . Under the terms of Billy's new agreement, Salomon partners in effect committed to leave most of their share of the future profits of the firm in their capital accounts, not only while they were working for Salomon but for five years after departure.

Billy ran the firm for the next 20 years. . . . Of course, it was Billy's family name that was on the firm. Retaining his unassuming, rather gentle manner, he became more of a dictator than Smutny had ever been. . . . And though he was an unusually courteous man outside the office, nobody can remember that he ever said thanks for a service done for him or the firm.

But among the hundreds of partners and "managing directors" who passed through Salomon Brothers in the years of his leadership, there are amazingly few who feel anything but loyalty to the point of love for the Salomon Brothers of the Bill days. (Even the failure to say thanks has its defenders: "You were *supposed* to be good," said one of them.) . . . "He had little compassion, and he did little stroking. He had . . . the Pit Theory of personnel management—put all these guys into a pit, and whoever walks out is the survivor. But he kept all the inmates walking in lockstep. He could play the traders and the salesmen and the bankers against each other—that was his genius. He was very comfortable making people decisions, and that's the greatest strength a manager can have."

It was the people Billy Salomon hired and socialized into his firm who made . . . Salomon Brothers . . . one of the most important investment banks in the world, hugely profitable and heavily capitalized with almost $200 million (only Merrill Lynch had more). Although some of these activities were still embryonic and would mushroom only in the dark world of the 1980s, Salomon in 1978 was already a pioneer in hedging as well as taking risks, in the creation of mortgage-backed securities, and in finding profitable swap financing for multinational corporations, governments, and international organizations. Its monetary and fixed-income (bond) research operations were the best in the world, certainly in the private sector. Eventually Billy even got some respect: He served on the board of governors of the New York Stock Exchange and as president of the Bond Club, an organization, as one of his partners said rather sourly, "formerly headed by people who had come over on the Mayflower."

For most of those years Bill was in physical pain, limping about the trading room to favor an arthritic hip joint that was replaced in a pioneering and successful operation in the early 1970s. Then another physical disability led him to resign as managing partner in 1978, a year before his sixty-fifth birthday. He had been diagnosed with a brain tumor, and while it proved operable and benign, he was concerned—or so one of his closest friends reported—that after he returned from the hospital he would not have the judgment to know that his judgment was impaired. Billy himself said his reason for taking early retirement was that he and his wife Virginia were entitled to take vacations of the kind they hadn't known since he had taken over the firm in 1957: "We wanted three weeks in Europe, and I could never do that while I was running the firm. The brain tumor told me it was time."

John Gutfreund

PAUL FERRIS

John Gutfreund, managing partner from 1978 to 1991, led Salomon
Brothers through an extraordinary transformation. Subsequently, a
major scandal involving fraudulent bids on Treasury securities forced
him out—and very nearly destroyed the firm.

"Stan's got an order for ninety-nine," "a million ninety-twos," "ninety-
eight to two thousand." The bonds had different maturities. "Ninety-
eight" meant 1998, "two thousand" was the year 2000, when the world
would be different, but money wouldn't. The longest bonds, almost two
thirds of the total, would not be paid off till July 1, 2023. These were the
most popular with investors; the syndicate status report that someone
pulled off a desktop printer for me showed that most of them had gone already. On July 1, 2023, I would be 94, if anything. The sales staff would
have moved on to something quieter.

John H. Gutfreund would be 94, too. In middle age he is quiet, gruff,
well manicured, and rich. He joined Salomon in 1953, became a partner 10
years later, and rose to the head of the firm in 1978 as managing partner.
There were 60 or 70 general partners, their private capital locked up in the
firm; altogether they owned but had little access to a fortune between $3
and $4 hundred million. In 1981 talks began with a possible purchaser who
would buy them out and enable them to realize their wealth. This was not
the only reason for the dialogue. The firm interested in Salomon Brothers
was the large and secretive Philbro Corporation, a commodity trader and
dealer in many countries, with annual sales of $20 or $30 billion. Philbro
and Salomon had done business for years, and there were logical reasons for
combining the two. Philbro's staples included ores, metals, grains, and the
commodity that (with one exception) trades in the greatest volume, petroleum. The exception was money and securities. Salomon Brothers knew all
about financial trading. The talks prospered and the deal was done by the
autumn of 1981. Salomon Brothers kept its autonomy under a holding company that was itself called Philbro-Salomon. There were those who said that
despite the size of Philbro, the bank would be the tail that wagged the dog.

Reprinted from *The Master Bankers: Controlling the World's Finances* (New York: William
Morrow and Company, 1984; originally published 1984 in Great Britain as *Gentlemen of
Fortune*), Chapter 4, pp. 125–127, by permission of Curtis Brown Group Ltd. on behalf of
Paul Ferris. © 1984 by Paul Ferris.

As for the former partners who changed overnight into managing directors, dazzling sums of money fell into their laps. Every partner seems to have
become a dollar millionaire if he was not one already: not that a plain millionaire in the United States nowadays excites much interest. The money
came from two directions. Philbro Corp. paid the partners $250 million in
Philbro securities for the firm. Some got more than others. Securities and
Exchange Commission figures showed that Henry Kaufman received just
over $10 million worth. Gutfreund's share was worth more than $13 million. Their value fluctuated, on the whole upwards. The other source was
the broken-up partnership capital. This must have been worth well over $10
million apiece to some of the senior Salomon people. John Gutfreund's total
prize from both sources was widely estimated, a couple of years after the
Philbro deal, to be worth more than $40 million.

He has a somewhat world-weary look. His gray hair is thinning. His
heavy face and the almost sullen set of his sensuous mouth don't change
much as he speaks. The hand looks too small for the cigar. Measured and
lucid, he sounds the epitome of the Wall Street professional. If there is a
trace of some different person, it is only a trace. Everybody knows who
Gutfreund is. He has never worked anywhere else.

I met him twice. The first time, he said, "One of the problems for me in
a proprietary business is that I'm really not very interested in removing
the mystique. It doesn't serve our purpose to lay ourselves bare. A nice
press is leaving us alone."

After that he was more helpful than his remarks suggested. He talked,
when asked, about his progress through the firm. "I graduated from college
in 1951," he said, "was drafted into the army, went to Korea. When I returned I wasn't poor but I wasn't terribly affluent. I was thinking of going to
graduate school, of teaching, of the arts. But I felt—I don't know, I thought
maybe I wouldn't be the greatest, and I always had an affection for wanting
to be the best in some way. In the arts it seemed to me that you really were
starved emotionally and financially if you were less than the best. I met a
friend who asked me down for lunch, and he said, 'Would you like to try
this, John?' I took the job, which was supposedly training. The training was
watching other people working. Then when somebody died or got fired or
they were expanding the department, they'd transfer you to that slot. And I
got placed in the municipal department. At that time you had to understand
simple numbers, have a good memory so you didn't make the same mistakes
over and over again, and have the ability to respond to the broadest set of
stimuli, which is what a good market person always has to have. I proved to
have a pretty good memory and a simple knowledge of numbers, and I did it
well for some years. As a result I was put in charge of sales and syndicate.

"I used to be very good at the syndicate business. It was a great deal of
fun. It was a game I understood. In our firm at that point in history it was
very important. My success was related to that, and to the fact that I had a

great information base. If one is successful it is only because one knows more facts, not because one is smarter. I had a better feel, because of our trading activities, because of our sales force, of what might happen. And I guess I was fairly aggressive in my time—that is, trying to get the best terms. We didn't have much inherited underwriting business, so most of it was through competitive bidding. . . . I just used the resources at hand."

I asked how long it had taken before he felt committed to the firm. "You get involved in working here," he said. "The world narrows, your horizons narrow. You drift—if you're like I am—you drift into something, then excuse it by saying, 'Anything else I do now, I'm too old, I'm 27, I'm 33, I'm 36. I'm too old to try for something new.'"

A ship's hooter was groaning in the bay. He said, "I'm not one of the great adventurers of the world. I think I've become more so as I've got older. Probably because I *am* older. Also probably because I'm richer." He said that one of the things he liked about the securities business was the certainty: "There is no room for half truths. It's not a gray world. There are no white lies. Either you made the bid or you didn't. Either you sold the bonds or you didn't. You lose money sometimes, you make money sometimes. It's a fairly simple-minded game. There is an absolute truth, which is rare in the human condition, that's quite satisfying for small people. Also, I would guess that I knew the people with whom I worked, better most of the time than I knew wife and family. The necessity for an absolute, unequivocal answer—I pay, I buy, I sell. It used to be *we* bought, *we* sold, but you get more egotistical as you get older. Which is an error, because it's not my money." He smiled as he said it: the only time.

John Meriwether

MICHAEL LEWIS

Michael Lewis sought to capture the personality of a great firm—to tell what it was *really* like—in a 1989 book about Salomon Brothers, his former employer. Here, the work's first chapter sets the stage and we very quickly learn the meaning of its title: "Liar's Poker." John Gutfreund played this round with John Meriwether. In 1998, Meriwether would play the largest round in history as his highly leveraged giant, Long Term Capital Management, sought acutely needed, massive financing to avert an ugly and dangerous disruptive collapse that could have been cataclysmic. With remarkable talent, nerve, and grace, Meriwether is back.

It was sometime early in 1986, the first year of the decline of my firm, Salomon Brothers. Our chairman, John Gutfreund, left his desk at the head of the trading floor and went for a walk. At any given moment on the trading floor billions of dollars were being risked by bond traders. Gutfreund took the pulse of the place by simply wandering around it and asking questions of the traders. An eerie sixth sense guided him to wherever a crisis was unfolding. Gutfreund seemed able to smell money being lost.

He was the last person a nerve-racked trader wanted to see. Gutfreund (pronounced *Good friend*) liked to sneak up from behind and surprise you. This was fun for him but not for you. Busy on two phones at once trying to stem disaster, you had no time to turn and look. You didn't need to. You felt him. The area around you began to convulse like an epileptic ward. People were pretending to be frantically busy and at the same time staring intently at a spot directly above your head. You felt a chill in your bones that I imagine belongs to the same class of intelligence as the nervous twitch of a small furry animal at the silent approach of a grizzly bear. An alarm shrieked in your head: Gutfreund! Gutfreund! Gutfreund!

Often as not, our chairman just hovered quietly for a bit, then left. You might never have seen him. The only trace I found of him on two of these occasions was a turdlike ash on the floor beside my chair, left, I suppose, as a calling card. Gutfreund's cigar droppings were longer and better formed than those of the average Salomon boss. I always assumed that he smoked a more expensive blend than the rest, purchased with a few of the $40 million he had cleared on the sale of Salomon Brothers in 1981 (or a few of the $3.1 million he paid himself in 1986, more than any other Wall Street CEO).

This day in 1986, however, Gutfreund did something strange. Instead of terrifying us all, he walked a straight line to the trading desk of John Meriwether, a member of the board of Salomon Inc. and also one of Salomon's finest bond traders. He whispered a few words. The traders in the vicinity eavesdropped. What Gutfreund said has become a legend at Salomon Brothers and a visceral part of its corporate identity. He said: "One hand, one million dollars, no tears."

One hand, one million dollars, no tears. Meriwether grabbed the meaning instantly. The King of Wall Street, as *Business Week* had dubbed Gutfreund, wanted to play a single hand of a game called Liar's Poker for a million dollars. He played the game most afternoons with Meriwether and the six young bond arbitrage traders who worked for Meriwether and was usually skinned alive. Some traders said Gutfreund was heavily outmatched. Others who couldn't imagine John Gutfreund as anything but omnipotent—and there were many—said that losing suited his purpose, though exactly what that might be was a mystery.

The peculiar feature of Gutfreund's challenge this time was the size of the stake. Normally his bets didn't exceed a few hundred dollars. A million was unheard of. The final two words of his challenge, "no tears," meant that the loser was expected to suffer a great deal of pain but wasn't entitled to whine, bitch, or moan about it. He'd just have to hunker down and keep his poverty to himself. But why? You might ask if you were anyone other than the King of Wall Street. Why do it in the first place? Why, in particular, challenge Meriwether instead of some lesser managing director? It seemed an act of sheer lunacy. Meriwether was the King of the Game, the Liar's Poker champion of the Salomon Brothers trading floor.

On the other hand, one thing you learn on a trading floor is that winners like Gutfreund *always* have some reason for what they do; it might not be the best of reasons, but at least they have a concept in mind. I was not privy to Gutfreund's innermost thoughts, but I do know that all the boys on the trading floor gambled and that he wanted badly to be one of the boys. What I think Gutfreund had in mind in this instance was a desire to show his courage, like the boy who leaps from the high dive. Who better than Meriwether for the purpose? Besides, Meriwether was probably the only trader with both the cash and the nerve to play.

The whole absurd situation needs putting into context. John Meriwether had, in the course of his career, made hundreds of millions of dollars for Salomon Brothers. He had an ability, rare among people and treasured by traders, to hide his state of mind. Most traders divulge whether they are making or losing money by the way they speak or move. They are either overly easy or overly tense. With Meriwether you could never, ever tell. He wore the same blank half-tense expression when he won as he did when he lost. He had, I think, a profound ability to control the two emotions that commonly destroy traders—fear and greed—and it made him as noble as a man who pursues his self-interest so fiercely can be. He was thought by many within Salomon to be the best bond trader on Wall Street. Around Salomon no tone but awe was used when he was discussed. People would say, "He's the best businessman in the place," or "the best risk taker I have ever seen," or "a very dangerous Liar's Poker player."

Meriwether cast a spell over the young traders who worked for him. His boys ranged in age from 25 to 32 (he was about 40). Most of them had Ph.D.'s in math, economics, and/or physics. Once they got onto Meriwether's trading desk, however, they forgot they were supposed to be detached intellectuals. They became disciples. They became obsessed by the game of Liar's Poker. They regarded it as *their* game. And they took it to a new level of seriousness.

John Gutfreund was always the outsider in their game. That *Business Week* had put his picture on the cover and called him the King of Wall Street held little significance for them. I mean, that was, in a way, the whole point. Gutfreund was the King of Wall Street, but Meriwether was King of the Game. When Gutfreund had been crowned by the gentlemen of the press, you could almost hear traders thinking: *Foolish names and foolish faces often appear in public places.* Fair enough, Gutfreund had once been a trader, but that was as relevant as an old woman's claim that she was once quite a dish.

At times Gutfreund himself seemed to agree. He loved to trade. Compared with managing, trading was admirably direct. You made your bets and either you won or you lost. When you won, people—all the way up to the top of the firm—admired you, envied you, and feared you, and with reason: You controlled the loot. When you managed a firm, well, sure you received your quota of envy, fear, and admiration. But for all the wrong reasons. *You did not make the money for Salomon. You did not take risk.* You were hostage to your producers. They took risk. They proved their superiority every day by handling risk better than the rest of the risk-taking world. The money came from risk takers such as Meriwether, and whether it came or not was really beyond Gutfreund's control. That's why many people thought that the single rash act of challenging the arbitrage boss to one hand for a million dollars was Gutfreund's way of showing he was a player, too. And if you wanted to show off, Liar's Poker was the only way to go. The game had a powerful meaning for traders. People like John Meriwether believed that Liar's Poker had a lot in common with bond trading. It tested a trader's character. It honed a trader's instincts. A good player made a good trader, and vice versa. We all understood it.

The Game: In Liar's Poker a group of people—as few as two, as many as ten—form a circle. Each player holds a dollar bill close to his chest. The game is similar in spirit to the card game known as I Doubt It. Each player attempts to fool the others about the serial numbers printed on the face of his dollar bill. One trader begins by making "a bid." He says, for example, "Three sixes." He means that all told the serial numbers of the dollar bills held by every player, including himself, contain at least three sixes.

Once the first bid has been made, the game moves clockwise in the circle. Let's say the bid is three sixes. The player to the left of the bidder can do one of two things. He can bid higher (there are two sorts of higher bids: the same quantity of a higher number [three sevens, eights, or nines] and more of any number [four fives, for instance]). Or he can "challenge"— that is like saying, "I doubt it."

The bidding escalates until all the other players agree to challenge a single player's bid. Then, and only then, do the players reveal their serial numbers and determine who is bluffing whom. In the midst of all this, the mind of a good player spins with probabilities. What is the statistical likelihood of there being three sixes within a batch of, say, forty randomly generated serial numbers? For a great player, however, the math is the easy part of the game. The hard part is reading the faces of the other players. The complexity arises when all players know how to bluff and double-bluff.

The game has some of the feel of trading, just as jousting has some of the feel of war. The questions a Liar's Poker player asks himself are, up to a point, the same questions a bond trader asks himself. Is this a smart risk?

Do I feel lucky? How cunning is my opponent? Does he have any idea what he's doing, and if not, how do I exploit his ignorance? If he bids high, is he bluffing, or does he actually hold a strong hand? Is he trying to induce me to make a foolish bid, or does he actually have four of a kind himself? Each player seeks weakness, predictability, and pattern in the others and seeks to avoid it in himself. The bond traders of Goldman Sachs, First Boston, Morgan Stanley, Merrill Lynch, and other Wall Street firms all play some version of Liar's Poker. But the place where the stakes run highest, thanks to John Meriwether, is the New York bond trading floor of Salomon Brothers.

The code of the Liar's Poker player was something like the code of the gunslinger. It required a trader to accept all challenges. Because of the code—which was *his* code—John Meriwether felt obliged to play. But he knew it was stupid. For him, there was no upside. If he won, he upset Gutfreund. No good came of this. But if he lost, he was out of pocket a million bucks. This was worse than upsetting the boss. Although Meriwether was by far the better player of the game, in a single hand anything could happen. Luck could very well determine the outcome. Meriwether spent his entire day avoiding dumb bets, and he wasn't about to accept this one.

"No, John," he said, "if we're going to play for those kind of numbers, I'd rather play for real money. Ten million dollars. No tears."

Ten million dollars. It was a moment for all players to savor. Meriwether was playing Liar's Poker before the game even started. He was bluffing. Gutfreund considered the counterproposal. It would have been just like him to accept. Merely to entertain the thought was a luxury that must have pleased him well. (It *was* good to be rich.)

On the other hand, $10 million dollars was, and is, a lot of money. If Gutfreund lost, he'd have only $30 million or so left. His wife, Susan, was busy spending the better part of $15 million redecorating their Manhattan apartment (Meriwether knew this). And as Gutfreund *was* the boss, he clearly wasn't bound by the Meriwether code. Who knows? Maybe he didn't even know the Meriwether code. Maybe the whole point of his challenge was to judge Meriwether's response. (Even Gutfreund had to marvel at the king in action.) So Gutfreund declined. In fact, he smiled his own brand of forced smile and said, "You're crazy."

No, thought Meriwether, just very, very good.

Michael Bloomberg

RICHARD L. STERN AND JASON ZWEIG

Michael Bloomberg is brilliant, irreverent, good-looking *and* fun. By serving the information needs of his former colleagues and competitors, he has made a larger fortune than almost any other Wall Street contemporary. As this profile reveals, "user-friendly" is a winning strategy.

Mike Bloomberg has all the standard trappings of wealth, the usual success statements and trophies: an apartment in Vail, Colorado, a townhouse on Manhattan's East Side, a country home in northern Westchester County and horses for his two equestrian daughters. He is licensed to fly both fixed-wing aircraft and helicopters. But his passion is his business, from which he unashamedly derives a sense of power. Says he: "Sunday night is the happiest night of the week. I can't wait to get back to work."

Fast-talking, profane, overflowing with self-confidence, always on the move, Bloomberg is easily a match for his relatively faceless competitors. He has strong ideas about how to run an organization, and he acts on his ideas. He has no secretary and answers his own phone at his desk in the back of the main newsroom of his wire service. He forbids job titles, even on business cards. At Bloomberg L.P. there are no private offices, the conference rooms have clear glass walls, and virtually nothing is partitioned off except for the photocopiers and bathrooms.

Although Bloomberg's headquarters occupies three floors of a Park Avenue skyscraper, the elevator opens only on the middle floor, so that all the employees must periodically rub elbows on the single spiral staircase. "I tried to put the bathrooms all on the same floor too," he says, but he abandoned the idea—tricky plumbing. . . .

Bloomberg personally watches every detail. He insists on signing every nonpayroll check and every contract. "I would like to know every goddamn thing that's going on," is the way he explains it.

Competitive? "Competitive" should be Mike Bloomberg's middle name. An employee who leaves is considered a deserter. "If you leave," barks Bloomberg, "I will not wish you the best. I will not go to a farewell party for you. You're a traitor, you're out to hurt everybody else in this company and take the bread out of their kids' mouths."

This hard-driving entrepreneur grew up in Medford, Massachusetts, a Boston suburb, the son of a bookkeeper for a dairy. He studied engineering and physics at Johns Hopkins University, working his way through as parking lot attendant at the faculty club. He graduated from Harvard Business School in 1966.

Even then Bloomberg was somewhat unconventional. Most MBAs go right for the green, grabbing at the highest-paying jobs. Bloomberg accepted a humble job in "the cage" at Salomon Brothers in Manhattan, as a clerk processing trades at $9,500 a year. Of course, he did not intend to stay long in the cage. Recalls Bloomberg: "I used to get in at 7 A.M. I was the only one in the trading room other than Billy Salomon, and so we chitchatted. Then I would stay till 7 at night, and after 6 the only other person in the room was John Gutfreund, and he'd give me a ride uptown. So the managing partner and the heir apparent became my friends when I was just starting as a clerk."

Bloomberg went on to become head of equity trading and sales for five years. His training made him a rare bird on Wall Street: As an engineer, he understands how the black boxes work and he knows how to use them for successful trading. "There might be better traders than me," says Bloomberg, "and there might be people who know more about computers. But there's nobody who knows more about both."

Integrating his training and his work experience, he has developed an information system that most people find exceptionally user-friendly, and he works hard at making it even more so. Bloomberg's data displays are so simple to analyze and manipulate that a neophyte can feel like an expert user in minutes.

But for Bloomberg's abrasive cockiness, the system might have belonged to Salomon. Because he knew a fair amount about computers, Bloomberg was put in charge of Salomon's systems when he lost out in the power struggle there. It was an obvious demotion, and Bloomberg stayed just long enough to collect a $10 million share of the loot when Salomon went public in 1981 in a merger with Philbro.

Bloomberg had no intention of retiring. At Salomon he built a computerized information, analytics and bookkeeping system. In 1982, he pitched a system for U.S. government bonds to an informal committee at Merrill Lynch.

Merrill's computer experts said they would need six months to study the practicability of such a system. Bloomberg pounced. "I'll deliver a finished product in six months," he said, "and if you don't like it you don't have to pay for it." Six months later he delivered a system that did complex calculations on government bonds as well as routine pricing of Merrill's inventory. Merrill quickly ordered 20 machines. Then Merrill made an extremely smart move. It put $30 million into Bloomberg's company in return for a 30 percent interest. Today that stake is worth at least $250 million.

Bloomberg still does business the same way: "Instead of doing what our bigger competitors do, which is to take two or three years to perfect a technology that is then a fossil when they put it into the market, we just throw it out there and work with our customers to perfect it."

From the start, Bloomberg's strategy differed from that of his giant competitors. He went a step beyond: Instead of just supplying information, he helped the customers utilize it. "Whenever you see a business that's done the same thing for a long time," says Bloomberg, "a new guy can come in and do it better. I guarantee it." . . .

Steven Fenster, a professor of finance at Harvard, was a Bloomberg classmate in business school and now is a director of Bloomberg's company. He recalls how Bloomberg reacted to a case study called Voltamp. The case involved an electrical equipment company that had secretly invented a new device that would transform the entire industry. Yet the company was loath to bring its product out because it could be so readily copied that profit margins on the product would almost instantly disappear. "Most students," recalls Fenster, "suggested improving other areas of the business to increase margins, or buying a competitor to get better market share. But Mike's solution was spectacularly creative. He said something like this: 'Cloak it under the same name as the old device, make it look the same on the outside, and the customers will buy it by the millions once they plug it in, while the competition won't even notice there's anything new to copy.'"

There, in a nutshell, is Bloomberg's formidable strategy. While his price has remained constant for eight years, he has been stuffing more and more data into his service. . . .

Bloomberg indulges in unbroken 10-minute monologs fired out at lightening speed, interrupted only by sips from alternating cups of coffee and instant chicken soup. Like any brilliant trader, he cuts complex ideas down to size with a few slashes of his sharp tongue. He expresses his contempt for his competitors with his favorite term, "horseshit," and throws in the F word for good measure. But don't conclude from these expressions of scorn that Bloomberg is growing complacent. He understands himself. Says he: "All repetitively successful people have an inferiority complex." So they keep pushing even when, to the world, they seem to have it made.

Richard H. Jenrette

JOHN W. MILLIGAN

Dick Jenrette built a career by taking on a series of "cellar" jobs and doing them well in a truly nice way—even when the task at hand required hard or unpleasant decisions. As a team leader he both builds consensus and makes bold independent decisions. Privately, he is a master antiquarian and restorer of great old houses. Almost always underestimated, he continues to gain in others' appreciation. Since this piece was written, most of Equitable Life's financial problems have been resolved.

Think of it this way: Gentleman Dick Jenrette pulled off the last great takeover of the 1980s.

Jenrette himself would no doubt object to the notion. So might the people who consider him sufficiently dignified to be the chairman of the New York Stock Exchange, a job he recently turned down. And it's not as if Jenrette became chief executive of the Equitable Life Assurance Society of the United States by means of junk bonds or a proxy fight.

Yet five years after selling little Donaldson, Lufkin & Jenrette to giant Equitable for $440 million and a promise of autonomy, Richard H. Jenrette has ended up running the whole company. In an era of poison pills, bear hugs and white knights, DLJ turned out to be a Trojan horse. Jenrette showed that an outsider can take over at an insular mutual life insurer after all–provided he has the right qualities and is in the right place at the right time. Rising to chief investment officer in 1986 and chairman one year later, he assumed the chief executive's job in May when Equitable's board of directors took the extraordinary action of forcing president and CEO John Carter, a 30-year company veteran, into early retirement.

Carter's forced departure shows how badly Equitable has stumbled and how sizable is the task that now confronts the 61-year-old Jenrette. Mutual companies have long been bastions of mediocrity, where no one, let alone the boss, ever gets fired. Carter nevertheless managed the trick. Now the board has put Jenrette in charge, and his assignment is large: cut costs, improve profits and inject some life into what has become a schizophrenic

Excerpted from *Institutional Investor* (September 1990). This copyrighted material is reprinted with permission from: **Institutional Investor, Inc.**, 488 Madison Avenue, New York, NY 10022.

company, one in which successful investment operations are weighed down by barely profitable insurance activities. Jenrette also must improve the parent company's standing with the rating agencies. Equitable's claims-paying rating is several notches below those of its biggest competitors, and in early August, Moody's Investors Service dropped it even further, from Aa3 to A1. Moody's is worried that profits from two consistent money makers in recent years—leveraged buyouts and commercial real estate—may nosedive in a worsening economy.

It was Carter's inability to solve these problems that cost him his job, and expectations for Jenrette are high. "Insurance companies have to have the total confidence of the consumer and the financial community," says attorney Arthur Liman, an Equitable director. "And in Dick Jenrette you have someone who is the very symbol of solidity."

Why is the board so high on Jenrette? Certainly not because of his great experience in insurance; he hasn't any to speak of. The confidence he inspires derives in part from his reputation as a statesman. Besides having been offered the NYSE chairmanship, which he turned down in favor of the job at Equitable, he's also a past chairman of the Securities Industry Association. Jenrette's greatest asset, though, is his experience as a foul-weather captain. "When the market would collapse and everyone would think it was the end of the world," says Jenrette, "I'd get optimistic—I'm a contrarian. I'm somewhat that way in the corporate world. I think I do some of my best work under adversity." Liman puts it this way: "You have to look at what he did at DLJ."

• • •

What Jenrette did there was to help build the firm and then, later, save it from disaster. Born in Charlotte, North Carolina, educated at the University of North Carolina and Harvard Business School, Jenrette accepted the invitation of Harvard classmates William Donaldson and Dan Lufkin to start a firm specializing in equity research on small growth companies. It later became the first New York investment bank to go public.

Donaldson and Lufkin eventually left DLJ for individual pursuits. Jenrette stayed on to run the firm as CEO, beginning in the mid-1970s when fixed commissions were coming to an end, the country was in a deep recession and Wall Street firms were disappearing like dinosaurs. John Chalsty, DLJ's current CEO and a 21-year veteran of the firm, describes Jenrette as someone to whom people will rally. "One of Dick's greatest strengths is serving as a kind of glue that holds people together," he says. Jenrette became, simply, the gravitational force that kept DLJ together when the rest of Wall Street seemed to be breaking apart.

He held it together in more ways than one. DLJ was starved for capital in this period, and many executives figured the best way to raise it would be to sell Alliance Capital Management, an institutional money management firm DLJ had started several years earlier. Jenrette said no, and Alliance ultimately made the far greater contribution of helping to fund the parent's subsequent diversification. Chalsty credits Jenrette with recognizing that DLJ couldn't survive as a one-product company. "He didn't hunker down and try to tough out the institutional research business, but used cash flow to grow into other businesses," he says. . . .

Chalsty likes to say that his old boss plays tougher than he looks—and certainly Jenrette neither acts nor talks very tough. Thirty-some years of living in New York haven't much hardened the sonorously Southern accent. And he seems almost too gentlemanly to be an effective chief executive. Donaldson calls him a romantic with an interest in the historical perspective. (Jenrette can quote unerringly from *Gone with the Wind.*) And consistent with this trait is his love affair with old houses. Jenrette owns five, including residences in Charlotte and St. Croix and an estate on the Hudson River where he spends his weekends. "He enjoys being the squire of the place," says Chalsty.

But this country squire is both decisive and willing to make the difficult call when necessary. Within two weeks of taking over from Carter, Jenrette announced his intention to cut $100 million in annualized expenses from Equitable's corporate office and insurance operation (the investment subsidiaries were largely spared the knife.) By mid-July that figure had risen to $156 million. He also took the early step of consolidating Equitable's sprawling organizational structure by eliminating two of its three holding companies. This required that he choose from among three chief financial officers—and he unhesitatingly fired one of them and demoted the second. "Dick is a strong person who forms his own opinions and does not lack for the courage of his convictions," says Alliance chairman Dave Williams.

By Jenrette's own admission, the five years following DLJ's sale were restless ones for him. As chief investment officer he put together a solid record running Equitable's investment subsidiaries. "I liked the people I was working with," Jenrette says. "I thought I was helping them fulfill their dreams, and that kept me going." But this clearly wasn't enough. "I learned that if I'm going to be coming into work every day, I want to be the boss," he says. "Looking back on it now, it was a wonder that I didn't leave." Jenrette is clearly delighted to be in charge again. "I can't think of anything else I'd rather do," he says.

WISEMEN AND RASCALS

Sidney Homer

MARTIN MAYER

Sidney Homer led the revolution in the valuation of fixed-income instruments and established at Salomon Brothers one of the world's largest and most respected financial research organizations. More than this, he kept it independent in its views.

Sidney Homer was the son of Louise Homer, one of the earliest great American singers, a mezzo-soprano much loved at the Metropolitan Opera and also a lieder singer on concert stages. Homer, who had gone to Harvard but considered himself a self-trained "bond man," worked for Scudder Stevens & Clark, an investment management firm for financial institutions. "I called Homer," [Salomon Brothers partner Charles] Simon remembered, "and asked whether I could take him to lunch at Massolletti's, which was then the best restaurant downtown, and he said, 'Yes, I'll come lunch with you. Who are you?' I knew he was solid gold when he told me the city of Vienna had had fives outstanding for 100 years, the loans rolled over from monarchy to monarchy. I just loved it; I was fascinated with him immediately. He would pontificate to anybody about the bond market and Wall Street. He was *the* example of the intellectual WASP on Wall Street. In those days I ran an annual investment seminar for New York State bankers, and I invited him to give a lecture at it."

Homer, who did some trading for Scudder Stevens & Clark, also became one of Simon's customers. "If ever there was a chiseling son of a bitch on price, it was Homer," Simon recalled. "It was always 'I have to call you back.' What a tough guy he was to do business with, but I admired him all the time. I used to tell him, 'You have to write a book.' It fell into my lap that he lived in Gramercy Park, in an ancient apartment that must have been used by Charles Addams, with the oldest furniture I ever sat on."

"Then I saw in the *New York Times* that Scudder Stevens & Clark had elected five new officers. Homer had never been an officer, and they hadn't elected him. I talked to Billy [Salomon], told him I thought we could hire Homer, and he gave me the go-ahead. We had lunch at '21,' and I told him. He made one condition: He would have to come in as a partner." In 1960, Homer became the first person to join Salomon as

Reprinted with the permission of Simon & Schuster from *Nightmare on Wall Street* by Martin Mayer. Copyright 1993 by Martin Mayer.

a partner, beneficiary (in part) of a killing the firm had made in the market for AT&T convertible bonds, which had left extra money for such a luxury. Homer was an apparently owlish man with a brush mustache, thick glasses, and a solemn manner that was quite deceptive, for he was in fact an amusing fellow; he wrote a continuing series of in-house articles called *Fun with Bonds*, pieces with titles like "Twenty-one Ways to Say No to a Bond Salesman."

At the beginning Homer's role was mostly to educate the traders, both by his presence at the partners' table (he was rarely on the trading floor) and by his writings. . . . Gradually the salesman recognized that Homer was giving them the raw materials of their trade: reasons why customers should swap from one bond to another, making two transactions through Salomon Brothers. A salesman could get a hearing on a much higher level of his customer's firm if he had Homer in tow.

"He thought up all those hedges," Billy Salomon remembered. "When you should buy the two-year and sell the five-year." In fact, what Homer did was far more significant than that: He revolutionized the valuation and the trading of fixed-income instruments . . . multiplying the volume and profitability of Salomon's business and transforming the investment and trading patterns of insurance companies and charitable foundations. Salomon's enormous strength in trading was in large part the result of Homer's work, which rested in the end on a single simple insight. What Homer and nobody else had seen was that all the tables in . . . [the standard] yield book, which every Salomon apprentice had memorized . . . were simply wrong. They assumed stable interest rates, and interest rates were not stable. . . .

The problem with this[standard] analysis was that it neglected the reinvestment of the twice-yearly coupons, "the interest on the interest." If interest rates were going up, a $900 price for a $1,000, 4 percent bond—a $100 discount—would leave its purchaser well behind the purchaser of the 5 percent bond, because the owner of the 5 percent bond would have more income from the interest payments to invest every year at the higher rates. On the other hand, if rates were going down, the $100 discount on the 4 percent bond would leave its purchaser ahead of the game, because it had been calculated to offset the difference between the 4 percent the bond would pay him and the prevailing market rate of 5 percent at the time he bought. If you carried this to its extreme, Homer and [his pupil and associate Marty] Leibowitz pointed out in an aside—not taking the possibility seriously themselves (as of 1972, no company or government had ever issued or seriously considered issuing such a piece of paper)—people who thought interest rates were going down should want to buy a *zero-coupon* bond. In such a bond the interest instead of being paid out would accumulate every year, compounding at the promised interest rate, until a final payment that returned principal and all the accumulated interest. In effect, such a bond guaranteed the purchaser that he would reinvest his annual earnings at today's interest rate until the day the bond was paid back.

A few years after [Homer's] *Inside the Yield Book* was published, Bill Brachfeld asked the Federal Reserve Bank of New York whether it would object to Salomon's "stripping" a 30-year Treasury bond, then selling its customers two separate investments. One of these instruments would be a zero-coupon bond, offering the face value of the bond as a lump-sum payment (at 6 percent interest, a $1,000 30-year bond would sell for about $175); the other would represent the right to the 60 semi-annual coupons (at $30 each, for a 6 percent bond). The first instrument would be for people who thought interest rates would go down and wanted to lock in their 6 percent; the second instrument would be for people who thought interest rates would go up and wanted the chance to reinvest the coupons at the higher rates. Because it would be tapping the two markets separately, Salomon would be able to sell the two pieces of the stripped bond for a total price higher than the going price on the whole bond. The Fed said it wished Salomon wouldn't do that, and for almost a decade Salomon didn't. . . .

For Salomon the significance of Homer's quick partnership was that research would not be subordinate to either the traders or the salesmen. It was understood that Homer's work was completely independent of their needs or desires: *He* would decide what would be useful to *them*. In fact, he put most of his time into a monumental book, *A History of Interest Rates*, a path-breaking survey that traced rates from Sumeria (how much corn did the farmer have to repay the merchant who lent him the seed corn?) to the modern money markets. In his 1977 preface to the revised edition of his book, Homer noted that "when this book was a mere 40 pages of jumbled notes and tables, my friend Mr. Charles Simon, a partner in the bond firm of Salomon Brothers, gave me that enthusiastic encouragement which was essential to convert the idea into a book." Homer's scholarly output was widely disseminated by the firm. . . . Homer's work . . . [gave] Salomon a bipolar image: They were tough traders who bought business with price, but they were also the house that supported and publicized fundamental research into financial matters, something the established houses, the Morgan Stanleys and First Bostons and Goldman Sachses, had never done.

Henry Kaufman

ANISE WALLACE

Henry Kaufman is a scholar and a gentlemen. Formal, gracious, courteous in style, he is also rigorously hard on the data and the way they are used. As a result, he has created for himself a highly respected role in economics and finance, both as a senior partner at Salomon Brothers—where he was when this profile was written—and more recently, as head of his own firm.

This time last year, very few people outside financial circles had heard of Henry Kaufman. . . . But now, Salomon Brothers' chief economist has been clutched to the bosom of the mass media; he might be billed as the Isaiah of economics—the man who told everybody what was going to happen to interest rates and then provided the after-chill of being horrifyingly right. Once a purveyor of merry quips about yield curves and interest rates, Kaufman now finds himself being quoted in all the "popular" publications and even appearing on TV's *Today Show*.

All this is not to say that the 52-year-old Kaufman is some kind of economic upstart who has suddenly burst upon the scene with a dazzling new theory about supply-side economics. . . . over the years he has made all the dutiful appearances that economists are wont to make before Congressional committees, organizations like the World Bank and the Council on Foreign Relations. Nor is he a flashy spellbinder in the image of the economic showmen of years past; "often," says one observer, "I suspect a lot of his analysis goes right over most people's heads."

All Henry Kaufman has done is to be right. Not only has he been so at a time when most other economists have taken their lumps for being so wrong, he has been on target in a pivotal area where accuracy can make—or prevent the loss of—huge amounts of money. After all, if you're right on the gross national product, all you have is a swell batting average. If you're right on interest rates, you can become a hero to the firms and institutions that are in the market with millions—or even billions—at risk daily. And Kaufman has been remarkably on target with key predictions at three pivotal moments for the U.S. economy: during the interest-rate scourges of 1970 and 1974, and most notably, prior to the latest—and unprecedented—

Excerpted from *Institutional Investor 14* (May 1980), pp. 45–48, 52. This copyrighted material is reprinted with permission from: **Institutional Investor, Inc.**, 488 Madison Avenue, New York, NY 10022.

flare-up in rates. As the prime touched 20 percent this spring, his pronouncements crowded out all the others. . . .

Setting Kaufman apart, moreover, is his skill as a communicator. His weekly "Comments on Credit" is widely quoted on both sides of the Atlantic. And he is constantly on the hook with Salomon's clients; in the wake of his pronouncements this year he has been on the road explaining his views as a representative of the firm.

• • •

Part of the credit for Kaufman's clout, of course, stems from his association with Salomon Brothers, which is, after all, the nation's premier dealer in fixed-income securities. Not only has the firm accumulated many decades of data and experience, its renowned trading room . . . provides Kaufman with unparalleled access to the minute-by-minute mood of the market. For one thing, Salomon for many years was the seat of Sidney Homer, the widely respected author of the seminal *A History of Interest Rates*. Homer gave Kaufman—who earned his Ph.D. at New York University, worked with the Federal Reserve and joined Salomon in 1962—responsibility for the firm's credit-flow analysis. (Homer retired in 1971, but the two men still see each other almost weekly.)

In addition, many of Kaufman's Wall Street followers speak of the fact that his views, before they are taken public, undergo the close scrutiny of Salomon's partners, who themselves are no slouches at the nuances of financial markets. As one Salomon partner puts it: "If Henry gets out of step with what we perceive to be the world, he is subject to considerable abuse. The partners lean all over him. So when he expresses a view, he has already fought his battle out here." Kaufman himself won't argue with that statement. "I don't sit on a pedestal in this organization," he says. "I'm fair game for anyone." Or as managing partner John Gutfreund puts it: "Salomon is not one voice."

But it *is* Kaufman to whom people listen, and for the reason that, in addition to his Salomon affiliation, he possesses the gift of being pithy. Even though he addresses audiences without notes, "he's the most articulate economist around," says one admirer. Kaufman often displays a genuine sense of humor and punctuates his remarks with rolling laughter. And he says he takes pains to avoid couching his comments in economic jargon because "I think it is a crutch to use esoteric terms in analysis." At the same time, he adds that he tries never to patronize his listeners. "I don't like it when people pull it on me," he explains, "and I wouldn't like to pull it on them."

Kaufman's writing can be as succinct as his speaking. He occasionally writes Salomon's "Memorandum to Portfolio Managers," a notable example being the March 1979 edition, which many clients regard as a classic. The memo dealt with the implication of trends in household credit activities, transformations in the financial markets to accommodate inflation and the developing public perception that the government was unwilling to brake inflation. In part, Kaufman then suggested that there were rocky times ahead for investors: "I believe that our economic and financial system has slipped away from some of its moorings that, in the past, kept our behavior within reasonable limits. The loss of these moorings poses grave risk and danger to us all."

· · ·

None of the above would matter, of course, if Kaufman hadn't been so maddeningly right in his predictions. And his secret, he contends, is that he has learned "to look at the economic side through financial eyes." Where so many other economists failed to see the force of the tide of inflation and the public's recognition of it in their economic data, Kaufman spotted and measured it through the behavior of the financial markets.

In other words, Kaufman has one inestimable advantage over other economists with their access to computer printouts and other lifeless data: When he walks through the Solomon Brothers trading room—which he does four or five times a day—he is standing at the center of what he calls the world's financial crossroads. And not a day goes by, Kaufman reports, that he doesn't pick up a crucial nuance to add to the printed matter upon which his rivals form their judgments.

· · ·

"He has more intuition than most economists," stresses one Boston-based fund manager, who adds that "there's an element to Henry, a sort of sixth sense."

Kaufman himself attributes some of his skills as a forecaster, in fact, to the degree that his intuition frees him from boilerplate economics. "I have felt that no particular economic or financial school of thought has a monopoly on wisdom," he says. The danger of being doctrinaire, he goes on, can be illustrated by the recent failings of the monetarists, who, absorbed by their narrow, elegant definition of the money supply, ignored the real upheavals that were occurring in the financial system as a whole. Kaufman, by contrast, did not. . . .

Kaufman's special perch also allows him to rely less heavily on the various economic models as forecasting tools, other economists note. Indeed, Kaufman believes that such reliance on models has actually hurt some forecasters because the models all generated forecasts that are based on historic economic relationships—when X goes up, Y goes up—whereas Kaufman believes recent financial developments reflect breakdowns in some of those relationships. "You have to treat econometric analysis with considerable reservation," he says, "rather than as the total wherewithal for evaluating future change."

· · ·

Whatever happens, there are those in Wall Street who suspect that Kaufman could be wrong for the next ten years and still be an extremely influential economist. They figure that by sticking to his guns during this troubled period—and saving money for those who followed his advice—he can just rest on his laurels. But Kaufman doesn't see it that way. "This is not an environment in which yesterday's accomplishments are going to carry you for the rest of your career," he concludes. "And that's the way it should be."

John J. McCloy

Jack McCloy was the acknowledged "Chairman of the Board" of the American establishment. He gave his country a distinguished public service career that was capped by his great success as High Commissioner in Germany following World War II. This brief profile was published just as he assumed command at Chase Manhattan Bank (then Chase National).

At the recent annual meeting of the Chase National Bank, John Jay McCloy, one week old as chairman of the board, prefaced his comments with the story of the horse thief standing on the gallows who said, "This is the first time I've ever done this, sheriff. Would you go a bit easy until I sort of get the hang of the thing?" The ingenious disclaimer may seem to reflect the ingenuousness of the man himself, who calls himself "a new boy," and who comes to the top job at the Chase without experience in commercial banking except for a schoolboy job, as runner for Drexel & Co., that imprinted on his memory the clearinghouse numbers of all the banks in Philadelphia. Such admission of inexperience on the part of the chairman of the Chase may seem also to suggest that banking, once an operation encrusted with glitter and enhanced with prestige, has somehow become an ordinary sort of business.

The immediate consequence, however, of Mr. McCloy's self-deprecating gambit was a remarkably smooth annual meeting. It even broke into spontaneous applause. The "new boy" is, of course, the former High Commissioner for Germany, the man who handled the transfusion of a billion dollars of U.S. aid into the German economy, who negotiated the Bonn Republic into the European Defense Community, and who worked out the contractual agreements that superseded the U.S. occupation of Germany. He is also the former president of the World Bank, a former assistant secretary of war, the man who helped write lend-lease, who presided during the war over the powerful State-War-Navy Coordinating Committee. Incidentally, he is the lawyer who won the Black Tom case, and a Republican. Henry Stimson said of him: "So varied were his labors and so catholic his interests that they defy summary . . . His energy was enormous, and his optimism almost unquenchable."

That a person of such experience finds the Chase chairmanship as challenging as other of his jobs (in comparison with the high commissionership, "less tense but almost as complex") suggests that commercial banking is something more vital than the safeguarding of moneys and the decorous investment of them in solid bonds and well-secured loans.

• • •

At the Chase the . . . result of making loans and investments, particularly in anticipating the needs of customers and seeking out business, is a perpetual conversation with industrial organizations all over the world, with 3,700 American and nearly 1,500 foreign banks, not to mention government departments and sovereign states. The conversation is, in sum, an immense and immeasurably vital interchange of economic intelligence. The particular reputation of the Chase, in fact, is based on its skill in this interchange, which is conducted with the weight of $5.4 billion assets, the dignity of its own name and that of its Rockefeller stockholders, and the delicacy that attends vast foreign involvements and makes for world trade. New Chairman McCloy is a man adept at talk that is affable, wide ranging, informative, discreet, and effective.

• • •

This adeptness is important within the bank as well as without. The Chase is a large organization with the regular complement of big-company staff activities. Mr. McCloy, who has worked for the largest organization in the country, the government, finds his past experience of distinct use. "The job is always," he says, "to recognize talent, advance talent, and work with talent. Infusing spirit, putting the right man in the right spot, is a thrilling experience."

William McChesney Martin Jr.

RICHARD AUSTIN SMITH

> William McChesney Martin Jr., a 48-year-old Democrat, was appointed
> chairman of the Federal Reserve Board by President Eisenhower in 1955.
> He came to the job with solid preparation: chairman of the New York
> Stock Exchange at 31, a U.S. Army Colonel (up from the ranks) in World
> War II, head of the Import-Export Bank, and the assistant secretary of
> the treasury who arranged the 1952 Accord between the openly hostile
> Fed and Treasury. This excerpt is from a blatantly unflattering article
> telling of his arrival at the NYSE. Once again, he was underestimated.

Ten years ago Yale's young class of '28 cast the traditional ballot for the man
"most likely to succeed." Seventy votes bestowed the wreath of classmates'
confidence upon a campus power who is now a clerk in a large New York law
firm. The ten runners-up for the prophetic honor included others of undergraduate eminence and a few sons of famous fathers. And at the tail end of
the count, with three lonely votes to his credit, dangled a bookish, bespectacled youth who belonged to no fraternity and who, as one newspaper recently put it, would have been considered a grease ball by such as Richard
Whitney. The youth was William McChesney Martin Jr., who on May 16
of this year became chairman of the Board of Governors of the New York
Stock Exchange.

The trio of unknown soothsayers who cast their votes for Martin must
have seen behind his shy, solemn front the stuff of which success is made.
They must have seen those quiet qualities of single-minded determination
and unaggressive ambition that he packs behind the same shy, solemn front
today . . . and the rare ability to impress by being tolerantly positive and
brilliantly dull. . . .

They could scarcely have foreseen the crash of '29 or the depression or
the nine almost unrelieved years of drought and occasional panic on the Exchange. They could not have conjured up Mr. Pecora's investigation nor Mr.
Roosevelt's Securities and Exchange Commission nor Messrs. Corcoran-
and-Cohen's Securities Exchange Act. They could not have guessed that the
same William O. Douglas who came to Yale to teach three months after
they left Yale would in ten years be the U.S. Government's head cop on the
Stock Exchange beat and would be waving a wicked regulatory night stick
over the head of the Exchange.

They could not have known, either, that those in control of the Exchange at the time would thumb their noses at the Douglas night stick. Nor that a rebel group on the Exchange would line up with Douglas and the SEC. Nor that Douglas and the rebels and public opinion and falling stock prices would scare the Exchange into the first significant reorganization in its 150-year history. Nor could they have known that proud, patrician Richard Whitney, symbol of the Exchange's Golden Age, would fall so low and, in falling when he fell, deliver the Exchange into the hands of the SEC, the reformers within its own ranks, and 31-year-old William McChesney Martin Jr.

For it was this series of events, far more than Martin's qualifications, however sterling, which made apparent oracles out of three of Martin's Yale classmates. It was this series of events that tossed young Martin, corklike, to the crest of precocious success. . . . The hero-hailing newspapers and newsreels have missed it completely, but the fact is that Martin's real success story, if any, still lies very definitely in front of him and not behind him. . . .

To Martin, the hard-working youngster whom nobody disliked and whom many did not even know, the lad who helped do the spadework for the reorganization, the compromise choice to whom the nominating committee's only objections were his youth and the fact that he did not wear a hat to work, went the chairmanship of the new Exchange. He walked into his job with 913 votes of confidence behind him—or 910 more than he got from his Yale classmates 10 years before.

The last thing Martin ever wanted to be was a stockbroker. From the time when he was first able to think about it at all, which was approximately at the age of 12, he thought of himself as a student, and he still does. . . . Figures have always been his dish, although at that early date the figures that got most attention were the batting averages of the St. Louis Cardinals.

By the time he was 16, young Bill had on tap in his head the averages of practically every major-league ballplayer, and he had, incidentally, been graduated from a public high school in St. Louis. He had also acquired a respect bordering on reverence for W. M. Martin Sr., who had already shown his son the way to precociousness by becoming at the age of 39 the Chairman of the Federal Reserve Bank of St. Louis. . . .

Hard work and hard play sum up his four years at Yale, and Martin retains no nostalgic affection for his college days. He was interested in economics, but majored in English, following his father's admonition to get a broad background and forget about a career. . . .

From Yale, Martin went back to St. Louis and back to playing with figures. First came a job under his father as bank examiner for the Federal Reserve. Then, in a few months, the post of head statistician for A. G. Edwards & Sons, brokers—and relatives. And less than three years later, in May 1931, Martin was made a partner, was sent to New York where he set foot in

Wall Street for the first time, and within a month was entrusted with his firm's Exchange membership.

The ticker was nothing new to Martin; he had participated mildly in the boom (investment, not gambling) and had been instructively brought to earth by the crash. But the scene on the Exchange floor was something new and fascinating. He would often stand staring about him with a vacuous grin on his face, trying to drink in what it all represented . . . instead of limiting his curiosity and his information to facts of some use in his business as floor broker, he burrowed about after hours in an effort to understand the whole structure and mechanism of the Exchange as an institution.

Nor did he restrict the scope of his studies to Wall Street, its workings, and its points of view. He took courses under Economists Alvin Johnson, Walton H. Hamilton, and E. W. Kemmerer at the leftish New School for Social Research. And he enrolled at Columbia University to study . . . such varying subjects as contemporary politics, . . . banking, . . . current economic theories, . . . the history of the World War, . . . and wages. . . . Attending classes almost daily before the Exchange opened and after it closed, he soon had nearly enough credits for a Ph.D. . . .

But Martin, despite this rigorous schedule of work and study, had not been neglecting his play. And there is nothing about himself that he will discuss with as much relish as his sports prowess. Tennis, which he has kept top rank ever since he left Yale, is his greatest love. . . .

Martin's favorite diversion, next to athletics, is the theatre. He goes to more than a hundred plays a year, often sitting in the balcony by himself, and he doubts that he has missed a single show in the past five years that has run as long as two weeks. His favorite play of all was *Yellow Jack*, which he knew practically by heart after he had seen it for the ninth time. . . .

Unmarried and uninterested, he has lived since he came to New York at the Yale Club with his college roommate, Sanford Kauffman, now an engineer for Pan American Airways. Martin's election to the chairmanship of the Exchange brought him dozens of requests for photographs from all over the United States—but no proposals.

The chairmanship (along with the duties of acting president of the Exchange, which he was delegated to carry simultaneously until a permanent president should be chosen) has, however, cut in a bit on his playgoing. And this despite the fact that he has made a habit of doing without breakfast so that he can catch fifteen minutes of extra sleep, which he feels does him more good, and still carry on his daily round of work, study, and play. But the most important change that his election has made in his waking routine is that he now, at the half-jesting request of the committee that nominated him, wears a hat to the office.

Though no shilly-shallyer, Martin is not out to court enemies for himself or his regime. He will not talk of the Old Guard as having been anything worse than "misguided." And in telling how and why he was hoisted to the chairmanship of the Exchange, he tends to soft-pedal such facts as the explosive nature of the whole situation, the rebellious part played by Shields and others of his group (such as quiet Edward Allen Pierce) in bringing about a genuine change of front, and the power of persuasive pressure from Douglas and the SEC. According to Martin, he had gradually and calmly talked himself into the accepted leadership of the opposition to the Old Guard on the governing committee. And when the Whitney scandal broke and carried the prestige of the whole Whitney crowd up the river with it, he, Martin, was the obvious choice to head the new setup on the Exchange. . . .

Martin was the obvious choice, not at all because he led the revolt against the Old Guard. But on the contrary, partly because though no Old Guardsman he was not so clearly associated with the rebels that his selection would look on its face like an abject surrender to the SEC.

There was still another reason for Martin's selection, and this Martin concedes. It explains, too, his rapid rise to a position of respect on the Exchange even before he was chosen to head it. Normally, such a meteoric record in any business or institution would betoken brilliance. But Martin is not and did not have to be brilliant. He is merely intelligent, inquisitive, and willing and able to concentrate on problems that do not promise an immediate money reward. That none-too-rare combination of qualities, however, made him stand out like a genius among his fellows on the Exchange, where serious study has never been a drug on the market. And it was that fact that really made Martin the obvious choice for the chairmanship.

Paul Volcker

WILLIAM R. NEIKIRK

Paul Volcker achieved a remarkable degree of distinction as chairman of the Federal Reserve Board. He broke inflation. Not only was he acknowledged to be effective, but he was also well-appreciated—no mean accomplishment for the head of a central bank in a democracy. In this profile, we get some background on the man and on the job.

Monetary policy is inherently slow in its impact on the real economy. An analogy would be if you applied your car's brakes and it didn't stop for at least six months. But what if the economy is already slowing down when

Excerpted from *Volcker: Portrait of the Money Man* © 1987. Used with permission of Congdon & Weed, Inc. and Contemporary Books, Inc. Chicago.

the brakes are applied? That could cause an unintended recession. These lags give the job that artistic flavor. Knowing when to move is as important as how to move.

Volcker fancied himself as good an artist and scientist of monetary policy as there was around. As president for the New York Fed, he sat as a permanent member of the policymaking Federal Open Market Committee (FOMC), where he often pressed for tighter money in the Carter years. Since the early 1950s, he had worked with or around monetary policy in one way or another, and he know its limitations.

At another point in American economic history, Volcker might never have been considered for the Fed chairman post. Technicians, no matter how talented, rarely rise to such heights when they must rely on the judgment of politicians to elevate them. Jimmy Carter's first instinct was to seek a big, well-recognized name like Rockefeller or Clausen, and although Volcker was Carter's reluctant, and perhaps third, choice for the key post, it turned out to be the best appointment the Georgian ever made in his four years in the White House. Though there were many occasions in 1980, when interest rates began soaring as a result of Volcker's policies, that Carter regretted his decision, there was very little he could do about it, and most financial and political leaders agree that Volcker turned out to be the artist the economy so desperately needed. . . .

The naming of Volcker as Fed chairman was in many respects a historical accident. It came about only because two points in history converged.

One, the banking system realized it was in deep trouble, with inflation raging throughout the world. Credit itself had become a joke, a one-way deal that favored the borrower, who could take out a loan, get a tax deduction for the interest, and pay back in cheaper dollars. Banks were actually receiving negative interest on their loans, meaning that, after discounting for inflation, they were losing. Financial institutions felt that a house of cards was being built that would soon collapse. They began to realize that it was time to apply tough medicine, and one of the strongest, most effective candidates they could imagine for this task was Paul Volcker.

The New York Times once described Volcker as one of a breed of eastern money men who have run U.S. economic and financial policy since Alexander Hamilton and the founding of the republic. To be sure, Volcker springs from that tradition, but he differs in many ways, too. For one thing, he is not a wealthy man, although he could have long ago abandoned public service and made millions. Second, Volcker doesn't consider himself one of the boys of an exclusive club and holds in contempt many of the bankers who have so vigorously pushed his name to the fore. He believes that many of them are inept and greedy and made bad loans in the 1970s when they should have known better.

Why, then did the financial institutions like him? Because he played the right music for their ears. He supported the preservation of financial assets, which were under threat because of a roaring inflation. The lack of confidence of financial institutions in the economic policies of the Carter administration forced a crisis that brought Volcker on the scene. In a real sense, this marked a change in the emphasis of economic policy. It moved away from the "real economy," where goods and services are produced, to the "paper economy," the financial assets that undergird the real economy.

The second historical point pushing Volcker to center stage was the death of Keynesianism as the intellectual driving force in American economics.

• • •

The inflation crisis of 1979 was to change many lives, but few as dramatically as Volcker's. As the 51-year-old president of the Federal Reserve Bank of New York, he had acquired an apartment on East 79th Street a few years earlier when the city was embroiled in financial crisis and housing was relatively cheap. On a $116,000 salary (not bad for the time), he managed to live comfortably with Barbara and Jimmy, then 21. Daughter Janice was married and living in Arlington, Virginia.

The White House's call for him to come and meet with Carter shattered that tranquility. It was not especially convenient for Volcker to give up his position in New York. Jimmy, a bright and highly personable man, was undergoing a difficult personal adjustment. At the time, he was coping with problems associated with the cerebral palsy that had affected his limbs since he was born. Here in New York, his father had grown closer to his son and was helping him to make the adjustments. "It wasn't an ideal time to be coming to Washington," he said.

Then, his wife, who suffers from severe arthritis and diabetes, decided to stay in New York, both to be close to her doctors and to stay in the city she loved and knew well, where she could get around easily. Although he would call frequently and often commute home for weekends, the separation would still be difficult, and both Paul and Barbara knew it. Finally, because of the bizarre pay system in the federal government, in which the pay of top officials is linked to that of members of Congress, the chairman's job at the time paid only $57,000, which put a strain on the family budget despite a compensation package Paul received from the New York Fed. He would have to pay for housing in two separate cities, two of the most expensive in the world.

So, Volcker said, he was racked with ambivalence. He really didn't want to be named chairman of the Fed. He also knew something else: "If the president offered it to me, I knew I couldn't turn it down." It would be the pinnacle of his career and it would offer him a challenge the likes of which he had never had before, a chance for instant stardom and ego gratification—a difficult opportunity for anyone to turn aside.

The offer from Carter touched a deeper nerve. Back in Teaneck, New Jersey, a town of 35,000, Volcker had grown up as the son of the city manager, Paul A. Volcker, Sr., who had hammered into his children the duties and satisfactions of public service. Here, too, as a young man who had grown up during the Depression, he had heard his father, the son of a German immigrant, preach the merits of thrift and economic conservatism and how debt can be injurious. . . .

To Volcker, the 1979 climate offered only one clear answer, and he laid it out to Carter in his interview with the president: tighter money plus independence for the Fed. . . . Volcker left with the distinct impression that he would not be appointed because of his blunt economic prescription. Volcker never knew about the infighting over his appointment, though he later found out that both Rockefeller and Clausen had been approached. . . .

As it turned out, Carter had *not* objected to his plan. When the call for the appointment came, it was confirmation from the president that more tightness was just the medicine needed. . . .

Volcker's confirmation hearing before the Senate Banking Committee on July 30, 1979, established a persona that was to become familiar with the American public—an imposing man hunched over in his witness chair, puffing a cheap Antonio y Cleopatra drugstore cigar that emitted plumes of smoke around his bespectacled, balding head. These, and the rumpled suit or the tie that was often too short for his long trunk, became Volcker trademarks.

His confirmation went smoothly, as Volcker displayed his remarkable talent for dodging questions or seeming to answer them without hemming himself in. But the bulk of his answers that day left little doubt that he was going into the Federal Reserve with the full intention of being tighter. When Senator William Proxmire (D., Wisconsin), the committee chairman, asked him if he intended to raise interest rates to an even higher level, Volcker said he was only one member of the board with only one vote, a bit of a misleading answer since this was hardly reflective of his full powers as chairman of the board. But then he added, "I don't think there's any feeling or any evidence around at the moment that the economy is suffering grievously from a shortage of money."

In addition, he made it perfectly clear that he had little respect for the view of liberal economic policy that had dominated American life for most of the postwar period. When Proxmire quoted a study . . . that tightening the money supply would exact a tremendous price from the economy in terms of lost production and jobs and would have little impact on inflation, Volcker was ready. Such studies didn't mean much, he said.

"And part of the difficulty—and part of what has helped to account for this—seems to me the fact that the prolonged nature of the inflation has changed expectations; it's changed the way people look at their personal lives and view the outlook for the economy, in an unfavorable way. . . . I think it's fair to say the economy probably doesn't react the way you and certainly I were brought up to think. In terms of economic analysis, we were taught that an expansionary dose by whatever technique would improve employment with maybe some risk of inflation. We proceeded on that assumption for a long time, and we found the risks of inflation became much greater and that reactions in terms of employment, output, and productivity got less. . . . I don't think we have any substitute for seeking an answer to our problems in the context of monetary discipline."

This man was going to be different, all right. After his confirmation, he set out to prove it. But in his first few weeks on the job, Volcker realized how difficult it was going to be—in convincing his own board and the financial markets that it was time for a new course.

Volcker found his board was split between the "hawks" and the "doves." The doves didn't like the idea of putting the economy "through the wringer," as they say, to squeeze out inflation. It would have, as Proxmire's question to Volcker implied, put too many people out of work and not even control inflation. The "doves" of Volcker's board were Charles Partee, Nancy Teeters, and Emmett Rice. The "hawks," on the other hand, believed there was no substitute for a sound dollar brought on by monetary restraint. The "hawks" were Henry Wallich, Phillip Coldwell, and a brand new appointment, Frederick Schultz. . . .

Volcker's first experience at being tighter was successful as the board voted unanimously to raise the discount rate from 10 to 10.5 percent. After that, it got much tougher for Volcker. The board secretly voted down another rise in the discount rate on August 31, and then, on September 18, it split four to three to push up the discount rate to 11 percent.

Volcker said a split vote was all right with him. As far as he was concerned, four to three didn't matter as long as he was winning. But financial markets interpreted that vote as meaning that it would be the last time the central bank could tighten, given the dynamics of voting within the board. It did not make sense, but as many central bankers have learned, they often have to react to irrational thinking if that is what is driving the markets. The dollar sank again, and this time the situation was more serious.

The Volcker rally and the Volcker honeymoon were over. Something had to be done and done quickly. And Volcker was marshalling his evidence internally to go to a new system and break through this wall of incrementalism that would send the Fed in an entirely different direction, one that would bring it some credibility and at least give it a chance to bring inflation under control. He began to sound out the Fed members on the new proposal to target the money supply.

Debate within the board on whether the plan would work was intense. "We were groping," said one close to the situation. "It became one big intellectual discussion. Volcker himself did not try to do much persuading."

• • •

It was ironic that one of the most Keynesian administrators in U.S. history should pick as the head of the central bank a man who did not hold the philosophy in highest esteem. It wasn't that Paul Volcker was not steeped in

Keynesian economics, such as the importance of the federal budget in influencing the economy and the need for national economic statistics to gauge the demand for goods and services. John Maynard Keynes, after all, had revolutionized economic theory and virtually invented the whole notion of macroeconomics. He had almost single-handedly written the language of modern economics. Volcker accepted many of the ideas of the famous British economist, but as with almost everything he encountered, he could not buy the almost romantic optimism that seemed to infect many of Keynes's followers.

Volcker made this distinction when asked if he was a Keynesian. "Whatever answer I give you, you will misinterpret or your readers will misinterpret," he said. "I'll give you a Nixonian answer: We're all Keynesians now—in terms of the way we look at things. National income statistics are a Keynesian view of the world, and the language of economists tends to be Keynesian. But if you mean by Keynesian that we've got to pump up the economy, that all these relationships are pretty clear and simple, that this gives us a tool for eternal prosperity if we do it right, that's all bullshit."

Alan Greenspan

KEVIN MUEHRING

Alan Greenspan and his private struggle to balance financial, social, political, intellectual, and historical ambitions are described in this illuminating profile. In the period since it was written, the struggle appears to have continued. While there is no clear resolution yet, Greenspan's very favorable place in Fed history appears secure.

"Suppressing inflation over the past decade has obviously not been without cost," droned Federal Reserve Board chairman Alan Greenspan, barely lifting his eyes from his text to survey the crowd at the New York Hilton. "And to fritter away this substantial accomplishment by failing to contain inflationary forces that may emerge in the future would be folly."

The applause was perfunctory; no one would confuse Greenspan with a great speech maker, and much of the rest of his talk was a rehash of earlier Senate testimony. But consider the subtext of his statement: The dragon of

Excerpted from *Institutional Investor* (June 1993), pp. 41–46, 51. This copyrighted material is reprinted with permission from: **Institutional Investor, Inc.,** 488 Madison Avenue, New York, NY 10022.

inflation was almost dead. He, Alan Greenspan, had just about completed what Paul Volcker had started in the dog days of Jimmy Carter's administration. And to the tough crowd at the Economics Club that April night, Greenspan was really saying, forget the politicians, trust *me*.

It must be terribly frustrating to Greenspan that this remains difficult for so many to do, even among the Wall Streeters who gathered that night in the Hilton ballroom. Here is the man who handled the 1987 crash, piloted the Fed through the head winds of corporate restructuring, and coped with overhanging debt and a tottering banking system. Despite the handicap of unreliable monetary targets, he did it all without a breakdown in U.S. borrowing power or a financial meltdown. And for all of that, the widespread perception of Greenspan, even among Washington insiders, is of a bureaucrat too easily snookered into sitting next to First Lady Hillary Rodham Clinton at the State of the Union address.

That cruel twist of public-relations fate neatly encapsulates Greenspan's dilemma. Greenspan is a complex personality operating in an intensely political environment. For now, he and President Bill Clinton share similar interests: Low inflation is a necessary prerequisite to the Clinton economic program. But they are an odd pair, this New York Republican apostle of price stability and devotee of Ayn Rand and this Democratic populist from Arkansas with a fondness for Elvis Presley. Eventually—and it now looks like it will be sooner rather than later—a day of reckoning will come, when Greenspan will have to defend price stability against populist stimulus and reflation tendencies. Whether he will be able to, whether his economic ideals can conquer his predilection for the political limelight, will determine his place in Fed history. . . .

His image as a shrewd—perhaps too shrewd by half—political operator undercuts his assertion that he will keep inflation low. "He is not seen in this town as a symbol of strength," says longtime Republican political analyst Kevin Phillips. After all, didn't Greenspan go just a little overboard in his endorsement of the Clinton economic plan? And didn't he sit between Hillary Clinton and Tipper Gore, at the big Clinton speech?

There is, more ominously, Greenspan's congressional problem. Over the past few years, both Senate and House Democrats have introduced bills to make the Fed more accountable to Congress. Those bills may have a chilling effect. If Greenspan tightens to quell inflation before official figures confirm it to be a problem, which of course is the best time to battle inflation, the Fed may find itself under legislative threat.

• • •

Greenspan's whole career has been built upon such tensions. "Alan is a man of contrasting passions," notes Leonard Garment, a longtime Washington power. . . . Garment has known Greenspan since 1944, when they played big-band jazz together. . . . There is the shy, softspoken Greenspan who has a striking ability to draw economic interconnections from masses of raw data. . . .

This is Greenspan the technocrat, the man who seems to extract an almost sensual pleasure from statistics. . . .

You can't truly understand Greenspan, friends say, without getting some sense of his youth. Greenspan was an only child, born and raised in Manhattan's Washington Heights; he went to high school with a German refugee named Henry Kissinger. His father, Hermann, a stockbroker, divorced Alan's mother, Rose, when Greenspan was a teenager. Young Alan found solace in music and economics. After studying economics at New York University and taking a job with the Conference Board studying the steel and aluminum industries, Greenspan joined economic consultancy Townsend & Associates. When he was 27 he met writer Ayn Rand . . . a flamboyant advocate of radical individualism and Darwinian capitalism. Greenspan remained active in the Rand circle through the mid-1960s and was briefly married to a member of the group. Randian analysis shaped his economics: He eschewed the mainstream Keynesianism of the day for a fiercely romantic, anti-big-government philosophy that was to draw him into Republican politics.

Indeed, Republican politics increasingly replaced his Randian enthusiasms. In 1965 Greenspan, by then president of renamed Townsend-Greenspan & Co., bumped into Garment on Broad Street in New York's financial district. They had lunch at the Bankers Club, where the conversation turned to Garment's recruiting efforts for Richard Nixon's upcoming presidential campaign. Garment introduced him to Nixon, who was impressed by Greenspan's understanding of the federal budget process. "Alan was fascinated with budgets," Garment recalls. "He said they were the central nervous system of American politics, that if you could understand the budget, it would give you a very good insight into the character and thinking of the administration." In 1968 Greenspan served as head of the Nixon campaign's economic-policy research team. "His line at the time was that the Nixon people pleaded with him to come to Washington, but he resisted. The fact is he wanted a position in Washington badly," recalls one friend.

After Nixon's resignation, his successor, Gerald Ford, named Greenspan chairman of his Council of Economic Advisors. As former Senator William Proxmire pointed out during Greenspan's Fed confirmation hearings in 1987, Greenspan's track record at the CEA was pretty lackluster: He regularly overestimated GNP growth and underestimated inflation rates. Whether that reflected poor forecasting skills or a willingness to skew the figures to serve the political agenda is unclear; but in any case, Greenspan was later to stick to his anti-inflation instincts by adopting a passive stance on the debate raging within the Ford administration on whether to introduce countercyclical measures to combat the 1974 recession. Ford didn't do so, and lost in 1976.

During the Carter years Greenspan was back at his lucrative consultancy, though he remained immersed in GOP politics. In 1980 he advised both Reagan and Ford during the Republican convention, and in the early years of the Reagan administration, he accepted several non-cabinet posts, including the chairmanship of the President's Committee on Social Security Reform, where he won plaudits for achieving consensus.

Greenspan's advancing career increasingly brought out the conflict in him between the romantic individualist and the high-level economic mandarin. Those contradictions persist on a variety of levels, both personal and professional. Despite making a tidy sum at his consulting firm, Greenspan, recalls one friend, never felt that he really "belonged": He was the outsider looking in, an economist who was neither a technical academician nor a Wall Streeter.

Greenspan's characteristic style of economics, with its focus on statistics, provides one haven from a very messy world. In his 1991 Senate testimony, he reminisced about watching the effect of the Persian Gulf war air strikes, not on CNN, but on his computer screen. "You could basically see not only the price of gold coming down very sharply around the world, but you could see the effects minute by minute in the exchange markets, in the interest rate markets, all arbitraged across and around the world," he said.

There is another side to Greenspan. This is the Greenspan who, like his schoolmate Kissinger, blossomed into an eligible bachelor-about-Washington, squiring the likes of NBC correspondent Andrea Mitchell and ABC anchorwoman Barbara Walters. In his pre-Fed days Greenspan was an aggressive name-dropper and networker who played tennis with violinist Isaac Stern at the Century Club in Rye, New York.

One social acquaintance who has known Greenspan since the early 1970s describes him as "a very ambitious and successful social climber, among those New Yorkers who came out of circumstances that were hardly privileged, who worked their way to the top and who are thrilled at being so successful." One woman who has known Greenspan for years says bluntly, "I think Alan has his principles, but he also has social ambitions, and I'm not sure if he wouldn't rationalize away the former if they ever intruded on the latter." And though one person who has worked with him counters that the remark is too harsh, he then adds, "You will note that I am not saying the opposite is true."

Much of this venom is just the price of power and fame—though there were a few occasions when Greenspan clearly trimmed monetary policy to political winds. On the day of the New Hampshire primary in February 1992, with President George Bush under attack by Patrick Buchanan, Greenspan announced a cut in bank reserve requirements, from 12 to 10 percent, though the cuts wouldn't take effect until April. A few months later, with Greenspan himself up for reappointment and Treasury Secretary Nicholas Brady back in Washington after an ineffectual plea to his fellow Group of Seven ministers to spur growth through interest rate cuts, the Fed conveniently cut the Fed funds rate. This isn't quite the equivalent of Arthur Burns pumping up the money supply to ease the reelection of President Nixon, but to many in Washington, Greenspan seemed to be skating close to the edge.

• • •

Greenspan did little to hide the fact that he wanted the job as Fed chairman after Volcker resigned in July 1987. Although he was considered a front-runner, his close ties to the Republican party raised hackles within the Senate Banking Committee. Proxmire openly questioned Greenspan's independence. That charge continued to haunt him. . . .

Perhaps the ultimate criterion for judging whether Greenspan will live up to his death-of-inflation promise is what Garment calls his "pride of place," his conviction that after all he has accomplished, he is not about to throw it all away by letting inflation back out of the bag. Greenspan has already confronted some formidable challenges—and survived. He has steered the economy through tumultuous change and has pioneered new methods of formulating monetary policy in volatile times, which seem certain to be exported to European countries as they begin to undergo financial deregulation. And he is proud of the job he has done.

But will he ever be viewed as a great Fed chairman? The competition is stiff, and the future, of course, unfathomable. But before Greenspan can even be considered to be in the league of giants such as Volcker; Franklin Delano Roosevelt's Fed chairman, Marriner Eccles, the first modern Fed chairman to wrestle with the role of big government in the economy; and [Benjamin] Strong, who expanded the powers of the Fed in the 1920s; he will have to fulfill his promise to really kill inflationary expectations—an enormous claim in a consumer-based, democratic country operating in a global economy.

And for all his political skills, Greenspan must face the inevitable day when he drops the political pretense and directly challenges the political establishment. "The reality is that whatever the administration, Democratic or Republican, we are bound to inevitably clash because we are operating under different agendas," says one Fed official. "All they want is growth, growth, growth. What we want is *sustained* growth."

Whether Greenspan can achieve that agenda will ultimately determine whether he will be a great Fed chairman or just another technocrat who mistakes numbers for reality.

Gary Lynch

ANDREW MARTON

Gary Lynch, now a partner at Davis Polk, was the classic model public servant, working long hours at low pay and confident that he could work through the system. A bit tall, modest, tough and—as it turned out—very effective at cracking insider trading networks for the SEC when he got his big chance. Then, he left as quietly as he had arrived.

It's a steamy July afternoon and the chief cop of the Securities and Exchange Commission—the guy who's been the scourge of Wall Street's white-collar criminals—has only 48 hours to clear out his office. It won't be easy. He's surrounded by reams of paper and dozens of overstuffed boxes, and he still has a long way to go.

"Please pardon the mess," Gary Lynch says as he plops into a government-issue vinyl armchair. Fortunately, he isn't the kind of guy who'll slow down to reread the two dozen commendation awards, plaques, and presidential thank-you letters that are piled up on his desk. In fact, he's so self-effacing that when he takes down a picture of himself shaking hands with Ronald Reagan, he says that the only thing he remembers about the event is that his wife, Donna, wasn't with him; she'd just given birth to their second child.

It's just the kind of remark you'd expect from Lynch. His image as a tough-as-nails government prosecutor and devoted family man inevitably leads people to compare him with Eliot Ness. After all, Lynch was to Wall Street's hotshots what Ness was to Prohibition's hoodlums. And there are other similarities: both men are Irish, both toiled in eras pocked with greed, both worked with a band of "untouchables," and both had a favorite target. Ness's was Al Capone; Lynch's was Michael Milken. Capone had his day in court and lost; Milken's is still to come.

"In the end, Gary Lynch was to securities law what Michael Milken was to finance—both unique contributors, unequaled by anyone else," says Peter Romatowski, a lawyer with Crowell & Moring who worked with Lynch when he ran the U.S. attorney's securities and commodities fraud division. "Frankly, going back to the beginning of the SEC in 1934, I don't think a single individual has made the same impact on securities enforcement that Gary has."

Excerpted from *Regardie's 10* (March 1990), pp. 89–90. Reprinted with permission.

In the 17 years that the SEC's enforcement division has been in business, only four men have worn its tin badge, and Lynch may have been the best. When he called it quits last year, he bequeathed a lawyer's gun notched with the names of the Wall Street crooks he'd bagged. His first big hit was Dennis Levine, a former head of mergers and acquisitions at Drexel Burnham Lambert, whose $11.6 million insider-trading settlement in 1986 was the largest in the SEC's history. The largest, that is, until Lynch brought in a $100 million settlement from Ivan Boesky, who put Lynch's posse on the trail of such Wall Street outlaws as Milken and Martin Siegel of Drexel Burnham and Boyd Jefferies of Jefferies & Company. But Lynch and his deputies weren't content to stop there. They pummeled Milken with a 200-page indictment that listed more than 100 counts of fraud and forced a crushing $650 million settlement on Drexel Burnham—perhaps the largest penalty ever paid in law enforcement. The case elevated Lynch to a police demigod.

"You see, I'm directed—*very* directed—in what I do," Lynch says matter-of-factly. "I've always liked to win, especially if it's worth the fight."

In his four years as the head of enforcement Lynch didn't often lose. By weaving a bit of testimony here and a plea bargain there, he braided a net of evidence that snared some of Wall Street's most accomplished market manipulators. He caught all kinds, from CEOs to arbitrageurs, to lawyers, accountants, clerks, printing-plant employees, and journalists. He didn't discriminate; he cleaned out upstart Drexel Burnham as readily as he took down blue-blooded Morgan Stanley. And through it all, he made sure that his marks suffered public humiliation. . . .

Despite the sea of changes that Lynch churned up, he remained curiously outside the limelight, his name all but obscured by the demise of yet another Wall Street fat cat. It was no accident; Lynch preferred it that way. But during his years at the SEC he faced a dilemma: he wanted to be a faceless, laconic bureaucrat, a governmental Gary Cooper, but he needed to grab headlines to ward off future miscreants. In the end, he became the ultimate not-ready-for-prime-time player. Unable to describe his latest triumph in a sound bite for the evening news, he remained a shadow gunslinger who rode into town, cleaned things up, and galloped off into a smoggy sunset. Now that he's gone, many are still asking, "Who *was* that masked man?"

Ivan F. Boesky

GWEN KINKEAD

Ivan Boesky's competitors used to say that they "couldn't believe" his incredibly astute timing when buying into stocks that then became "deals." They were, we now know, more right than they knew. This unblinking piece was written in 1984—before his ignominious fall and subsequent incarceration. It helps explain why he couldn't pass the "sniff test."

Ivan F. Boesky, 47, wants an empire. To get that, he needs capital to build it. To get that, he plays fast and tough in a Wall Street profession in which capital can be accumulated rapidly—risk arbitrage, the secretive, arcane business of trading securities of companies involved in mergers or reorganizations. "I don't take any particular pride in being big," says Boesky. "I do take a certain amount of pride in creating wealth."

Within the compass of Ivan Boesky, most things hinge on money and getting more of it. He has built one of the largest arbitrage firms on Wall Street. The Ivan F. Boesky Corp., his private holding company, started this fiscal year with $834 million in assets and $210 million in total capital. Investors in the corporation and its predecessor, a private partnership, have done well, but nowhere near as well as Boesky. He had made a fortune investing their money.

He regularly plunges into the largest positions taken by any "arb," a habit that has made him widely feared and envied—and led to his nickname on Wall Street: "Piggy." He has earned his wealth and fame by pressing to the legal limits of his profession. Charming and amusing though he can be, he won't talk about many aspects of his business and personal life and when he does, occasionally shades the truth.

Son of a Russian émigré who owned a chain of Detroit delis, Boesky says he was always "very eager to earn my way." At 13, without a driver's license, he drove a truck through the city selling ice cream. In conversation with *Fortune* Boesky left the impression that the only high school he had attended was Cranbrook, a private boys' school outside Detroit. He did go to Cranbrook but left after his sophomore year; school records and documents from the Securities and Exchange Commission show that he graduated from a public high school. Boesky also said that he "went to the University of Michigan as an undergraduate." But university officials say that he spent only one term there. He passed through two other Michigan colleges without getting a degree before graduating from Detroit College of Law in 1964.

During law school Boesky married Seema Silberstein, a daughter of the owner of the Beverly Hills Hotel. In the early days, at least, he was scorned by his wealthy father-in-law. In 1966, attracted to arbitrage by the enthusiasm of a former college roommate, Boesky and his wife moved to New York, where by 1972 he was running the arbitrage department for the firm of Edwards & Hanly. During his tenure there, the New York Stock Exchange censured Boesky and fined him $10,000 for selling securities short in excess of the firm's ability to deliver.

In 1975 he boldly launched his own partnership with $700,000, half from his wife's mother and stepfather, he says, and half from his wife and himself. Boesky's was the first partnership devoted to securities arbitrage; until he came along, arbitrage had been practiced only by investment banks. His diligence and confidence gave him the aura of a winner and drew investors. Says one: "I was very taken by Ivan, by his personality and intensity. I felt this guy was going to be successful no matter what he did."

After four strong years, the partnership weakened in 1980. During the first quarter, two deals in which Boesky had huge stakes ran into difficulties: Imperial Group's tender for Howard Johnson Co., and ERC Corp.'s proposed merger with Connecticut General Insurance. That caused the partnership's capital to fall by about $40 million. In midyear Boesky told investors to withdraw their money. He passed the firm to a friend after the close of the year, and started over as a corporation in early 1981. . . .

Most of the profits of the [Boesky] corporation flow to Boesky and his family. The corporation has two classes of equity: preferred and common. Preferred holders receive fixed dividends, which last year totaled less than 3 percent of net profits. After these, the preferred holders receive 45 percent of the net profit, which goes to their retained earnings account. Common stockholders get 55 percent, also held in retained earnings. As of last February, outside investors owned 82 percent of the preferred stock but only 2 percent of the common. So, as the arithmetic works out, outside investors got 38 percent of the year's profits vs. 62 percent for Boesky.

When fate turns against the company, however, Boesky gets off relatively easy, while outside investors get soaked. Boesky Corp.'s preferred holders bear 95 percent of all losses; common holders bear only 5 percent. The way the shares were divided in the unprofitable year of 1982, the outside investors lost $9.3 million vs. Boesky's $1.8 million. Of the $52 million the corporation has earned after taxes since its founding, investors have received only $14.9 million.

Boesky, for his part, has accumulated $37 million on an initial investment of $4.1 million. In the future he could make out even better in good times (though worse in bad times). At the close of the last fiscal year he parceled out dividends of preferred stock to all shareholders—with a disproportionate share to himself. The dividends pushed the percentage he and his family own from 18 percent to 41 percent. As a result, he will receive 72 percent of future earnings and 44 percent of losses.

Why do investors stay with Boesky if he pounces on most of the profits himself? Says Steven Oppenheim of Oppenheim Appel & Dixon, the corporation's accountant: "Ivan Boesky will increase your wealth only if he can increase his own. I don't find that repugnant. It's disclosed: every investor knows that going in." . . .

Boesky's money lets him live the good life. A limousine ferries him between his midtown office and a 200-acre estate outside New York City, where he resides in splendid isolation with his wife and four children. Boesky calls the property "a farm." A friend describes it this way: "It's definitely how people live in books: there are formal gardens and gardeners all over the place, indoor handball and racquetball courts, saunas, spas, pools, pool houses, indoor tennis courts, outdoor tennis courts, art, antiques, etc." Boesky plays tennis and squash often, eats abstemiously, and says he sleeps three hours a night.

Devoted to his family, he also gives copiously to numerous charities. He and his wife have donated about $2.5 million and a collection of rare Judaic and Hebraic books to the Jewish Theological Seminary. Boesky has also contributed to a visiting fellowship for journalists at the Harvard School of Public Health, whose recently retired dean, Howard Hiatt, has been a Boesky investor for years.

Boesky has yet to prove himself in one cherished goal—becoming an investment banker or, as he puts it in British terminology, a merchant banker. Arbitrage has not yielded the capital he needs to both remain an arbitrager and do what else he wants: buy companies outright, or purchase large stakes and over time help a company's management raise the value of its stock. Though he says he won't greenmail or participate in unfriendly takeovers, his most recent target apparently didn't believe him.

Scott & Fetzer, an Ohio door-to-door sales company for vacuum cleaners and *World Book* encyclopedias, rejected his proposed leveraged buyout this spring, even though Boesky offered $10 a share more than Scott & Fetzer's management did. Asked why he has not been successful as a merchant banker, Boesky says, "Sometimes people don't know what's best for them."

"We want to be wanted," Boesky says, adding: "Companies can use the advice of experienced banking mentalities." As he looks for companies that want him, he is up against his lack of managerial experience and his hardnosed reputation. A broker who has known him for years says that Boesky is brilliant but avaricious, "all take and no give." This broker adds that Boesky's image prevents him from doing some of the things he wants, like merchant banking. Boesky views it differently. "It's a question of people getting to know, understand, and believe, and all these things take time. People kind of have to sniff you to know what you're about." Until Boesky passes the "sniff test," as he says, the merchant banking empire he wants to build on the profits from arbitrage will remain a dream.

Dennis B. Levine

DENNIS B. LEVINE

A principal in an insider trading scandal of the late 1980s, Dennis Levine pleaded guilty to four felony counts, was fined $362,000 and sentenced to four concurrent two-year terms in prison. Further, he was barred for life from the securities business even though his testimony led to indictments of Ivan Boesky, Martin Siegel, Michael Milken, and others. He tells us something about his fall in this brief sketch.

Sometimes, in those scarce moments when I allowed myself time to reflect, it all sent me reeling. When I started in the business world in 1977, I earned $19,000 a year. Now, a mere, magical nine years later, as a managing director of the investment-banking house of Drexel Burnham Lambert, I had an annual salary, bonus, and investment income of more than $2 million. My wife, Laurie, and I had more than $1 million socked away in legitimate investments.

We lived in a beautiful, freshly refurbished Park Avenue co-op. Laurie was pregnant with our second child. Parked in the garage nearby was a 1983 BMW 633CSI and a fire-engine-red Ferrari Testarossa, my fantasy embodied in steel, so fresh that it still had only about 3,000 miles on it.

Making money was my passion, more than ever, and the $10.6 million I had stashed in a secret account at Bank Leu in the Bahamas represented not so much buying power as points on the scoreboard.

I was not yet sophisticated enough to realize a basic truth: I didn't need the money in the secret account. Only on this day, Monday, May 12, 1986, in the thirty-third year of this crazy life, would I begin to learn.

I was in a bubbly mood when I met with my staff to review the day's agenda. I then attended some other meetings and returned to my own office shortly after 11 A.M. My secretary, Marilyn Stewart, announced, "There were two gentlemen here looking for you. They didn't look like clients."

"Tell them I'm not here. Refer them to Legal and Compliance."

"Okay," Marilyn said. Then she added, "Oh, by the way, they're from the Department of Justice."

The Justice Department? Not the SEC? I saw my fist pound involuntarily upon my desk. I've got to get the hell out of here, I said to myself. But somehow I found the composure to say to Marilyn, "No problem, I'll take care of this."

Grabbing my briefcase, I slipped out of my office from a side exit and edged toward the reception area to get a good look at these men. One of them was huge, perhaps six feet nine, with shoulders that seemed to span the width of the room. His partner was of average height, but the giant's commanding presence made the pair appear like Mutt and Jeff.

I needed time to think. Get out of here, Dennis, I told myself. Call in. Get the facts. Assess the situation. Preserve your options. Get help.

Once on the street, I hailed a taxi and commanded, "Ninety-third Street and Park Avenue."

"What's the matter?" Laurie asked. She had been napping and was trying to shake the sleep from her head.

"I might be in a lot of trouble," I stammered. "I don't know. But if somebody comes here to see me, or calls for me, you don't know anything. You haven't seen me. Say nothing to anybody."

"Dennis, what are you talking about?"

"I can't tell you about it now," I said. "I have to get the car." I raced toward my desk, and as Laurie followed, I issued directions. "Call for the car," I said. "No, I'm going to get it. Tell them . . . no, call for the car." I wanted the BMW because it had a cellular phone and because it was far less conspicuous than the Ferrari.

She called the garage. Then she asked, "Where are you going?"

• • •

One of our biggest concerns was our five-year-old son, Adam. . . . Adam needed to know why Daddy was going away. We were at my brother Robert's house, sitting in the den, when I tried to explain. I drew Adam onto my lap and began, "You know, when little people make mistakes, they have to be punished. Well, it's the same for big people. They get punished by a judge."

"I went to see a judge," I said. "A judge is a man who punishes big people."

Adam asked fearfully, "What did he do?" . . .

My body went numb. I felt paralyzed.

Laurie tried to explain: "The biggest punishment that an adult can have, especially if he has children, is to be taken away from his family for a time. The judge is probably going to take Daddy away from us for a while."

Through tears Adam asked, "Daddy, did you know what you were doing was wrong?"

Through my own tears I replied, "Yes."

"So then why did you do it?"

Martin Siegel

JAMES B. STEWART

Marty Siegel was a senior executive of Kidder Peabody when he started to break the securities laws, enriching himself while helping to enrich Ivan Boesky. He once received a payoff in the form of a suitcase full of cash delivered to a telephone booth. By the time he made up his mind to quit the game, it was too late.

Somehow, Siegel knew . . . information was finding its way into the marketplace in advance of market-moving corporate announcements. Anyone could see the trading volume and price increases, and it wasn't hard to trace the identity of the purchasers. A whole cottage industry grew up on Wall Street consisting of self-styled arbitragers who simply tracked the trading patterns of the club members, blindly buying and selling in copycat fashion.

The Carnation deal was in full swing when Freeman[1] called, reinforcing Siegel's suspicions about the arbitrage community. Freeman mentioned that he knew Boesky owned a million shares of Carnation. Siegel was doubly astounded, both by the magnitude of Boesky's position—he had had no idea how heavily Boesky had invested—and by the fact that Freeman knew. Obviously, there were no secrets in the Boesky organization, at least when it came to powerful arbs like Freeman. No wonder rumors were appearing in the press. Siegel's mind raced as Freeman talked on. Then he heard something that gave him another stab of anxiety: "You should be careful," Freeman said. "There are rumors that you're too close to Boesky."

"I'm not talking to him anymore," Siegel blurted out. "I used to."

Freeman's comment was the last straw. Siegel vowed that the Carnation disclosure would be his last. He had to distance himself from Boesky, fast. Otherwise he'd be dogged by rumors forever.

Then . . . Siegel received a call from reporter Connie Bruck, who was at work on another profile of Boesky, this one for *The Atlantic*. She . . . was prepared to mention Siegel by name as the subject of the rumors. Siegel

[1]*Editor's note:* Robert M. Freeman was a Goldman Sachs partner who in 1990 pleaded guilty to one charge of illegal insider stock trading and received a four-month sentence to a Federal prison camp.

begged her to keep him out of the article, to no avail. He went again to De-Nunzio [his boss at Kidder] to warn him, saying that something had to be done. Something was. When Bruck turned in her manuscript with the reference to Siegel, she was told by lawyers for the magazine that the article would not be published unless she deleted the material about Siegel. She protested, but they were adamant. The article appeared in the December issue, with no mention of the Siegel rumors. Only later did Siegel learn that Kidder, Peabody's lawyers had intervened, threatening suit if the offending material wasn't dropped from the manuscript.

For the rest of the year, Siegel remained determined to sever his ties with Boesky. His almost daily phone contacts with Boesky fell off dramatically. He gave him no new inside information. And yet, as the end of the year approached, and despite all the anxiety, Siegel began to contemplate his year-end "bonus." Even for Siegel, it was hard to make a rational case that he really needed the money. He had had a terrific year in 1984, and his legitimate salary and bonus at Kidder, Peabody had crossed the $1 million mark; he was paid $1.1 million in cash and Kidder, Peabody stock. Still, the renovations on the apartment were costing more than he expected, approaching $500,000. And he had earned the "bonus," after all, with the incredibly valuable tips and insights. Why shouldn't he share in Boesky's outsize profits?

In January 1985, Siegel and Boesky settled down again at Pastrami 'n Things. As he had vowed, Siegel upped his request to cover the anticipated skimming. He asked for $400,000, expecting to realize about $350,000. With that cash, he could pay off all the building contractors on the apartment. Boesky readily agreed; the value of the Carnation tip didn't even have to be discussed. But this time Boesky had a new plan for the cash drop-off. He didn't want to risk another transfer in the Plaza lobby.

Boesky instructed Siegel to be at a pay phone booth at 55th Street and First Avenue precisely at 9 A.M. Siegel would pick up the receiver and pretend to be making a call. While he was on the phone, the courier would stand behind him as though he were waiting to make a call. He would place a briefcase by Siegel's left leg, then disappear. Siegel thought this scheme sounded even more ridiculous than the Plaza plan, like something out of a bad spy novel, but Boesky was insistent.

Siegel arrived at the pay phone early on the appointed date. To kill time, he sat down at a table in the window of a coffee shop across the street. As he sipped his coffee, he spotted someone who had to be the courier: a swarthy man with a briefcase milling about the small plaza where the pay phone was located. He was wearing a black pea coat.

Then Siegel saw someone else. About a half block up the street, he spotted another dark-skinned man walking back and forth on the sidewalk, keeping an eye on the man Siegel suspected was the courier. Siegel started to feel panicky. What was going on? Was someone else involved? Suddenly all of Siegel's fears about Boesky and his reputed CIA involvement surged to the fore. "They're going to kill me," Siegel thought. That was the reason for the bizarre plan to have the courier come up behind him: he was going to be murdered. Siegel finished his coffee, paid the check, and fled, stranding the courier with the briefcase filled with cash.

The same day, soon after Siegel arrived at his office, Boesky called. "How did it go?" he asked.

"Nothing went," Siegel answered.

"Why not?" Boesky sounded disturbed.

"There was more than one person there," Siegel explained. "Someone was watching."

"Of course," Boesky exclaimed. "There always is. I want to make sure they deliver."

Siegel was astounded. Boesky didn't even trust his own courier.

Boesky insisted Siegel repeat the exercise at the phone booth. "I've gone to all the trouble to get this cash, you might as well take it," Boesky argued. Siegel was wary, but he couldn't bring himself to disengage. After holding Boesky off for several weeks, he gave in. This time the hand-off went without a hitch. As usual, some of the money had vanished, but Siegel didn't even bother mentioning it to Boesky. "This is the last time," Siegel vowed to himself. He didn't intend to keep living in fear.

In Siegel's mind, the scheme was over, the last payment made. Siegel stopped calling Boesky entirely, and when Boesky called, he was evasive, busy, eager to get off the line. It didn't take Boesky long to realize what was happening.

One afternoon, as Siegel took Boesky's call but then tried quickly to end the conversation, he sensed a softening in Boesky's tone, a genuine sadness. "What's the matter, Marty?" Boesky asked quietly. "You never want to talk to me. You never call anymore. I never see you.

"Don't you love me anymore?"

Michael Milken

JAMES B. STEWART

Michael Milken made a larger fortune faster than anyone else in Wall Street history. In about equal parts, this was because he was in the right place at the right time, because he *made* it the right place and the right time, and because he broke the law. Also, it was because he played for keeps—and enough was never enough. He wanted all of it. This revealing vignette is from a book aptly titled *Den of Thieves*.

Jim Dahl took a deep breath and walked into the conference room for his annual salary review. This year, 1986, he was prepared to insist on more than Milken offered. He never knew the exact size of the high-yield operation's bonus pool, but he knew it had to be big. Other employees . . . had succeeded in wheedling large amounts out of Milken. This year, Dahl had been indisputably the top salesman, coming through even in the most difficult situations, as in the $100 million of Boesky debt he sold Charles Keating.

Milken went right to the point. "You're going to be paid $10 million this year," he told the 33-year-old Dahl. This was more than Dahl had ever dreamed of making, but he stuck to his resolution. "I really think I'm entitled to more," he insisted, ticking off his achievements. Milken listened sympathetically, but quickly disagreed. "Jim, I really can't pay you any more," he said in a soft voice, "or you'd be making more than me. Now that wouldn't be fair, would it?"

"I guess not," Dahl said. He was surprised at the low amount, but he guessed that Milken was plowing a larger share of the department's profits back into the firm than he'd suspected. Dahl now owned nearly 1 percent of Drexel's stock, so he admired Milken's apparent selflessness.

In New York, Fred Joseph was grappling with the issue of Milken's pay. That spring, Joseph had been elevated from head of corporate finance to chief executive officer when Robert Linton stepped down. In some ways Joseph hadn't wanted the promotion. *Institutional Investor* had just named him the best corporate finance manager on Wall Street, and he was enjoying himself, feeling he was accomplishing something as his department capitalized on the Milken phenomenon. He also liked having some free time to spend with his wife at their working farm in northwestern New Jersey.

Milken made no secret of his opposition to Joseph's appointment. He complained about it to Joseph, claiming Joseph was too important to him in corporate finance. Yet Milken, who could have placed anyone he chose in the top position, didn't offer any alternatives. He first suggested his own nominal boss, Edwin Kantor, but even he had to acknowledge that Kantor's wasn't the image the firm wanted to project. The personable Joseph was the nearly inevitable choice.

Drexel had soared even beyond Joseph's own ambitious projections. In 1986, Milken's high-yield department was entitled under Drexel's compensation formula to approximately $700 million in bonuses. Approximately half was attributable to finder's fees, allocated to Milken for referring clients to services elsewhere in the firm. By comparison, the corporate finance bonus pool was about $140 million, reflecting the disproportionate weighting of compensation and underlying power wielded by the Beverly Hills [Milken's] operation.

Once Joseph approved the overall bonus pool of $700 million, it was up to Milken to divide it up as he saw fit. Milken doled out about $150 million to his colleagues in Beverly Hills, including the $10 million he'd promised Dahl. But Milken didn't keep just $10 million for himself, as he'd implied. Nor did he plow the remainder into the firm's capital, as Dahl had surmised. Dahl had no way of knowing this at the time, but Milken bestowed $550 million on himself. That was more than the $522.5 million in profit that Drexel itself—the entire firm—had earned.

Yet Milken didn't think $550 million was enough. Milken was actually angry with Joseph about the size of the bonus pool.

Robert Maxwell

BRONWEN MADDOX AND JIMMY BURNS

Robert Maxwell was a man who was forever in motion. He was also a bully who treated his family badly, erected a seemingly-successful multinational complex of companies that, however, required extensive fraud to keep it going, and who, within days of the inevitable discovery, was found dead in the sea. The wonder of it is that although British regulators in 1971 had declared him unfit to run a public company, it wasn't until two days after his 1991 death that agents of the Serious Fraud Office went looking for evidence. What had transpired in the 20-year interval revealed a record of ongoing deceit and dissimulation.

The Rolls-Royce swung out of London's Park Lane into Knightsbridge heading for the Royal Albert Hall, where the Queen was attending a recital of Handel's Messiah.

Excerpted from *Financial Times* (June 15, 1992), p. 9. Reprinted with permission.

As the car threaded its way through the evening traffic, Robert Maxwell told his French wife, Betty, he couldn't go with her as he had a business meeting. He suggested she get out and catch a taxi.

"What am I going to tell the Queen?" Betty pleaded. "Tell her I'm a busy man," came the reply. Maxwell left his wife near the Albert Hall and headed for Henry Ansbacher, the merchant bank. He stayed until late that night, drinking vintage champagne with Lord Spens, the corporate financier who was later to become involved in the second Guinness trial. "I was bored, I felt like having a drink with the boys," Maxwell told Spens.

Maxwell was a bully when alive; when he died, he left his wife and family a terrible legacy. He also robbed 30,000 past and present employees of their pensions.

The portrait that emerges from his treatment of both his family and his employees is one of a man enslaved by egotism with delusions of omnipotence.

He had some good qualities: many found him an inspiration. Some shared the sentiments of Betty Maxwell, who said the day after he died: "Looking back on our close-on-50 years together, I can see a kaleidoscope of never-ending adventures, projects, achievements, tragedies, holidays, work and more work. With him life was often tough, but the rewards were great."

At heart, however, Maxwell was a tyrant, and it is that which holds the key to the fraud. He built around himself a medieval court which fed his enormous ego. This allowed him to believe he could do anything and created the culture—fantastic, absurd, domineering, lawless, chaotic and paranoid—that made the fraud possible. Those who opposed his rules were banished; those who flattered, soothed or entertained him stayed. In the same way that he left others to pick up his dirty towels and clothes, Maxwell used the people who worked for him to run the wheels of his empire.

The inner core of his court was his family. From his seven children, Maxwell drew two—Kevin and Ian—into the heart of his empire. They became its crown princes. Maxwell was fiercely proud of his family, but also fiercely critical. He believed their lives belonged to him. This pressure on them began early. George Ireland, a schoolfriend of Kevin, remembers that Maxwell insisted that his son write home from school each week listing his achievements. Kevin complained that "no-one else in the school had to write in such detail." . . .

Maxwell took his obsession with his empire wherever he went. John Pole, Maxwell's head of security from 1986, says: "He would go home to celebrate Christmas and be bored by Boxing Day. The family would gather for what they thought was going to be a holiday only to find out that they were going to work, but in a different country. He treated them like employees. Gradually they needed to look to other things to maintain sanity and some family life of their own."

All but two of his seven children worked for part of his empire at some point—but, unable to stand the pressure, most built separate lives . . .

Betty Maxwell was stoical under the pressures of life with her husband, insulated by her French upbringing and her château in south-west France. However, just before Christmas 1990, she confided in Pole how sad it was that her family was not only divided by the Atlantic, but no longer had the reunions she remembered from when the children were younger. . . .

• • •

Peter Jay—the former ambassador to the United States and once described as the cleverest young man in Britain—who became Maxwell's "chief of staff," the organiser of his office, says: "It was like a medieval court—people milling around in the courtyard with their petitions, or waiting to grab the king's cloak as he rushed by." . . .

Maxwell rejected all constraints. To him, "Have a nice day," was a presumption; "I'll have whatever kind of day I like," he would reply.

Jay says: "He was not just disorderly, he actively abhorred order. The key to the man was that he had the lowest threshold of boredom. He would come in and say: "What shall I do?" He'd get an idea and start ringing people. They would turn up and wait to be told what to do, by which time he would be on to something else . . . from grotesque schemes for transforming the world to fantastic rows about running newspapers."

This "whirling chaos" which Maxwell created around him, in Jay's words, obscured the truth and, ultimately, made the fraud possible.

In a satirical note to his successor as chief of staff, Jay warned: "The job is essentially administration, a process of which the chairman is deeply suspicious and profoundly uncomprehending."

Jay says: "Maxwell never read anything unless it arrived by fax." The Maxwell House post became unmanageable. Several hundred letters a day, many with cheques enclosed, would pile up unopened.

Maxwell hired a bizarre coterie of courtiers. Anyone who took his fancy could be found a role in some corner of the empire. Many stayed, at least for a while. But many others moved away, finding it intolerable. In the frantic last two years of his life, the inner circle dwindled to an even smaller band. Many of those who opposed him left. . . .

Maxwell particularly liked to collect people with titles, badges or rank. . . . Once these people had joined Maxwell's staff they had to suffer the same absurd decrees as other members. Pole says: "It didn't matter whether you were a City banker, a member of his family or a peer of the realm, all got treated equally. Once you took the king's shilling and accepted the salary and the conditions, Maxwell believed he had bought you lock, stock and barrel." . . .

Molloy says: "There were Thomas Mores in the court as well as fools. Some would not put up with his nonsense and were not pushed. Others were treated despicably. He instinctively, intuitively knew what people would take—he was very feminine in many ways."

As part of that calculation, like a feudal baron, Maxwell would bestow praise and rewards. "Look at that, that is true service," he would say, pressing $200 into Cole's hand. "Get something for your wife." But he was generous only in front of an audience, says Cole, and could be astonishingly mean. To compensate Cole for staying late on his wife's birthday, Maxwell said: "Give the man a bottle of champagne"—but then overruled the receptionist's selection of Dom Perignon in favour of a cheaper bottle of Mumm.

Formal job titles counted for nothing; what counted was whether someone was in or out of favour. It made the directors' jobs impossible, stripping them of information and authority. Pole adds: "Maxwell would put you in a cupboard and open it only when he wanted you to do something for him. Often there would be three or four people doing the same job for him without knowing about the others."

This led to an atmosphere of intrigue, ingratiation and backstabbing.

Nicholas Leeson

HOWARD G. CHUA-EOAN

Nick Leeson, former back-office clerk and internal fraud investigator-turned-high-octane derivatives trader, was only 28 years old when he propelled 232-year-old Baring Brothers into bankruptcy. Ironically, the firm itself had had to get Mr. Leeson's SIMEX trading license for him, he being unable to get one for himself in London when regulators discovered that he had neglected to tell them of a court judgment against him for debt. This account details the whole sordid mess.

The week before he disappeared, Nicholas Leeson kept throwing up in the bathroom at work. Colleagues didn't know why. He had been working hard, perhaps harder than usual. For two months, the security guard at his luxury apartment building in Singapore had been complaining about the noise from Leeson's computer printer. It was grinding out copy from 8 P.M. to 4 A.M.—the hours Wall Street did business 12 time zones away. During the daytime, the young Englishman appeared distracted, almost dour. In the trading pit of the Simex [Singapore International Monetary Exchange], where Leeson worked from dawn to 7 P.M. among the other

Excerpted from *Time Inc.* (March 13, 1995), pp. 40–47. © 1995 Time Inc. Reprinted by permission.

men who yelled at numbers careening across video screens, a fellow trader remembers that people would say hello to him and he wouldn't seem to hear them. At least he didn't respond.

Yet on Tuesday, February 21, amid the pit's uproar, Leeson replied quite evenly to a question from an A.P.-Dow Jones reporter curious about rumors that the Englishman was making huge purchases on the Japanese and Singapore exchanges on behalf of his London-based investment bank. Leeson coolly explained that he was "buying Nikkei futures here and selling them there." As simple as that, nothing out of the ordinary. One of Leeson's colleagues at another Barings office in Asia told . . . of a phone call with Leeson two days later. "He sounded really weird on the phone, like he was in a really good mood," said the man, who often partied with him in London and Tokyo. "He asked me, 'How's life?' He never asked me anything like that before. It was completely out of character. We talked again later in the day, when he must have already known he was in trouble, but he was still joking around. I asked him to change something in the way he sent reports to us and he said, 'Do you want me to tell you which hand I wrote the report with?'"

At the end of trading that day, Leeson gathered up his notes, walked off the floor and began his getaway. By 11:30 that night, he was out of Singapore, checking into a hotel in the Malaysian capital of Kuala Lumpur, 200 miles to the north. At 7 A.M. on Friday, his wife reportedly jumped into a cab and headed for the airport. In his wake lay a venerable 232-year-old British banking empire rendered suddenly and irretrievably insolvent; half the financial world was reeling in fear, the other half in astonishment. On his office desk was a handwritten note that said "I'm sorry."

It seemed beyond imagining that a bank like Barings could be utterly undone, sapped of more than a billion dollars—nearly twice its available capital—in a few weeks of reckless financial gambling by a single person. Around the world staff members were in shock. Many were about to receive their annual bonuses. Now, in Barings outposts outside Britain, passports were being confiscated, properties frozen, company credit cards rescinded, salaries withheld—just as tax time approached. "We were a bank with a crest, not a trademark," said one Hong Kong employee in dismay. Indeed, Barings was one of the Queen's banks, and the founding family currently boasts five different hereditary peerages, more than any other English clan since the Middle Ages. The Princess of Wales is a great granddaughter of a Baring. But last week control of Barings P.L.C. appeared to be going to the Dutch firm ING—for the decidedly nominal amount of $1.60.

How could such an illustrious institution come to such an ignominious end? Was it mismanagement or conspiracy? Was it fraud or simply more proof of the treacherousness of those chimerical financial instruments called derivatives? At the moment Leeson, detained in Germany after a week on the run, is the only one who knows the answer to those questions, and last week he wasn't talking. Still, what is already known of his strategy and what could be teased out through interviews with far-flung friends and colleagues suggest a tale of arrogance and greed on a grand scale. . . .

At one point last year, another bank was thinking of hiring Nick Leeson away, but a corporate headhunter contracted to analyze Leeson's abilities recommended against it. There was nothing wrong with his background or performance. The headhunter just "didn't trust him." His report went on to describe Leeson as "very bright but it might be quickness without any underlying depth. . . . After you have Leeson for six months he might hold you up for a bigger package."

In 1989, he was hired in London as a back office clerk doing settlement work, making sure all transactions were accounted and paid for. As the bank continued to ponder its commitment to derivatives, he focused on them. By 1992 he had moved from that job to a position as a roving troubleshooter, jetting off to Indonesia to help set up an office or to Tokyo as part of a team investigating allegations of internal fraud. At the time the Singapore International Monetary Exchange was trying to set itself up as Asia's hot new trading floor. Barings wanted a presence—and Leeson was put on the team assigned to help get it. At first he did settlements as he had done in London. Then, because Barings was short staffed, Leeson began executing trades himself. He was only 25, but as a former colleague puts what must have been the bank's position: "So what? No one else knew anything about developing this kind of business."

Before long Leeson was bringing in tens of millions of dollars. Last year, when the Asian markets were sagging, he was thought to have made $20 million to $36 million for Barings. Just a couple of weeks before the bank's collapse, he boasted to friends that he had been promised a $2 million bonus for the work, in addition to his $350,000 salary, company-financed apartment and limitless travel budget. In Singapore he developed a following. Says one trader: "When all the charts said sell, he would push the market even higher and the locals would go with him." His immediate boss in Singapore was so enamored of Leeson's success that the young man operated virtually without supervision—even though other traders were warning SIMEX authorities that Leeson was a "gunslinger" who should be watched carefully. Singapore traders came to feel that Leeson considered himself invincible. As a currency trader put it, "He began to believe his own press clippings."

The accolades—and the monetary rewards—were gratifying, particularly to a working-class kid, the son of a plasterer from the London suburb of Watford. "He doesn't exactly throw money around," his sister Victoria, 21, told the Watford *Observer*, "but he feels we shouldn't go without and if he can help us, he does—he's our big brother. He loved his

work and would put in up to 20 hours a day. He wanted to make something of himself because he knew he could. The press," she added, "seem
to be saying that if you are working class, you don't deserve a top job, that
you should work as a dustman or a shop assistant." Leeson never attended
college. At 18 he became a junior clerk at Coutts & Co., another prestigious bank. In 1987, he became a clerk at Morgan Stanley. That American
corporate pedigree, a mark of aggressiveness, was enough to help him
land a job at Barings.

• • •

Barings believed it was not exposed to any risk because Leeson said he was
executing the huge purchase orders at a client's behest—and presumably
with the client's funds. Furthermore, to Barings' delight, Leeson was also
making a tidy profit by making those trades in conjunction with the bank's
separate and official holdings of Nikkei 225s in Osaka and SIMEX. "I won't
tell you how good," says a Barings employee, "but it was a good business."
Little did Barings know that it was responsible for error account No. 88888,
which was unhedged and would turn out to be fatal to the company.

In later November or December, Leeson decided to wager that the Nikkei
index would not drop below about 19,000 points on March 10, 1995. It
seemed to be a safe bet: the Japanese economy was already rebounding after
a 30-month recession. Using the account No. 88888 also had a special advantage, one that Leeson had probably learned about in his old back-office
job in London when he made sure cash flowed into the right accounts. Both
Osaka and Singapore demand prompt margin payments on contracts—that
is, the difference between what the contracts were sold for and their value at
the close of each trading session. Since the account was technically Barings'
property, it appears that the company automatically made some of the payments. "It was a free bet," says one colleague.

In addition, while Leeson could call up the error account on the company computer, most of his colleagues, who lacked the special password,
did not have access to it. And last week members of Leeson's trading team
in Singapore admitted to police that he had instructed them to put only a
certain number of specific trades in the error account.

Still, in December 1994 and early January 1995, the Nikkei 225 seemed
headed for 19,000. On the morning of January 17, 1995, however, an
earthquake measuring 7.2 devastated the Japanese city of Kobe—and the
erstwhile stable Nikkei index plummeted more than 7 percent in a week.
Despite that, over the next three weeks Leeson bought thousands more
contracts betting that the Nikkei would stabilize at 19,000. "He was going
for the big kill," says the director of one trading house in Singapore. . . .

There were no hedges, no bets the other way to protect Barings' huge ex-
posures. Leeson attempted to trade in Japanese government bonds as well,
but these too incurred large losses. In what apparently was a breakdown in

internal controls at Barings' treasury, the bank continued to fund Leeson's activities, going as far as taking out an $850 million loan in the four weeks leading up to the collapse.

Barings may have wanted to look the other way. It had allowed Leeson to remain chief trader while also being responsible for settling his trades. At most banks the two jobs are split because allowing a trader to settle his own deals makes it simpler for him to hide the risks he is taking—or the money he is losing. As early as March 1992, an internal fax warned that "we are in danger of setting up a structure which will prove disastrous, in which we could succeed in losing either a lot of money, client goodwill or both." But an internal audit from August obtained by the *Financial Times* last week concluded that though Leeson was a risk in this situation, his departure would "speed the erosion of Baring Futures' profitability . . . [W]ithout him Baring Futures would lack a trader with the right combination" of experience, contacts, trading skills and local knowledge.

Despite this conclusion, Anthony Hawes, acting as a troubleshooter for the Barings inner circle in London, flew to Singapore on February 8 to talk to Leeson and his team. On Monday, February 20, Leeson's regional supervisors in Tokyo asked him to reduce the company's holdings of the Nikkei contracts. "It's almost getting to be a problem," a Barings top manager explained to a friend. No one yet suspected the crisis awaiting the company in account No. 88888. By the time internal auditors did suspect, the amount of credit extended to cover those positions had exceeded the bank's capital.